Also by Elaine Hatfield, Richard L. Rapson, and Jeanette Purvis

Elaine Hatfield

Interpersonal Attraction
Equity: Theory and Research
A New Look at Love
Human Sexual Behavior
Mirror, Mirror: The Importance of Looks in Everyday Life
Psychology of Emotion

Richard L. Rapson

Britons View America: Travel Commentary, 1860–1935
Individualism and Conformity in the American Character
The Cult of Youth in Middle-Class America
Major Interpretations of the American Past
Denials of Doubt: An Interpretation of American History
Fairly Lucky You Live Hawaii! Cultural Pluralism in the 50th State
American Yearnings: Love, Money, and Endless Possibility
Amazed by Life: Confessions of a Non-Religious Believer
Magical Thinking and the Decline of America

Elaine Hatfield and Richard L. Rapson

Emotional Contagion
Love, Sex, and Intimacy: Their Psychology, Biology, and History
Love and Sex: Cross-Cultural Perspectives

Jeanette Purvis

Strategic Interference and Tinder Use: A Mixed-Method Exploration of Romantic Interactions in Contemporary Contexts

What's Next in Love and Sex

Psychological and Cultural Perspectives

ELAINE HATFIELD, RICHARD L. RAPSON,
AND JEANETTE PURVIS

OXFORD
UNIVERSITY PRESS

OXFORD
UNIVERSITY PRESS

Oxford University Press is a department of the University of Oxford. It furthers
the University's objective of excellence in research, scholarship, and education
by publishing worldwide. Oxford is a registered trade mark of Oxford University
Press in the UK and certain other countries.

Published in the United States of America by Oxford University Press
198 Madison Avenue, New York, NY 10016, United States of America.

Library of Congress Cataloging-in-Publication Data
Names: Hatfield, Elaine, author. | Rapson, Richard L., author. |
Purvis, Jeanette, author.
Title: What's next in love and sex : psychological and cultural
perspectives / Elaine Hatfield, Richard L. Rapson, and Jeanette Purvis.
Description: New York, NY : Oxford University Press, [2020] |
Includes bibliographical references and index.
Identifiers: LCCN 2019040679 (print) | LCCN 2019040680 (ebook) |
ISBN 9780190647162 (hardback) | ISBN 9780190647186 (epub) |
ISBN 9780190647179 (updf) | ISBN 9780190647193 (online)
Subjects: LCSH: Man-woman relationships. | Love. | Sex. |
Interpersonal relations. | Interpersonal attraction.
Classification: LCC HQ801.A3 H373 2020 (print) | LCC HQ801.A3 (ebook) |
DDC 306.7—dc2 3
LC record available at https://lccn.loc.gov/2019040679
LC ebook record available at https://lccn.loc.gov/2019040680

3 5 7 9 8 6 4 2

Printed by Integrated Books International, United States of America

Contents

Preface   vii
About the Authors   xiii
Acknowledgments   xv

  1. The Way We Are   1

  2. The Business of Love and Sex: The History of Computer
     Matching from the "Happy Family Planning Service"
     to Tinder   21

  3. The Globalization of Western Love via the Internet   52

  4. Going, Going, Gone: A Market View of Love and Sex   73

  5. The Nature of Love: Its Ups and Downs   88

  6. Sexual Behaviors   104

  7. The Hookup Culture: Cultural, Social, and Gender
     Influences on Casual Sex   122

  8. From Monogamy to Swingers and Polyamory   151

  9. Pornography: The Private Enters the Public   169

 10. Sex Dolls and Robots   191

 11. The End of the Affair   201

 12. The Future of Love and Sex   220

References   229
Name Index   259
Subject Index   271

Preface

In 1969, Drs. Ellen Berscheid and Elaine Hatfield wrote the first book summarizing what was known scientifically about the psychology of interpersonal attraction, love, and sex:

Berscheid, E., & Hatfield, E. (1969). *Interpersonal attraction.* New York: Addison-Wesley.

More research was brought together in 1978:

Hatfield, E., & Walster, G. W. (1978). *A new look at love.* Reading, MA: Addison-Wesley.

While matters of love and sex had previously been thought to be "taboo," "beyond the reach of science," "mysterious,"—or even too "trivial" to permit reliable, verifiable scientific inquiry, these texts attempted to view love through a scientific lens. Since the publication of these two books there has been a virtual explosion of scholarly papers and texts on these topics, no longer seen as trivial or beyond the reach of reliable understanding. Since those lonely days, we now see "experts" on TV, in newspapers, all over popular culture, telling us about romance, sex, and passionate love. There is even a TV show, *Married at First Sight,* in which a panel of experts match up couples who are "right" for each other, who then get married on the show before ever meeting. Much of the research has been splendid. But we're also surrounded by unfounded claims, often based on research that wouldn't rate a D+ in a middle school science fair.

What is missing from this outpouring? In recent years, the world has changed radically. Internet use has expanded, globalization accelerates daily, the women's movement continues apace, and our expectations of love and partnership evolve significantly from generation to generation. More changes are in the offing. For many years, the three of us have taught classes at the University of Wisconsin and the University of Hawaii on love and sex

(Hatfield), human sexuality (Hatfield and Purvis), and the history of love, sex, and marriage (Rapson).

Increasingly, our students' questions, and most of the excitement in discussion groups, come from debating topics not covered in standard textbooks. A sampling: "Do men secretly hope for the same thing from a one-night stand as women do?" "Are hookup sites like Tinder making it more difficult to commit to a long-term relationship?" "Does pornography warp your brain?" "Does watching interactive pornography constitute adultery?" "When does flirting become sexual harassment?" "How do we know whether of not to believe it when a woman cries 'rape'?" "Is it OK to end an affair with a text message?" . . . Well, you get the idea.

When we first started searching the literature for answers to such an array of new questions, we didn't know what we would find. We were surprised to discover that there exist many studies designed to address the topics looked at in this book. Scholars from a wide variety of disciplines (cultural psychology, anthropology, social psychology, sociology, sexology, history, communication studies, biology, and the neurosciences) have amassed a great deal of evidence concerning the nature of love and sex.

This is not surprising, as most people at some point in their lives will find themselves genuinely curious about love, sex, hooking-up, and romantic partnerships. These topics cross many disciplines and enter the lives of nearly everyone. Just as there have been millions of songs, poems, and books on the complexities of love, academic works are now increasingly present. For example, The Kinsey Institute currently has 80 different academic journals listed on their website as being related to sex and sexuality. This means there are easily hundreds, if not thousands, of love and sex-related articles published each month within the scientific community. For the millions of people who say they don't understand the mysteries of love and sex—well, scientists are clearly on the job, trying to help.

Given this flood of new research, we have to wonder about its dissemination. Why aren't these path-breaking studies better known? Why aren't they included in the popular sexuality texts, let alone the media?

With over 80 different journals, how can anyone be expected to sort through these decentralized sites? And perhaps most importantly, what's the point of all these studies if only a select few academics can understand them? We began to wonder if these studies were banished from major texts because they weren't considered "serious enough" or "scientific enough" for a social psychology text—that old hurdle for love and sex researchers.

In *What's Next in Love and Sex: Psychological and Cultural Perspectives*, we plan to address these issues, among others, by reviewing diverse, contemporary research on these topics. We anticipate only one problem. The world is changing so fast that as we review the status quo or predict the future, the world keeps zipping by us. The romantic robots that were supposed to be developed by scientists in 2020 appear for sale on the Web today, crafted by Japanese junior high school students, in love with Scarlett Johansson, for the price of a 3D printer, $50 in plastic, and an iPhone. The landscape of love is evolving before our eyes, and people find it hard to keep up with so many transformations. That being so, we aim to do our best to catch up, and try to describe the ever-changing world of love and sex.

Main Themes and Objectives

The main objective of *What's Next in Love and Sex* is to provide a probing, comprehensive, and accessible look at the way love and sex exist in modern society. We will use contemporary scientific findings to provide an explanation for why we do the things we do when we're in love, searching for love, making love, attempting to patch up a faltering relationship, or breaking up. We will try to give readers an in-depth, scientific understanding of the nature of love and sex across cultures, while still providing an unpretentious, accessible, and entertaining read. And we will try to make some informed guesses about where all this is going in the years ahead.

Throughout the book, we will attempt to look into our cloudy crystal ball and demystify the future of love and sex—while still accepting that there are no absolutes in predicting human behavior. As folk artist Conor Oberst once wrote, "If someone says they know for certain / They are selling something certainly."

With humility, we will make some guesses as to where love life will be going in the developed, urban world over the next two or three decades. We wish we had a magic carpet so we could sail into the future and discover what's next. While our book makes a serious attempt to anticipate future trends in love and sex, the fact remains that *no one* can predict the future. There are simply too many unknowns, and genuine "psychics" simply don't exist. The best strategy for trying to predict the future has always been to rigorously look at past and current realities and attempt to project their continuation into the future.

We will also try to factor in the effects of globalization as it stretches across the developed and developing countries alike, linking the global population in new, perhaps profoundly significant ways. Additionally, we will discuss how culturally accepted options for love and life are evolving alongside new technologies, such as increased access to the Internet through mobile use, the global accessibility of Western media, social networking, and much, much more.

While we may not possess an authentic crystal ball to predict the future of love and sex, we do have some theories in regard to what challenges the next generation will face. For example, many kinds of behavior that were once considered taboo, sinful, or illegal are gaining increased acceptance at unprecedented rates. According to a recent Gallup poll, 60% of Americans state they accept gays and lesbians' rights, up from 41% in 2012 (McCarthy, 2016). That is still far from Spain's 88% acceptance rate, or Nigeria's 1% acceptance rate (Pew Research Center, 2013). Another Gallup poll found that attitudes toward premarital sex are evolving substantially as well. In 1989, 68% of Americans said it was wrong to engage in premarital sex. Today, that number is 34% (Rifkin, 2014). While this is a big shift, Americans still differ from the citizens of France, where only 6% think premarital sex is wrong (Pew Research Center, 2013).

All this reflects the extraordinary growth of individualism and the enlarged spaces for personal freedom in the West, but these trends are hardly everywhere in our planet. We will discuss how these shifts in cultural attitudes affect how we love, have sex, and form interpersonal bonds across a variety of cultures.

The major area for behaviors *unlikely* to be accepted by even freedom-loving people will fall in the realm of non-consensual behaviors: sex trafficking, rape, child molestation by religious or parental figures, sexual violence in all its many manifestations—all huge and profoundly ugly matters. Though we will not be focusing on non-consensual matters in this book, such as the horrors of sex trafficking, it is only because we cannot cover everything. This also includes all matters relating to gender identity. Nor will we cover sexual preferences. These are rapidly changing and very important matters best left to other writers. These topics deserve a bookshelf of works by other authors. Rather than being the last word and a comprehensive look at love and sex, we hope that what we *do* include here will only serve as a stimulant for others to add to and enrich the story we must tell here. We present an early word—and far from the last word.

The desire to understand the various facets of love and sex knows no boundaries in age, gender, class, or race. As the longing for love and sex makes us immensely vulnerable, there is a powerful desire to seek additional understanding as to why they can affect us in such profound ways. Our hope is that, through these various chapters, we will demystify how modern-day love and sexuality act with politics, the social media, online dating, new developments in healthcare, contemporary music and movies, and other current issues. Although this book will be empirically based, we do hope to arouse the curiosity of anyone interested in the subject, and, considering that most of us are affected at some point in our lives by love and sex, we should have little to worry about here. We hope readers of all backgrounds can walk away from this book with an up-to-date understanding of contemporary sex and sexuality research as it applies to the modern world. We hope this book will aid our readers in making better personal choices as well.

About the Authors

Elaine Hatfield is Professor of Psychology at the University of Hawaii at Manoa and past president of the Society for the Scientific Study of Sex. In 2012, she received the William James award for a Lifetime of Scientific Achievement from the Association for Psychological Science. In recent years, she has received Distinguished Scientist Awards from the University of Hawaii, the Society of Experimental Social Psychology, the Society for the Scientific Study of Sex (SSSS), the International Academy for Intercultural Research (IAIR), and the Alfred Kinsey Award from the Western Region of SSSS. She also recently received the Methodological Innovator Award from the Society for Personality and Social Psychology (SPSP).

Richard L. Rapson is a Professor of History at the University of Hawaii at Manoa; he has also taught at Amherst College and Stanford University. He has written more than a dozen books, most of which focus on the psychological side of American life, past and present. His most recent books are

Amazed by Life: Confessions of a Non-religious Believer (2004) and *Magical Thinking and the Decline of America* (2007).

Jeanette Purvis is an Adjunct Lecturer in Social Psychology currently working in the private sector. Her research focuses on the intersection of modern romantic relationships and new technologies. She also works in the community as a social worker for the homeless and is a former Chandler Fellow in Public Policy at the University of Hawaii at Manoa.

Acknowledgments

We enlisted a number of younger star students, current and past (and from different countries), to help us with this book. Many of them, after all, are far closer than we are to the actual dating scene and its market pressures—and thus could offer on-the-scene observations with a power, precision, and knowledge based on personal experiences that we found of inestimable value. We wish to thank them for their significant contributions to this work; they made it better. They are:

Holly Brandt
Paul Hogan
Kendall Horan
Madison Kingsbury
Dr. Sarah Peoples
Dr. Sabine Prokscha
Sara Silverman
Dr. Xiaomeng (Mona) Xu

1

The Way We Are

If we are to make informed guesses about the future of love and sex, we need to take an unblinkered look at where we were in the past and where we are today. Maybe then our crystal ball will be less opaque. So let's start with today and get our terms clear.

Passionate love is a universal emotion (see Fischer, Shaver, & Carnochan, 1990; Shaver, Morgan, & Wu, 1996). Yet despite its universality, culture has a profound impact on people's definitions of love and on the way they think, feel, and behave in romantic settings. Cross-cultural studies provide a glimpse into the complex world of emotion and allow us to gain an understanding of the extent to which people's emotional lives are written in their cultural and personal histories, as well as "writ in their genes," their evolutionary history, and in the interaction of the two (Tooby & Cosmides, 1992).

Passionate and Companionate Love

Poets, novelists, and social commentators have proposed numerous definitions of love. Ahdaf Soueif (1999), an Arab novelist, once poetically described the multitude of meanings that "love" possesses in Arabic:

> "Hubb" is love, "ishq" is love that entwines two people together, "shaghaf" is love that nests in the chambers of the heart, "hayam" is love that wanders the earth, "teeh" is love in which you lose yourself, "walah" is love that carries sorrow within it, "sababah" is love that exudes from your pores, "hawa" is love that shares its name with "air" and with "falling," "gharm" is love that is willing to pay the price. (pp. 386–387)

Cultural theorists have long been interested in the impact of culture on the meaning that men and women ascribe to "love." Scholars usually distinguish between two kinds of love: passionate love and companionate love (Hatfield & Rapson, 1993).

What's Next in Love and Sex. Elaine Hatfield, Richard L. Rapson, and Jeanette Purvis, Oxford University Press (2020). © Oxford University Press.
DOI: 10.1093/oso/9780190647162.001.0001

Passionate Love

Passionate love (sometimes called "obsessive love," "infatuation," "lovesickness," or "being-in-love") is a powerful emotional state. In this book we will define such love as:

> A state of intense longing for union with another. Passionate love is a complex whole including appraisals of the situation, one's subjective feelings, expressions, patterned physiological processes, action tendencies, and instrumental behaviors. Reciprocated love (union with the other) is associated with ecstasy and a sense of fulfillment. Unrequited love (separation) is associated with feelings of emptiness, anxiety, and despair. (Hatfield & Rapson, 1993, p. 5)

People in all cultures recognize the power of passionate love. In South Indian Tamil families, for example, a person who falls head-over-heels in love with another is said to be suffering from *mayakkam*—dizziness, confusion, intoxication, and delusion. The wild hopes and despairs of love are thought to "mix you up" (Trawick, 1990).

The Passionate Love Scale (PLS) was designed to tap into the cognitive, emotional, and behavioral indicants of such longings (Hatfield & Sprecher, 1986). The PLS has been found to be a useful measure of passionate love with men and women of all ages, in a variety of cultures, be they heterosexual or homosexual (Graham & Christiansen, 2009).

In order to investigate passionate love, psychologists have created several scales to assess this captivating emotion (Hatfield, Benson, & Rapson, 2009). The PLS (Hatfield & Sprecher, 1986) is the most commonly used of the scales. The PLS was designed to tap the cognitive, emotional, and behavioral components of passionate love (see Table 1.1). (The PLS comes in two versions—a 15-item scale and a comparable 30-item scale, for use by researchers.) This instrument has been translated for use in several countries, such as France, Germany, India, Indonesia, Iran, Italy, Japan, Korea, Peru, Poland, Spain, Sweden, and Switzerland. Cyrille Feybesse (2015) includes a table listing all the countries that have used the PLS and discusses the reliability and validity of the scale in each country. He argues that these data provide evidence of the universality of passionate love. We encourage you to pick up a pencil and pad and take this test to find out how your feelings when you are in love compare to those of your peers.

Table 1.1 Passionate Love Scale

We would like to know how you feel (or once felt) about the person you love, or have loved, most *passionately*. Some common terms for passionate love are *romantic love, infatuation, love sickness,* or *obsessive love.*

Please think of the person whom you love most passionately *right now.* If you are not in love, please think of the last person you loved. If you have never been in love, think of the person you came closest to caring for in that way. Try to describe the way you felt when your feelings were most intense. Answers range from (1) Not at all true to (9) Definitely true.

	Not True					Definitely True			
I would feel deep despair if _____ left me.	1	2	3	4	5	6	7	8	9
Sometimes I feel I can't control my thoughts; they are obsessively on _____.	1	2	3	4	5	6	7	8	9
I feel happy when I am doing something to make _____ happy.	1	2	3	4	5	6	7	8	9
I would rather be with _____ than anyone else.	1	2	3	4	5	6	7	8	9
I'd get jealous if I thought _____ were falling in love with someone else.	1	2	3	4	5	6	7	8	9
I yearn to know all about _____.	1	2	3	4	5	6	7	8	9
I want _____ physically, emotionally, and mentally.	1	2	3	4	5	6	7	8	9
I have an endless appetite for affection from _____.	1	2	3	4	5	6	7	8	9
For me, _____ is the perfect romantic partner.	1	2	3	4	5	6	7	8	9
I sense my body responding when _____ touches me.	1	2	3	4	5	6	7	8	9
_____ always seems to be on my mind.	1	2	3	4	5	6	7	8	9
I want _____ to know me—my thoughts, my fears, and my hopes.	1	2	3	4	5	6	7	8	9
I eagerly look for signs indicating _____'s desire for me.	1	2	3	4	5	6	7	8	9
I possess a powerful attraction for _____.	1	2	3	4	5	6	7	8	9
I get extremely depressed when things don't go right in my relationship with _____.	1	2	3	4	5	6	7	8	9

Now add up all your points. The total will tell you how much in love you are compared to your peers.

Total: _____

Results:
- 106–135 points = Wildly, even recklessly, in love.
- 86–105 points = Passionate, but less intense.
- 66–85 points = Occasional bursts of passion.
- 45–65 points = Tepid, infrequent passion.
- 15–44 points = The thrill is gone.

In recent functional magnetic resonance imaging (fMRI) studies of brain activity, the PLS was found to correspond well with certain well-defined patterns of biochemical and neural activation. For example, Aron and his colleagues (2005) discovered that PLS scores are tightly linked with activation in a region of the caudate associated with reward (see Cacioppo & Cacioppo, 2016, and Hatfield & Rapson, 2009, for a review of recent neuroscience research correlating the PLS with participants' fMRI reactions). The PLS has also been found to be highly correlated with a variety of measures of love, intimacy, and sexuality (see Feybesse, 2015, for a summary of this voluminous research).

Companionate Love

Companionate love is a far less intense emotion, but not necessarily a lesser form of love. It combines feelings of attachment, commitment, and intimacy (Hatfield & Rapson, 1993). It has been defined as:

> The affection and tenderness we feel for those with whom our lives are deeply entwined. (Hatfield & Rapson, 1993, p. 9)

Psychologists have used a variety of scales to measure companionate love. Since Sternberg (1988) postulated that companionate relationships require both commitment and intimacy, many researchers have assessed such love by measuring those two components of his scale. Take up your pencil again and see how you score (see Table 1.2).

Other Definitions of Love

Scientists have proposed a variety of definitions and typologies of love (see Hendrick & Hendrick, 1989; Shaver & Hazan, 1988; Sternberg, 1988). According to Sternberg (1988), for example, types of love are determined by various combinations of passion, intimacy, and commitment. Possible combinations result in romantic love, infatuation, companionate love, liking, fatuous love, empty love, and consummate love. Sternberg tells us that the ideal form of love is consummate love, which includes passion, intimacy, and commitment.

In this chapter we will focus on passionate love and sexual desire; we will touch on other varieties of love only briefly, if at all.

Passionate Love: A Cultural Universal

Bridegroom, let me caress you,
My precious caress is more savory than honey,
In the bedchamber, honey-filled,
Let me enjoy your goodly beauty,
Lion, let me caress you,
My precious caress is more savory than honey.
Bridegroom, you have taken your pleasure of me,
Tell my mother, she will give you delicacies,
My father, he will give you gifts.

This inscription, dating from the 8th century BCE, is the world's oldest known love poem. It was written on a clay tablet by a Sumerian bride, to be sung at the New Year's banquets and festivals and accompanied by music and dance.

Passionate love is as old as humankind. The Sumerian love fable of Inanna and Dumuzi, for example, was spun by tribal storytellers in 2000 BCE (Wolkstein, 1991). World literature abounds in stories of lovers caught up in a sea of passion and violence: Daphnis and Chloe (a Greek myth), Shiva and Sati (Indian), Hinemoa and Tutanekai (Maori), Emperor Ai and Dong Xian (Chinese), the VhaVhenda lover who was turned into a crocodile (African), and Romeo and Juliet.

Here is a quote from the Bible that illustrates the antiquity of passion:

Love is as strong as death, its jealousy unyielding as the grave. It burns like blazing fire, like the very flame of the LORD. Many waters cannot quench love; rivers cannot wash it away. . . . (Song of Solomon 8:6)

Today, most anthropologists argue that passionate love is a universal experience, transcending culture and time (Feybesse, 2015; Hatfield & Rapson, 1996/2005; Jankowiak, 1995; Tooby & Cosmides, 1992).

Jankowiak and Fischer (1992) draw a sharp distinction between "romantic passion" and "simple lust." They propose that both passion and lust are universal feelings. Drawing on a sampling of tribal societies from the

Table 1.2 Sternberg's Triangular Love Scale

What are the components of your love relationship? Intimacy? Passion? Decision/Commitment? All three components? Two of them?

To complete the following scale, fill in the blank spaces with the name of one person you love or care about deeply. Then rate your agreement with each of the items by using a nine-point scale in which 1 = "not at all," 5 = "moderately," and 9 = "extremely." Use points in between to indicate these values. Then consult the scoring key at the end of the scale.

Intimacy Component

_____1. I am actively supportive of _____'s wellbeing.

_____2. I have a warm relationship with _____.

_____3. I am able to count on _____ in times of need.

_____4. _____ is able to count on me in times of need.

_____5. I am willing to share myself and my possessions with _____.

_____6. I receive considerable emotional support from _____.

_____7. I give considerable emotional support to _____.

_____8. I communicate well with _____.

_____9. I value _____ greatly in my life.

_____10. I feel close to _____.

_____11. I have a comfortable relationship with _____.

_____12. I feel that I really understand _____.

_____13. I feel that _____ really understands me.

_____14. I feel that I can really trust _____.

_____15. I share deeply personal information about myself with _____.

Passion Component

_____16. Just seeing _____ excites me.

_____17. I find myself thinking about _____ frequently during the day.

_____18. My relationship with _____ is very romantic.

_____19. I find _____ to be very personally attractive.

_____20. I idealize _____.

_____21. I cannot imagine another person making me as happy as _____ does.

_____22. I would rather be with _____ than with anyone else.

_____23. There is nothing more important to me than my relationship with _____.

_____24. I especially like physical contact with _____.

_____25. There is something almost "magical" about my relationship with _____.

_____26. I adore _____.

_____27. I cannot imagine life without _____.

_____28. My relationship with _____ is passionate.

Table 1.2 *Continued*

_____29. When I see romantic movies and read romantic books I think of _____.

_____30. I fantasize about _____.

Decision/Commitment Component

_____31. I know that I care about _____.

_____32. I am committed to maintaining my relationship with _____.

_____33. Because of my commitment to _____, I would not let other people come between us.

_____34. I have confidence in the stability of my relationship with _____.

_____35. I could not let anything get in the way of my commitment to _____.

_____36. I expect my love for _____ to last for the rest of my life.

_____37. I will always feel a strong responsibility for _____.

_____38. I view my commitment to _____ as a solid one.

_____39. I cannot imagine ending my relationship with _____.

_____40. I am certain of my love for _____.

_____41. I view my relationship with _____ as permanent.

_____42. I view my relationship with _____ as a good decision.

_____43. I feel a sense of responsibility toward _____.

_____44. I plan to continue my relationship with _____.

_____45. Even when _____ is hard to deal with, I remain committed to our relationship.

Scoring Key:

Add your ratings for each of the three sections—Intimacy, Passion, and Commitment/Decision and write them on a sheet of paper. Divide each subscore by 15 to get an average subscale score. An average rating of 5 on a particular subscale indicates a moderate level of the component represented by the subscale; for example, an average rating of 5 on the intimacy subscale indicates a moderate amount of intimacy in the relationship you chose to measure. Following this example further, a higher average rating would indicate a higher level of intimacy, and a lower average rating would indicate a lesser amount of intimacy. Examining your ratings for each of the three subscales will give you an idea of how you perceive your love relationship to be composed of various amounts of intimacy, passion, and decision/commitment.

Sternberg's Triangular Love Scale (adapted) from *The Triangle of Love* by Robert J. Sternberg. Copyright © 1988 by Basic Books, Inc. Reprinted by permission of Basic Books, a division of HarperCollins Publishers, Inc.

Standard Cross-Cultural Sample, they found that in almost all of these far-flung societies, young lovers talked about passionate love, recounted tales of love, sang songs of love, and spoke of the longings and anguish of infatuation. When passionate affections clashed with parents' or elders' wishes, young couples often ran away together. Social anthropologists have explored folk conceptions of love in such diverse cultures as the People's Republic of China, Indonesia, Turkey, Nigeria, Trinidad, Morocco, the Fulbe of North Cameroun, the Mangrove (an Aboriginal Australian community), the Mangaia in the Cook Islands, Palau in Micronesia, and the Taita of Kenya (see Jankowiak, 1995, for a review of this research).

Culture and Passionate Love

A spate of commentators once argued that the idealization of passionate love is a peculiarly Western institution. Recently, cultural researchers have begun to investigate the impact of culture on how individuals define love, what they desire in romantic partners, their likelihood of falling in love, the intensity of their passion, and their willingness or unwillingness to acquiesce to arranged marriages (Ghimire, Axinn, Yabiku, & Thornton, 2006; Riela, Rodriguez, Aron, Xu, & Acevedo, 2010; Schmitt et al., 2009). They find that, throughout time, people have embraced slightly different attitudes toward romantic and passionate love, have ascribed to somewhat different meanings of "love," have desired very different traits in romantic partners, and have differed markedly in whether such feelings were to be proclaimed to the world or hidden in the deepest recesses of the heart.

In the real world, romantic sexual attitudes and behavior seem to be forever in flux. Nonetheless, from recent research, it is clear that although cultural differences do in fact exist, cultures often turn out to be more similar than one might expect (Feybesse, 2015; Feybesse, Hatfield, & Neto, 2013). In most cultures, men and women are equally likely to fall in love (Hatfield & Rapson, 1993). And, given the ubiquity of modern-day communication, it appears that cultures are becoming more similar in their yearning for passion (Levine, Sato, Hashimoto, & Verma, 1995). Around the world, there appears to be a swing toward passion being more positively regarded and yearned for more intensely than ever before. So more and more people, throughout the world, are coming to value passionate love (Hatfield & Rapson, 1996/2005).

What might that portend, both for individuals and cultures? Let us now consider this research.

A Bit of Background

The world's cultures differ profoundly in the extent to which they emphasize individualism or collectivism (although some cross-cultural researchers focus on related concepts: independence or interdependence, modernism or traditionalism, urbanism or ruralism, secularism or religion, affluence or poverty). Individualistic cultures such as the United States, Britain, Australia, Canada, and the countries of Northern and Western Europe tend to focus on personal goals. Collectivist cultures such as China, many African and Latin American nations, Greece, southern Italy, and the Pacific Islands, on the other hand, press their members to subordinate personal interests to those of the group (Markus & Kitayama, 1991; Triandis, McCusker, & Hui, 1990). Triandis and his colleagues point out that in individualistic cultures, young people are allowed to "do their own thing"; in collectivist cultures, the group comes first.

A half-century ago Hsu (1953, 1985) and Doi (1963, 1973) took it for granted that passionate love was a Western phenomenon, almost unknown in China and Japan; it was so incompatible with Asian values and customs that it was unlikely ever to gain a foothold among young Asians. Hsu (1953) wrote: "An American asks, 'How does my heart feel?' A Chinese asks, 'What will other people say?'" (p. 50). Hsu pointed out that the Chinese generally use the term *love* to describe not a respectable, socially sanctioned relationship, but an *illicit* liaison between a man and a woman.

Chu (1985; Chu & Ju, 1993) also argued that although romantic love and compatibility are of paramount importance in mate selection in America, in China such things matter little. Traditionally, parents and go-betweens arranged young peoples' marriages. Parents' primary concern was not love and compatibility but *men tang hu tui*. (Did the families possess the same social status? Were *they* compatible? Would the marriage bring some social or financial advantage to the two families?)

On the basis of such testimony, cross-cultural researchers proposed that romantic love would be common only in modern, industrialized countries. It should be less valued in traditional cultures with strong, extended family ties (Simmons, Vom Kolke, & Shimizu, 1986). It should be more common in modern, industrialized countries than in developing countries (Goode, 1959; Rosenblatt, 1967).

These claims are wrong. Over the next few sections, we will see that throughout the world men and women fall passionately in love with equal frequency and equal intensity. Where they differ is in whether or not they idealize love and whether or not they are able to express their feelings—specifically, do they assume they will be allowed to marry for love? But, as we shall see, that is changing too.

Culture and Susceptibility to Love

Compelling evidence suggests that men and women in a variety of cultures (industrializing as well as industrial) are every bit as romantic as those in the West. Susan Sprecher and her colleagues (1994), for example, interviewed 1,667 men and women, all college students, in the United States, Russia, and Japan. "When asked, 'Are you currently in love?' similar percentages of men and women in the various countries agreed that they were. Passion was surprisingly high in all the societies—averaging around 59%. In all three cultures, men were slightly less likely than women to be in love at the present time. Surveys of Mexican-American, Chinese-American, and Euro-American students have also found that in a variety of cross-national groups, young men and women show high rates of reporting being in love at the present time.

How to explain this? Not one to give up on a good hypothesis, the group decided that although college students claimed to be in love, they probably differed in the *intensity* of their feelings. This hypothesis, too, proved to be wrong. In one study, Hatfield and Rapson (1987) asked men and women of European, Filipino, and Japanese ancestry to complete the Passionate Love Scale. Men and women from the various ethnic groups seemed to love with equal passion. William Doherty found similar results with Euro-Americans, Chinese-Americans, Filipino-Americans, Japanese-Americans, and Pacific Islanders.

Subsequent research indicates that young people may (1) ascribe slightly different meanings to passion and (2) differ in whether or not passionate love is the sine qua non of marriage.

The Meaning of Passionate Love

One impact of globalization (and the ubiquitous MTV, Hollywood, and Bollywood movies, chat rooms, and foreign travel) may be that when people speak of "passionate love," they are talking about much the same thing. Yet there are some differences in their visions of love.

Shaver, Wu, and Schwartz (1991) interviewed young people in the Unites States, Italy, and the People's Republic of China about their emotional experiences. In all the countries, as per our definition, love was seen to be a bittersweet experience. Culture had an impact, however, on whether they emphasized the bitter or the sweet. Shaver and his colleagues found that Americans and Italians tended to equate love with happiness and to assume that both passionate and companionate love were intensely positive experiences. Students in Beijing, China, possessed a darker view of love. In the Chinese language, there are few "happy-love" words; love is associated with sadness. Not surprisingly, then, the Chinese men and women interviewed by Shaver and his colleagues tended to associate passionate love with ideographic words such as infatuation, unrequited love, nostalgia, and sorrow love.

Other cultural researchers agree that cultural values may, indeed, have an impact on the subtle shadings of meaning assigned to the construct of "love" (Cohen, 2001; Kim & Hatfield, 2004; Kitayama, 2002; Luciano, 2003; Nisbett, 2003; Oyserman, Kemmelmeier, & Coon, 2002; Weaver & Ganong, 2004). There is, however, considerable debate as to how ubiquitous and important such differences are. When social psychologists explored folk conceptions of love in a variety of cultures—including the People's Republic of China, Indonesia, Micronesia, Palau, and Turkey—they found that people in the various cultures possessed surprisingly similar views of love and other "feelings of the heart" (for a review of this research, see Fischer, Wang, Kennedy, & Cheng, 1998; Jankowiak, 1995; Kim & Hatfield, 2004; Shaver, Murdaya, & Fraley, 2001). In a typical study, for example, Shaver and his colleagues (2001) argued that love and "sexual mating, reproduction, parenting, and maintaining relationships with kin and reciprocally altruistic relationships with friends and neighbors are fundamental issues for humans" (p. 220). To test the notion that passionate and companionate love are cultural universals, they conducted a "prototype" study to determine (1) what Indonesian (compared to American) men and women considered to be "basic" emotions and (2) the meaning they ascribed to these emotions. Starting with 404 Indonesian *perasaan hati* (emotion names or "feelings of the heart"), they asked people to sort the words into basic emotion categories. As predicted, the Indonesians came up with the same five emotions that Americans consider to be basic: joy, love, sadness, fear, and anger. Furthermore, when asked about the meanings of "love," Indonesian men and women (like their American counterparts) were able to distinguish passionate love (*asmara,* or sexual/desire/arousal) from companionate love (*cinta,* or affection/liking/fondness). There were some differences in the American and Indonesian lexicons. The Indonesian conception of love may place more emphasis on yearning and desire than the American conception, perhaps because the barriers to consummation are more formidable in Indonesia, which is a more traditional and mostly Muslim country. Much more research needs to be done, of course, before scientists can state this conclusion with any certainty.

Love and Marriage

In the West, before 1700, no society ever equated *le grand passion* with marriage. In the 12th century, in *The Art of Courtly Love,* for example, Andreas Capellanus (1174/1957) stated:

> . . . everybody knows that love can have no place between husband and wife . . . . For what is love but an inordinate desire to receive passionately a furtive and hidden embrace? But what embrace between husband and wife can be furtive, I ask you, since they may be said to belong to each other and may satisfy all of each other's desires without fear that anybody will object? (p. 100)

And Capellanus wasn't even talking about passionate love—just love. To make his argument perfectly clear, he added:

> We declare and we hold as firmly established that love cannot exert its powers between two people who are married to each other. (p. 106)

Shakespeare often wrote about passionately mismatched couples hurtling toward marriage, but his plays were the exception. Until 1500, most courtly love songs, plays, and stories assumed a darker ending—passionate love was either unrequited or unconsummated, or it spun down to family tragedy and the suicide or deaths of the lovers.

As late as 1540, the Italian philosopher Alessandro Piccolomini could write peremptorily that:

> Love is a reciprocity of soul and has a different end and obeys different laws from marriage. Hence one should not take the loved one to wife. (Hunt, 1959, p. 206)

True to his times, Piccolomini began to change his mind just before he died.

In the great societies of Asia—China, Japan, and India (lands of arranged marriage)—at least since the end of the 17th century, and in thousands of *haiku* poems, *Noh* plays, and heroic legends later, the notion that passionate love and sexual desire go together with thwarted hopes for marriage and suicide has been embedded in the Eastern psyche as an Eternal Truth. Classical tales recount the couple's journey together to the chosen place, leaving forever behind them familiar scenes, agonizing mental conflicts, and the last tender farewells (Mace & Mace, 1980). To today's young individualistic Americans and Europeans, such tales of forbidden romance may seem ridiculous. But to Asian young romantics, who knew that passion had little chance of flowering into marriage, the tales were sublime tragedies.

In traditional cultures, it was the lovers who had to adapt, not society. Individual happiness mattered little; what *was* important was the maintenance of social order and the well-being of the family. As one modern Chinese woman asserted, "Marriage is not a relation for personal pleasure, but a contract involving the ancestors, the descendants, and the property" (Mace & Mace, 1980, p. 134).

In contemporary societies, however, both East and West, most young men and women do meet, fall in love, feel sexual desire, and live together or marry. In the next section, we will discuss the revolution that is occurring in the ways young men and women from a variety of cultures (be they heterosexual, homosexual, or bisexual) currently select their romantic, sexual, and marital partners. We will see that throughout the world, parental power is crumbling and arranged marriages are being replaced by the ideal of love marriages.

Arranged Marriages

Throughout history, cultures have varied markedly in who possessed the power to select romantic, sexual, and marital partners. In the distant past, in most societies, parents, kin, and the community usually had the power to arrange things as they chose. Marriage was assumed to be an alliance between two families (Dion & Dion, 1993; Lee & Stone, 1980). Families might also consult with religious specialists, oracles, and matchmakers (Rosenblatt & Anderson, 1981). When contemplating a union, parents, kin, and their advisors were generally concerned with a number of background questions. What was the young person's caste, status, family background, religion, and economic position? Did his family possess any property? How big was her dowry? Would he fit in with the entire family? In Indian families, for example, men and women observed that what their families cared most about in arranging a marriage was religion (whether one was a Hindu, Muslim, Sikh, or Christian), social class, education, and family background (Sprecher & Chandak, 1992). If things looked promising, parents and go-betweens began to talk about the exchange of property, dowries, the young couple's future obligations, and living arrangements.

Some problems were serious enough to rule out any thought of marriage. Sometimes religious advisors would chart the couple's horoscopes. Those born under the wrong sign might be forbidden to marry (Bumroongsook, 1992). Generally, young people were forbidden to marry anyone who was too closely related (say, a brother or sister, or a certain kind of cousin). Sometimes, they were forbidden to marry foreigners. (In Thailand, Thais are often forbidden to marry Chinese, Indian, Japanese, Mons, or Malay suitors [Bumroongsook, 1992].) Similar assets and liabilities have been found to be important in a variety of countries, such as India (Prakasa & Rao, 1979; Sprecher & Chandak, 1992), Japan (Fukuda, 1991), Morocco (Joseph & Joseph, 1987), and Thailand (Bumroongsook, 1992).

Today, in many parts of the world, parents and matchmakers still arrange their children's marriages. Within a single society, arrangements often vary from ethnic group to ethnic group, class to class, region to region, and family to family (Bumroongsook, 1992). Arranged marriages are common in India, in the Muslim countries, in sub-Saharan Africa, and in cultural enclaves throughout the remainder of the world (Rosenblatt & Anderson, 1981). Even in the United States, although arranged marriages are rare, parents and kin might well express strong opinions as to the suitability of potential mates (objecting to a suitor's social class, race, religion, education, or family background, for example), and for some young people these objections might loom large.

Compromising on Love

Cross-cultural surveys document the variety of types of mate-selection systems that exist throughout the world (Goode, 1963; Goodwin, 1999; Rosenblatt, 1967; Stephens, 1963). These surveys indicate that, currently, in most of the world, prospective brides and grooms, parents, elders, and the extended family consult with one another before arranging a marriage. The *Ethnographic Atlas* contains anthropological information on more than 1,000 preindustrial societies throughout the world. When Broude and Green (1983) sampled 186 of these groups, they found, again, that in most societies, parents, kin, and young men and women are supposed to consult with one another in this most important of family decisions. In most societies, men have considerably more power than women to determine their own fates. In only a minority of societies are men and women allowed complete power in choosing their own mates.

Today, however, even in the most traditional societies, parents and husbands are generally forced to balance conflicting interests. The Moroccan tribal world, for example, is definitely a man's world. Men possess absolute authority over their wives and children. They possess the power to take several wives. They often promise their sons and daughters to potential allies at very young ages. Yet, in families, things do not always happen as they are supposed to; men may possess all the power in theory, but in fact they may not. Joseph and Joseph's (1987) vivid descriptions of Moroccan family life make it clear that even in Morocco compromise is often required. When "all-powerful" Moroccan fathers try to force their children into unappealing marriages, sympathetic family members may employ an avalanche of strategies to thwart them. Young lovers may enlist an army of mothers, uncles, brothers, neighbors, and business partners to plead, threaten, and haggle on their behalf. Mothers may warn prospective brides about their sons' "faults." Young men may whisper that an undesirable bride is a witch. Young men and women may threaten to kill themselves. Many young men and women rely on witchcraft or magical charms to get their way. Sometimes these desperate stratagems work; sometimes they don't.

In a discussion of the confusion of attitudes toward marriage in Zawiya, Morocco, Davis and Davis (1995) quote two young people he interviewed. One 18-year-old high school boy said the couple's wishes were what was important:

> If that boy gets married to the girl he likes, they will certainly live happily. Because money is not happiness; happiness is something the heart feels. The boy must have the feeling that the girl likes him. This is why I say that if the boy is hooked on a girl and he truly loves her, he should go and propose to marry her no matter what she's like. It is not the father who should choose for the son a girl he doesn't like. It is the son who should decide what he likes. . . . It is not the father who is getting married.

A 19-year-old woman, still in primary school, disagreed.

> She should follow her parents' decision. Parents come first. . . . If she goes against their wishes it will be her own responsibility. She'd be ungrateful [literally, cursed by them], very much so. If she marries him against their will, she'll face a catastrophe, an accident or something—or even death, some kind of death. They may have an accident or something—she shouldn't. Her parents told her not to marry him: she shouldn't marry him, period. . . . Since she has grown up, [her parents] have taken good care of her: they clothe her, give her money, provide for her needs. Whatever she asks for they provide, and then at the end they give an opinion and she rejects it. This is not possible; it is not admissible that she doesn't accept that advice.

Marriage for Love

In the West, romantic love has long been considered to be the sine qua non of marriage (Kelley et al., 1983; Sprecher et al., 1994). Men and women generally assume that couples should be romantically in love with whomever they choose to marry. In the mid-1960s, William Kephart (1967) asked more than a 1,000 college students: "If a boy (girl) had all the other qualities you desired, would you marry this person if you were not in love with him (her)?" He found that men and women had different ideas as to how important romantic love was in a marriage. Men thought passion was essential (only 35% of them said they would marry someone they did not love). Women were more practical. They said that the absence of love would not necessarily deter them from considering marriage. (A full 76% of them said they would be willing to marry someone they did not love.) Kephart suggested that while men might have the luxury of marrying for love, women did not. Women's status was dependent on their husbands'; thus, they had to be practical and take a potential husband's family background, professional status, and income into account. Since the 1960s, sociologists have continued to ask young American men and women this question. They have found that, year by year, young American men and women have come to demand more and more of love.

In the most recent research, 86% of American men and 91% of American women answered the same question with a resounding "No!" (Allgeier & Wiederman, 1991). Today, American men and women assume that romantic love is so important that they insist that if they fell out of love, they would not even consider *staying* married (Simpson, Campbell, & Berscheid, 1986). Of course, with more experience they might find that they are willing to "settle" for less than they think they would. In the half-century since Kepart's original study, gender differences in considering love a sine qua non for marriage have all but disappeared. Generally, today, it is now *women* who rate love as more important as a basis of marriage (Sprecher & Toro-Morn, 2002). It would be fascinating, of course, to investigate the choices men and women make once they are married. As yet, this research is not available.

How do young men and women in other countries feel about this issue? Many cultural psychologists have pointed out that cultural values have a profound impact on how people feel about the wisdom of love matches versus arranged marriages. Susan Sprecher and her colleagues (1994) asked American, Russian, and Japanese students, "If a person had all the other qualities you desired, would you marry him/her if you were not in love?" (Students could only answer yes or no.) The authors, of course, had expected that only the individualistic Americans would demand love *and* marriage; they predicted that both the Russians and the Japanese would be more practical. They found that they were wrong. Both the Americans and the Japanese were romantics (see Table 1.3); few of them would consider marrying someone they did not love. (Only 11% of Americans and 18% of the Japanese said yes.) The Russians were more practical; 37% of them said they would accept such a proposal. Russian men were only slightly more practical than men in other countries. It was the Russian women who were most likely to "settle." Perhaps the Russian caution is due to the fact that these data were

Table 1.3 The Importance of Love for Marriage

Question 1: "If a man (woman) had all the other qualities you desired, would you marry this person if you were not in love with her (him)?" (Note: Answers are all in percentages)

	India	Pakistan	Thailand	United States	England	Japan
Yes	49.0	50.4	18.8	3.5	7.3	2.3
No	24.9	39.1	33.8	85.9	83.6	62
Undecided	26.9	10.4	47.5	10.6	9.1	36.7

	Philippines	Mexico	Brazil	Hong Kong	Australia
Yes	11.4	10.2	4.3	5.8	4.8
No	63.6	80.5	85.7	77.6	80.0
Undecided	25.0	9.3	10.0	16.7	15.2

collected when Russia was in political and economic chaos and women were in dire need of masculine support.

Other cross-cultural research documents the importance of love for marriage worldwide. True, couples viewed love as more important for entering marriage than for maintaining marriage, but it nonetheless remains important (Sprecher & Toro-Morn, 2002).

In a landmark study, Levine and his colleagues (1995) asked college students in 11 different nations if they would be willing to marry someone they did not love even if that person had all the other qualities they desired. (Students could answer yes or no or admit that they were undecided.) In affluent nations such as the United States, Brazil, Australia, Japan, and England, young people were insistent on love as a prerequisite for marriage. Only in traditional, collectivist, Third World nations, such as the Philippines, Thailand, India, and Pakistan, were students willing to compromise and marry someone they did not love. In these societies, of course, the extended family is still extremely important and poverty is widespread (see Table 1.3). It would be fascinating, of course, to conduct research to determine whether or not the poor in Western countries are like those in traditional societies—considering love to be a luxury and choosing mates for more practical reasons.

Conclusion

The preceding studies suggest that the large differences that once existed between Westernized, modern, urban, industrial societies and Eastern, modern, urban industrial societies may be eroding. Those interested in cross-cultural differences may be wise to search for differences in only the most underdeveloped, developing, and collectivist societies—such as in Africa, Latin America, China, or the Arab countries (Egypt, Kuwait, Lebanon, Libya, Saudi-Arabia, Iraq, or the United Arab Emirates).

However, it may well be that even there, the winds of Westernization, individualism, and social change are blowing. In spite of the censure of their elders, in a variety of traditional cultures, young people are increasingly adopting "Western" patterns—placing a high value on "falling in love," pressing for gender equality in love and sex, and insisting on marrying for love (as opposed to arranged marriages). Such changes have been documented in Finland, Estonia, and Russia (Haavio-Mannila & Kontula, 2003) as well as among Australian Aboriginal people of Mangrove and a Copper Inuit Alaskan Indian tribe (see Jankowiak, 1995, for an extensive review of this research).

Naturally, cultural differences still exert a profound influence on young people's attitudes, emotions, and behavior, and such differences are not likely to disappear in our lifetime. In Morocco, for example, marriage was once an alliance between families (as historically it was in most of the world before the 18th century) in which children had little or no say. Today, although parents can no longer simply dictate whom their children will marry, parental approval remains critically important. Important though it is, however, young men and women are at least allowed to have their say (see Davis & Davis, 1995).

Many have observed that today, two powerful forces—globalization and cultural pride and identification with one's country (or nationalism)—are contending for men's and women's souls. True, the world's citizens may, to some extent, be becoming "one," but in truth the delightful and divisive cultural variations that have made our world such an interesting and simultaneously dangerous place are likely to add spice to that heady brew of love and sexual practices for some time to come. The convergence of cultures around the world may be reducing the differences in the ways passionate love is experienced and expressed in our world, but tradition can be tenacious, and the global future of passionate love cannot be predicted with any certainty.

In the next few chapters, we will discuss the impact that globalization might be expected to have on the way young people throughout the world view passionate love and marriage. The extraordinary rise of social media and the Internet open the door to a world of rapid and breathtaking change, and our look into the future of love and sex aptly continues there.

2

The Business of Love and Sex

The History of Computer Matching from the "Happy Family Planning Service" to Tinder

Any time a new form of communication appears—from the "penny dreadfuls" to Morse code and the telegraph, skywriting, the wireless radio, TV, computers, and smartphones—men and women have found creative ways to use that technology to find love and sexual partners. In this chapter, we discuss the evolution of modern-day matchmaking services.

In the 1950s, almost as soon as computers hit Stanford University, two computer science students, Jim Harvey and Phil Fialer, decided to create a date matchmaking service, christened the "Happy Family Planning Service," as their final class project in Math 139. The students asked 49 Stanford men and 49 Stanford women to fill out questionnaires (which asked 30 questions about their attitudes, preferences, and behavior). Then they cranked out a matching program, assuming (for some reason) that while men and women generally prefer partners who share their attitudes and opinions, when it comes to personality, opposites attract. Data were then punched into IBM cards, and using the new IBM FORTRAN computer language, they matched couples up on Stanford's new IBM 650 mainframe computer (see Illustrations 2.1 and 2.2). Alas, the matches weren't very successful. For example, in one instance, a 30-year-old single mother with several children ended up paired with an 18-year-old freshman member of the Stanford Marching Band (Harmon, 2003).

The problem in the 1950s and 1960s wasn't how to match couples but how to match them well. Thus, various social psychologists set out to determine what sort of factors would accurately predict which couples would get along and which ones would not.

In July of 1969, three social psychologists, Elaine Hatfield, George Levinger, and Zick Rubin, were offered $100,000 by Todd Gittleson, a wealthy trustee of the University of Massachusetts, who was upset by his daughter's

What's Next in Love and Sex. Elaine Hatfield, Richard L. Rapson, and Jeanette Purvis, Oxford University Press (2020). © Oxford University Press.
DOI: 10.1093/oso/9780190647162.001.0001

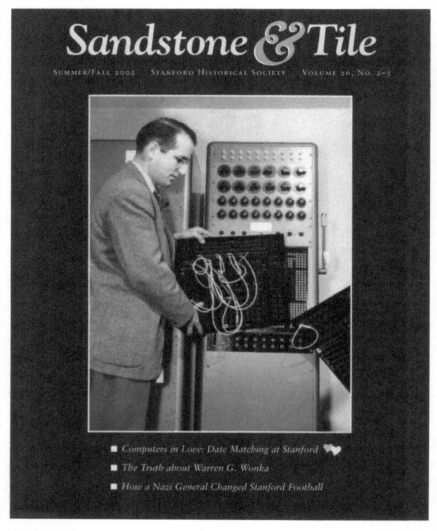

Illustration 2.1 The first computer matching program, Stanford University, 1950.

failure to find suitable dating partners, to craft a matching system. They set out to craft Project Cupid, a nonprofit dating service. After many meetings designed to devise reliable and valid instruments, the authors gave up. They had little confidence in psychology's ability to guarantee successful matches. A typical problem: the people who signed up for Project Cupid were either

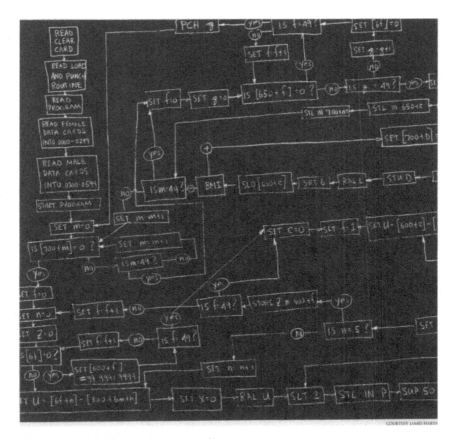

Illustration 2.2 The mathematics of love.

elderly women or teenage men; no matches there. The problem of balanced sex ratio between men and women and differences in age—and preferences in the age of partners on dating websites—has persisted to this day.

Searching for Love in the Digital Age

Over time, as computers became faster, cheaper, and more powerful, the high-speed Internet was created, and a new generation of computer match-making sites was founded. Since the 1970s, the online dating business has gone through three stages: it started with online personal advertisement sites, moved to supposedly "scientific" algorithm-based matching sites, and recently onto smartphone-based dating applications.

Match.com, launched in 1995, was the first commercial site for online dating. Subscribers were encouraged to post "personal advertisements" in hopes of finding a romantic partner. Today, these postings read like ancient history—it's like perusing the classified ads posted in the *Jewish Daily Forward* in the early 1900s, in which bewildered young European immigrants in search for a soul mate. On Match.com, young people posted profiles, which included a photograph, demographic information, personality descriptions, and a statement of interests. Members could then browse the ads of potential romantic partners and contact those they deemed promising.

In the early days, people who posted on sites like Match.com were often assumed to be nerds, the desperate, and the socially inept. People worried that the people who posted might be sexual predators or psychotics. One commentator suggested that there was a kernel of truth in those stereotypes, observing that, originally, participants were "a little on the shy side or a little on the sleazy side" (Orr, 2004, p. 29).

All that has changed. Online dating has lost much of its stigma—15% of American adults have used online dating sites or mobile dating apps, with 59% of American adults stating that online dating is a good way to meet people (Smith & Anderson, 2016). In 2016, Statistics Brain Research Institute (2016a) calculated that there were 54,250,000 single people in the United States. Out of this sample of single folks, 49,250,000 stated that they had tried online dating. Older people (who may find it hard to meet dates and mates) are twice as likely to use online dating sites now as in 2013 (Smith & Anderson, 2016).

In recent years, approximately 22% of couples have met on the Internet—coming just behind friends in popularity of meeting. Among same-sex couples, the numbers are markedly higher (61%) (Rosenfeld & Thomas, 2012). According to *Online Dating Magazine* (Tracy, 2012), there are over 2,500 dating services in the United States and 5,000 online dating services worldwide. This number is certainly higher as this book to press. Only a handful of these innovative sites will survive; a full 99% of new sites fail.

Of course, certain sites, such as those that offer hookups or extramarital sex, may still carry a stigma. Kendall Horan, one of our reviewers and a University of Hawaii athlete, observed:

One day I had a talk with my really good friend about Tinder. She wanted to get on Tinder, but she said she didn't want to be labeled as a "hoe." I told her that many people have Tinder just to talk to people, and she laughed at me and said yes but if you see anyone you know on Tinder they automatically know you are just trying to get laid. I personally do not have a Tinder [profile], but many of my friends do and they do tell me their fears of this stigma.

There are many steps in the Business of Love. The first step is choosing a dating site(s). Then, one must create a profile and/or browse others' profiles, initiate a contact or receive one, embark on communication, meet face to face, and then (hopefully) develop a relationship offline (Finkel, Eastwick, Karney, Reis, & Sprecher, 2012). But first things first: how does someone know which site to choose?

Profile of Users

Scholars have examined the personality characteristics of people who date online compared to those who do not, finding that users aren't very different from those who abstain. They are similar in terms of self-esteem and on the Big Five personality dimensions. (The Big Five is the most popular personality test. It measures openness to experience, conscientiousness, extraversion, agreeableness, and neuroticism.) There is still a debate as to whether online daters are more or less socially skilled than their peers. Online daters are generally more liberal in social attitudes than the general American public and, often, are also more liberal than other Internet users. More specifically, Internet daters tend to be less likely to define themselves as religious, less likely to believe in traditional gender roles, and more likely to experiment with new ideas. The profiles of users are, quite naturally, skewed in different ways on the various specialty sites. For example, religiosity will be higher at Christianmingle.com, and education will be more salient at TheRightStuff.com, a dating service for people from elite Ivy League colleges and universities (see Finkel et al., 2012, for a summary of this research).

In subsequent sections, we will discuss some of the most common questions that people entering the dating market tend to ask:

Should I try online dating?

What are the most popular online dating sites and apps?

How much do the various sites and apps cost?

How can I separate myself from the pack?

Once we meet, what should I look for in a match?

How can I get to know someone more intimately?

What are the advantages and disadvantages of searching for love on the Web?

What are the dangers of going online?

How do most matches work out?

Should I Try Online Dating?

The first question young people must consider is: "Do I really want to try online dating?" In their clinical practice, when Hatfield and Rapson (1993) were working with shy or lonely clients, or clients who were hoping for a little magic in their lives, they usually recommended the following strategy for gay and straight folks. Keep in mind that Web matching didn't exist yet.

1. People who long for an active social life should *not* begin by trying to find the perfect mate. If they follow that approach, they are likely to make a commitment to the first promising person who comes along, invest a great deal of exclusive time in the relationship, only to find out months or years later that the person who once seemed so perfect turns out to have fatal flaws. Not all frogs that come into view turn out to be princes (or princesses).

2. Rather than search for the first acceptable frog that hops into view, people do far better if they concentrate at first on making a few friends. They should go out of their way to say hello and to chat with the men and women they bump into at school, at work, or while participating in daily activities. They should make an effort to meet the most appealing and interesting men and women in their classes, dance groups, computer workshops, car repair shops, or Sierra Club hikes. They needn't worry about the age, marital status, or attractiveness of these acquaintances or whether they are mate material. What they are looking for are casual friends. They should ask those acquaintances they like best to lunches,

walks, or the movies. Eventually, after a weeding-out process, people are bound to make a social connection with a new friend.

3. Once having established a network of friends, it is usually a short and easy step to begin to find suitable dates. People can ask their friends to introduce them to potential dates. (Instead of one person searching for possible dates, now several matchmakers are involved in the project.) When in doubt about whether to date someone or not, the best strategy is to give it a try. Usually, it takes only a few shared interests to make a *date* interesting. Imagine that, potentially, men and women can "fit" one another on 100 traits. To make a serious love affair or marriage go well, couples probably have to match on, say, 85 or 90 of those traits. (In close relationships, little differences can cause big problems.) If casual dates fit on just a trait or two, they can probably still have an okay time together now and then. Some dates might share an interest in Marvel Universe movies. . . and nothing else. Another might be a great dinner date and serious conversationalist. Still others might be just right for spur-of-the-moment sailing trips. Another date, impossible one-to-one, may sparkle at parties. The criterion for a casual date is simply this: "Would I rather be alone tonight, or with my friend for an hour or two this evening?" The distance between what is required for an enjoyable date and what it takes to make a successful, serious relationship succeed is gargantuan.

There were some people for whom the traditional strategy we recommended didn't work. They ended up with a lot of friends but no lovers. Today, the typical American has one more tool to try out: the Internet.

If you choose to go on the Internet, keep the following in mind: Some sites and apps, because of their emphasis on good looks, youth, fun (and the fact that they are free), attract men and women who are primarily interested in casual dating (Tinder is often associated with this). Other sites (say, eHarmony), given the time, effort, and money required to join, are particularly appealing to people who are interested in searching for serious, long-term relationships. (Romance seems to cost far more than a date.)

What Are the Most Popular Online Dating Sites and Apps?

Today, the most popular sites in the United States (in order of popularity) are Match, PlentyofFish, Zoosk, OkCupid, eHarmony, Badoo, and

ChristianMingle (although rankings can change from moment to moment; see Statistica, 2016).

Some sites stick to the original tried-and-true Match.com strategy, namely asking people to compose profiles and then allowing them to sort through other people's profiles until they find someone who interests them. But as far back as August 2000, e-Harmony was launching a site claiming to take a "scientific approach" to matching. The site asked members to complete a "scientifically proven" questionnaire (consisting of 400 items), then e-Harmony's statisticians could feed their answers into a high-speed computer, so a (secret) "compatibility algorithm," presumably also based on scientific studies, could provide a match. For this effort and a monthly fee, members were promised a list of potential dates and mates who were "perfect" or "compatible" matches. Such presumably scientific sites soon became popular.

Some sites like Chemistry.com and GenePartner have attempted to match people, not on the basis of personalities, but on their genetic or immunological compatibility. GenePartner, for example, allows matchmakers or couples to order a DNA kit for $99 and mail in a saliva sample to discover their score on biological compatibility. Chemistry.com asks men and women to answer 56 questions—things like: "Which image (which they provide) most closely matches your right hand?" The assumption is that people possess different levels of dopamine, serotonin, estrogen, and testosterone. It is assumed that these differences in brain chemistry have a powerful effect on people's personalities—determining in which of four categories they fit: the explorer, the builder, the negotiator, or the director. (The site attempts to tell people what type, or combination of types, they are, based on physical characteristics, i.e., finger length, etc.) Clients are then matched with compatible types, on the basis of similarity or complementary.

Some sites target special niches of the population. Others are designed to appeal to various age groups (e.g., Mylol, OurTime), political groups (ConservativeMatch and LiberalHearts), religious groups (CatholicSingles.com, Jdate.com, ChristianCafe.com, and HappyBuddhist.com), race (blackpeoplemeet.com), and sexual orientations (Grindr or Her). There are sites for those yearning for an extramarital affair (Ashley Madison and VictoriaMilan). Dating sites and apps also exist for people who possess mental and physical disabilities, unusual sexual preferences, and so forth. Even people who wish to find dates for themselves and their favorite pets can sign on to a site (DateMyPet.com)! (See Table 2.1 for a list of some of the popular dating sites.)

Table 2.1   A Sampling of Matchmaking Websites and Phone Apps

Type of Site
Sites where people select their own dates and mates from a large pool of profiles: Match, PlentyofFish, OkCupid
Virtual dating sites: Users create an avatar and go on virtual dates in an online setting: OmniDate, Weopia, VirtualDateSpace
Sites where people are matched with dates and mates on the basis of their self-reports (via algorithms): eHarmony, Chemistry, Perfectmatch
Sites where people are matched with dates and mates on the basis of genetic or immunological compatibility GenePartner, ScientificMatch, FindYorFace,Mate, Chemistry
Social networking sites: Users can meet friends of friends Facebook, MySpace, Friendster, Whatsapp
Specialized niches: JDate, Gay, SilverSingles, ConservativeMatch, Catholic Singles, Manhunt, PinkCupid, SugarDaddie, Grindr, Scruff, Her, Jack'd

Smartphone Apps
GPS-enabled apps alert users of partners in their vicinity: Zoosk, Badoo, Grindr, Tinder, Happn, Bumble, Coffee Meets Bagel, Hinge
Sex or hookup sites: OnlineBootyCall, ManCrunch, AdultFriendFinder, Gettingon
Infidelity sites: Users can pursue extramarital sex: AshleyMadison, IllicitEncounters, Waiting Room

Some men and women use sites such as Sugar Daddy or Sugar Mama, to earn money for tuition, rent, or books. Rich elderly men (and women) will pay beautiful young men and women to accompany them on dinner dates, concerts, and the like. Whether sex is involved depends on the man or woman.

Given that 12,000 to 15,000 sites exist, Table 2.1 is obviously not intended to be all-inclusive. We are merely providing examples of the type of choices available to users. This information is current as of 2017; since things change rapidly, it may be different in later years.

But, as predicted, the third wave of matching has arrived. There now exist a plethora of smartphone apps, such as Tinder, Hinge, Bumble and others, which let their users post and then scan photos and short profiles of potential dates. With the swipe of a finger, people can decide if they want to chat or pass on a prospect. Many of these sites use Facebook data in their mathematical algorithms, so people can identify friends of friends and contact them. (Social networks have become inadvertent matchmakers.) Dating apps such as Tinder, Happn, Scruff, Her, Grindr, Badoo, Zoosk, Online BootyCall, and ManCrunch use Internet technology and GPS information to identify users' current locations and offer men and women, gay and straight, the chance to chat with strangers in their neighborhood. Participants can thumb through postings of people interested in chatting or, on the spur of the moment, engaging in casual sex, hookups, one-night stands, or even long-term relationships and friendships. People can now attach their Instagram and Spotify accounts to their Tinder and Bumble profile to further personalize their profiles. Both apps show what people have liked on Facebook, which further increases matching opportunities.

The most popular dating app to date is Tinder. In fact, nearly 26% percent of dating app consumers use Tinder, followed second by PlentyofFish (19%), then OkCupid (10%) (Priceonomics, 2016). Currently, Tinder has been downloaded over 100 million times, with one million of those downloads being for the "premium service" in which users get unlimited swipes. (Users without premium service have a limit to viewing a number of profiles in a 24-hour period; Chang, 2016). Tinder is immensely popular on college campuses. One study conducted at a major U.S. university found that 96% of its respondents had at one point used Tinder (Hildebrandt, 2015).

Tinder is unique in several ways. For one, it is hard to create a fake Tinder account, because Tinder connects to users' Facebook account and uploads photos directly from their Facebook page. However, aside from the Facebook link, there is little else required for users to quickly sign on and start swiping. While many other online dating platforms require completing lengthy personality tests, filling out profiles in which they must present themselves as a good potential mate, or have strict requirements regarding who the user can send messages to, Tinder in comparison is largely barrier-free. Since selecting mates relies only on the user's pictures (six to eight in total), age, location, and a brief bio, there's not much "up-front" time cost to signing up. After a user has signed up, they are presented with photos from other users in their immediate geographic area. Users then drag their finger across the screen to the right if they like the potential mate, and to the left if they do not. If the other person also swipes right, a "match" is created. At this point, a notification is sent to both users and the messaging feature between these individuals is enabled. Unlike most other dating websites, Tinder makes no effort to match its users, aside from age and location. There are no algorithms that place similar users together, no personality tests to compare scores between users. As such, Tinder is unlike any other dating service and provides a very unique, unfiltered look at mating behaviors (Tyson, Perta, Haddadi, & Seto, 2016).

These convenient mobile apps have taken over the market. Mobile technology is progressing at a pace that may make visiting the traditional online dating website obsolete. In fact, smartphone penetration in the United States is at 80%, while mobile use now makes up over 65% of all Internet traffic worldwide (comScore, 2016). As such, people are increasingly using dating apps instead of online dating websites. This shift to apps has happened in just a few years. In 2013, for example, 65% of users searched via a desktop computer. By 2014, 60% were making a connection via a mobile app. This is a remarkable change. Fig. 2.1 is a graph showing the unprecedented rise of Tinder, which now has over 50 million users worldwide—and counting.

We should note that which sites are "hot" and which are not can change with lightening speed. Sara Silverman, an athlete at the University of Hawaii, who served as one of our reviewers, observed:

> Chat rooms aren't really that popular anymore, at least in my experience. Social networking dating apps such as Tinder, Bumble, etc. are much more popular. Bumble is especially popular since women are the only ones who can initiate a conversation. The man's profile disappears within 24 hours [after making a match]. In addition, the new phenomenon of "sliding

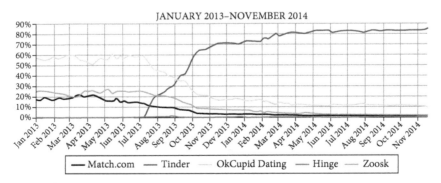

Fig. 2.1 Popularity of various dating sites over time.
Source: 7ParkData (2015).

into someone's DM" (sending someone a direct message on Instagram) is increasing in popularity as well, or the action of adding someone on Snapchat.

How Much Do the Various Sites and Apps Cost?

Sites and apps vary greatly in price. There are an array of free dating sites and mobile apps, such as Grindr, Tinder, Badoo, Clover, and Craigslist's "no-strings-attached" section, that are arguably geared toward finding casual sex or casual dating. (These sites rely on advertising to support them.) For those sites and apps that charge, it's tricky to say how much a given site will cost. Most offer a free get-acquainted service (which allows you to "lurk"—i.e., to scan postings), but require you to actually become a subscriber if you spot a potential date or mate that you want to contact and/or chat with. (Zoosk falls in that category; it is free to search the postings of subscribers but costs $29.95 a month to become a participating member.) PlentyofFish and OkCupid have Basic Accounts that are free. Then the various subscriptions increase in price, depending on the services they provide. Match, for example, charges $35 for a 1-month membership; e-Harmony charges $60 for the same period. ScientificMatch charges $2,000 for a lifetime membership, matching on personal preferences, personality, and values, as well as genetic and immunological compatibility. MillionairesClub123 charges $25,000 a year. The fee includes image counseling, date coaching, hypnotherapy, and relationship advice. It also gives one access to hair stylists, plastic surgeons, and personal trainers. To find out the cost of any sites of interest, you merely have to access that site and study the various options. Word of mouth provides a lot of information, too. Price is of special concern, since (as we will see in a final section) there is no compelling evidence that any of these sites are effective.

How Can I Separate Myself from the Pack?

Once a user selects a dating site, the first step is often to create a profile or fill out a questionnaire. Heino, Ellison, and Gibbs (2010) have compared a profile to a "résumé, a promotional tool designed to market one's "best self" rather than provide a complete or accurate representation. Naturally, people want to attract a reasonable number of potential mates and dates. Thus, just as products are marketed to appeal to certain demographic groups, participants emphasize qualities they think will appeal to the specific kinds of potential dates and mates they hope to meet. A posting typically includes one or more photos of oneself (people who don't provide a photo are rarely contacted), basic demographic information (e.g., age, sex, education, profession, number of children, geographic location, religion, relationship status, sexual orientation), and information about interests and behaviors (e.g., smoking and drinking habits, hobbies).

There are any number of online sites that give newcomers advice about crafting a profile. Of course, one can only list a few of one's assets (enough to give readers a feel for one's personality and interests). In one study, Hitsch, Hortaçsu, and Ariely (2010) studied the profiles of 6,485 users of a major self-selection dating site in the United States. They wanted to know what worked and what didn't. They found that both sexes were especially likely to initiate contact with potential partners who were physically attractive and earned a high income. They also tended to contact partners who were similar to themselves in characteristics such as race, religion, political orientation, educational achievement, single versus divorced status, parenthood status, and smoking habits. In personality, people who were agreeable, emotionally stable, and extroverted (possessing definite beliefs and hobbies) were the most desirable partners. Interestingly, people with these latter profiles tend to experience greater satisfaction and longevity in relationships (Weidman, Cheng, Chisholm, & Tracy, 2015).

We would argue, though, that postings that help potential suitors get a real feel for their personality work better than stereotyped presentations. How useful is it when men and women confront 8,500 postings that say "My favorite activities are sipping a glass of wine in front of a roaring fire, hiking, and strolling along a beach?" Does it mean anything if they omit "gazing at a beautiful sunset"?

Surprisingly, most participants say that listing all their assets made them feel better about themselves. They hadn't realized they possessed so many good traits until they constructed the profile! Many women said, given the number of responses they received, it felt like an "ego boost." The few who said it had lowered their self-esteem said it taught them to be less picky over time (Heino et al., 2010, p. 439).

In an ideal profile, you would list all your desires and all of the traits you know are deal breakers for you (see the next section for suggestions). But you can't. That sort of winnowing comes later in the get-acquainted process—when you finally meet face to face. Inefficient to be sure, but that's the way it is. In your initial posting you can only describe a few of your traits and mention a few of your pet peeves. Later on, you will have the chance to get to know people at a deeper level.

You will note that almost all these dating sites employ market metaphors in their ads. They take a very pragmatic approach to romance. Throughout most of history, families arranged marriages; love was a practical matter. Then came Shakespearian comedies, romantic poetry, and Hollywood. Increasingly, many young people came to think of love as something magical, sparked by destiny . . . or Disney. Love at first sight would be accompanied by an explosion of fireworks. In those times of love as magic, social psychologists (often in the face of much criticism and outrage) would point out that market conditions matter, too (Hatfield, Walster, & Berscheid, 1978). (We'll talk more about love and the market in Chapter 4.)

Now the pendulum has swung so far the other way that all of the capitalist metaphors that dominate advertisements for matching sites get to be annoying. We think it may be overdue for scholars to acknowledge that people can hope for a little sprinkling of enchantment when searching for a mate. But currently that's not the way it is. Perhaps the scholars of love and marketers could be reminded that there is some magic and unpredictability when it comes to finding love. But that's not where we are now. Matching sites still claim, just get your algorithm right, and perfect love is likely to follow.

Which Traits Should I Look for in a Mate?

Heino and her colleagues (2010) have conceptualized online dating as "relations shopping." People flip through the "advertisements" until they find something they like. One online dater illustrated this shopping cart mentality: ". . . this one yes, this one no. You know. 'I'll take her, her, her'—like out of a catalog" (p. 437). There is no reason not to aim for the best (maybe you will get lucky), but a little experience suggests that in making selections, you want to be realistic. People do best if they don't aim too high or settle for too little. But how does one know what constitutes an "equitable" or suitable mate?

Experience helps. In real life, discovering how you "stack up" may be a long and painful process. Online, it's faster. As one woman said: "I don't pick the models because I know they won't pick me. So I pick the Joe averages."

One man mentioned that as he aged and his online response rate suffered, he broadened his age and weight criteria for potential dates (Heino et al., 2010, p. 439). In the online marketplace, participants come to understand that their own desirability is made explicit by the number and types of responses received. However, the online dating market is not like the real-world one. Sending messages is easy, and it can be tempting to misinterpret sex ratios and your own marketability in the strange world of profile swiping and message sending. In fact, studies show that online dating causes both men and women to "shoot for the stars" and consistently send messages to the best-looking people on the site, regardless of their own attractiveness level (Hitsch et al., 2010). There may be several reasons why this happens so often in digital spaces.

Studies suggest that men are more likely than women to desire a variety of sexual partners across their lifespan (Bailey, Gaulin, Agyei, & Gladue, 1994) and are more likely than women to seek different partners who indicate signs of youth and fertility (Baumeister, Catanese, & Vohs, 2001). Additionally, men are much more likely to pursue romantic partners by using direct and quick methods of approach and proposition (Clark, Shaver, & Abrahams, 1999), and they spend more time and energy looking for short-term mating opportunities than do women (Townsend, Kline, & Wasserman, 1995). These dating strategies result in men sending more messages, likes, or swipes to more women, more indiscriminately on online dating sites where the interface of apps such as Tinder facilitate these selection methods (Tyson et al., 2016). Women, in response to what appears to be a "buyer's market," as their inboxes are regularly flooded with short messages from many men, send fewer messages and only to the most attractive men. Hey, if there's this much to choose from, why settle for less than the hottest thumbnail pic you can find? Ironically, it is the most attractive men who are the most likely to send the most messages (Cooper, 2015), which then may cause this confusing game of cat-and-mouse to perpetuate itself ad nauseam.

However, these gender differences may not be as salient as previously believed. In Dr. Jeanette Purvis' recent dissertation studies, experiences on Tinder were analyzed in an Internet survey, an analysis of an online forum, and through an experimental paradigm. There were no significant gender differences in likelihood to engage in casual sex, partner preferences, or desired relationship length between male and females who used Tinder. The only gender difference detected was that males were more likely than females to indicate a willingness to engage in sex on a first date, but that difference was not reflected in actual reported behavior (Purvis, 2017). These findings offer support for the gender similarity hypothesis (Hyde 2005), which suggests males and females are more similar than they are different, the most reliable difference being expressed as willingness to engage in casual sex.

But no matter if men and women are more the same or more different, finding love online is not futile, and indeed, many people are smart to continue the search. This makes some sense. It's hard to hit the mark. One sample of users reported that they spent an average of 5.2 hours per week browsing profiles and another 6.7 hours writing and responding to e-mails—a process they did not really enjoy and which yielded only 1.8 hours of face-to-face interaction (Frost, Chance, Norton, & Ariely, 2008). However, as online dating becomes less stigmatized, and online dating apps make it increasingly simple to meet in offline places, it may be that people will be able to meet more people offline more quickly, saving hours of time spent trying to express one's "true self" via email beforehand.

Then people usually have to try out a number of dates. This mode of meeting multiple potential mates through online interfaces may increase one's likelihood of finding a mate. Heino and his colleagues (2010) recount the advice a computer sales person gave to one online dater:

> The example he used was, out of 100 phone calls there might be 20 potential prospects, and meeting with them there might be three or four sales out of that 20. It's a trial and error thing, it's a numbers game. He said to her, "You've got to meet 100 guys! Out of 100 guys, there's [sic] bound to be a few." . . . And she met them and went on a lot of first dates and finally met somebody. So maybe it is a numbers game. (p. 438)

Once you meet, of course, you can allow your partner to know you at a more honest and perhaps deeper level.

Once We Meet, What Should I Look for in a Match?

When it comes to selecting a long-term mate, choices become more critical and more complex. It is very difficult to make wise choices. We pick up some attitudes from TV and from our family and friends, but only experience can tell us with any certainty what works for us. People who have been married a long time, or are on the brink of divorce, or are older often lament: "If only

I had known." Dating several people helps us separate what we think we *should* want from what we do in fact want.

In one study, Elaine Hatfield and her students (Young & Hatfield, 2011) interviewed 1,000 dating couples, 100 newlyweds, and 400 elderly women, asking them what rewards (or the lack thereof) they considered to be most important in their relationships. The authors expected young people to differ wildly in what they wanted in a date versus a mate, but they found this not to be the case. Maybe in a club or a one-night stand only looks mattered, but by the time men and women had dated for awhile, they had developed a pretty good idea of what they would look for "next time." The characteristics the men and women found to be most important were clustered in four areas: personal concerns, emotional concerns, day-to-day concerns, and opportunities gained and lost.

The *personal rewards* include how attractive partners are, how sociable, and how intelligent.

The *emotional rewards* touch on such matters as how much partners like one another, their understanding of each other's needs, their sexual relationship, and their commitment to one another.

Day-to-day events concern the amount of money they both bring in, daily maintenance of the house, fitting in with each other's friends and relatives, and the like.

That brings us, finally, to *opportunities gained and lost.* One thing we rarely consider when assessing the happiness of a relationship is the fact that irrespective of one's partner, having a steady date or mate provides some advantages (and disadvantages). These include the chance to be married and have children. But they also showcase opportunities foregone, such as the chance to have married someone else. For a complete (and more detailed) list of what people wish for in a serious dating relationship and a marriage, see Young and Hatfield (2011).

Your Own Personal Deal Breakers

When thinking about love, people usually focus on what they want—not what they want to avoid like the plague. With experience, people learn the hard way what they will avoid next time. We encourage you to pick up a pencil and scratch pad and make a list of the things you wouldn't put up with in a relationship. How did you learn that these traits were deal breakers for you?

Here are some things that most young people say would be deal breakers for them—next time.

When asked what constituted "deal breakers" in their own failed romantic relationships, the young people we interviewed (Hatfield, Feybesse, & Rapson, 2016) quickly compiled a list:

Alcoholism
Drug addiction
Opposite wishes on having children
Mates who turned out to be stupid
Sloppy/Piggy partners
Controlling
Verbally abusive
Physically violent
Jealous
Disparaged my taste and values
Racist/Sexist/Homophobic
Irresponsible or mean to children, or a child molester
Dismissive of my friends
Dismissive of my work
Wouldn't share housework/childcare
Procrastinated/Always late/Didn't pay taxes, etc.
A cheater
Broke the law
Made no money/Refused to get a job/Lazy
Spent all my money
Admired Donald Trump

For other traits that turn romance into boredom and disgust and push a relationship into dissolution, see the work by Burkett and Kirkpatrick (2006) and Jonason and his colleagues (2015).

Cunningham, Shamblen, Barbee, and Alt (2005), in a series of studies with U.S. college students, identified major categories of behaviors that are often responsible for the termination of a relationship. These included *uncouth habits* (e.g., poor grooming, failure to clean the bathroom, and the like), *inconsiderate acts* (e.g., being late for appointments, demanding too much attention), *intrusive behaviors* (e.g., physical abuse, being overly controlling, being overly critical of the partner), and *norm violations* (e.g., partner drinks too much, flirts with other people, etc.) Among them, *intrusive behaviors*—harmful behaviors that are intentionally directed toward the partner—best predicted relationship dissatisfaction and termination. *Norm violations*—intentional behaviors that violate societal standards—also predicted relationship dissatisfaction and termination. *Having undesirable personality traits* may also force the partner to terminate the relationship.

In a longitudinal study of American couples followed from courtship (in the 1930s) to the 1980s, the strongest personality predictors for divorce were neuroticism or negative emotionality and lack of impulse control by the male partner (Kelly & Conley, 1987). Men and women may possess reproductive interests and sets of evolved sexual strategies that are at odds with each other. It then follows that there should be gender differences in what constitutes a romantic deal breaker, with men and women becoming offended by the other's preferred sexual strategy. Consistent with this assumption, research has found American women to be more upset by their partners' sexual assertiveness and aggressiveness, whereas men are more upset by their partners' sexual withholding. In addition, women were upset by their partners' inconsiderate, neglecting, and condescending behavior, whereas men were upset by their partners' moodiness and physical self-absorption (Buss, 1989).

Across six studies, Jonason and his colleagues (2015) identified some standard relationship deal breakers. He found that deal breakers were associated with unattractiveness, undesirable personality traits, unhealthy lifestyles, differing religious beliefs, limited social status, divergent mating psychologies, and differing relationship goals. Naturally, people had different preferences in short-term versus long-term relationships. There were some individual differences. People who are more appealing (i.e., who possess higher mate value) were more demanding—that is, reported more deal breakers.

It may be worth noting that by far the primary deal breaker, in movies and on TV, and in popular culture is described as "cheating," or "adultery," or "infidelity." (Language matters. If people used words like *sampling*, or *experimenting*, or *fooling around*, lazy screenwriters and authors of soap operas might explore more fully the many other, often more telling, reasons for breakups—such as physical violence, humiliation of children, drug addiction, or alcoholism. As of now, *cheating* is the easy shorthand, and for many consumers of pop culture, it has become the main reason for ending a relationship. "Cheating" supposedly says it all.)

There is some confusion, however about what cheating is. Is it messaging a girl on Instagram? Liking a picture of a friend of a friend you find attractive on Facebook? Hugging a friend? Kissing? We will discuss this later. It is somewhat puzzling that some people often consider casual sex (as in hookups) to not be a problem when they are single, but once they are in a relationship, monogamy becomes critically important. These individuals often say they would divorce if they caught their partner straying even once. We do not have a good explanation for this anomaly.

A variety of researchers have suggested ways to increase the passion, intimacy, and commitment in relationships. Arthur Aron (in Ehrenfeld, 2013), for example, suggests that young people can increase the intimacy of their relationships by spending time discussing the following 36 questions with one another. For many, such discussions, which naturally occur over the course of a relationship, can foster a sense of intimacy.

How Can I Get to Know Someone More Intimately?

After the small talk, how can I find out a bit more about my partner? Aron (Ehrenfeld, 2013) proposed that couples can find their way to greater intimacy by discussing these telltale questions:

1. Given the choice of anyone in the world, who would you want as a dinner guest?
2. Would you like to be famous? In what way?
3. Before making a phone call, do you ever rehearse what you're going to say? Why?
4. What would constitute a perfect day for you?
5. When did you last sing to yourself? To someone else?
6. If you were able to live to the age of 90 and retain either the mind or body of a 30-year-old for the last 60 years of your life, which would you choose?
7. Do you have a secret hunch about how you will die?
8. Name three things you and your partner appear to have in common.
9. For what in your life do you feel most grateful?
10. If you could change anything about the way you were raised, what would it be?
11. Take four minutes and tell you partner your life story in as much detail as possible.
12. If you could wake up tomorrow having gained one quality or ability, what would it be?

13. If a crystal ball could tell you the truth about yourself, your life, the future or anything else, what would you want to know?

14. Is there something that you've dreamt of doing for a long time? Why haven't you done it?

15. What is the greatest accomplishment of your life?

16. What do you value most in a friendship?

17. What is your most treasured memory?

18. What is your most terrible memory?

19. If you knew that in one year you would die suddenly, would you change anything about the way you are now living? Why?

20. What does friendship mean to you?

21. What roles do love and affection play in your life?

22. Alternate sharing something you consider a positive characteristic of your partner. Share a total of five items.

23. How close and warm is your family? Do you feel your childhood was happier than most other people's?

24. How do you feel about your relationship with your mother?

25. Make three true "we" statements each. For instance, "we are both in this room feeling . . . "

26. Complete this sentence: "I wish I had someone with whom I could share . . . "

27. If you were going to become a close friend with your partner, please share what would be important for them to know.

28. Tell your partner what you like about them: be honest this time, saying things that you might not say to someone you've just met.

29. Share with your partner an embarrassing moment in your life.

30. When did you last cry in front of another person? By yourself?

31. Tell your partner something that you like about them already.

32. What, if anything, is too serious to be joked about?

33. If you were to die this evening with no opportunity to communicate with anyone, what would you most regret not having told someone? Why haven't you told them yet?

34. Your house, containing everything you own, catches fire. After saving your loved ones and pets, you have time to safely make a final dash to save any one item. What would it be? Why?

35. Of all the people in your family, whose death would you find most disturbing? Why?

36. Share a personal problem and ask your partner's advice on how they might handle it. Also, ask your partner to reflect back to you how you seem to be feeling about the problem you have chosen.

... and a few variations:

1. If you could choose the sex and physical appearance of your soon-to-be-born child, would you do it?
2. Would you be willing to have horrible nightmares for a year if you would be rewarded with extraordinary wealth?
3. While on a trip to another city, your spouse or lover meets and spends a night with an exciting stranger. Given that they will never meet again, and could never otherwise learn of the incident, would you want your partner to tell you about it?

These questions are said to help you gain insight into the thoughts and feelings of family members and friends as well.

Next we turn to a question that is especially critical for people considering using the Web:

All in all, what are the advantages and disadvantages of choosing to add the Web to our armamentaria for finding a mate?

What Are the Advantages and Disadvantages of Searching for Love on the Web?

That girl is really hot. I'd definitely swipe right for her.
—The Urban Dictionary

Swipe Right: The Advantages of the Web

Theorists have long noted that the number of suitable men and suitable women in the "dating market" determine how much one can expect from a pairing (Hatfield, Forbes, & Rapson, 2012). Given this logic, it is no surprise to find that the degree to which people are attracted to the Internet is related to the qualities (or lack thereof) of the "singles scene" in which they find themselves. The Internet and apps can ameliorate the problem of scarcity. Merkle and Richardson (2000) noted that a person can sample scores of potential partners via Internet matching services and apps. The potential exists for connecting with large numbers of people, who may be spread across a large geographic region, in a relatively short period of time.

Furthermore, presumably, the people with whom one connects at matching services are available, eligible, and interested in making a connection—information that is harder to find out from in-person meetings in public settings. As another special attraction, Internet services provide considerable help in matching people according to age, occupation, wealth, physical looks, psychological qualities including values and attitudes, lifestyle preferences, and many other factors. Use of the Internet increases one's chances of connecting with like-minded (or "like-bodied") people, owing to the computer's ability to rapidly sort along many dimensions. In fact, the biggest attraction to matching services may be the hope that one can obtain a soul mate, "the love of one's life," a special partner who is unlikely to be found through normal channels. Many matching services promote this hope. Finding a compatible mate through an Internet matching service may be possible, although it may take time and investment.

Some of the most enthusiastic proponents of online dating are people who live in isolated geographic locations (such as in a small town or the countryside) or work at jobs that make it difficult to find partners, particularly partners who share their values and interests. These include men and women who have moved to a new community, are over 30, who have experienced a breakup or are divorced, who have children, who possess limited time to meet potential partners because they are single parents or work long hours, or who don't feel comfortable in the bar scene or clubs (Finkel et al., 2012).

The Internet as well as apps are also godsends for those who have atypical interests (surfing or anime), who possess a minority sexual orientation— who are, say, LGBT (lesbian, gay, bisexual, or transgender), or who possess "kinky" interests or certain stigmata (such as being HIV positive). Such people may be likely to find a partner or at least someone to chat with online by casting a wide net.

It is no surprise, then, that generally gays, lesbians, bisexuals, and those who are interested in interracial relationships are often the first to go online (Rosenfeld & Thomas, 2012). In places like China or India, for example, where gay sex is taboo, Grindr and local gay sites like Blued have attracted millions of gay male users. Bengali and Kaiman (2016) report that one user observed:

> In America, if you don't use Grindr, you can go to a gay bar. You can find gay people around. In China, apart from Beijing, Guangzhou and Shanghai—in smaller cities and in the countryside—you can't find any gay organizations or gay bars whatsoever. (p. 2)

It is people in these categories who are likely to be most satisfied with their online matchings.

Swipe Left: What Are the Dangers of Going Online?

Given all the potential advantages of matchmaking services, why wouldn't all singles who are looking for love choose to use the Internet?

For a few, there are practical barriers to finding partners in this way: these include the costs involved; illiteracy in the use of computers, iPhones, and online services; and the investment of time. These fees, however, are probably not overwhelming for most, especially compared to the costs of going to clubs and bars to meet others, taking trips with singles groups, and engaging in other elaborate ways of meeting people in person.

There is, however, a set of more imposing social psychological barriers to the use of the Internet. In particular, for a few there still is a stigma associated with Internet matchmaking. Some people do not want the stigma and negative stereotypes they believe they might encounter if they admit to using such services. Although the stigma is dissipating with millions of Internet users, it nonetheless affects some—in Smith and Anderson's (2016) survey, 29% of American adult respondents agreed that people who engage in online dating are desperate. The stigma still exists, but to a much lesser extent.

Another barrier is that occasionally online searchers need to settle for matches that are at a great geographic distance, which can introduce costs to the relationship. Although most online daters request matches that are nearby, those who do not live in geographic areas with high-density populations may need to expand the radius in order to find any matches. In contrast, people traditionally fell in love with the person next door—or at least just down the lane (e.g., Bossard, 1932). Although it was unlikely that the person next door would have a similar score on the type of compatibility test utilized by popular Internet matching services today, neither person had to travel more than a few blocks to find the other, and neither had to be uprooted in order to move in together. Now, people may be connected through Internet sites with people from other cities or states (or even other countries), which creates all kinds of logistical and financial challenges. The fact that these kinds of relationships require commuting to see one another can exacerbate a related barrier: a pair formed over the Internet does not have the opportunity to gain support from family and friends. Often, family and friends do not even know about the developing online relationship, and when they do learn about the Internet-initiated romance, they may not always be supportive (Wildermuth, 2004).

> How could you believe me
> When I said I loved you
> When you know
> I've been a liar all my life?
>
> —Burton Lane and Alan Jay Lerner

In addition, some singles may be reluctant to try online dating because they assume that potential matches may be lying in their profiles. The anonymity of the Internet is a key issue for all parties in using this medium for communication. In particular, an abiding concern is that potential partners listing their wares on dating sites are not being honest about their marital status, their current romantic involvements, the age of photos posted, their financial status, their personal health, and the like. Singles have reason to be suspicious if someone looks too good to be true. Hitsch, Hortaçsu, and Ariely (2010) compared data presented in profiles with national averages. Men claimed to be 1.3 inches taller and women claimed to be an inch taller than the national average. Women reported weighing from 5.4 pounds less (in the 20–29 age group) to 22.9 pounds less (in the 50- to 59-year-old age group) than the national average; men's reported weight generally aligned closely with national averages.

More direct evidence comes from a study comparing the profiles of 80 online daters with their actual characteristics (Toma, Hancock, & Ellison, 2008). When the researchers assessed height with a tape measure, weight with a scale, and age as reported on an individual's driver's license, they discovered that 81% of these online daters reported inaccurate information on at least one of these three characteristics on their profile. About 60% lied about their weight, 48% about their height, and 19% about their age. Most people reported themselves to be above average in looks; only 30% of users reported themselves as average in looks, and a mere 1% said they were "less than average." Generally, the degree of deception was small and it would be difficult to detect face-to-face. But these findings do recall Garrison Keillor's praise of Lake Wobegon, where "all the children are above average." This may explain why many "swipers" tend to shoot for the stars by swiping profiles much more attractive than their own!

One Ghanaian published this description of computer matching gone wrong: He describes his first face-to-face meeting with a computer match:

> It was too late to run away or pretend I wasn't the guy she had come to meet. I don't expect too much from women: moderate curves, a Master's degree, and a dimple will be a bonus. Instead, a scruffy lady with a roomy stomach suspending on thin legs was smiling towards me. Her bottom was as flat as a pancake and her body distribution was laughable: huge arms, the size of 16th century queens used as billboards to display the royal jewelry and a neck so short that her torso tucked under her chin. The face powder she was wearing was thicker than shaving foam I had used that morning. As we sat eating, I wondered whose photographs she sent me. . . . We parted honorably. Strangely, it turns out, she also didn't like me. God is always faithful. (Tawiah, 2007, cited in Fair, Tully, Ekdale, & Asante, 2009)

There is also a more sinister side to the Internet that may serve as a formidable barrier to the most cautious of singles. Although they may be fewer in number now that the online dating industry has become mainstream and background checks exist at some sites, Internet predators still exist.

Catfishing

On rare occasions the scams are serious. One kind of scam is called "catfishing," which means to pretend to be someone you are not in order to inspire romantic feelings in a hapless victim. One of the most infamous cases of catfishing happened to Manti Te'o, a football star at Notre Dame who went on to play in the NFL. The catfishing began when Te'o received a picture of a beautiful Hawaiian woman on social media, claiming she was "Lennay Kekua." Te'o and "Lennay" posted and talked on the telephone for almost a year, never meeting, and soon Te'o was wildly in love with her. Then, weeks after Te'o's grandmother died he was told that

Lennay had died from leukemia. Soon he learned that the whole romance had all been a hoax by a man named Ronaiah Tulesosopo, a rumored friend of Te'o's. The grief and shame are thought to have contributed to the ruining of Te'o's very promising football career. The drama and shame surrounding the act of catfishing are part of the reason the MTV documentary show *Catfish*, which uses investigative journalism to uncover suspected catfishers from all over the country, is now entering its wildly popular sixth season.

Scams

According to the FBI, romance scams bilked victims of all ages and orientations out of more than $200 million in one year (Murphy, 2016). The scammers pose as the perfect soul mate. Then, after a series of passionate letters, come the requests for money. The soldier needs a new cellphone so the lovers can better communicate or needs cash so he can get the necessary papers to go on leave so they can finally meet. The model or nurse may need money to pay lawyers' fees to get a restraining order against an abusive ex. In the latest twist, scammers coax victims into sending nude photos or explicit texts, and then threaten to distribute them to their Facebook contacts if they don't help them launder money.

The many scams that come out of Africa are the stuff of legend and *Saturday Night Live* skits: the social media "soul mate" who wants to award you a fortune, if only you will send a few thousand in processing money (called the Nigerian 419 scam) or who needs money for a family emergency (this is called the Nigerian/Ghana emergency scam); the fake kidnap scam; and requests to cash a money order ("I can't cash a money order in Ghana. Would you cash it and send me the money?"). Actually, the money order was originally for $20, doctored to indicate it is worth $20,000. When the money is sent to Ghana, Nigeria, or Lagos and cashed, the lover disappears. The FBI follows soon thereafter, demanding that the dupe pay back the scammed money.

Profiles picture stunning African movie stars or handsome African princes, generals, or sportsmen (temporarily impoverished by this or that war). In response to these desperate pleas, many lovers have sent tickets for travel and money, waited at the airport for a flight from Zambia, a bouquet in hand, only to be disappointed as reality dawns.

Similar to what can occur in face-to-face interaction, some men may initiate a first date in order to isolate a woman and sexually assault her (Shotland,

1989). For further discussion of Internet stalking, see Spitzberg and Cupach (2007).

And at the extreme: "Facebook's 'teen dating' groups are every parent's nightmare come to life" blared a *Washington Post* headline (Dewey, 2016). Nicole Lovell, a 13-year-old girl who had been ill most of her life, posted a plaintive plea on a Facebook dating site called KIK or Teen Dating and Flirting; "Am I ugly?" she asked. She received some bullying replies, many of which are heartbreaking. One man was interested, however—an 18-year-old Virginia Tech student, David Eisenhauer. They arranged to meet. She snuck out of her bedroom window after her curfew—and he killed her. *The New York Times* warned parents about smartphone apps that allow users to conceal their identities, posing significant risks for teenagers: these include Kik, Yik Yak, Whisper, After School, Snapchat, and Photovault (Stolberg & Pérez-Peña, 2016).

Lately, and horrifically, young people are being seduced into joining the Islamic State through offers of romance and marriage as enticements. Young women are promised a "jihottie" (jihadist hottie) of their choosing for a husband. Young men are offered an attractive and devoted wife. Of course, when they join ISIS they are sorely disappointed and tragically misused and abused.

> After growing wildly for years, the field of computing appears to be reaching its infancy.
>
> —John Pierce

How Do Most Matches Work Out?

Almost all of the matching sites make extravagant claims as to their efficacy. For example, eHarmony states:

> Out of all of the single people you will meet in your life, only a very few would make a great relationship partner for you. By combining the best scientific research with detailed profiling of every member, we screen thousands of single men and single women to bring you only the ones that have the potential to be truly right for you. (Assimos, 2011)

OkCupid.com states on their "About" page that "We use math to find you dates. You should see the work that goes into this bad boy. Algorithms, formulas, heuristics—we do a lot of crazy math stuff to help people connect faster" (2016). Clearly the promise is that scientists, with their esoteric ability to turn all human behavior into a complex yet successful algorithm, have somehow cracked the code on love.

Chemistry.com probably makes the most outrageous claims, as outlined next.

DNA Matching and the Magic of Chemistry

When you share chemistry with someone, you significantly increase your chances of realizing these amazing benefits:

1. You'll love their natural body fragrance—they'll smell "sexier" than other people.
2. You'll have a more satisfying sex life.
3. If you're a woman, you'll have a higher rate of orgasms.
4. There will be less cheating in your exclusive relationship.
5. As a couple, you'll be more fertile.
6. Your children will be healthier.(Taken from Cacioppio, Bianchi-Demicheli, Hatfield, & Rapson, 2012)

Lots more orgasms? Healthier children? Such modest promises!

In support of these wild assertions, the Chemistry.com authors cite a slew of articles published in prestigious social psychological, neuroscience, evolutionary psychology, and neurobiochemistry journals. Alas, none of these articles are really relevant to the efficacy of the sites' matching procedures.

What evidence, then, is there to support such claims? Really, none. The date match companies are all for-profit entities and so they are not enthusiastic about revealing their theories (probably that similarity, complementarity, or both are important), the variables emphasized in compatibility matching (for good guesses, see Finkel et al., 2012), their strategies for matching (the algorithms are trade secrets), or how much they supposedly spend evaluating the success of their services. They are much happier promising the world and spending their money on advertising than on transparency.

So, in deciding whether or not the sites are likely to meet your needs, consider the frank admissions of the scientists who have crafted many of these sites.

We contend: "the various sites are for fun; they shouldn't be taken too seriously."

Helen Fisher (2004a, on Match.com) writes:

> ... it's a misnomer that they call these things "dating services." They *should* be called "introducing services." They enable you to go out and go and meet the person yourself. . . .

"We, as a scientific community, do not believe that these algorithms work," Eli J. Finkel (2012) has observed. To him, dating sites like eHarmony and Match.com are like peddling snake oil. "They are a joke, and there is no relationship scientist that takes them seriously as relationship science."

Psychologists have learned a great deal about the factors that make for happy relationships. They are fully aware that, as yet, even the most brilliant scientists are unable to predict how love affairs will work out.

Conclusion

For common folk, computer matching sites have the imprimatur of Science (with a capital *S*). Some argue that no one takes the claims of these sites seriously. How satisfied you will be with these sites depends on how modest your expectations are. If you access them just for fun, you will probably be satisfied. If you are shy or live in a geographic location or work at a job or have preferences that make it difficult or impossible to find partners (particularly those who share values and interests), you will have the chance to meet dates and mates that might never come your way. But if you truly believe that scientists can match you with an ideal Prince Charming or Sleeping Beauty, you are likely to be disappointed.

Some supporters point out that commercial matching services are still in their infancy. Since social psychologists, neuroscientists, and neurobiologists are working for these sites, in time—given the money that is being lavished on these commercial enterprises—it is reasonable to hope that in the future the business of love sites will craft more complex versions of relationship science to inform their questionnaire construction, website construction, and matching algorithms. Thus, in time, these matching sites may provide increased opportunities for men and women to find dating and marital relationships that are fulfilling.

Other scientists cringe, arguing that these sites can't possibly fulfill their promises of the great match. Currently, as we said, these matching sites— arguing that they are businesses not scientific enterprises—are reluctant to explain in any detail how they match people and how successful such matches are. Critics point out that only charlatans, crooks, and con men sell "elixirs" that cure nothing. People who join these sites looking for love are being cheated. Worse yet, false claims make people who get burned skeptical about the scientific enterprise itself. When people are disappointed—and they are bound to be—they will blame science for their disappointment (see Sprecher et al., 2008, for a longer discussion of these issues.)

Life may be wonderful or painful, because love and relationships are no simple matter. People should look in all possible places for the experience, most definitely including the Internet. The experience of putting oneself on a somewhat public interface to be evaluated for love is obviously an intimidating process. Wanting and searching for love can certainly leave one feeling vulnerable. However, when you look around and see there are millions of others doing the same thing, it can be better understood as a regular human process, now extending across technological frontiers. It may be convenient to blame computers for our struggles at forming and keeping interpersonal relationships when, in fact, technology may sometimes be bringing us together; it's the difficulties of life, love, and relationships themselves that tear us apart. Just so one goes in to this search with open eyes, a spirit of fun, and realistic expectations, participation should be rewarding.

3

The Globalization of Western Love via the Internet

People have always exchanged information and goods. Twenty thousand years ago, tribesmen from Jiangxi Provence in China learned how to throw pots and brought those skills with them as they traveled the world. In Papua New Guinea, tribes organized vast Kula Rings, so tribal members could paddle to nearby islands once a year, gifting the next tribe in a circle with shell necklaces, beads, and armbands. The exchange was thought to build trust and solidarity. But today it is the processes of Westernization and globalization that are the most relevant to our interests.

Westernization and Globalization

In the realms of love and sex, a profound revolution has taken place in the last three centuries, and it is still happening (for better or for worse). It started in Europe, spread to the United States, and now appears to be reaching deep into the traditions of many non-Western societies. It is part of the dominant tendency of modern history, a tendency given the names of "Westernization" and "globalization." It is important to describe, however briefly, the general nature of this ongoing revolution, because from the point of view of world historians, it underlies practically everything we see going on about us (McNeill, 1963; Rapson, 1988; Roberts, 1976). The historical model with which most scholars interested in world history operates, goes like this.

Throughout the centuries, four cultures possessed the most political and economic power and the most influential cultural traditions. These four were the *East Asia* area (today's China, Japan, Korea, southeast Asia); *South Asia* (India, Pakistan, Afghanistan, Sri Lanka); the *Middle East* or *West Asia* (Egypt, Persia [Iran], Mesopotamia [Iraq], Palestine, Syria, and other Arab countries); and *Western* civilization (Europe and, recently, Canada

What's Next in Love and Sex. Elaine Hatfield, Richard L. Rapson, and Jeanette Purvis, Oxford University Press (2020). © Oxford University Press.
DOI: 10.1093/oso/9780190647162.001.0001

and the United States). There have been other strong, original cultures—in Africa, North and South America, the steppes of Asia, Polynesia, Oceania, and other places—but none of them could match the power and influence of the Big Four. Until 1500, the four major groups were by and large separate and independent cultural units. They tended to move on parallel tracks, intersecting at times, but generally swerving away from one another. There barely existed even the *concept* of one world. In the realms of passionate love and sexual desire, different cultural groups possessed somewhat different ideas about the social rules governing them (Braudel, 1966; Stavrianos, 1981).

All that changed after 1500. Large transformations followed in the wake of the Renaissance, the Scientific Revolution, and the Industrial Revolution. By the late 18th century, the West began to alter its view of love and almost everything else. Western culture began to "invent" a number of unique and modern ideas. In the *material sphere*, "Westernization" has meant the rapid expansion of urbanization, industrialization, and technology. In the *economic and political spheres*, it has meant a move toward democracy, capitalism, socialism, or totalitarianism systems. In the *philosophical sphere*, it has meant an increasing faith, first in Christianity and then humanism, secularism, and science. And (perhaps most importantly for our purposes) in the *psychological sphere*, it has meant an increasing insistence on individualism, the desirability of the goal of personal happiness and the reduction of pain, accompanied by personal and artistic freedom and more fluid class systems. Looming large in the psychological arena has been a metamorphosis in European-American approaches to love and sex, many of which are now being emulated in corners of the non-Western world (McNeill, 1963; Roberts, 1976; Stavrianos, 1981; Toynbee, 1934; Wallerstein, 1974).

The West initiated such ideas and practices (among many) as placing a high value on romantic and passionate love; marriage for love (as opposed to arranged marriage); egalitarian families (as opposed to patriarchal, hierarchical arrangements); sexual freedom for men *and* women; a movement toward equality for women; sexual permissiveness; and childhood as a separate phase of the life cycle, with children deserving special treatment (instead of treating very young children as miniature adults sent out to farm the fields as soon as they could walk) (Ariès, 1962; Coontz, 1988; Ladurie, 1979; Stone, 1977). By 1800, the West had been transformed by these ideas.

The Rise of Western Dominance

Between 1750 and 1914, a combination of political and economic factors converged which allowed the West to dominate the rest of the world. From China to the Muslim states to Africa, virtually all other parts of the world came under the sway of colonial powers. Illustration 3.1 portrays the stunning array of countries that came under the influence of the West. It is unsettling to look at the tiny European countries that succeeded in controlling vast areas of land in this era.

The West (a tiny land mass) was in almost in complete control of its colonies until 1914—when the Great War sent convulsions smashing through all of the world's hallowed institutions. One by one, the West lost its colonies. In nationalistic fervor, the colonies took control of their own territories.

Now the global village is upon us. No longer a utopian vision, we can see it materializing through the mist. Regardless of how we may feel about it, the revolution in communications and information stands as one of this century's monumental transformations. Our century is defined by globalization.

Visit the most remote, rudest village in India, and you will come upon farm communities gathered around the settlement's television set to watch old reruns of *House of Cards, The Simpsons*, or other programs brought down to earth by satellite. Plop down on the living room couch in a home in Paris or Jerusalem or Beijing to tune into the war with ISIS being fought in Afghanistan, Syria, Aleppo, or Paris. Bring your laptop computer to some distant corner of China and have instantly available to you quantities of information that a Leonardo or even an Einstein could only have dreamed about. And FAX machines, email, interactive television, and i-pads and palm-held iPhones, with a worldwide reach, clearly represent only the beginning of the global shrinking to come.

The implications for our intellectual and personal lives are enormous, and nowhere are they greater than in the intensely private spheres of love, sex, and marriage. No matter the part of the planet from which we come, the ways in which we think about love and sex are no more immune from change than are the ways we organize our political lives, dress, eat, or hear music. West is meeting East and East is meeting West (and North and South).

One particularly intriguing and important phenomenon is that it took the West over 500 years to embrace (though still not unanimously) "modern" ideas of love, sex, and intimacy. In some non-Western cultures, however, many of these same changes are occurring in less than 50 years (Bendix,

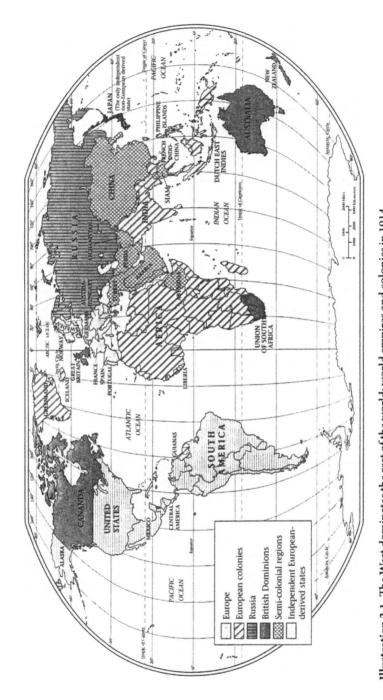

Illustration 3.1 The West dominates the rest of the world: world empires and colonies in 1914.

By Andrew0921 (own work) (CC BY 3.0 [http://creativecommons.org/licenses/by/3.0]), via Wikimedia Commons.

1964; Dunn, 1989; Wittfogel, 1957). It looks as though history is hurtling through these societies at an ever-accelerating pace.

Recently, of course, there has begun to be a fierce backlash against Western ideas and hegemony. Non-Western ethnic groups have begun to celebrate their own cultures, to resist wholesale Western cultural imperialism. Throughout the world, people have begun to speculate about the possibilities of taking only the best that the West has to offer and integrating it with the cultural traditions that are uniquely their own (Axtell, 1981; Kagitçibasi, 1990; Skocpol, 1979). Some feel it is best to reject Westernization entirely (which many associate with racism, drugs, crime, licentiousness, divorce, and greed) and try to turn back the clock. The dialectic between Westernization and resistance to it defines much of international life today.

The Web and Globalization

The Current State of Global Internet Access

According to Internet World Stats (2016), nearly 3.5 billion people on earth have access to the Internet—which marks an astounding 722% increase in Internet usage since the year 2000. Compared to in 2000, an additional three billion people are now able to access new forms of media, ideas, education, and other people. Generally speaking, scientists agree that, on a macro level, this is a good thing. Studies make it clear that increased Internet access can vastly improve various health outcomes, economic productivity, employment rates, literacy rates, gender equality, and overall feelings of social inclusion (Deloitte, 2015). While many debates continue regarding the negative effects of high Internet use, especially within developed countries (i.e., the kids are online all day instead of outside playing), there seems to be a clear indication that societies generally benefit from increased Internet access.

It must be noted, however, that just because "advanced" economies, with greater Internet access, have higher gross domestic product (GDP) rates and a cornucopia of other economic benefits, does not necessarily mean that "developing" economies, which lack these "advantages," are thus inferior in some way. GDP is one way to measure wealth, but it ignores other factors that contribute to the global index of happiness. These factors include caring, freedom, generosity, honesty, health, income, and good governance. (The winners in these world happiness rankings are almost always

Norway, Denmark, Iceland, Switzerland, and Finland. The United States ranks 14th; Helliwell, Layard, & Sachs, 2017.) But even use of the words *advanced* and *developing* can have pernicious effects—suggesting that one country is better in every way than another. Although these words denote economy, the implications of this power differential represent the current hierarchical structure of our globalized world: Those countries with economic power are "good" and have access to "good things," such as the Internet and other modern-day technologies. Those countries without economic power, it suggests, should strive to become developed countries and to absorb the values and ideas of the dominant culture.

Nevertheless, for good or ill, Internet access has been skyrocketing in the developing world with the invention of the mobile device—specifically in populations that previously did not have access to the Internet because of the high expense of at-home Internet access. Historically, home–Internet connections required (1) a working computer, (2) residence in an area that had the infrastructure to access the Internet, and (3) the ability to pay an expensive monthly fee. According to the World Bank Group (2013), close to one billion of the global population live on the equivalent of $1.90 a day or less, making at-home Internet a pipe dream for most global citizens. As such, it's not surprising to see that most of the world does not—and has never had—at-home broadband Internet access, also known as fixed broadband Internet. This trend does not appear to be declining. A recent study by the International Telecommunication Union found that developing countries and least-developed countries have barely 8 fixed-broadband users per 100 inhabitants. This means most people in the world have never had, and are not on a trajectory to ever have, access to the Internet at their homes through a fixed-broadband connection.

Currently, the global rate of fixed-broadband Internet is at roughly 32% and shows only moderate gains over the past few years (Morales, 2013). Surely this is understandable—the idea that the nearly 700 million people globally who live in poverty are anywhere close to having the capital to purchase a computer with an Internet plan sounds silly. And historically the idea that low-income people could access the Internet *was* indeed far-fetched. However, people no longer need a cumbersome computer or underground cables to go online. Millions of people have discovered that there is a much more practical solution: mobile phones. For the past decade, cellular devices have been flooding the global market (see Illustration 3.2). Competition brings prices down, as it is much easier to enter the market as a mobile provider than as a fixed-broadband provider. Improved technology means that every year, more of the planet is covered with cell phone service, and this trend will continue apace. It is undeniable that the world is going mobile, and it is providing individuals all over the world from a variety of different socioeconomic backgrounds a way to get online. The implications of this new global intercommunication may be far-reaching indeed.

Illustration 3.2 Advertisements for used cell phones are ubiquitous in Ghana.
Copyright Lucea Spinelli: http://work.luceaspinelli.com/. Used with permission.

The Rise of the Mobile Device

One of the unique contributions that mobile devices have made to the global Internet market is that they circumvent many of the barriers to Internet access that existed in previous years. As competition has continually lowered mobile market prices, billions of people who have never had Internet access before are now going online en masse. Currently, 92% of adult Americans have a smartphone, compared to 73% who have a laptop, which is a 10% drop in laptop ownership since 2010 (Anderson, 2015). In fact, a recent study by comScore found that 65% of all Internet traffic in the world now comes from some kind of mobile device, while desktop use shows some decline for at-home, personal use as compared to tablets and mobile devices (comScore, 2016).

There are many reasons for this shift. For one, mobile usage overcomes the problems of infrastructure. Cellular coverage increases daily and prices for plans decrease as more companies enter the competitive market. Individuals who do not possess the capital to purchase a computer can find a multitude of cell phones for sale at rock bottom prices. Many cellular plans offer deals with which one can receive a phone for free in exchange for a subscription. Additionally, apps used within cellular devices, such as WhatsApp, Viber, or Skype, allow people to make phone calls or send texts for free, making mobile usage that much more appealing. For example, while only 10% of sub-Saharan Africa has access to the Internet through a home computer, many sub-Saharan African countries are reporting mobile use at rates up to 90%. Amazingly, this increase has occurred mostly over the past few years (Poushter & Oates, 2015). When we asked one of our interview participants, journalist Eric Wainaina, based in Nairobi, Kenya, to describe how access to mobile phones has changed over the past 10 years, he responded:

Dramatic is the word. 10 years ago, we hardly knew what the Internet was but we currently have one of the highest Internet penetration in a developing economy. This has been as a result of several reasons: a) The government invested heavily in increasing fiber outlay across the country; b) Telco took advantage of the network investment by the government to extend services of both 3G and 4G across the country. With these developments, Kenyans were not only able to access the Internet but were able to do so cheaply. Finally, cheap smartphones selling for as little as $40 allowed even people in the villages to access the Internet.

The implications of increased mobile device use are massive. Billions more people are now connected to one another in unprecedented ways, augmenting social connections, access to information, and cross-cultural exchange. For example in India, 80% of the 462 million Internet users access the Web through a mobile device (Internet and Mobile Association of India, 2016). For many Indians, access to the Internet fits perfectly with their close-knit family orientations. Amazingly, in 2016, India surpassed the United States for total number of Facebook users with nearly 200 million registered users (Statistica Digital Market Outlook, 2016a). Additionally, a recent poll found that Indians' top concern while traveling is "not having a working mobile network." Respondents rated this concern above overspending and pickpocketing (Punit, 2016).

While these are just a few examples of how developing countries are getting online, all measurable outcomes point to the global population using mobile devices at a rapidly increasing rate to access the Web. So, if the world is going online, what are people doing once they get there? What are they looking at? How do they interact and interpret the images and messages that are now a tap of a finger away? While globalization used to mean planning decades-long shipboard sojourns to gather information on new people, cultures, and foods, people are now transmitting and receiving culture from around the world without even sitting up in bed.

Western Love on the Internet

The content of the Internet is not an egalitarian representation of the global population. Most major sites are created by Western companies, originally for Western use (Google, Yahoo, Facebook, YouTube, etc.). Since Western countries have wielded global economic power that facilitated the development of the Internet, it has since been populated by and constructed by Westerners. As such, in many ways, large portions (if not all) of the Internet are built on and perpetuates ideals of Western culture. For example, when people go online for the first time, they are almost immediately faced with the most Western construct there is—the English language. Over 54% of all websites on the Internet are in English (W3Techs, 2013), despite only approximately 27% of Internet users being native English speakers (Zuckerman, 2013). This suggests that to access a lot of the Internet, individuals either have to understand some English, attempt to understand it, or be prepared for half of the Internet to make no sense. Again, this can have the reinforcing message that

Western culture—the cradle of the English language—is somehow the *ideal*. In this scenario, to gain the ability to speak English, then, is to gain access to more information.

Many people who access the Internet, however, do not and will never speak English. This does not mean that they are not receiving countless messages about Western notions of romantic love. First, many popular music videos that are widely viewed online transmit a lot of messages about love and sex from just their images alone. For example, billions of people all over the world use video-sharing websites like YouTube, Vevo, and iTunes in order to watch music videos of their favorite songs. Within these videos, images dominate, and they tell a very particular tale of what love should look, sound, and feel like. For example, former boy band member-turned-solo artist, Zayn, released a music video for his song "Pillow Talk" in January, 2016. By August of that same year, the video had received 597,032,621 views on YouTube. That is more than the entire population of North America and nearly double that of South America. Since 80% of YouTube users are from outside the United States, there is every reason to believe that viewers of this particular media, and others, came from any and every part of the globe.

So why does it matter if someone in Madagascar watched "Pillow Talk" or Taylor Swift's ode to lost love, "Blank Space" (1.7 billion views as of August, 2016)? Studies show that interaction with pop culture through online engagement influences identity construction and performance (Williams, 2008). In other words, young people are actively constructing their concept of self through, and in reaction to, media presented in online formats. This suggests that consumption of pop culture through music videos or social media is not a passive event. Instead, individuals from all over the world may be reconstructing their ideas about themselves and their social environments based on the pictures, songs, and videos they encounter online.

Many of these pieces of media represent the story of passionate love, which is a moment of transcendence within the Western ideal of love. In the music video by Zayn, the singer is seen repeatedly kissing a beautiful young woman while their images become blurred together in a sequence of graphic patterns. These images harken back to Plato's quest for the predestined other half as identities blend mid-kiss, suggesting these two young lovers have *at last* found love and, thus, found themselves as well. By watching this video, viewers may perhaps long for this kind of love, as it is presented as such a delicious goal. Perhaps that's also why the most liked Instagram photo of all time is an image of singer Justin Bieber kissing his then-girlfriend Selena

Gomez. This photo has garnered almost four million "likes." Comments on the photo suggest some viewers interpreted the photo in ways that mirror Western concepts of idealistic, passionate love. One commenter wrote: "I don't think he posted This Without a Meaning [sic], true love never dies He cares about selena [sic] and so does she about him."

Surprisingly, a large portion of the comments on the Bieber photo were not in English. Even a quick scroll through the 100 most recent comments revealed postings in Portuguese, Spanish, French, Russian, Tagalog, Turkish, and Arabic. This is especially interesting because Justin and Selena are Canadian and American citizens. As such, people online are interacting with Western images in their native languages. This is important to consider when we think about the globalizing effects of contact with Western culture via the Internet—Can individual cultures and languages continue to exist and express themselves? Or does the Internet stifle the expression of local cultures and languages?

Hongladarom (2000) has proposed that, on the contrary, the Internet provides an "umbrella" under which many different cultures and languages can converge and participate in some variation of interchange. According to his analysis of a popular Thai message board, pantip.com, Hongladarom found that posters rapidly and continuously juggled global expectations and local identities. For example, many topics posted by users addressed global issues such as hairstyles, education, and love, but young people generally gave them a local spin and conformed to local expectations: Why do middle schools enforce hair length? Do you have sympathies for the current prime minister? And although Thais were perfectly comfortable talking frankly about love and sex, they scrupulously avoided any inflammatory or critical comments about the current king, knowing full well that such chats would result in immediate expulsion from the site.

Another way that Western media is being interpreted locally is through the rise of Internet piracy. Currently, across the world, billions of people can sign on to the Internet and download American and European TV shows, movies, or popular music albums without paying a dime. This is done using illegal "torrenting," or downloading sites like thepiratebay.org or kickasstorrents.com. These sites allow users from all over the world to directly upload or download movies, albums, or software from their friends without using a centralized server. Over 80% of all piracy downloads occur outside of the United States, which suggests a massive global interest in procuring foreign media or software. Because online piracy is relatively easy to do and hard to track because of its peer-to-peer networking, it's estimated that illegal downloads have cost the movie industry upwards of $20.5 billion globally (Norkey, 2015).

But while Hollywood hurts, people from all over the world are able to not only download Western movies but also download subtitles in their native language. For example, it is estimated that the popular American erotic romantic film, *Fifty Shades of Grey*, was downloaded illegally by over 32 million people across the globe. If all of those people paid $10 to see the movie, that would equal over $320 million in revenue losses for the industry. Part of the popularity of online piracy is not just that it's free, but that it can be localized. Users simply have to download the movie from a pirating website and then download an accompanying subtitle through popular free sites such as subscene.com. A quick Internet search yielded a list of languages that subtitles are currently available for download for the film *Fifty Shades of Grey* (see Table 3.1).

Accessing Western films with foreign subtitles may be another example of the "umbrella effect" offered by the Internet. Instead of being forced to learn English, or being shut out of over half of what the Internet has to offer, global citizens are finding their own localized and enterprising ways to access Western media. What's especially interesting about the many foreign subtitles available for *Fifty Shades of Grey* and for many other movies is that the subtitles are created by bilingual volunteers who then upload the files to subtitle-sharing sites, absolutely for free.

But are global cultures simply watching *Fifty Shades of Grey* when they get online? Or simply liking pictures of Justin Bieber? Certainly not. As mobile devices become more and more popular, so do many practical Internet

Table 3.1 Translations Available for *Fifty Shades of Grey* on the Web

Albanian	Dutch	Indonesian	Russian
Arabic	Estonian	Italian	Serbian
Bengali	Farsi	Korean	Sinhala
Brazilian Portuguese	Finnish	Malay	Spanish
Chinese	French	Norwegian	Swedish
Croatian	German	Persian	Thai
Czech	Greek	Portuguese	Ukrainian
Danish	Hebrew	Romanian	Vietnamese

applications that make real-world living much easier, such as email, accessing news, or even dating. Many Internet users would be unlikely to know about these artists and movies without the creation of social media sites. And as the messages of entrepreneurial, idealistic love permeate the Web, it makes sense that people may begin looking for love through their mobile devices as those options become increasingly popular and available. Certainly waiting for love has its romantic interpretations, but for billions of people across the world, just a few taps or swipes can accelerate the process of finding it.

The Rise of Dating Apps

All around the world, citizens are accessing news, sharing information, and downloading and using apps. *Apps* are software programs that can be downloaded directly onto mobile or tablet devices to accomplish a particular task. For example, some people have apps that keep their contacts organized, or apps that notify them whenever they receive an email or a message.

Other apps are games—in 2016, Pokémon Go was the number one app in the world. It allows users to walk around in real time and "catch" digital characters that have been geographically placed through online servers in real-world settings. The rapid growth in popularity of the Pokémon Go app has been attributed largely to the app's ability to engage the individual with their real-world environment. In general, this is what most people look for in apps—real-world engagement or apps that help them solve real-world problems. In a recent study, respondents indicated that the second most important aspect to future apps would be the ability seamlessly to integrate online and real-world experiences. This was ranked just behind the desire for future apps to provide more functionality so multiple apps would no longer be necessary (Aggarwal, 2015). Being able to engage with an app outside of an at-home computer means individuals can integrate their technology use into their day-to-day lives, further blurring the line between online and offline selves.

It is no surprise, then, that mobile dating apps are now eclipsing online dating sites in number of active users and new registrations. In the United States in 2013, only 5% of young adults reported using an online mobile dating app. By 2016, that figure had grown to 22% (Smith & Anderson, 2016). In fact, use of online dating websites has recently been surpassed by online dating apps. As people become more and more accustomed to compartmentalizing their tasks into easy-to-use, on-the-go mobile apps, it is not surprising that people have come to expect online dating to better integrate the online search to real-world success. Additionally, the West values entrepreneurship and independence. As Western values become more widespread, dating apps that focus on individual choice in choosing, meeting, and selecting a mate are bound to gain in popularity. Many individuals who may not have ever signed on to the Internet before, or who have never considered looking for love on their own, may suddenly be drawn to the choices and flexibility that online dating apps provide.

One of the most widely used dating apps on the planet is Tinder. Tinder was created from Hatch Labs in 2012, a subsidiary of Match.com. Within a few short years, Tinder has grown enormously, with over 100 million downloads worldwide and with over 10 *billion* digital "matches" made. (A match occurs when a person mutually indicates that they "like" the other person.) Tinder's format is simple and appealing. According to the analytics firm Similarweb (2016), Tinder has been downloaded over 100 million times and has become the highest grossing lifestyle app in the Google Play Store for Android phones (1.4 billion people use Android) in 99 countries worldwide.

What is most interesting is Tinder's cross-cultural appeal. It has reached the #1 most downloaded app in the lifestyle category, everywhere from Botswana to Ireland. There is something universally enticing about Tinder. Its fast-paced, split-decision swiping mechanism fits the criteria for an interval schedule reward system. This means that people are encouraged to swipe repeatedly, but they do not know which swipe may lead to a reward— finding an attractive face, or maybe even a new romantic or sexual partner. Many people report that Tinder usage is "like a game" and "highly addictive." In fact, there's a growing group of people designated as "Tinder tourists" or "lurkers," who borrow a friend's account with no interest in actually meeting a romantic partner; they are simply engaged by its fast-paced interface (Krupnick, 2014).

Tinder is popular in almost every language and in every market in which it exists, because it provides both a cognitively satisfying way to browse for potential partners as well a realistic one. In the real world, people who go to bars or parties to meet potential romantic partners have to make quick judgments, based mostly on looks, in deciding whether or not to approach someone they don't know. With Tinder, the user quickly "swipes" through potential partners with similar criteria: an image, a name, an age, and short bio. Another important aspect of Tinder is that matches appear on the basis of their proximity to the user—allowing one to screen the potential dating field without having to leave the couch. In fact, in the premium version of Tinder, you can search for people in other geographic locations. One of our interview participants explained to us that he travels often for business. Before leaving, he "spends hours and hours and hours" looking at possible matches in the country or state he is visiting, making arrangements so he will be able to "hook up" while in town:

> I've even had matches come and pick me up at the airport. Never met them before or anything. We just message back and forth beforehand and hope that the other person looks as good in real life as they do in their pictures.

While Tinder is growing in popularity every day across the world, there are many other dating apps that are very popular as well. The dating app Badoo is a social networking site that is also largely photo based, where users can "like" one another's photos, sending a notification of the "match" to both users. Badoo claims over 300 million downloads worldwide, with a large user base in South America and Europe. Other similar dating apps that are popular include Lovoo, Whosthere, and Frim. Table 3.2 presents each country listed alongside its most downloaded dating app, according to a recent article by the BBC News (2016).

The rise in online dating apps across the globe suggests that more and more individuals are getting online, and once they're online, they are searching for romantic or sexual partners. Most of these apps follow a model similar to Tinder: An individual looking for a dating partner downloads the app, looks through potential partners' profiles, selects a potential match, and independently pursues and arranges a subsequent romantic encounter.

Arranged Marriages to Marriage for Love

This kind of *entrepreneurial* approach to love is unusual for most of the world. Traditionally, throughout human history, most partnerships were made through familial arrangements (Apostolou, 2013; Tannahil, 1992). These romantic partnerings and marriages were systematically arranged to best benefit the *families* involved and thus provide an ongoing source

Table 3.2 Where Apps Are Most Popular

Badoo	Frim	Tinder
Argentina	Egypt	Australia
Brazil	Russia	Belgium
Bulgaria		Canada
Chile	**Heartbeep**	Denmark
Columbia	South Korea	Finland
Czech Republic		India
Hungary	**iPair**	Ireland
Indonesia	Taiwan	Israel
Italy		the Netherlands
Kenya	**Lovoo**	New Zealand
Kuwait	Austria	Sweden
Malaysia	Switzerland	
Mexico		**WhosHere**
Nigeria	**Momo**	Saudi Arabia
Portugal	China	
Romania		**YYC**
South Africa		Japan
Spain		
Thailand		
Turkey		
Ukraine		

for growing resources. In fact, selecting one's own mate without parental or community input or outright control—the transition from arranged marriages to love matches—did not really happen until the Industrial Revolution, when there occurred a global shift from agrarian communities to urbanized centers.

Even today, arranged marriages make up over half of all marriages in the world (Statistics Brain Research Institute, 2016b), in spite of the fact that such arrangements have declined over the past 100 years in some areas by as much as 40% (Rubio, 2014). While this trend is likely to continue in the near future, arranged marriages are still a massive organizing structure in contemporary global society. So, how do these cultural practices react to something like Tinder? Is there a clash between the tradition and the new technology? Does one destroy the other? It seems the truth lies somewhere in between. Given the nuances of human history, humans and cultures prove to be highly adaptable. Old ways and new ways can and do often merge, even when it comes to love, sex, and marriage. How does this merging manifest itself?

The Effect of Globalization via the Internet
on Love and Marriage

Even before the invention of the Internet, Western ideas of passion, love, and marriage were already becoming increasingly popular around the world. Industrialization brought people in from their farms into urban centers. There they would meet far more potential romantic partners than they ever would have back home. Graham Robb (2008), in his book *The Discovery of France*, observed that *as late as the mid-19th century*, a Parisian scullery maid would see more people in a single glance out her window than she would have in an entire lifetime in her village. Now, instead of working their own or their family's land, people were trading their labor for wages. With the move to cities, young men and women gained freedom from their immediate and extended families, lessening family influence in mate selection and in day-to-day decisions.

In addition, urbanization meant privatization. People were no longer living in close proximity to their families. They tended, rather, to live in small apartments. Families became nuclear families instead of extended families. Pair bonds had less to do with resources, because resources were different and shared in different ways in major cities than in rural areas. As such, the way people selected partners changed as well, moving in the direction of love marriages. Later, telephones and automobiles gave couples even more privacy than they had once had.

It can be tempting to assume that since the West wields economic and political power that Western values must be "better" than others, that once a "developing" nation encounters these ideals, it will only be a matter of time before they adopt these values. Especially by examining the historical trajectory of capitalism, one could easily come to the conclusion that we are heading toward a global village in which we all share the same principles, philosophies, and ideals. This notion is incorrect. Members of non-Western societies are not passively receiving information about love, sex, and partnership, ultimately consumed into the Western mainframe. They are instead constantly interpreting and navigating between global norms and localized applications. As we mentioned earlier, the use of Internet becomes a perfect way to reinterpret and construct identity as both a global and local citizen. For example, our interview participant Eric from Kenya told us that when it comes to online dating, in Nairobi:

People still want to forge relationships the traditional way. There is still belief among most people that online dating is a foreign thing or people you meet online are not genuine. I conducted an informal survey within the office and most people said they would feel better if they met someone offline than online.

This response indicates that while many people are using systems such as Tinder that are created by Westerners, they are still reinterpreting the uses of these sites into ways that are locally familiar. Eric, for example, talks about meeting on Tinder as being "not genuine." Kenyan society is more collectivist in nature that American society (Ma & Schoeneman, 1997), and in many of these collectivist societies, meeting romantic partners is a deeply organic process in which partners familiar to one another trust in-groups in forming pair bonds. As such, Kenyan users of Tinder may experience a sense of caution in the use of Tinder, as the social bonds formed there are often independent of any pre-existing social structures familiar to the users. Another one of our Kenyan interviewees, Wawerungigi, told us that using Tinder is still considered "desperate." Instead, he explained, many Kenyans prefer the chatting app Whatsapp:

> Whatsapp has really helped dating though because it's like an endless platform to talk as much as you want before going on a date. Because of this, dates usually occur a month after speaking to someone rather than before.

Again, we have evidence here of the navigation between global ideals and local applications. Wawerungigi explained that more personal and intimate forms of communication may be preferred to the fast-paced and impersonal structure of a dating app like Tinder. The effects of the Internet on the Kenyan experience of love is that a new tool has been added to the toolkit and can be used in its own, specifically constructed ways in specific towns and places. This process of interpreting the global into the local is not a new phenomenon.

Further evidence of this can be seen in India, where young Indians are modernizing the way their marriages are arranged with online arrangement sites. One such website, Shaadi.com, is fairly indistinguishable from any other online dating website, except for a few key differences. For one, while Tinder just asks what age and gender the user is looking for, Shaadi also asks about religion and language. Moreover, while Tinder users may indicate that they are interested in anything from hookups to marriage, Shaadi is specifically for arranging marriages. These marriages are expected to happen relatively quickly after the two Internet partners have met, but other than that, most of the online dating format is similar. Here, again, we see a reinterpretation of the globalizing Western ideal—choosing a romantic partner from a large selection of suitors based mostly on information potential suitors have put online—as applied to local realities—specifically, the culture of arranged marriage and the value of religion. One Indian young woman posted about her experience using Tinder on a popular Internet message board called *Quora*:

> Except one guy to whom I found sane as he just asked me to 'like' his fb page further adding he himself swiped him left with a wink emoticon, all men were like 'meri bann jaw (be mine), meet me, marry me, will you give name to my son and what not!

This message is interesting because most of the women we spoke to in America who used Tinder stated that most American men began conversations with "What's up" or "Hey." We see once more that utilization of Tinder was reinterpreted to local cultural scripts: If you think you've found your match, you may quickly offer to marry that person instead of dating multiple people throughout your young adulthood. This makes sense, considering that Indian women are expected to remain virgins until marriage, which may increase the urgency on both sides to quickly enter a marital partnership.

So while Western-made systems and ideals may seem omnipresent and powerful, their applications are by no means invariable. This is especially true for individuals who live in societies where pursuing their sexual interests can get them arrested or, worse, killed. For members of the lesbian, gay, bisexual, transgendered, and asexual (LGBT+) community, the Internet can provide an opportunity to meet potential romantic partners for the first time or in safer ways than going to bars or public spaces. It does appear that those who live in oppressive, homophobic communities are in fact using the Internet to find romantic partners and even friends and support. Egypt, for example, has some of the most conservative attitudes toward homosexuality in the world, with a near unanimous 95% of citizens stating they do not believe homosexuality should be accepted in society. In 2014, after a video of a wedding ceremony between two gay men surfaced (it was ceremonial in nature, as gay marriage is not legal), the eight men who were seen in the video were arrested and sentenced to eight years in prison (Tadros, 2016). Clearly, it is a terrifying time to be homosexual in Egypt, which is why it is most surprising that the popular gay dating app Grindr is currently the seventh most downloaded app in the iTunes store in Egypt (according to AppAnnie, July 4, 2016)! As we have seen before, when people are young, many are willing to risk everything for love and sex.

Grindr, which has over five million downloads, is generally considered to have been the "original Tinder." It allows users to search for potential romantic partners who are currently within a person's immediate area. Because of its long-standing role as the first and largest gay hookup app, its popularity is impressive. The Grindr homepage boasts over two million daily active users and is the most downloaded app for gay men in the United States, Mexico, Bahrain, and Indonesia, just to name a few.

While there are many horror stories of local governments using Grindr to track down, humiliate, threaten, or extort gay men, many more men find the app to be a transformative and positive way to meet other men who would otherwise be inaccessible. In an interview with the *LA Times,* Indian gay rights activist Ashok Row Kavi (Bengali & Kaiman, 2016) stated, "At any one time on Grindr, there are 100 to 200 gay men in a one-kilometer [half-mile] radius." In a country that has a history of fanatical homophobia, many men feel isolated or ashamed of their sexuality. To open an app and realize that there are hundreds of others just like you may be one of the many reasons for the app's popularity.

Dating apps are not the only way LGBT+ individuals around the world are negotiating the global with the local. The Internet has innumerable message boards and Facebook groups in hundreds of languages created to help members of the global gay community connect with and navigate their cultural environments. For example, there is a particularly large Internet message board designed for Muslims in the UK to meet and discuss issues such as "Islam and sexuality" or "for Muslims resisting their same-sex attractions." In Namibia, there is a Facebook group where gay men regularly post "polls" about sexual positions, share links to porn sites, and offer their phone numbers to men who want to chat with one another.

For gay men all over the world who are looking to find partners for sex in public spaces, the website cruisinggays.com offers an interactive map where individuals can find public places to meet men. These locations are usually discreet parks, bathrooms, or beaches. For individuals who may not be able to come "out" and who struggle to find partners, sites like these provide the opportunity to reinterpret their identity through these globalized systems for finding sexual partners, while still maintaining and applying these experiences to immediate local contexts.

Still, one can imagine an eventual decline in homophobia in these societies, in which case the more purely Western model could, for better or worse, eventually prevail. Similarly, one can also imagine arranged marriages (in any form) giving way to love marriages.

Conclusion

This chapter has discussed the history of passionate love in the West and how it is transforming global identities, not replacing them. The Internet offers new platforms to experience love and relationships within local contexts. While Western romantic love is often seen as the "ideal," and perhaps even as a symbol of modernity itself, billions of people throughout history and across the world experience and express love in different ways.

Some experience love through transactional sex. Others find happiness through arranged marriages with individuals who have access to resources. Others may engage in polygamy so that more people will tend to their land. Passionate love is evident in all cultures, but its expressions may not always look like the expensive music videos on YouTube or images in Hollywood movies. Instead, each culture develops their own interpretations of Western love, and they will continue to use the Internet to express and explore those interpretations.

While the influence of Western love through globalization is occurring with great power and speed, the interpretations of those influences are what truly define the individual's experience. There is not yet a global village for love. Instead, there's a world filled with millions of villages. But the movement is as much toward that homogeneous global village modeled in the West as it is toward variability. Stay tuned for the outcome, as it is yet unknown.

4

Going, Going, Gone

A Market View of Love and Sex

And What am I Bid for the Handsome Hunk Lurking in the Shadows

Illustration 4.1 Babylonian marriage market (Edwin Long [1829–1891]). An auction in ancient Babylon of women whose families have not been able to afford a dowry. They are being auctioned off as wives.

Source:https://commons.wikimedia.org/w/index.php?search=Babylonian+Marriage+Market&title=Special%3ASearch&go=Go&ns0=1&ns6=1&ns12=1&ns14=1&ns100=1&ns106=1#/media/File:Babylonian_marriage_market.jpg

Marriage markets have existed since ancient times (see Illustration 4.1). Parents in traditional cultures have routinely negotiated for the best deal possible. This fact is so taken for granted, that when queried about "markets," parents attempting to arrange such pairings have trouble even understanding the question. How could it be otherwise? In the West, for much of the past two centuries, young Romeos and Juliets have insisted they will marry for love. (It didn't work out very well for Shakespeare's young couple;

What's Next in Love and Sex. Elaine Hatfield, Richard L. Rapson, and Jeanette Purvis, Oxford University Press (2020). © Oxford University Press.
DOI: 10.1093/oso/9780190647162.001.0001

both killed themselves.) We tell each other that all you need is love. To think otherwise would be crass and unfeeling. Is it possible that we are now coming full circle? People on websites are often eminently practical, using blatant metaphors of the marketplace. Advice books talk about "selling yourself," "creating your brand." They advise men and women to "shop around," to realize there are always "trade-offs," to do a "cost-benefit analysis," and not to "settle for damaged goods." It's wise to "invest in a relationship before your market value plummets." Finally, they advise, try to "position yourself" to "optimize your romantic options," to be aware that there are "opportunity costs" in committing to the wrong partner.

The Current State of Affairs

Most people yearn for an ideal mate. In fairy tales, Prince Charming often falls in love with the scullery maid. In Hollywood, love often appears "at first sight." In musical comedies, love can become instantly obvious if you meet "a stranger across a crowded room." After a little trouble (to keep it exciting), all misunderstandings are cleared up and the couple marries and lives happily ever after. In real life, however, dating couples generally end up with a "suitable" partner—which means the most appealing partner they can attract in a competitive dating market. As the sociologist Erving Goffman (1952) dryly observed:

> A proposal of marriage in our society tends to be a way in which a man sums up his social attributes and suggests that hers are not so much better as to preclude a merger. (p. 456)

Since the 1960s, scientists have conducted a flood of research documenting that people tend to pair up with romantic and sexual partners who are similar to themselves in physical attractiveness and a host of other traits (see Hatfield, Rapson, & Aumer-Ryan, 2008, for a review of this research).

In one early experiment, Elaine Hatfield and her students invited freshmen at the University of Minnesota to a get-acquainted dance. Couples were promised that an IBM computer would match them with a blind date that was just right for them (see Hatfield, Aronson, Abrahams, & Rottman, 1966). (In truth, the students were randomly matched with one another.) When the freshmen arrived to purchase their tickets for the dance, a trio of ticket sellers surreptitiously rated their physical attractiveness. They assessed their intelligence by consulting transcripts of their high school grades and their scores on the Minnesota Scholastic Aptitude Test. They gauged their personality traits by recording their scores from a battery of tests, including the prestigious Minnesota Multiphasic Personality Test and the California Personality Inventory.

At the dance, the 400 couples chatted, danced, and got to know one another. Then, during the 10:30 P.M. intermission, the experimenters swept through the dance hall, rounding up couples from the dance floor, lavatories, and fire escapes—even adjoining buildings. Researchers asked the students to tell them frankly (and in confidence) what they thought of their dates. Did they plan to ask their date out again? If *their date* asked them out, would they accept? Six months later, the researchers contacted couples again to find out if they had, in fact, dated. Here are some of the things they found:

1. All young men and women yearn for the stars. When asked what kinds of dates they desired, everyone, regardless of what *they* looked like or how dismal their personalities, preferred (in fact, insisted) on being matched with the best-looking, most charming, brightest, and most socially skilled partner possible. As one young man said, "I think every man is entitled to a beautiful and charming date."

2. Those whom fate had matched with handsome or beautiful dates were eager to pursue the relationships. Keep in mind that some of the handsome men and beautiful women had expressed total disinterest in their computer dates, especially if they were unattractive; some even admitted to treating them rudely. No matter. Everyone wanted to see the good-looking computer matches again. When couples were contacted six months after the dance, participants (whether they were good looking or homely; well treated or not) had, in fact, attempted to wangle a date with the best-looking person. The more handsome the man and the more beautiful the woman, the more eagerly that person was pursued.

3. In this study, every effort to find anything else that mattered failed. Men and women with exceptional IQs and social skills, for example, were not liked any better than those who were less well endowed.

4. Finally, *men and women cared equally about their dates' appearance.* (Recent research documents that in speed dating and Tinder matches, both men and women care equally about looks; see Purvis, 2017.) This

contradicts the claims made by evolutionary psychologists that only men care about looks (for recent replications of these results, see Reis, Aron, Clark, & Finkel, 2013).

This study demonstrated that young people predictably yearn for perfection—especially in appearance. There is a difference, alas, between what people desire (perfection) and what they can get. Subsequent research makes it clear that, all too soon, young optimists discover they must be more realistic. Aim too high and you discover (after undergoing the humiliation of rejection) that the one you yearn for is "out of your league." Settle for too little, and friends counsel, "Don't be a sap; you can do better." Eventually, like Goldilocks, people settle for someone who is "not too hot, not too cold, but just right."

In a series of follow-up studies, Silverman (1971) observed couples in a variety of natural settings—in movie theater lines, in singles bars, and at assorted social events. Regardless of what they might once have wanted, in fact, most couples were found to be remarkably similar on the attractiveness dimension. A beautiful woman was most likely to be standing next to a handsome man. A homely man was most likely to be spotted buying a drink for a plain woman.

Furthermore, similarity did seem to "breed content." The more alike couples were in physical appeal, the more delighted they seemed to be with each other, if intimate touching is any indication of one's feelings. Sixty percent of the couples comparable in attractiveness were engaged in some type of fondling, while only 22% of mismatched couples were touching.

In the dating and mating "marketplace," physical appearance, of course, is not the only thing young people care about. Couples can be well or ill matched in a variety of ways. For example, socialite and fashion designer Mary-Kate Olsen recently married French banker Olivier Sarkozy, who is 17 years her senior, and arguably not entirely representative of traditional standards of physical beauty. Or take Justin Long, an actor famous for appearing in early Macintosh advertisements and several mainstream films. While not being traditionally attractive, he has been linked to many high-profile, beautiful female actresses, such as Amanda Seyfried, Kirsten Dunst, and Drew Barrymore.

Different people may care about personality, fame, socioeconomic status, or kindness. These various assets all contribute to one's "mate value"—a general indicator of how desirable a person is in the dating market. Certain assets, such as wealth, status, and beauty, increase one's social desirability while simultaneously increasing the *number* and *quality* of potential partners from whom one may choose.

In different cultures, different people get to make the selections, and different traits are deemed important. The Shanghai Marriage Market (Chinese: 人民公园相亲角; *pinyin: rénmín Gōngyuán xiāngqīn jiǎo*; literally: "People's Park blind date corner") is a marriage market held at People's Park in Shanghai, China. Parents of unmarried adults flock to the park every Saturday and Sunday from noon to 5 P.M. They write information about their children's age, height, occupation, income, education, family values, Chinese zodiac sign, and personality on a piece of paper and attach it to a long string that contains other people's advertisements. Then parents walk around, chatting with other parents to see if they can find a match. Young people scornfully describe this as "Match.com meets farmers market." It has a low success rate. Parents might like this system, but young Chinese prefer regular computer matching—where they are in control. But just how different are the criteria of the young?

Equity Theory

In the 11th century, St. Anselm of Canterbury argued that the will possesses two competing inclinations: an affection for what is to a person's own advantage and an affection for justice. Equity theory, too, posits that, in personal relationships, two concerns stand out: first, how rewarding are people's societal, familial, and work relationships? Second, how fair and equitable are those relationships? According to Hatfield, Walster, and Berscheid (1978), people consider a relationship equitable when the rewards they reap from a relationship are commensurate with their contributions to that relationship. According to the theory, couples feel most comfortable when their relationships are rewarding and they are getting exactly what they deserve from their relationships—no more and certainly no less. (Of the two, profit is generally thought to be a more important determinant of relationship satisfaction than are fairness and equity.)

Psychometricians have developed a variety of complex measures to assess how fair and equitable people perceive a given relationship to be. Scholars have found that a relationship's fairness and equity can be reliably and validly assessed with the use of a simple, one-item measure—the Equity Global

Measure. This simple measure has been translated into a variety of languages and used in a variety of romantic, marital, altruistic, friendship, and work settings. Also in common use is a 25-item multi-item scale—A Multifactor Measure of Equity (see Hatfield, Rapson et al., 2008, for a discussion of the reliability and validity of these scales).

Readers might wish to get out a pen and paper and indicate how fair and equitable they consider their current romantic relationship to be.

Assessing Equity

Technically, *equity* is defined by a complex mathematical formula (Traupmann, Peterson, Utne, & Hatfield, 1981; Walster, 1975). In practice, however, a relationship's fairness and equity can be assessed reliably and validly with the use of a simple measure. Specifically, participants in a social exchange are asked the following:

> Considering what you put into your current romantic relationship, compared to what you get out of it . . . and what your partner puts in compared to what (s)he gets out of it, how does your relationship "stack up?"

Respondents are given the following response options:

+3: I am getting a much better deal than my partner.
+2: I am getting a somewhat better deal.
+1: I am getting a slightly better deal.
  0: We are both getting an equally good, or bad deal.
−1: My partner is getting a slightly better deal.
−2: My partner is getting a somewhat better deal.
−3: My partner is getting a much better deal than I am.

On the basis of their answers, persons can be classified as over-benefited (receiving more than they deserve), equitably treated, or under-benefited (receiving less than they deserve).

Equity theorists (Hatfield et al., 1978) have assembled voluminous evidence documenting the critical importance of the "marketplace" in mate selection. Specifically, scholars find that attractive men and women—whether they are gay, lesbian, or heterosexual—place more importance on a "suitable partner" I.E., one being more socially desirable (i.e., more attractive, intelligent, personable, rich, well adjusted, and kind) than do their less attractive peers. Perceived equity has been found to be important in sparking passionate love, sexual attraction, and sexual activity. Market considerations have been found to affect both gay and straight romantic and sexual choices.

The market also affects the sexual bargains men and women craft in prison and the amount prostitutes charge for "risky" sex. Couples are likely to end up with someone fairly close to themselves in social desirability. Couples are also likely to be matched on the basis of self-esteem, looks, intelligence, education, and mental and physical health (or disability). People rarely get matched up with someone who is either "out of their league" or "beneath them."

Equitable relationships (i.e., well-matched relationships) are satisfying and comfortable relationships; inequity is associated with distress, guilt, anger, and anxiety. Those in equitable relationships (well-matched relationships) are less likely to risk extramarital affairs than are their peers. Equitable relationships (well-matched relationships) are correspondingly more stable than are inequitable relationships (Hatfield, Forbes, & Rapson, 2012).

Are there serious gender differences in the assets and liabilities for which men and women search (and consider to be "deal breakers") in the dating marketplace? Here, the evidence isn't so clear.

Evolutionary theorists contend that men are willing to pay a somewhat higher price for good looks, virginity, fidelity, and chastity, while women willingly pay more for status, support, and kindness (Baumeister & Vohs, 2004; Buss & Schmitt, 1993). These preferences in partner qualities are, according to evolutionary theorists, largely attributable to our biological predispositions. That is to say, women prefer men who can provide resources and support because this would ultimately benefit them in child rearing. Men, on the other hand, prefer women who are beautiful and chaste because, among other reasons, physical attractiveness is a cue of good health (increasing the probability of conception) and chasteness will provide assurance that any offspring are indeed their own and not those of another man. Men sometimes say they don't want a woman who has "been around the block" too many times because this may threaten the paternity status of potential children, or lead to a male having to devote resources to offspring that is not their own (Buss & Schmitt, 1993).

It should be noted, however, that there are always exceptions to the rule. Research on sociosexuality (i.e., willingness to engage in casual sex) has shed some interesting light on the mating preferences of men and women by suggesting that, though many men tend to prefer shorter-term relationships with multiple partners and women may tend to prefer longer-term relationships with fewer partners, there is considerable crossover between the genders on these preferences.

To explain this crossover, evolutionary theorists argue that women who prefer short-term partners typically seek out men who are more physically attractive in order to procure "good genes" for their resulting offspring. On the other hand, men who prefer long-term mating do so because they possess a relatively low mate value (in terms of attractiveness, wealth, and status) and as such must sweeten the pot, so to speak, by putting stability and emotional investment on the table.

We should note a problem with that line of reasoning: Although a few gender differences certainly exist, in general, men and women are far more similar than different (Hyde, 2005). Within each gender, variance is always far greater than between genders. A person's tactics for achieving one's goals will obviously vary depending on cultural, social, personal, and environmental constraints.

Some evolutionary psychologists assume that, in general, men care about looks, and women care more about power and status. In reality, those differences are exaggerated—especially when talking about casual encounters. When you *ask* men and women how much they care about, say, looks, power, and status (when, for example, they sign up for a matching service, or in a typical academic self-report study), they often reflect the conventional wisdom. When, however, you look at actual behavior (at mixers, in speed dating, in bars, in Web hookups, etc.), you get a far different picture. When selecting real flesh-and-blood casual partners, men and women turn out to be surprisingly similar in their desire that the partner be good looking and "hot." Good looks seem to be the sine qua non of a pickup. This is true whether those "cruising the scene" are gay, straight, or lesbian; American or foreign born (see Eastick & Finkel, 2008; Hatfield, Forbes, & Rapson, 2012; or Taylor et al., 2011, for a summary of this research).

As one of William Butler Yeats' beautiful ladies asks, "Do you love me for myself alone, or for my yellow hair?" Yeats' sage reply, truthfully and sadly, is: "Only God, my dear, could love you for yourself alone, and not for your yellow hair."

And as one of our informants observed:

Image is huge in my generation. I think we are coming into a world where a lot of girls and boys are trying to become this "perfect" person with the use of social media. There are apps that you can use to change your eye color, make you look skinner, make you look tanner, or you can add a filter. Even makeup "techniques" are becoming so advanced that people can actually change their faces by using "contouring" or "highlighting." My two roommates are huge on makeup. I am not the judging type, but I am actually concerned for their self-image and worth. Every morning they wake up two hours before class to glue on fake eyelashes, "cake face" (apply so much makeup it like frosting a cake) their entire face with liquid foundation, powder their face, then add eyeliner, mascara, eye shadow, and some highlights. I can't even get them to walk to the store with me if they don't have on makeup.

In addition, men and women in the modern world appear to be becoming more similar in their attitudes, feelings, and behaviors with the passage of time (Oliver & Hyde, 1993; Petersen & Hyde, 2010.)

In conclusion: Research seems to indicate that in the early stages of a dating or sexual relationship, considerations of the marketplace prevail. Men and women will attempt to attract a socially desirable partner and will be profoundly concerned with how rewarding, fair, and equitable their budding relationships are. As for personal attributes and overall mate value, it appears as though people are not only aware of their own value but also the value of others, and as such may adapt specific mating strategies to compensate for either their strengths or shortcomings. In all these matters, gender differences appear to be declining.

Recent Theorizing

Sex Ratios

> Don't the girls all get prettier at closing time?
>
> —Mickey Gilley

In 1973, Gary Becker, an economic sociologist interested in microeconomics, argued that marriage could be understood within an economic framework. Marriage is voluntary, and men and women compete for the best

mate possible. In this competition, he argued, sex ratios are a powerful determinant of the quality of the mate one can attract. A population's sex ratio is
defined as the number of sexually receptive men compared to the number of
sexually receptive women in a given population. Becker won a Nobel Prize
for his theorizing in 1992.

Students can see a mini-example of this in a singles bar on a Saturday
night. Pennebaker (Pennebaker et al., 1979) visited three campus bars. He
asked patrons to rate the women drinking there on a scale ranging from 1
to 10. He surveyed men at 9:30, 10:00, and midnight. As predicted, he found
that as the odds of finding an attractive woman to take home diminished,
men began to rate the other female patrons as better and better looking. This
accounts for the phenomenon that college students sometime wake up, after
a night of celebrating, to find that the tousled head on a pillow next to them is
a 3 rather than the 10 they thought they were taking home.

In a classic text, *Too Many Women? The Sex Ratio Question*, Marcia
Guttentag and Paul Secord (1983) provide a theoretical model for understanding the impact of gender inequalities (in number) on a society. They
point out that in all societies there are two kinds of power: *structural power*
(throughout the world, men generally are more powerful in agencies of government, justice, business, etc.) and *dyadic power* (who has the most power
in the dating and mating market). If, in a given society, sex ratios are markedly skewed—and such imbalances can be caused by a variety of factors,
such as religious practices, societal preferences for boys or girls (infanti-
cide), migration, wars, and differentials in deaths—it should have a profound impact on men's and women's social power. If a society has too many
men (if it is male biased) or too many women (if it is female biased), young
people may find themselves in an impossible situation; some will inevitably
end up without a partner. (In China, men who never marry are called "bare
branches"; women who never marry are called [stale] "Christmas cakes").
When many young men were killed in World War II, for example, young
women were often forced to forgo hopes of marriage and to seek out jobs
as teachers, secretaries, sales girls, and factory workers in order to support
themselves. These women soon developed more "modern" notions as to
what was fair in the world of work—and life. According to Guttentag and
Secord, in male-biased populations (where there is a premium on women)
women will be highly valued and seen as coveted possessions. Traditional
roles and divisions of labor will prevail, and there will be a stress on sexual
morality.

An article published in *The New York Times*, entitled "For Many Chinese Men, No Deed Means No Dates," provides an excellent illustration of this fact (Jacobs, 2011). Given a cultural preference for sons, China has found itself with a surplus of approximately 40 million men. This, as you can imagine, has had a considerable influence on the Chinese mating market. Chinese women have their "pick of the litter" when it comes to finding a sweetheart. As a consequence, only the most desirable men are lucky enough to find a mate. In such societies, women tend to marry at a relatively young age, while men tend to marry when they're older—and only after they have amassed considerable status, power, and wealth. In terms of sexual practices, fidelity and monogamy tend to be the standard, as men must adhere to women's sexual preferences in order to attract and keep a partner. It should be noted, however, that in societies with too many men, the sex industry (i.e., prostitution) tends to be widespread—making the transmission of sexually transmitted illnesses (STIs) and AIDs a particular concern.

When men are at a premium, however, women are the ones who have to vie for men's affection. In these societies, male sexual permissiveness and promiscuity are widely accepted, as women are viewed as sex objects. Men often say they want to "test drive" the car before they buy it. Furthermore, in these societies, women are less likely to get married and more likely to get divorced than when balanced sex ratios prevail. Adultery is also commonplace, and illegitimate births are quite widespread.

Evidence for these propositions can be found in the population statistics of post–World War II Russia. After losing millions of men in the war (more than in any of the Allied nations), the Russian population was substantially skewed, leaving men in extremely short supply. This resulted in a number of societal changes. First, it meant that women had to enter the workforce to help provide for themselves and their families. Additionally, owing to the lack of men, marriage rates took a nosedive, and out-of-wedlock births skyrocketed. In this society, domestic violence and extramarital affairs also increased markedly.

In addition to these societal impacts, sex ratios have profound economic implications. As you have perhaps gleaned from the examples just provided, the accumulation and spending of wealth differs depending on sexual market conditions. In a comparative study of two cities in Georgia (U.S.), namely in Macon and Columbus, researchers found that men's spending and saving habits during courtship differed greatly. In Columbus, where there were too many men, men spent more on their dates and were more willing to go into debt during courtship than were men in Macon, where there was an over-supply of women. This demonstrates once again that mating strategies differ with market conditions and sex ratios.

Changing Gender Roles

In some of the research we have discussed thus far, a number of scholars have generally assumed that (1) men and women possess traditional (and unchanging) desires for love and sex, and (2) that the markets they confront are closed systems. Both of these assumptions are more appropriate to 1950 (if not 1500 A.D.) than today. Recently, Richard Rapson and his fellow historians catalogued the many changes that have occurred since 18th-century Enlightenment and have made predictions as to the social, economic, and technological advances that might be expected in the next 50 years as a consequence of these changes (see Chapter 11 for a discussion of these predictions). In this section, let us consider the impact of two major social changes: (1) the marked increase in the status of women—which has granted them increased power and freedom, and (2) the possibility that men and women (especially those who find themselves in severely limited markets) can use modern cybertechnologies to increase their options.

In the Middle Ages, in Europe, according to the legal system, women were valued below the horses but above the sheep, pigs, and cows. The horses were well-esteemed "workers" after all. Since the Enlightenment, women's status has been steadily improving (Dabhoiwala, 2012). The women's movement of the past century stands, arguably, as the most culturally significant revolution of modern times. Every aspect of society has been affected by the movement toward gender equality in the modern world. That includes the workplace, politics, sports, reproduction, health, social mores, and much else. But nowhere has the approach to gender equality (still not nearly fully achieved anywhere outside of, perhaps, Scandinavia) mattered more than in manifestations of gender itself: in what it means to be a woman, in marriage, in love, in body image, and in sex.

Feminism has fought, at its core, for women to have the same choices in life as men. But there has been and continues to be considerable pushback against that simple idea. Gender equality continues to occupy a contested battleground.

Take the word *feminism* itself. In our classrooms we have asked students, men and women alike, whether they consider themselves to be "feminists." Our sample is generally a good deal more progressive than the American population at large. Yet, generally speaking, no more than one-quarter of women (and less among the men) will raise their hands expressing—timidly in most cases—their willingness to call themselves feminists.

Then, when we ask the question this way, "Suppose 'feminism' is defined as the belief that women should have the same choices in life as men. Would you now be willing to label?" Almost every hand shoots unhesitatingly up to the sky, men as well as women. And, really, that's what feminism is *in fact* mostly all about.

What's going on here is the success of the opponents of the women's movement to paint a feminist as a man-hating, angry, strident, often ugly woman. It is part of the ongoing backlash.

Our female students frequently express, healthily, the sense that, without question, they can be what they want to be, have any career they wish, live the lives they wish. They often take that for granted. Less wisely and concomitantly, they underestimate the discrimination that they will likely confront in the workplace and other areas of life. Thus, they are not much interested in organizing politically to protect and expand their rights, that is, to be "feminists."

In recent years, seismic shifts in men's and women's roles have occurred. Specifically, women, who were historically thought of as achieving fulfillment only as wives and mothers, have entered the realms of education and work force en masse. In fact, women are now more prominent in college settings, more successful in degree attainment, and have higher earnings growth than do men. Traditional family structures have been supplemented with two-income families, single-parent families, gay families, and various other structures.

So what does this mean for equity, sex ratios, and the overall mating market? Well, for one, it reduces the necessity for women to find a partner who can support them and their children. Does this alter women's preferences and choices? There is some research that suggests women with resources are likely to demand more in mates—insisting they be young, egalitarian, and attractive as well as possessing other assets—than are their less advantaged peers. This raises the definite possibility that—if men and women possess comparable economic power and status—women will come to value the same traits that men typically do when seeking partners. We suspect they will. Interestingly, there are some studies that suggest that as women gain financial resources, they rate financial resources in their partners as being more important than before. It's the "wanting it all" theory: Additionally, with men and women both earning a livable wage, how will relationships be renegotiated in terms of equity? Will men be taking on new roles as women become economic contributors? A growing body of research suggests that this is indeed the case and that change is well under way. As women play a greater role in the workforce, men are beginning to contribute more to household work and childcare, though not quite to the same extent as women do. Will women be more willing to pair up with other women (who offer love and intimacy) than with men, who offer less? How, if at all, this will continue to change is yet to be seen. We are not living in static times.

Expansion of Dating and Mating Markets

Most scholars who have studied the impact of dating markets and sex ratios on love and sex have written as if men and women were restricted to local markets—to their own campus, the neighborhood bar, or other local places. Obviously, this is no longer the case. As noted, recent developments—like the Web, dating websites, Facebook, Skype, speed dating, mail order brides (for Russian and Third World women), and easy transportation—mean people can search for sexual partners anywhere in the world. Compare this to pre-modern Western villages, where individuals often failed to come across more than 200 individuals in their entire lifetime (Robb, 2008).

Will this technology circumvent the impact of skewed sex ratios? Future research should seek to be more global in scope, as people are no longer confined to their towns, states, or even countries when seeking a potential mate.

Conclusion

We have seen that there is compelling evidence that men and women are influenced by market conditions in selecting potential mates and dates. The extent to which men and women desire the same or very different things in a casual and more serious mate is subject to debate—as is the extent to which the genders are becoming more similar in their attitudes, desires, and sexual behaviors. The profound social, economic, and technological changes that are occurring may well have an important impact on what men and women desire in their "exchanges." Failing to adapt to the kinds of changes we might expect to see in the next 50 years could lead to the condition that futurist Alvin Toffler famously described as "future shock." When it comes to gender, love, and sex, nothing is settled.

5

The Nature of Love

Its Ups and Downs

People's desires are variable. When men and women are young, they assume everyone wants the same thing—a passionate love affair, a rose-covered cottage with a white picket fence, a house full of children. Don't they? But with a little experience, they find that their personalities and their desires are quite unique. Some examples from our interviews:

Martin, a man in his late 40s, said:

> I don't know why it is. I'll fall madly in love with some woman, I really love her, and then after a couple of years, my feelings for her just die. I want out. When I was young, I didn't know this about myself. That for me love lasts two years max. These days I tell women up front. Truth in advertising. They don't believe me, of course. Everyone thinks they can work the magic, be the one. But, when I leave I feel morally justified. And they feel betrayed.

Marcia, an elderly woman, countered:

> Just you wait a few years. When you are young, all the young men sound like you, not wanting a commitment. But I am 80, and the worm has turned. Now it's all the old women who want companionship. It's the old men who want marriage and commitment. But I've been there, done that. When my husband died, I vowed "never again." What all these old duffers want is someone to boss around . . . and a nurse—especially a nurse. And I say: Tough luck. Too late. You can take me to the theater, but that's it.

Sylvia, a college student, said:

> I'm having a lot of fun, being young. I want romance, but nothing heavy. Not until graduate school is over and I have a good job. Then I might think about commitment and a family.

What's Next in Love and Sex. Elaine Hatfield, Richard L. Rapson, and Jeanette Purvis, Oxford University Press (2020). © Oxford University Press.
DOI: 10.1093/oso/9780190647162.001.0001

Her roommate, Mary, shook her head.

> I hate dating. Romance and all that fake stuff. There are a lot of jerks out
> there. I want to meet a nice sensible man, settle down, and start a family. It's
> one of those rose-covered cottages, with a white picket fence, for me.

Men and women today have far more choices than they once did. Ask "What kind of life are you hoping for in the next five years?" and some people would admit that in the foreseeable future they would like to experiment with love and life—like a bee, going from flower to flower. Maybe when they get to be 35 or 40, they would like to settle down, but not yet. Others are eager for a traditional relationship, the sooner the better. They would like to meet the right man or woman, settle down, and start a family. Others want neither. Activities and work take all their time. Maybe someday. . . .

When people are young, they often possess the happy delusion that potential dates and mates will share their own values. A bit of painful experience soon shatters that illusion. There is great diversity in what people want in their romantic lives—if they want anything at all. And this is true for both men and women. As Rapson, in Chapter 4, observed (personal communication):

> The women's movement of the past century stands, arguably, as the most
> culturally significant revolution of modern history. Every aspect of society
> has been affected by the movement toward gender equality in the modern
> world. That includes the workplace, politics, sports, reproduction, health,
> social mores, and much else. But nowhere has the approach to gender
> equality mattered more than in manifestations of gender itself: in what it
> means to be a woman, in marriage, in love, in body image, and in sex.

While women were once pretty much required to choose between a traditional married life (usually with children) or a celibate life of service as a teacher, nurse, or maiden aunt, today the world is open to women, and men, and to their definitions of what it means to be a man or woman. The culturally accepted possibilities have been smashed wide open. There is, contemporaneously, an increasing acceptance of LGBT+ (lesbian, gay, bisexual, transgendered, and asexual) rights. Technological developments (such as the Web [see Chapter 2], birth control pills, treatment for once devastating sexually transmitted infections [STIs], etc.) have made buying in to this new diversity even easier.

However people choose to live their lives, they will reap benefits and confront some predictable challenges. In this chapter, we will discuss the pros and cons one faces when focusing on the desire for passionate love, companionate love, both, or neither one. Of course, one's desires might change over the lifespan.

Researchers have found that people in love enjoy many advantages: Love is known to improve psychological, emotional, and physical health. When things go badly, however, lovers may suffer the pangs of rejection, jealousy, sadness, and anger. People can learn from both the joy of fulfilling relationships and the pain they suffer from the affairs that go wrong.

Passionate Love: The Gift of Angels or Devils?

The middle class and bourgeois of the time [in the Victorian era] had conflicting views about love because it could be viewed "as a divine blessing, a potent energy, an infectious disease, a slow poison"
—Peter Gay (1986, p. 44)

As is clear from our definition, passionate love is a profoundly complex and bittersweet emotion. We define *passionate love* as:

A state of intense longing for union with another. Passionate love is a complex functional whole including appraisals or appreciations, subjective feelings, expressions, patterned physiological processes, action tendencies, and instrumental behaviors. Reciprocated love (union with the other) is associated with fulfillment and ecstasy. Unrequited love (separation) is associated with feelings of emptiness, anxiety, and despair. (Hatfield & Rapson, 1993, p. 5)

When we yearn for romantic love, we are accepting the possibility of experiencing a tumble of emotions—unbounded joy and ecstasy as well as anxiety, sadness, anger, fear, and despair (Lamy, 2011).

The Joys of Love

When people speak of love, they usually associate it with positive emotions such as joy, well-being, and happiness. No one doubts that love is a high, that the joys of love generally spill over and add sparkle to everything else in life. Sappho, a Greek lyric poet (born 630–612 BCE), described the intense experience of being love:

> Sweat pours down me, I shake all over, I go pale as green grass. I'm that close to being dead.

Neuroscientists have found that there are good chemical and biological reasons for these profound reactions. According to Helen Fisher, Arthur Aron, and Lucy Brown (cited in Fisher, 2004a), three chemicals (dopamine, norepinephrine, and serotonin) play a crucial role in romantic passion (see also Takahashi et al., 2015). Arthur Aron and his colleagues (2005) conducted a series of fMRI studies. They first posted the question, "Have you just fallen madly in love?" on a bulletin board on the SUNY Stony Brook campus. They received a flood of replies. From the replies, they selected 17 men and women who scored high on the Passionate Love Scale.

The authors then asked lovesick men and women to view pictures of their beloved and "a boring acquaintance," while an fMRI imager recorded the activity (blood flow) in their brains. Fisher and her colleagues (Fisher, 2004a) found that when lovesick men and women gazed at their beloved, activity was sparked in many brain areas. Two areas were found to be critically important: the caudate nucleus (a large, C-shaped region deep in the center of the brain) and the ventral tegmental area (VTA), a group of neurons at the very center of the brain. Xu and his colleagues (2011) found similar results in a Chinese sample. Fisher (2004b) observed:

> I had hypothesized that romantic love is associated with elevated levels of dopamine or norepinephrine. The VTA is a mother lode for dopamine-making cells. With their tentacle-like axons, these nerve cells distribute dopamine to many brain regions, including the caudate nucleus. And as this sprinkler system sends dopamine to various parts of the brain, it produces focused attention as well as fierce energy, concentrated motivation to attain a reward, and feelings of elation—even mania—the core feelings of romantic love.
>
> No wonder lovers talk all night or walk till dawn, write extravagant poetry and self-revealing e-mails, cross continents or oceans to hug for just a

weekend, change jobs or lifestyles, even die for one another. Drenched in chemicals that bestow focus, stamina and vigor, and driven by the motivating engine of the brain, lovers succumb to a Herculean courting urge. (p. 79)

Lucy Brown added: "That's the area that's also active when a cocaine addict gets an IV injection of cocaine. It's not a craving. It's a high" (quoted in Brink, 2007, p. 3). These reactions are depicted in Fig. 5.1.

Fisher (2004a) concluded by observing that the chemistry of romantic attraction generally elevates sexual motivation. For more detailed descriptions of this research, see Aron et al. (2005) and Fisher et al. (2002).

Not surprisingly, these authors' pioneering research sparked a cascade of fMRI research (see Hatfield & Rapson, 2009). Recently, Cacioppo and Cacioppo (2016) conducted quantitative meta-analyses in order to integrate this burgeoning research. Overall, their fMRI meta-analyses revealed that passionate love increased activity in the subcortical brain areas sustaining basic emotions, euphoria, reward, and motivation, and in cortical brain

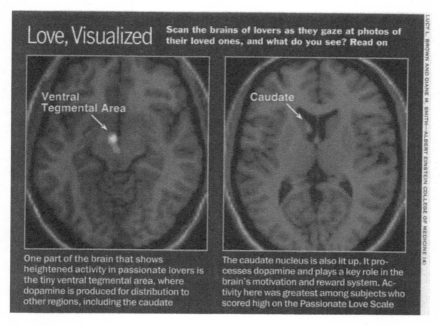

Fig. 5.1 Love visualized.
Permission granted by Cambridge University Press.

areas involved in more complex emotional and cognitive processing (e.g., embodied cognition, body image, and attention). Not surprising, then, that as our definition of passionate love states: "Reciprocated love (union with the other) is associated with fulfillment and ecstasy."

Interestingly, in one study, Zeki and Romaya (2010) found that although love, sexual desire, and hate generally involve very different patterns of brain activity, in two cases they overlap—producing activity in the right putamen and the medial insula. The authors offer some speculations as to why the two very different emotions spark similar brain activity in these two areas:

> We note with considerable interest that the parts of the right putamen and the medial insula activated in this study correspond closely to the parts activated in our earlier study of romantic love . . . the insula may be involved in responses to distressing sensory stimuli . . . there are also conditions in which a loved face may constitute a distressing signal. The putamen could also be involved in the planning of aggressive motor acts within the context of romantic love—for example, when a rival presents a danger. . . . This linkage may account for why love and hate are so closely linked to each other in life. (p. 6)

Whether or not this will prove to be so awaits further research. Brain research is still in its infancy and one must be cautious in assessing results' meaning and reliability.

Data indicate that at any given moment, more than 50% of young people are passionately in love (Feybesse, 2015). A wide array of studies have documented that for young people, passion is associated with a plethora of positive feelings. Infatuation is associated with positive emotions such as euphoria (Fisher et al., 2002). In a meta-analysis, Karandashev and Clapp (2015) found that passionate love is associated with idealization of the other, with commitment, with curiosity about the other, caring about the other, a desire to put the other first, and the sharing of intimate thoughts and feelings. Romantic relationships enhance happiness and life (Kim & McKenry, 2002).

Passionate love is important for young people's health and well-being. College students who are in stable romantic relationships experience fewer mental health problems, have fewer problems with overweight and obesity, and tend to drink less often than single people. In the same way, married couples are less likely to suffer from long-term medical conditions and have a longer life expectancy (Braithwaite, Delevi, & Fincham, 2010).

Passionate love has been found to have an important impact on the well-being and health of older people, too (Hatfield & Rapson, 2006; Slatcher & Selcuk, 2017). In one study, Traupmann and Hatfield (1981) interviewed a random sample of women living in Madison, Wisconsin, who ranged in age from 50 to 82. The authors found that passionate love (as well as companionate love, sexual satisfaction, and financial status) had a significant impact on mental health, physical health, and relationship satisfaction (Debrot, Meuwly, Muise, Impett, & Schoebi, 2017; Hatfield, Brinton, & Cornelius, 1989; Wang & Nguyen, 1995).

Aron and Henkemeyer (1995) interviewed married couples and found that, for women, passionate love was moderately correlated with marital satisfaction and overall happiness, relationship excitement, frequency of sex, and shared activities. For men, there were no significant correlations with passionate love.

The presence of romantic love has also been found to promote satisfaction in long-term relationships (Acevedo & Aron, 2009). As Noller (2005) observes:

> The environment created by romantic love has been analyzed as one of interdependence, equality, and open communication, where each partner supports the other in efforts at growth and self-development. (p. 112)

She concludes that

> relationships that combine the passionate and companionate sentiments of romantic love are conducive to the [type of] love that supports marriage and family. (p. 97)

Love has also been found to be related to patterns of sexual activity. People who are in love are more likely to give and receive oral sex, as well as to engage in sexual activity in general, compared to people who are not in love (Kaestle & Halpern, 2007; Regan, 2000). Although passionate love typically wanes through the course of a relationship (Hatfield, Pillemer, O'Brien, & Le, 2008), if a couple is able to sustain passionate love (for example, by engaging in novel and arousing activities; Aron, Norman, Aron, McKenna, & Heyman, 2000), then relationship satisfaction will increase.

Marriages based on romantic love also have numerous consequences for mental and physical health and well-being. Being in a long-term relationship (e.g., cohabitation or marriage) is associated with lower morbidity and mortality rates. Increasingly, however, research is demonstrating that it is not being in an intimate relationship per se, but the *quality* of that relationship that matters (Jaremka, Glaser, Malarkey, & Kiecolt-Glaser, 2013; Leach, Butterworth, Olesen, & Mackinnon, 2013). In a meta-analysis, Robles, Slatcher, Trombelleo, and McGinn (2014) found strong evidence for that contention. Low relationship quality is a risk factor for poor health.

There is considerable evidence that passion, love, and intimacy can assuage the negative psychological impact of stress (Laurenceau, Barrett, & Pietromonaco, 1998). Neurobiological and psychology studies document that feelings of "love, compassion and joy make our immune system function better and help to battle diseases" (Esch & Stefano, 2005). Joyful activities such as being in love have been shown to

> activate areas in the brain responsible for emotion, attention, motivation and memory (i.e., limbic structures), and it may further serve to control the ANS [autonomic nervous system], i.e., stress reduction. . . . Thus, love and pleasure clearly are capable of stimulating health, well-being and (re)productivity" . . . [making life] a deeply rewarding and pleasurable experience. (p. 265)

Thus, romantic love plays a role in developing and maintaining the overall social and biological health of partners.

Companionate love has been found to be a strong predictor of subjective well-being in both collectivistic and individualistic cultural samples, especially for women (Kim & Hatfield, 2004). Like passionate love, however, companionate love can also decrease over time in relationships (Hatfield, Pillemer et al., 2008), and then its benefits decline as well.

The Badlands of Love

> When I am in love I am INSANE. . . . And although a great glory shines around, the main results are anxiety, misery, despair, destruction, inability to work, etc.
>
> —Iris Murdoch

Besotted lovers yearn for love, certain it will bring them joy and fulfill-ment, but passion has a dark side, too. Men and women frequently know that others they love so fiercely do not return their affection. Often they are torn by jealousy. When things cool down (which is not a rare occurrence), people discover their lover is not all they'd hoped for. The reasons for these disappointments can be many.

First, love is associated with a variety of negative emotions. Infatuation, for example, is very stressful (Marazziti & Canale, 2004). Unrequited love and romantic breakups elicit sadness and shame (Leary, Koch, & Hechenbleikner, 2001). Love can be accompanied by jealousy (De Silva, 1997). The death of a romantic partner typically elicits intense grief (Rosenzweig, Prigerson, Miller, & Reynolds, 1997).

Second, difficulties in love may reduce general well-being. It has been shown, for example, that romantic breakups are a main risk factor for devel-oping a major depressive disorder in adolescents (Monroe, Rohde, Seeley, & Lewinsohn, 1999). Also, dysfunctional romantic relationships and romantic breakups are associated with a decrease in happiness and life satisfaction (Amato, 2004; Proulx, Helms, & Buehler, 2007).

Third, people who are infatuated often neglect their responsibilities or work because they think about their beloved all the time (Langeslag, Van der Veen, & Fekkes, 2012; Van Steenbergen, Langeslag, Band, & Hommel, 2014). This might not bother the infatuated individual, but it certainly results in a loss of productivity.

Fourth, unrequited love plays a role in several mental and sexual disorders, including sexual dysfunctions, paraphilic disorders, and erotomanic and jealous delusions (American Psychiatric Association, 2013), as well as sparking suicidal behavior (Canetto & Lester, 2002).

Finally, love is associated with various forms of criminal behavior, in-cluding stalking (Meloy & Fisher, 2005), domestic violence (Garcia-Moreno, Jansen, Ellsberg, Heise, & Watts, 2006; Wilt & Olson, 1996), and homicide (Wilson & Daly, 1993). Taken together, these negative effects of passionate love cause substantial social and economic burdens. (For a discussion of these problems, see Feybesse, 2015.) None of these findings are probably shocking for those who have gone through heartbreak themselves. And, of course, one needs only to look to works of literature, the movies, or TV shows to see the ubiquity of heartbreak and the human desire to understand and ameliorate the pain caused by heartbreak. Let us consider a few of these problems of the heart in more detail.

Unrequited Love

At the time of the French Revolution, novelist Benjamin Constant fell in love with Mademoiselle Germaine de Staël (1766–1817), the most impressive woman of her generation—beautiful, intelligent, and very rich. In his diary, Constant details the couple's tumultuous relationship. They quarreled incessantly. Words like *torture, fury,* and *anguish* poison every page. He despised her, yet he couldn't leave. It was a nightmare for both of him. In a novel, he details these feelings.

> The scene became stormy. We broke out in mutual recriminations. . . . There are things which for a long time are left unsaid, but once they are said, one never stops repeating them. . . . Had I loved her as she loved me, she would have been calmer. . . . A senseless rage took hold of us. All circumspection was abandoned, all delicacy forgotten. It was as if the Furies were urging us on against each other. (Constant, 2001, pp. 31–39)

Country music, novels, and films are filled with laments of lovers who loved and lost. Roy Baumeister and Sara Wotman (1991) asked young people to write stories about times when their love was unrequited and times when someone loved them but they often just didn't return that love. They found, to their surprise, that it is generally more painful to reject someone than to be rejected. As Carson McCullers (1951) says, "Most of us would rather love than be loved. And the curt truth is that in a deep secret way the state of being beloved is intolerable to many" (p. 54).

Why Should That Be?

For many, unrequited love is a bittersweet experience. At first the besotted are filled with love and hope. They wallow in the drama of their misery. They view the beloved with incomprehension. How could X not love them when they love X so intensely? They blame X for not reciprocating their love; they feel angry, annoyed, and resentful at X's stubbornness. They blame themselves: "I'm not good enough." They feel released from normal moral constraints ("all's fair in love and war"). When it finally sinks in that their case is hopeless, they sometimes feel their heart has been ripped to shreds. Sometimes, the rejected lover's pursuit of the other turns into harassment. In years to come, the unrequited lover remembers the infatuation as a bittersweet affair despite the poison of disappointment. And sometimes the consequences are deadly.

Things are not so rosy for the beloved. At first, their self-esteem may be slightly bolstered by all the adoration they receive from the supplicant. Soon, however, they find themselves in an impossible situation. They feel guilty for rejecting someone who obviously cares so much about them. (It is hard enough to tell someone you are not interested, much less why.) It feels even worse to lead someone on. But, if the supplicant persists, guilt soon turns to irritation and then to rage. People begin to feel trapped and persecuted. What could be motivating the besotted lover? Why won't she go away? Is he insane? How could she deceive herself this way? Didn't he see he is driving her crazy? (See Baumeister, Wotman, & Stillwell, 1993, for further information on this process.)

Disillusionment

We may start out idealizing our romantic partner but as we get deeper into the relationship we discover facts about him or her that give us pause. In fact, Diane Felmlee (2001) found that the very traits that attracted us to a romantic partner in the first place often come to annoy us with the passage of time. The kind and gentle man soon starts to be dismissed as a wimp; the strong, silent type begins to seem like a tyrannical bore.

Jealousy

> Love is as strong as death, its jealousy unyielding as the grave. It burns like blazing fire, like the very flame of the LORD. Many waters cannot quench love; rivers cannot wash it away. . . .
>
> —Song of Solomon 8:6

The American Psychological Association defines jealousy (VandenBos, 2007) as

> a negative emotion in which an individual resents a third party for appearing to take away (or likely to take away) the affections of a loved one. (p. 506)

Cultures differ markedly in what sparks jealousy, in how jealous people get, and in whether they have the power to do anything about their feelings (Fitness & Fletcher, 1993; Hupka, 1991; Hupka & Ryan, 1990).

What sparks jealousy? Men and women can use a number of clues to tell them that someone they love is drifting away and that jealousy is in order. Hupka (1981) illustrates the point that cultures define very different things as threats to self-esteem, relationships, and property through this scenario about an Ammassalik Eskimo husband and wife:

> On her return trip from the local watering well, a married woman is asked for a cup of water by a male resident of the village. Her husband, resting on the porch of their dwelling, observes his wife giving the man a cup of water. Subsequently, they approach the husband and the three of them enjoy a lively and friendly conversation into the late evening hours. Eventually the husband puts out the lamp, and the guest has sexual intercourse with the wife. The next morning the husband leaves the house early in order to catch fish for breakfast. Upon his return he finds his wife having sex again with the guest. The husband becomes violently enraged and mortally stabs the guest. (pp. 324–325)

At what point in the vignette might one expect the husband to be jealous? Why was he calm the first time he witnessed their intimacy and murderous the second time? In the first instance, the husband gave his permission for the sexual encounter. In the second, the woman and traveler engaged in sex simply because they wanted to; this is taboo.

Hupka, an anthropologist, points out that it depends, of course, in which culture we place the husband. A husband in the Pawnee Indian tribe in the 19th century, for example, bewitched any man who dared to request a cup of water from his wife. The Toda of Southern India, who were primarily polyandrous at the turn of the century, on the other hand, would consider the sequence of events described in the vignette to be perfectly normal. The Todas had the custom of *mokhthoditi,* which allowed husbands and wives to take on lovers. When, for instance, a man wanted someone else's wife as a lover, he sought the consent of that wife and her husband or husbands. If consent was given by all, the men negotiated an annual fee to be paid to the husband(s). The woman then lived with the new man just as if she were his real wife. Or, more commonly, the man visited the woman at the house of her husband(s).

It is evident from these illustrations and many others that culture is a potent determinant of when people will (or will not) evaluate a rival as a threat to self-esteem and to the relationship (Guerrero, Spitzberg, & Yoshimura, 2004).

Buunk and Hupka (1987) found that there are also cultural differences in the kinds of things that trigger jealousy in modern, industrialized nations. They interviewed 2,079 college students from seven industrialized nations of the time—the United States, Hungary, Ireland, Mexico, the Netherlands, the Soviet Union, and what was then Yugoslavia. Students were asked to take a look at several statements regarding the following: *flirting* ("It does not bother me when I see my lover flirting with someone else"); *kissing* ("When I see my lover kissing someone else my stomach knots up"); *dancing* ("When my lover dances with someone else I feel very uneasy"); *hugging* ("When somebody hugs my lover I get sick inside"); *sexual relationships* ("It would bother me if my partner frequently had satisfying sexual relations with someone else"); and *sexual fantasy* ("It is entertaining to hear the sexual fantasies my partner has about another person"). They were then asked to indicate to what extent they agreed with each of these statements.

There were some notable cross-national similarities in the kinds of things that people found threatening. Behaviors such as dancing, hugging, and talking about sexual fantasies were taken in stride. Explicit erotic behavior—flirting, kissing, or having sexual relations with someone else—evoked strong feelings of jealousy.

There were a few striking cultural differences in *exactly* what people found upsetting, however. U.S. citizens, for example, took hugging for granted. In the Netherlands, kissing, hugging, and dancing evoked less jealousy than in most other countries; but citizens got more upset by the idea of their partner's having sexual fantasies about other people than did others. Hungarians found both hugging and kissing most provoking. Citizens from the Soviet Union were upset by dancing and sexual relations.

The data also highlighted the importance of power in determining how people respond to jealous provocations. In most tribes, women, who are usually physically weaker than men, possessed less political and economic power. Although neither men nor women liked infidelity, only the men were in a position to do much about it. In general, women were "supposed to" respond to adultery with only the gentlest forms of aggression. They could express righteous indignation, cry, threaten to walk out, or divorce. The men were allowed to bring out the really big guns when offended; they were permitted to banish or murder their mates.

Thus far, we have focused on cultural differences in jealousy. Evolutionary psychologist David Buss (2000) argues that jealousy is more deeply and universally ingrained in humankind than one might think. Although jealousy is primarily a sad and negative emotion, he argues that it is adaptive because it contributes to romantic relationship maintenance:

> Jealousy, according to this perspective, is not a sign of immaturity, but rather a supremely important passion that helped our ancestors, and most likely continues to help us today, to cope with a host of real reproductive threats. Jealousy, for example, motivates us to ward off rivals with verbal threats and cold primate stares. It drives us to keep partners from straying with tactics such as escalating vigilance or showering a partner with affection. And it communicates commitment to a partner who may be wavering, serving an important purpose in the maintenance of love. (p. 26)

Several of our informants detailed the lengths the jealous person can go to in the modern world:

> Dating. I know dating is changing. Because of all this social media people really cannot define cheating. In my generation girls stalk on social media to see everything that the boys they like are doing. They check who they "follow," who likes their posts, who likes their comments, what they are commenting, what they are liking. Everything. My roommate was telling me the other day that she was so mad at her boyfriend because he followed a girl on Instagram, and when he refused to "unfollow" her she said he had to delete his entire Instagram or she would break up with him. It was crazy in my eyes, but MANY girls are like that. I know a lot of friends also "check up" on their friend's boyfriend/girlfriends. Friends will tell their friends if they see their boyfriend doing anything on the Internet. I even had one of my friends ask to use my cell phone. And of course I was like "Sure do whatever on it." And she texted her boyfriend on my phone, saying, "hi its Sarah, you want to come out with us tonight?" And when he replied "Sarah who?" She texted him off her phone saying "you would go out with girls and not tell me." I was mad because I think that is absolutely insane, and then she used my phone to do it. But that's how girls are using social media. . . . It's unhealthy and sad.

Vengeance

Some jealous lovers, as we've just seen, react very violently. In the 17th century, Richard Burton (1621/1927) wrote, in *The Anatomy of Melancholy*:

> Those which are jealous proceed from suspicion to hatred; from hatred to frenzie; from frenzie to injurie, murder and despair. (p. 428)

Historically, since men had the most power, they were allowed to let their "frenzie" lead to murder. Women had to be content with more tepid responses.

Arapaho (American) men might beat wives they suspected of having sexual relations with anyone else. Occasionally a suspicious man calmly sent his wife away, either to her paramour or to her home. More often he became angry and jealous. Usually he whipped her, and cut off the tip of her nose or her braids, or both. According to Kroeber, he also slashed her cheeks. This treatment of an unfaithful wife was conventional and neither her parents nor the tribe did anything about it (Hilger, 1952, p. 212). The king of the Plateau tribes of Zimbabwe executed men caught with any of his wives. The wives were grossly mutilated (Gouldsbury & Sheane, 1911).

In Western cultures, men are far more likely to beat or murder their girlfriends and wives than their rivals (White & Mullen, 1989). In America, family peace centers report that about two-thirds of wives who are forced to seek shelter do so because their husbands' excessive or unwarranted jealousy has led them to repeatedly assault the women (Gayford, 1979).

Male jealousy is the leading cause of wife battering and homicide worldwide (Buss, 1994/2003; Daly & Wilson, 1988). Until recently, such vengeance was approved of or treated leniently. The 18th-century English jurist Blackstone commented that killing in a situation where a man or woman is caught in the act "is of the lowest degree of manslaughter; . . . for there could not be a greater provocation" (quoted in Smith & Hogan, 1983, p. 288). In many countries, the courts have been (and sometimes still are) sympathetic to such "crimes of passion." Traditionally, it was considered a man's right to defend his "honor." In Morocco, for example, the law excuses killing one's wife if she is caught in the act of adultery, but a woman would not be excused for killing her husband in the same circumstances (Greenhouse, 1994). In Sao Paulo (Brazil's most populous city), in 1980–1981, 722 men claimed "defense of honor" for murdering their wives. Brazilian women then adopted the slogan "Lovers don't kill" and campaigned against allowing such a defense in murder trials. Once again, we see that, worldwide, the world is changing. (See Brooke [1991] for a discussion of the changes that globalization has brought to views of "honor" and crimes of violence in one culture—Brazil.)

Perhaps jealousy and the acts of vengeance that follow are universal and based in biology. But perhaps they are based on the raw power of men over women; men are generally bigger and stronger. What happens when the power differential diminishes? Will jealousy and the violence that follows begin to wither as powerful factors in relationships? Might jealousy be more culturally derived than biological and immutable?

These questions will surely continue to be contextual and mutable in nature, especially as gender equity continues to develop across the globe. However, we can predict that no matter what the future brings, there will still be an intense desire for many, if not most, humans to connect with another human. That connection may be short or long, passionately sexual, or companionate and platonic. But beneath these connections will be "love" in all of its varied expressions. And the stronger those feelings around love are, the more chaos will ensue when they're taken away, like a wire full of electricity yanked from its power source. There are so many songs, books, and movies about love because it elevates, and at times, devastates us in ways we seem to have no control over. While we may find solace in the artistic expressions of the ups and downs of love, science is also now able to show us the nuts and bolts of the experience itself.

6

Sexual Behaviors

At the start of our Human Sexuality course at the University of Hawaii at Manoa in the fall of 2015, we asked our students to submit three hand-written questions about love, sex, or sexuality that they hoped we would answer over the course of the upcoming semester. Students were given five minutes to write their questions on a small note card and return it to the front of the room when they were finished. After five minutes, many students were still writing furiously, carefully guarding their cards from prying eyes, or ribbing one another while sharing a muffled giggle. Excited to see such an involved response, we set out after class to analyze their answers in order to better understand how we should formulate the direction of the course.

Questions varied from "Why do people like sex?" to "Do women like anal?" to "What's the best position for achieving a vaginal orgasm using a strap-on?" While these questions demonstrated the variety of student curiosities, one common theme was omnipresent. Surprisingly, by and large, unlike these questions, the students weren't focused on what is "most pleasurable" or "most satisfying in sex." Instead, what they wanted to know most often was simply, "What is normal?" Normal penis size. Normal amount of sex a couple should have in a month. Normal rate of female orgasm. "Is it normal to feel attracted to the same sex, but not be gay?" "What is the definition of a normal sexual relationship?" they asked, the handwriting anxious and pressed deep with a ballpoint pen.

This presented us with a particular problem. As sex researchers, we typically eschew the concept of normalcy in regard to sexual behaviors. Since "normal" has so often been equated with white, Western, heterosexual standards, we've seen too often how categorizing certain sexual behavior as "good," "bad," or "normal" disproportionality marginalizes sexual minorities or variations in sexual expression. "THERE IS NO NORMAL!" we declared the next day in class, enthusiastic that students would embrace the ambiguity of the unknown. We followed up our declaration with a well-known quote

What's Next in Love and Sex. Elaine Hatfield, Richard L. Rapson, and Jeanette Purvis, Oxford University Press (2020). © Oxford University Press.
DOI: 10.1093/oso/9780190647162.001.0001

by sex researcher Dr. Milton Diamond: "Nature loves variety, society hates it." The students looked on, blankly. We could tell they weren't buying it and we realized at this point that untangling the concept of "normal" from their concepts of sex would take a bit more work.

Problems with "Normal"

The issue about sex and normalcy is that, generally speaking, there exists no foolproof way to keep an ongoing tab of everyone's regular sex behaviors, mapped out on a two-dimensional graph. Sex is expansive, diverse, and fiercely private. It's hard to study a topic to which people have been conditioned, and perhaps even explicitly told, not to talk about. Particularly in the United States, this may have to do with the powerful legacy of sexual puritanism, where sex is not to be seen, nor discussed in explicit terms. This would be true generally of religious and rural cultures worldwide. Sex is often referred to as something that "goes on behind closed doors" or is known as a "bedroom issue" and spoken about in poetic euphemisms in public and in explicit slang between friends. Still, the actual words themselves are rarely spoken.

The cultural norm in America of private sex is thought to have arisen from early Protestant settlers' orientation toward the nuclear family, which brought sex squarely within the bedrooms of married men and women and established privacy as the norm for subsequent American life (see D'Emilio & Freedman &, 2012). This concept of sex as a sacred bond between a man and wife is rooted strongly in Abrahamic religions, namely Christianity, but also in orthodox Judaism and Islam. According to Hebrews 13:4 (the New King James version), "Marriage should be honored by everyone, and husband and wife should keep their marriage pure. God will judge guilty those who take part in sexual sins." Currently, 76.5% of Americans are affiliated with an organized religion (Pew Research Center, 2015). While it is true that, overall, Americans are becoming less religious, the decline comes mostly from fewer individuals stating they are Protestant or Catholic compared to 10 years ago. Evangelical Christians, however, have only dipped slightly in number, with a 1% decline in the American population since 2007 (Pew Research Center, 2015). While new studies have demonstrated the role of Christianity in America to be nuanced in regard to its impact on sexuality (Sands, 2000), it still is by far the most popular religion in America and continues to have a lasting impact on our concept of sexual behavior as belonging to carefully delineated private spheres.

For these reasons, it has been a difficult struggle for researchers to get an accurate picture of modern human sexual behavior in Western as well as non-Western societies. Asking people about sex point-blank is not typically something that is culturally acceptable, except for those particular circumstances that involve friends or trusted confidants. For example, if you are a researcher, interviewing participants may be easy when the questions are about age, ethnicity, and whether or not someone is left- or right-handed. But asking the average American "How many times do you masturbate in a week?" may be met with more resistance. In one of our first surveys assessing sexual behavior, a frequent complaint by our participants was that the question "How many people have you slept with in the past year" came immediately after "How old are you?" One person went so far as to write in the comment section, "I wasn't warmed up yet enough to answer that question. Next time, ease into it." Point taken.

Speaking specifically of the United States, where research into sexual behavior is most ample, it is impossible to suggest this is a country of tightly laced Puritans, wildly waving Bibles over their heads as they heap judgment on all those around, with no desire to discuss matters of sex and sexuality. In reality, Americans have a complex and layered relationship to sex and its many presentations. In fact, American's attitudes toward sex, sexuality, and the nuclear family have become increasingly more liberal over the past several decades.

Since 1972, there has been a 13% decline in the number of people who think sex before marriage is wrong, bringing the grand total of individuals who don't believe in sex before marriage to 21% (Smith & Son, 2013). In addition, while in 1987 nearly 76% of Americans stated that they believed homosexual sex to be wrong, that number dropped to 43% in 2012 (Smith & Son, 2013) and continues to decline dramatically.

Other dimensions such as pornography consumption, extramarital affairs, and gay marriage have all shown significant shifts toward being increasingly morally acceptable in America, especially within younger generations (Smith & Son, 2013). There is still considerable disapproval of porn, of course. One of our informants said:

> For most of my friends it is very looked down on. If my friend asked what I was watching and it was porn they would find it strange. Girls do not openly talk about watching porn. It is a hidden secret.

Many women get angry if they "catch" their boyfriend watching porn. "Aren't I good enough for you?" they ask. Men and women, even those who have had extramarital affairs, disapprove of porn, too. But attitudes are changing even here (Smith & Son, 2013).

There has been a greater change in the acceptance of homosexuality. Additionally, a number of churches from a variety of Christian religions not only teach acceptance of homosexuals but also fully sanction gay marriages and even allow gay individuals to serve in leadership positions (Masci & Lipka, 2015). In fact, the mainline Protestant denomination the Presbyterian Church (United States) recently changed its definition of marriage from being between "a man and a woman" to being between "two people," and the Unitarian Universalist Church has maintained an Office of Gay Affairs since 1973. Does this mean that the days of sexual puritanism are fading, and research into modern sex behaviors will benefit from newly discovered sexual openness? Well, just as American's attitudes toward sex are complex, so are the results we gather from our research. The problems with understanding "normal" sex behavior extend beyond even the general reluctance of many folks to talk about it.

Studies on sex behavior have a long history of being especially prone to report biases given the sensitive nature of the topic (Gribble, Miller, Rogers, & Turner, 1999). People lie about their sex lives. Perhaps this is because so many individuals don't know what "normal" sexual behavior is and thus are influenced to respond in certain ways in many survey or interview formats, whether consciously or otherwise, by gender or cultural stereotypes. For example, one of the most replicated findings in social psychology is that males overreport the number of sexual partners they have had, while women underreport the number (Brown & Sinclair, 1999). Interestingly, women appear to stretch the truth even more so than men (Alexander & Fisher, 2003).

Since endorsement of the traditional sexual double standard is still common (Allison & Risman, 2013), and traditional gender roles are still dominant in contemporary dating scenarios (Serewicz & Gale, 2008), it is likely that these realities are absorbed by the participants, greatly influencing their responses. Research by Brown and Sinclair (1999), for instance, indicated that one of the factors contributing to the differences between male and female reports of number of sexual partners has to do with the fact men are more likely to make "rough estimates" of their previous partners, while women rely on more specifically recalled, discrete events. Accordingly, men usually report more sexual partners than do women. In this study, both genders had a certain percentage of participants who acknowledged that their estimates were not accurate. Many, however, were confident that their estimates were correct. One possible explanation is that these divergent "counting strategies" were developed differently by each gender because the end result for each gender-linked strategy fits more with sexual double standards that are still common in our society, in which men are encouraged and rewarded socially for having many sexual partners, while women are still punished. As such, men may benefit socially from overreporting, and women may benefit socially from underreporting, and they unconsciously adopt reporting strategies that fit these expectations.

While newer studies suggest that this reporting bias regarding gender-linked differences in number of sexual partners may not be as large as it once was (Hamilton & Morris, 2010), the fact that many people misrepresent their overall number of sexual partners indicates that there may be a high social cost for engaging in sexual behavior that violates social norms. People are aware that behaving in sexually gender-typical ways may be a safer bet than not. A logical reason for this is the need for social inclusion. There are significant evolutionary and cultural reasons for pursuing and maintaining social inclusion. In many past societies, it would have been certain death to be cast out from one's family or clan, as resources, protection, procreation, and socialization would no longer be available. Some evolutionary theorists contend that humans have evolved certain cognitive structures designed to detect and prevent social exclusion. For example, recent research with fMRI imagery found that the brain reacts similarly to social exclusion as it does to physical pain—a unique cognitive trick to motivate the individual to avoid further or prolonged instances of social separation (Eisenberger, Lieberman, & Williams, 2003).

Social exclusion hurts, and there has been perhaps no greater risk to social exclusion historically than engaging in sexual behavior outside of expected social norms. In 17th century Plymouth country, there were strict rules against "immoral" sexual behaviors as determined largely by tenets derived from the Christian faith. Rape, anal intercourse, or sex with animals could result in a death sentence (Lauria, 1998). In 1778, Thomas Jefferson went so far to state:

Whosoever shall be guilty of Rape, Polygamy, or Sodomy with man or woman shall be punished, if a man, by castration, if a woman, by cutting thro' the cartilage of her nose a hole of one half inch diameter at the least.

While these laws may sound antiquated, sodomy laws were not struck down in the United States until 2003, and it took a Supreme Court case to do it (*Lawrence et al. v. Texas*, 2003). To this day, America is the only major industrialized country that still has laws against adultery on its books. In fact, 21 states currently have some form of law against adultery, although they are not commonly enforced (Bronner, 2012). That said, sometimes these anti-adultery laws are enforced, as was the case when North Carolinian woman Cynthia Shackelford successfully sued her husband's mistress to the tune of $9 million. According to local North Carolina lawyer Lee Rosen, the historic anti-adultery law that helped Shackelford win her case hasn't been struck down because "our conservative legislators don't want to be known as the people that voted to, in effect, legalize adultery" (Gomstyn & ABC News Business Unit, 2010). Clearly, there is still a deep intersection between the government and the regulation of "proper" sexual behavior. Again, with stakes this high, many people, especially minority members, may not be particularly motivated to share with strangers information about their sexual behaviors.

Sexual Behavior—From Kinsey to the Present

What are we left with? To answer that question, we look to the first person ever to attempt to conduct a large-scale population study of male and female human sexual behavior, zoologist Alfred Kinsey, in his highly publicized *Kinsey Reports* (Kinsey, Pomeroy, & Martin, 1948; Kinsey, Pomeroy, Martin, & Gebhard, 1954). In these two volumes, *Sexual Behavior in the Human Male* and *Sexual Behavior in the Human Female*, Kinsey combined data collected from thousands of interviews that assessed sexual orientation, frequency of sex acts, sexual satisfaction, orgasm rates, and many other variables relating to recalled sexual behaviors.

While the reports caused widespread moral panic, as they revealed that the sexualities of both men and women were diverse and varied, it modeled the importance of gathering large-scale data on sexual behavior.

Even though Kinsey's studies have since been criticized for methodolog-ical and statistical problems, by creating this taxonomy of human sexual be-havior, the first glimpses into human's sexual behaviors were finally made available to the general public. In addition, by creating such a large database of human sexual behaviors, the *Kinsey Reports* illuminated an interesting finding: human sexuality appeared to be surprisingly fluid.

According to Kinsey (1948), "The living world is a continuum in each and every one of its aspects," and he viewed sexuality as no different. Through his thousands of interviews, Kinsey and his colleagues realized that many indi-viduals indicated same-sex sexual interest, or even had previous same-sex encounters, although many considered themselves heterosexual or led reg-ular heterosexual lives with wives or husbands and had children.

In an attempt to measure this fluidity, Kinsey developed the "Kinsey Scale": a seven-point scale that placed an individual's sexual orientation on a continuum, rather than locking it into one of three discrete categories (gay, straight, bisexual). While this scale has been improved and expanded over the years, this finding regarding sexuality as a continuum has fostered a significant and lasting insight into human sexual behavior. It does appear that sexual orientation may not commonly be exclusively gay or exclusively straight for many—if not most—humans. Contemporary research on sexual fluidity has also been conducted. Epstein, McKinney, Fox, and Garcia (2012) distributed online surveys to over 17,000 participants across 47 countries, utilizing 18 items to assess sexual orientation. This survey took attitudes and desires into account as well, by asking participants such questions as "Have you ever had a waking fantasy about a sexual encounter with a member of the same sex?" or "Would you be willing to have sexual relations with someone of the same sex?" Results from this study demonstrated a smooth distri-bution of scores across a sexual orientation continuum, with only 7.4% of the participants indicating a completely straight or completely gay orienta-tion (Epstein et al., 2012). Additionally, just as Kinsey found, Epstein and his colleagues also concluded that there was a higher likelihood that women would indicate more sexual fluidity than men (see also Diamond, 2008).

Sexual fluidity has become a popular topic in contemporary culture. Recently, 27-year-old Nico Tortorella, star of a popular TV show on TV Land called *Younger* "came out" as sexually fluid. "It's just a fluidity. ... We're all kind of moving into this one situation" he stated when referencing his sexu-ality in a recent interview with Access Hollywood. While gender attitudes to-ward homosexuality and different sexual expressions are not what they used to be, it is still a unique and bold action for a handsome, young, rising male TV star to speak openly about his sexual fluidity.

Indeed, millennials seem to be especially prone to discredit traditional identity categories, be they gender, religious, political, or sexual. Social changes may be giving permission to men in particular, perhaps for the first time, to be open about having varied sexual interests outside the traditional male–female binary. In fact, the Centers for Disease Control and Prevention (CDC), in a recent survey of American adults, found that although more women than men considered themselves to be bisexual (5.5% vs. 2%, $n = 10,000$), there was a 0.8% increase in men identifying themselves as bisexual compared to just five years ago (Copen, Chandra, & Febo-Vazquez, 2016). Perhaps if the CDC had included a scale for participants to indicate their sexual orientation on a wider continuum they might have captured even more reports of sexual fluidity.

Not only has Kinsey's contribution to better understanding sexual fluidity been impactful, so has his taxonomical approach to human sexual behaviors. Kinsey's alma mater, Indiana University, has continued his legacy in collecting data from a large population sample to assess the frequency of particular sexual behaviors in their *National Survey of Sexual Health and Behavior* report (Herbenick et al., 2010).

Since so many of our students were interested in what is "normal," we spent part of class one day discussing the results of the Indiana University study, which was distributed to nearly 6,000 individuals from the ages of 14–94, and discussed the frequency of sexual behaviors such as oral sex, penile-vaginal sex, masturbation, and anal sex across the lifespan, broken down by gender. Some revealing findings included a high rate of female masturbation, with 72% of women ages 25–29 indicating that they had masturbated in the past year compared to 85% of men. Additionally, 33% of women over the age of 70 had masturbated over the past year, only slightly lagging behind males over the age of 70, at 46%.

Another fact we discussed was the prevalence of sexual activity among older adults. According to Lindau and colleagues (2007), of the adults 75 to 85 years old surveyed in their study, 54% were sexually active. A full 23% were sexually active once a week or more; 54% were engaging in some form of sexual activity two to three times a month. Surprisingly, older adults' reported sexual activity was similar to that of adults aged 18–59 in prevalence, contradicting the long-standing stereotype that "older adults have less sex."

Sadly, even though sex has been found to positively affect the life quality and satisfaction of older people (Weeks, 2002), stigmatization of sexuality among older adults is still common in Western cultures (Bauer, McAuliffe, & Nay, 2007). We encountered this stigma when discussing this very statistic with the class. When we referenced the 33% of women of age of 70 who had masturbated within the last year, we heard several laughs and an audible "Eww" come from somewhere in our lecture class of 150 students. Stopping for a moment, we asked the class if anyone wanted to volunteer their reaction to this information and talk about how this statistic made them feel. "I dunno, it's just gross," said one student hiding behind a laptop screen in the back of the room. "Nooo! Not grandma!" laughed another.

We did our best at this point to convey that sexual needs continue for many individuals throughout life (Foley, 2015; Nikolowski, 1980), regardless of gender, and that this was a positive thing because healthy sex lives are often correlated with positive health outcomes (Weeks, 2002) (see also Chapter 5). In fact, these stigmas are often internalized by the elderly, both from society and directly from some health professionals as well. In one of our grandmothers' nursing homes they tied down the hands of inmates caught masturbating. Another old man was deprived of his 90th-birthday cake when he was caught sneaking into his wife's bed. The nurses assumed he was senile instead of just lonely for his wife's touch. This stigma may lead many older people to refrain from disclosing important sexual health information to their doctors and to neglect receiving necessary and helpful STI and HIV screenings (Slinkard & Kazer, 2011).

To help our class overcome their ageism, we went on to assign the documentary *Still Doing It: The Intimate Lives of Women Over 65*. In it, various women discuss their burgeoning postmenopausal sexuality. One character featured was having regular sex with a man 40 years her junior. Another woman spoke openly about a sexually satisfying relationship she had recently started with another woman. In an especially telling statement, a 70-year-old woman featured in the documentary explained, "I found the yearnings were still present. At first I tried to ignore them, and think 'oh my gosh, you're much too old for this.' But then I thought, you know, why would I be feeling this if my body was too old?" After the students had watched the film, we conducted an informal poll of the class and asked them what they thought of the woman in the film. "BAD ASS!" came a voice, sailing from the back of a room. We felt that by seeing female sexuality in older women in an interesting and enjoyable documentary, we made a little progress into making postmenopausal sexuality "normal" in ways it was not before.

Oral Sex: The New Normal?

Indiana University's National Sex Survey not only dispelled some commonly held beliefs regarding elderly sexuality, by demonstrating that older Americans were absolutely "still doing it," but also indicated a shift in sexual behaviors among younger heterosexual couples. This shift, compared to previous generations, was found in the frequency of oral sex. When Kinsey first recorded his data, oral sex was reported by 10–19% of participants outside of marriage and around 50% of participants within a marriage (Kinsey et al., 1954). In 2010, according the data from the National Sex Survey, 75% of all men and women between the ages of 25 and 29 had engaged in oral sex over the past year (Herbenick et al., 2010).

Research by Kaestle and Halpern (2007) found similar results, with 85% of emerging adults in a current romantic relationship indicating that they had engaged in oral sex with their partner. However, these sexual behaviors are not occurring symmetrically by gender. Vannier and O'Sullivan (2012) found that 90% of reported oral sex encounters by emerging adults included fellatio, while only 46% of all interactions included cunnilingus. This means that women are giving head more than they are receiving.

These findings are consistent with those that Peggy Orenstein (2016) reported in her book *Girls & Sex*, which consists of interviews with young women from across the country with regard to their sexual experiences. Many of the young women Orenstein interviewed did not count oral sex as "sex." In an interview with two young women, Ruby and Rachel, Orenstein transcribed a conversation the young women had:

"It's not '*sex*,'" Devon countered.

"It's like a step past making out with someone," said Ruby. "It's a way of hooking up. A way to have gone farther without it being seen as any big deal."

"And it doesn't have the repercussions that vaginal sex does," Rachel added. "You're not losing your virginity, you can't get pregnant, you can't get STDs. So it's safer" (p. 53). (Note: Of course you *can* get STIs from oral sex.)

So how should this gender difference in giving and receiving oral sex be interpreted? Are the attitudes expressed by these young women in Orenstein's book the norm? The answer is, perhaps. It appears that modern females are caught between a rock and a hard place. They are told on a macro level to adhere to traditional gender and sex roles, minimizing the number of casual sex partners they have, while at the same time, experiencing on a micro level the pressures from individual men to engage in casual sex.

Women may be receiving extremely mixed messages in regard to sexual expression, pleasure, and identity. In an interview with *Rolling Stone*, Paris Hilton once stated, "My boyfriends always tell me I'm not sexual. Sexy, but not sexual" (Grigoriadis, 2003). This quote was then picked up in Ariel Levy's contemporary feminist manifesto *Female Chauvinist Pigs* (2006) and subsequently replicated in countless blogs and articles as an example of the competing messages women receive regarding their sexuality. On the one hand, women are supposed to serve as an object of desire, or the means by which males find and experience pleasure. This is sexy. Performing oral sex is, in many ways, perhaps a performance in which women can star as the sexy actress.

Being sexual, however, would involve acknowledging a need for female pleasure. Receiving oral sex may also necessitate accepting, or at least liking, one's own body. Studies suggest that women who have lower body-image self-esteem have lower rates of sexual satisfaction compared to men, and this may be due to the socialized notion that sexual satisfaction can only be achieved by those who meet certain criteria of physical attractiveness (Dove & Wiedermann, 2000). Women with lower body-image self-esteem are also more likely to engage in risky sexual behaviors (Littleton, Breitkopf, & Berenson, 2005). Possibly, since they feel they are lacking in social desirability, yet yearn for a relationship, they try to give men what they want, ignoring their own needs, in hopes of attaining a relationship.

This is not to suggest that giving oral sex is a zero-sum game in which women cannot enjoy themselves. In a recent article in *Bustle,* titled "Do You Like Giving Oral? 16 Women Share How They Really Feel About Performing Oral Sex," one young woman stated, "Under the right circumstances I love it—love the reaction it gets, love the power and gratification that comes from giving someone else pleasure. I also actually like the experience of it, as long as I'm in the mood to be doing it" (Chatel, 2015). Again, we do not advocate for a normal standard in sexual behavior, and we use this quote as yet another example of a diverse and powerful experience when women give as well as receive oral sex. Contemporary asymmetries, however, in oral sex behaviors may serve as a mirror to deeper asymmetries in modern dating markets.

Same-Sex Sex Life

Oral sex cannot be analyzed just within heterosexual couples. Oral sex is an often central component of modern same-sex sexual behavior, perhaps even more so than for heterosexual couples. For homosexual men, 72% of respondents in a large nationwide survey ($n = 24,787$) that explored recent sexual behavior in men who have sex with men indicated that they had engaged in oral sex during their last sexual encounter (Rosenberger et al., 2011). Interestingly, this survey found that only 37.2% of men who have sex with men reported having engaged in anal sex during their last sexual encounter (Rosenberger et al., 2011). This is a stark contrast to the widely held belief that all gay men engage in anal sex regularly. In fact, there are many men who have sex with men who not only do not engage in anal sex but also self-identify as what is called a "side," as a way of designating their sexual preferences within the gay community. According to gay blogger Joe Kort (2015), "sides" have an active and diverse sex life; it just doesn't involve anal penetration:

> Sides prefer to kiss, hug and engage in oral sex, rimming, mutual masturbation, and rubbing up and down on each other, to name just a few of the sexual activities they enjoy. These men enjoy practically every sexual practice aside from anal penetration of any kind.

As such, the sex lives of gay men should be considered in the many dynamic behaviors that they include. This will allow a more accurate and inclusive understanding of modern gay male experiences, instead of the largely HIV and condom-use focus, characteristic of many studies on gay sex. When the search terms "homosexual, male, love" were entered into our university's electronic journal search, 58 peer-reviewed articles came up. When we typed in "homosexual, male, HIV," an astounding 1,037 articles came up. Clearly, a less pathologizing orientation toward the sex lives of men who have sex with men is necessary.

The previous quote from Joe Kort (2015) illustrates the diversity of sexual behavior that can still constitute "having sex," specifically within same-sex couples. For women who have sex with women, sex also involves a diverse variety of sexual behaviors. These behaviors are most commonly oral sex, digital penetration, and mutual masturbation (Bailey, Farquhar, Owen, & Whittaker, 2003). Interestingly, compared to straight and bisexual women, lesbians report higher rates of orgasm (Garcia, Lloyd, Wallen, & Fisher, 2014). There are probably several reasons for this. One, as previously mentioned, asymmetrical sex roles and internalized negative body-images may be causing many straight women to struggle with exploring sexual pleasure. Then, too, men may lack the intimate knowledge to understand what women want. Women have an easier time guessing what another woman wants, given their physical similarity to one another. Thus, it is harder for men to "feel" what a woman feels. The difference in sex roles between heterosexual men and women may mean that male pleasure is prioritized over female pleasure. As such, vaginal pleasure or fellatio may be considered more desirable than cunnilingus, rubbing, or mutual masturbation. Indeed, research suggests that while lesbians have sex less frequently than heterosexual couples, they have sex for almost twice as long (Blair & Pukall, 2014). These factors may contribute to a higher likelihood of orgasm.

The Female Orgasm

Aside from asking our class what they wanted to learn about sex, we also maintained an active social media site on the microblogging Web host *Tumblr*. Here, students could share interesting sex-related videos or news stories or post their thoughts on any topic covered in class. Additionally, *Tumblr* offers an anonymous "Ask Me Anything" email link through which students can submit questions to the professor in a safe and secure way, without revealing their identity. Then, we would post the answers we wrote to their questions on the main page of our *Tumblr* site for the rest of the class to read. Students quickly latched onto this interactive tool and began filling our inbox daily with questions about sex, love, and their bodies. Again, most were concerned about whether or not their thoughts, ideas, and behaviors were normal. And one topic that nobody seemed to feel normal about was the female orgasm. Women were wondering why they weren't having one, and men were wondering how they could give one.

The truth is, when it comes to heterosexual penetrative sex, men and women are not statistically likely to have the same kind of orgasms, the same way. Men generally assume that, since orgasm is so important for *them*, it is crucial for women, too. In fact, in Elisabeth Lloyd's book, *The Case of the Female Orgasm*, she reviews 33 studies on the female orgasm and arrives at the conclusion that roughly 25% of women consistently experience orgasm from vaginal intercourse. Many women report faking orgasm in order to make their male partner happy, with studies putting the figure at around 64% (Thompson & Muehlenhard, 2003), although relying on recalled self-report may not be totally reliable. Several studies have demonstrated that a central reason females fake orgasms is to avoid hurting the feelings of their male partner (Fahs, 2014; Schaefer, 1973). Indeed, men do report that having a woman experience orgasm during penile-vaginal intercourse is one of the most sexually satisfying experiences. That, in turn, may put pressure on both genders for the woman to experience orgasm (Salisbury & Fisher, 2014). This may relate again to the asymmetrical sex roles between men and women, where men's sexual prowess is correlated to positive social outcomes. As such, the orgasm itself can become an object of male desire, which women may thus feel pressure to provide in order to please the man (see MacKinnon, 1989). Additionally, lack of proper sex education may lead to inaccurate assumptions about female anatomy. A study by Wade, Kremer, and Brown (2005) found that 37% of men incorrectly believed that the clitoris was directly stimulated by the penis during penetration. Improved sexual education programs and more open dialogue about sex in context with pleasure may assist in advancing these forms of knowledge into the 21st century, where they belong.

While the female orgasm may not be experienced in every sexual encounter, it is important to note that many women also state that orgasm is not necessary for sexual pleasure. In fact, in Kleinplatz and her colleagues' (2009) interviews with a wide range of men and women who reported having "great sex," these interviewees insisted that orgasm was neither necessary nor sufficient for the experience. In interviews conducted by Salisbury and Fisher (2014), one woman clarified this in the following way:

> [Female orgasm during intercourse] is not important, but it is a plus. As long as the woman enjoys herself, why is an orgasm important? The whole point is to have a good time. An orgasm would just be icing on the cake. (p. 621)

In the end, we explained to our students that "normal" was going to elude us once again. The role of orgasm in pleasure would ultimately be a process and an experience that was defined and experienced by the sex partners themselves.

Sexting

Sexting is the sending or receiving of sexually explicit messages or photographs, usually via mobile phones. The generational differences in attitudes toward sexting is an example of how rapidly the world is changing. A surprising number of young people, mostly women, report that they have been pressured to text sexually explicit messages.

Many young people report that they have sent sexts—usually to their boyfriend or girlfriend. A 2012 study conducted at the University of Utah found that in a survey of 606 teenagers aged 14–18, nearly 20% of students said they had sent a sexually explicit image of themselves via cell phone, and nearly twice that many said that they had received such a picture. Of those receiving such a picture, over 25% indicated that they had forwarded it to others (Strassberg & McKinnon, 2013).

Sexting, according to young people, is often a positive experience. It is fun—much of sexting occurs between friends, as a joke. It allows people to experiment with sex (sexting often precedes, or is a substitute for, sexual activity), it allows couples to get closer, and has been found to increase relationship and sexual satisfaction in romantic partnerships. This is especially true in long-distance relationships. But there are dangers associated with texting, too.

Sexting, though enjoyable for many, can sometimes negatively impact not only one's relationship but one's life as well. One click, and the photo is posted online for everyone to see. When a relationship crumbles and a couple splits up, a newly single person, bitter at a former lover, may release a partner's pornographic pictures to the world—this is called *revenge porn*. (Horrified that her parents and classmates would see what she had done, one young woman, Jesse Logan, committed suicide when her photo was posted on the Web.) Research by Internet Watch Foundation calculated that 88% of self-made social explicit images are stolen from their original site (usually social networks) and posted on other sites (often porn sites featuring children and teens [Topping, 2012]).

Worse yet, parents, older people, and legal agencies often consider sexting to be a crime, especially if the young people are under age. There is a certain irony that when a young man or young woman sends a photo to his or her sweetheart, police authorities often prosecute both of them for participating in child pornography. And the penalties are often serious. In addition to a jail sentence, the offender may lose the chance to attend college and may be put on the sex offender register for a mandatory 25 years. This means they will have trouble finding jobs, be forced to live in certain designated areas, and be classed with pedophiles and serial rapists on the offender list.

In the course of time, it is likely that the sex laws will come to reflect community attitudes toward sexting, but that day has not yet arrived.

Conclusion

There have been many remarkable inventions in the 20th century, including antibiotics, television, the computer, the mobile phone, the Internet, air travel, space travel, and many, many more technological "miracles."

But in cultural terms, perhaps none has been more life-changing than the relatively taken-for-granted invention, championed by the unsung Margaret Sanger after the Second World War, of the birth control pill. (This followed her pioneering work trying to teach poor women, who already had more children than they could feed, how to avoid getting pregnant, for which she was rewarded with several trips to prison.)

In the past, sexual activity for women could not be separated from pregnancy. In fact, in Catholic Europe (and to this day) the Church teaches that the entire purpose of sexual activity is procreation. The notion that women could enjoy sex for the pleasure of it, barely existed; the type of woman who might do it for pleasure (and not money) was considered a "fallen woman," a sinner, someone meant to be ostracized, condemned, and humiliated. Even for those women who fell through the historical cracks, who may have enjoyed sex, there was still no serious way by which they could safely avoid pregnancy, had they engaged in sexual activity. (This was true of the courtesans as well, for whom sex offered some pitiful bit of power.)

The cultural meaning of the invention of the birth control pill meant that, for the first time in history, women could enjoy sex without the fear of pregnancy and procreation. Slowly but surely, it began to become clear that women could be as sexual as men, could enjoy it as much, and could take initiatives, all with reduced (but still extant) cultural stigma.

This discovery has had revolutionary implications. It has changed the way the Western world, and increasingly the non-Western world, has come to view sexual activity. It has demystified the sexual act, made it more frequent, more egalitarian, less forbidden, less magical, and more matter-of-fact.

Historically, even sex for love is a relatively new idea, not fully coming into cultural acceptance before the middle of the 19th century. And sex for fun, particularly for women, was not considered culturally acceptable until our time—and after The Pill.

Now, in the 21st century, we find that sexual motives—beyond procreation, power, love, and pleasure—have multiplied exponentially. In addition to these, we now find couples (and others) having sex for revenge, for exercise, to decrease the chance of or to resolve fights, for practice, for stress reduction, for hurt and for hate, as a rite of passage, to get a job, for status, for that part in the movie, to counter boredom, for money, for duty (that's an old one!), for erotic discovery, for research, for couples therapy, and for so many more reasons (Hatfield, Luckhurst, & Rapson, 2012).

What this may add up to as we look into the future is that sexual activity has become and will continue to be demystified. And as the motives multiply, as the platforms on which sex can be activated grow larger—for example, the Web or on pornographic sites or with sex dolls, robots, avatars, and operating systems—both guilt and magic may find their force withering.

One may venture the possibility that as the taboos, sense of sin, and stigma erode (along, perhaps, with those mysteries and fears, some of the enchantment and romance), sex may increasingly come to be seen as (as we say in Hawaii): "no beeg teeng." What long-term consequences ensue are hard to prophesize, but it may be possible to suggest that sex in the near future will become more quotidian, more various, and more normalized than ever before in history. For some this will signal "the decline of Western Civilization," while for many others it may come to be seen as a welcome change from the prohibitions, puritanism, and punishments of the past.

Modern sexual behaviors take many forms and expressions. While many people feel anxiety about whether or not their behavior is "normal," the truth is that normalcy continues to elude sex researchers at every turn. The focus of future sexual education and sex research should include a focus on pleasure and satisfaction, with careful consideration of how current asymmetries within modern gender roles may negatively affect that focus. As the attitudes of Americans become more open to accepting the many variations and nuances of sexual behavior, the more pleasure can be included and integrated into our understanding of self and others.

When reading our teaching evaluations for that semester, our favorite was from a student who wrote, "I'm glad I took this course. I'm not wondering what's normal anymore. I'm wondering all the ways things and people aren't the same."

7

The Hookup Culture

Cultural, Social, and Gender Influences on Casual Sex

Introduction

In 1978, Russ Clark and Elaine Hatfield (2003) conducted an experiment designed to test the classic evolutionary theory that men are generally more receptive to sexual offers than women. In their experiment, their students approached fellow college students and asked one of three questions: (a) "Would you go out with me tonight?" (b) "Would you come over to my apartment tonight?" or (c) "Would you go to bed with me tonight?" Men and women differed markedly in their receptivity to casual sexual offers. Seventy-five percent of men accepted the offer of stranger sex while none of the women did (see Table 7.1).

Since its publication, this study has attracted a great deal of attention. In 2003, *Psychological Inquiry* designated the study "a classic, an experiment that scholars will still be talking about 100 years from now." Several TV science programs in the United States, Austria, Canada, and Germany have discussed the study and have conducted partial or full replications of the original experiment. In fact, YouTube users have replicated the study with hidden camera "social experiments" and garnered tens of millions of views. In recent years, this study has sparked heated debates in *Science,* News in Brain and Behavioural Sciences, and Sexnet, the last two being scholarly Web-based discussion groups. In these postings, readers were both laudatory of and annoyed by the study. Some thought the results were obvious, others thought they couldn't possibly be true. Some asserted that the study was a landmark experiment, while others asserted that it was a trivial and frivolous experiment (see Clark & Hatfield, 2003, for a compendium of these comments). The study has been turned into an electronic song, called "Would You?" by the band Touch and Go (Lowe, 1989).

What's Next in Love and Sex. Elaine Hatfield, Richard L. Rapson, and Jeanette Purvis, Oxford University Press (2020). © Oxford University Press.
DOI: 10.1093/oso/9780190647162.001.0001

Table 7.1 Percentage of Agreement by Gender and Type of Request

	Type of Request		
Gender of Respondent	Date	Apartment	Sex
Men	50%	69%	75%
Women	56%	6%	0%

Note: The higher the number, the greater the percentage of people agreeing to the request.

What accounts for these striking results? Currently, cultural psychologists, feminists, and evolutionary psychologists are engaged in a great debate as to why men and women differ so markedly in their enthusiasm for recreational sex—and if they do. Is it because men are more sexual beings, or is it because women who engage in casual sex face more stigma and dangers? As the sexes become more equal in opportunities—and the risks of stigma, physical danger, and unwanted pregnancies decline—will existing differences disappear? In this chapter, we review current theorizing as to the impact of cultural, social, gender, and biological factors on young people's attitudes toward casual sex and their desire and willingness to engage in such activity.

Definitions of Casual Sex

In this chapter, we define casual sex as follows:

> A person engaging in sexual activities (such as sexual caressing, oral sex, sexual intercourse, or anal sex) outside of a "formal" relationship (dating, marriage, etc.) and without a "traditional" reason (such as love or commitment) for doing so.

Such brief encounters may occur between close friends, acquaintances, or total strangers, and they frequently "just happen." Research has estimated that between 60 and 85% of college men and 50 and 85% of college women have engaged in casual sex, hookups, or friends with benefits (Grello, Walsh, Harper, & Dickson, 2003; Paul, McManus, & Hayes, 2000; Puentes, Knox, & Zusman, 2008).

Here, too, *casual sex* will serve as an umbrella term for a wide range of sexual activities. Other common names for these activities are *one-night stands, hookups, fuck buddy, friends with benefits, anonymous sex, no strings attached, booty calls, chance encounters,* and *cruising.* There is wide variation in how these terms are used. *Hookups,* for example, can range from kissing a stranger to fooling around, to having intercourse with someone who was picked up. Surely, in time, other slang terms for casual sex will arise. It is, of course, also likely that these terms represent somewhat different phenomena (Bay-Cheng, Robinson, & Zucker, 2009; Jonason & Balzarin, 2016; Jonason, Li, & Richardson, 2010). In this review, of necessity, however, we will focus on similarities, not differences, in the various forms of impromptu sex.

So let us turn now to the perspectives of theorists from a variety of disciplines that speculate about the antecedents and consequences of casual sex. We will see that while many scholars increasingly emphasize cultural factors and others emphasize evolutionary factors, most scholars (including us) take an interactive approach—pointing out that it is the intersection of culture, personal experience, social context, and biological factors that shapes young people's attitudes and willingness to participate in such encounters.

The Nature of Casual Sex

In this section, we discuss what scholars from a variety of disciplines have learned about the nature of recreational sex. We will survey people's attitudes toward such offhand encounters, try to ascertain how common such activities are, why people choose to engage in them (rather than searching for a committed relationship), and how such flings generally work out.

Attitudes Toward Casual Sex

As we observed earlier, throughout the world men generally possess more positive attitudes toward casual sex than do women. Petersen and Hyde (2010), in their meta-analysis of the attitudes of men and women from 87 countries, found that young men worldwide reported moderately more permissive attitudes toward casual sex than those of young women. In a survey of 289,452 college students at 421 different American colleges and universities, researchers asked students whether they agreed or disagreed with this statement: "If two people really like each other, it's all right for them to have sex even if they've known each other for a very short time." A full 58.1% of the men, but only 34.1% of the women, strongly or somewhat agreed with this statement. (Interestingly, these numbers have decreased since 1990, when 64.8% of men and 37.2% of women agreed; see Pryor, Hurtado, Saenz, Santos, and Korn [2007].) Similar gender differences were found by Milhausen and Herold (2001), the National Center for Social Research & London School of Hygiene and Tropical Medicine (2001), and Petersen and Hyde (2010). Asian-Americans possess more conservative attitudes about casual sex than do their Black, Hispanic, or Euro-American peers (Sprecher, Treger, & Sakaluk, 2013). Sexual attitudes have been found to be a strong predictor of whether or not young people (of various races) actually participate in casual sex (Zimmer-Gembeck & Helfand, 2008).

Aubrey and Smith (2013) developed a scale, the Endorsement of the Hookup Index (EHCI), to see to what extent people endorsed the culture associated with casual, commitment-free sexual encounters. We encourage you to take the test to see to what extent you endorse positive statements about flings: the idea that hooking up is harmless, that it is fun, that it enhances one's status in one's peer group by participating; believe that hooking up allows one to assert control over one's sexuality; and believe that hooking up is a reflection of one's sexual freedom. Indicate the extent to which you agree with each of the items on a five-point scale, ranging from 1 = strongly disagree to 5 = strongly agree.

Hookup Culture Index

Hooking up is not a big deal.	1 2 3 4 5
A hookup is just a hookup.	1 2 3 4 5
Hooking up is harmless.	1 2 3 4 5
Hooking up is just for fun.	1 2 3 4 5
I overlook some of the questionable parts of hooking up because it is fun.	1 2 3 4 5
I hook up to have a good time.	1 2 3 4 5
I like hooking up because it provides immediate gratification.	1 2 3 4 5
Hooking up is pleasurable.	1 2 3 4 5
Hooking up would be a way to make a name for myself.	1 2 3 4 5
It would improve my reputation to hook up with someone who others find appealing.	1 2 3 4 5
Hooking up would make me more popular.	1 2 3 4 5
Hooking up would improve my status among my friends.	1 2 3 4 5

I feel I can control what I want to have happen
    during a hookup.   1 2 3 4 5

I assert my needs during a hookup.   1 2 3 4 5

I feel powerful during a hookup.   1 2 3 4 5

Hooking up is fun when I am in control.   1 2 3 4 5

College is a good time to experiment with hooking up.   1 2 3 4 5

College is a time to experience sex.   1 2 3 4 5

Hooking up allows me to be sexually adventurous.   1 2 3 4 5

Hooking up is a natural thing to do in college.   1 2 3 4 5

On the EHCI scale, students' replies averaged a little above the mid-point (M = 2.82). On the groups of items EHCI–fun, they averaged a bit higher: 3.20. On the EHCI–harmless, answers averaged 3.12, on EHCI–status, considerably lower: 1.70; EHCI–control, 2.87; EHCI–sexual freedom, 2.98. In this study, the authors found no gender differences in men's and women's attitudes and endorsement of hooking up!

Cultural Differences in Attitudes Toward Premarital Sex, Chastity, and Casual Sex

Cultures vary markedly in their attitudes toward people's impromptu sexual activity. Not all premarital sex is casual sex, of course, but it seems reasonable to assume that if a society condemns *all* premarital contact and strongly values chastity, it is almost certain to disapprove of young people's casual sexual encounters as well.

In a cross-cultural survey of over 10,000 people from 37 countries, representing a diversity of cultural, geographic, political, ethnic, religious, racial, economic, and linguistic characteristics, Buss (1989) asked young men and women to indicate what characteristics they most valued in potential mates. Although participants in most cultures agreed on the importance of such traits as love, character, emotional stability, and maturity, one thing they disagreed about was whether or not premarital sexual activity ought to be taboo. In China, India, Indonesia, Iran, Israel (the Palestinian Arabs), and Taiwan, young men were insistent that chastity was "indispensable" in a potential bride. In Finland, France, Norway, the Netherlands, Sweden, and West Germany, on the other hand, chastity in a bride was considered to be of trivial importance—or even a disadvantage. A few respondents even jotted notes in the margin of the questionnaire, indicating that, for them, chastity would be a *disadvantage*.

In an alternative analysis of Buss's (1989) findings, Wallen (1989) attempted to determine which was most important, culture or gender, in shaping young people's mate preferences. He found that for some traits— such as good looks and financial prospects—gender had a great influence on preferences. For other traits, such as chastity, ambition, and preferred age, culture mattered most. (In those instances, gender accounted for only 5–16% of the variance, whereas geographic origin accounted for 38–59% of the variance.) Wallen concluded that, in general, the cultural perspective may well be more powerful than evolutionary heritage in shaping young people's preferences in mates. There is considerable evidence that culture is, in fact, a powerful determinant of young people's attitudes toward premarital sex, chastity, and thus (and most importantly for our purposes) casual sex.

Desire and Willingness to Engage in Casual Sex

Almost all men and women (78–99%), in almost all countries, consider "a faithful marriage to one partner" to be the ideal arrangement (Stone, Goetz, & Shackelford, 2005). Nonetheless, there appear to be marked gender differences in the desire for recreational sex prior to marriage. Men desire more sexual partners, pursue casual sex with multiple partners, and are more willing to accept sexual "come-ons" from strangers, acquaintances, and friends than are women (Clark & Hatfield, 1989; Fischtein, Herold, & Desmaris, 2007; Petersen & Hyde, 2010). Surprisingly, many young people do not worry about the possibility of acquiring STIs and AIDs. One of our students observed:

> I do not think my generation even worries about getting AIDs. That is the last thing young people think about before they have sex with someone. Since so many girls use birth control now, people are not so worried about hooking up because they know their birth control will stop pregnancy. If someone gets an STI, they are shocked. They can't imagine who gave it to them.

Schmitt and his colleagues (2003) provide cross-cultural evidence for gender differences in the desire for multiple partners. In a survey of 16,288 people from 52 nations, men expressed a greater desire for a variety of sexual partners than did women. Other studies have shown that American and Australian men yearn for sex with a far greater number of partners (in both the near future and over a lifetime) than do women. This is true whether the sexual encounter seems risky or safe (i.e., when one is drunk, taking drugs, dating strangers, or in dangerous settings (Clark & Hatfield, 2003; Fenigstein & Preston, 2007; Surbey & Conohan, 2000 [Australia]).

Mathes, King, Miller, and Reed (2002) interviewed men in their teens, 20s, and 30s who were students at Western Illinois University. As men matured, their desire for casual sex and sexual variety decreased; women's desire for casual sex remained relatively constant over the years. Why this decrease happens has not been fully explored.

How Prevalent Is Casual Sex?

Historians argue that in the West (and to some extent throughout the world), there have been momentous changes in young people's willingness and opportunity to engage in sexual liaisons. As Beth Bailey (1988), in *From Front Porch to Back Seat* observes, until the early 20th century, in small-town America, courting couples were usually confined to front parlors and front porches, where family members (and neighbors) could keep an eagle eye on their shenanigans. In 1908, the invention of the Model T gave young people increased freedom to experiment with sex away from prying eyes (Bailey, 1988; Collins, 2009). For the first time, couples could evade chaperones and find privacy in the back seat of a "flivver." Dating became the dominant script. A suitor was expected to invite a woman out to dinner and a movie. He brought her flowers and paid the bills.

At first there might be kissing, then petting. Couples might have sex, but they were supposed to "save themselves for marriage." In the late 1960s and early 1970s, the sexual revolution revved up, fueled in part by the ready accessibility of birth control pills (such as Enovid), which were virtually 100% effective. These allowed young men and women to participate in romantic encounters and casual sex without worrying about pregnancy. True, in the 1980s, with the advent of STIs and AIDs, the dangers of casual sex increased yet again. But that may have been just a bump in the road. New medical advances may well reduce those impediments to recreational sex as well. We would expect a continuing, upward trajectory for such trysts. Today, throwaway sexual activities appear to be gaining a considerable degree of cultural acceptance, if not universal approbation.

The Rise of Recreational Sex

Today, among college students, casual sex appears to be surprisingly common. In a recent paper, Garcia and Reiber (2008) observed that "'Hooking up' has become a normative sexual experience on American college campuses today" (p. 193) (see also Jonason et al., 2010). Confirmation of this assertion is described in a study by England, Shafer, and Fogarty (2008). (Just what this term means, as we observed, is still a bit vague—some people mean kissing, others oral sex, others intercourse.)

In nationally representative samples, 70–85% of sexually experienced American adolescents, ages 12–21, reported engaging in intercourse with a casual sex partner during the previous year (Grello, Welsh, Harper, & Dickson, 2003). More than three-quarters of American college students have experienced at least one hookup (but typically more) with partners they did not consider to be romantic partners (Aubrey & Smith, 2013). Similar results were secured by England et al. (2008), Lambert, Kahn, and Apple (2003), and Paul and Hayes (2002). Most often, such casual liaisons are with friends or ex-boyfriends or ex-girlfriends, and less frequently with strangers (Manning, Giordano, & Longmore, 2006). In non-college samples, the percentage of young Americans experimenting with casual sex may be even higher (Lyons, Manning, Giordano, & Longmore, 2013). As such, it could be that young people aren't hooking up more, just using the label to identify their relationships. In fact, as previously mentioned, contemporary American college students have more negative attitudes toward casual sex than they did in 1990 (Pryor et al., 2007).

In the West, both men and women, regardless of race and age, report high (and equal) rates of engaging in sex for fun (Herold & Mewhinney, 1993 [Canada]; Lyons, 2009 [United States]). As with many other sexual behaviors—masturbation, attitudes toward casual sex, age at first sexual encounter, number of sexual partners, and the like—gender differences in participating in casual sex seem to be steadily decreasing (Oliver & Hyde, 1993; Petersen & Hyde, 2010).

In a random sample of 2,997 Norwegian adolescents ages 17–19 years, Traeen and Levin (1992) asked respondents, "Have you ever had sexual intercourse with a person you met *for the first time* the same night as the intercourse took place?" About one-third of them said "Yes."

Gender Differences in Participation in Casual Sex

It is unclear to what extent men and women differ in their actual willingness to experiment with casual sex. However, it is one of the most replicated findings in social psychology that men are more likely than women to indicate a *desire* for short-term mating, that is, casual sex (Hyde, 2005). Teri Conley (2011) recently proposed that mitigating factors such as unfamiliarity and negative perception of the proposer of casual sex may also influence the likelihood of casual sex acceptance. Conley found that women displayed a willingness to engage in casual sex equal to that of men if the target individual was perceived to be both safe and sexually skilled. In other words, women may not think highly of men who randomly propose casual sex, and other factors such as familiarity and likelihood of sexual pleasure may be more significant. It will be important to examine differences in men's and women's participation in casual sex in context with their different experiences regarding social expectations of behavior, perceived threat from potential partners, and gendered reproductive realities.

Evolutionary Perspectives on Casual Sex

Since Darwin's (1859/1988) classic *The Origins of Species,* anthropologists have been interested in how men and women go about selecting sexual partners and mates. Many evolutionary psychologists point out that one trait that has stood *Homo sapiens* in good stead is their ability to adapt. Humankind can survive (and prosper) in a wide range of climates (from the Arctic to sub-Saharan Africa), physical settings (from seashore, to forest, to desert), and social structures (polygamous, monogamous, and polyandrous; democratic, authoritarian, capitalist, and communist). No surprise for Darwinians, then, is the fact that in Homo *sapiens* societies, as well as in primate groups, there exists an impressive variety of sexual behavior. Men and women appear to respond more to cultural and social conditions than to genetic imperatives (Hrdy, 1997).

On the other hand, currently, most prominent evolutionary theorists are interested in gender differences that are "bred in the bone." In a pioneering book, Symons (1979), for example, argued that men and women are programmed to desire very different things in a mate or sexual partner. His argument proceeds as follows:

> According to evolutionary biology, an animal's "fitness" is a measure of the extent to which it succeeds in passing on its genes to the next generation. (p. 6)

It is to the evolutionary advantage of humans, regardless of gender, to produce as many progeny as possible. But men and women differ in one critical respect—how much they are required to invest to ensure the survival of their offspring. Men need to invest a trivial amount of time and energy in any one child. A single man can conceivably father an almost unlimited number of children. In recent times, Abdul Aziz married more than 300 wives in order to ensure the loyalty of the desert tribes. His sons now rule Saudi Arabia. One Saudi ruler claims to have more than 5,000 children (Sasson, 1992).

Women, by contrast, must invest a great deal of time and effort in their offspring if they are to survive. In tribal societies, most women are lucky to produce even five surviving children (Hrdy, 1981). Howell (1979) followed the reproductive careers of 166 Kung women over 11 years. She reported that the maximum number of births for any woman was five; the minimum, zero. Women must usually sacrifice a year or two in nursing, protecting, and teaching children to survive on their own. And Symons (1979) observed:

> The enormous sex differences in minimum parental investment and in reproductive opportunities and constraints explain why *Homo sapiens,* a species with only moderate sex differences in structure, exhibits profound sex differences in psyche. (p. 27)

In an important paper, Buss and Schmitt (1993) proposed a "sexual strategies theory" of human mating. They argued that men and women are programmed to desire different traits and to employ very different strategies in short-term relationships (such as one-night stands) than those used in long-term (marital) relationships. Following is a brief recap of what their theory has to say about gender and casual sex.

In short-term relationships, *men* should tend to be interested in "playing the field," or engaging in as much casual sex with as many fertile partners as possible. In casual encounters, it is to men's advantage to be sensitive to clues to women's reproductive fitness. They should be "turned on" by women who are easily available and "turned off" by women who are sexually inexperienced, conservative, or prudish or who possess a low sex drive. They should care a great deal about good looks, youth, and health. They should be eager to have numerous, fleeting sexual encounters. In the absence of an ideal sexual partner, men should be willing to engage in casual sex with almost anyone, under almost any circumstances. They should try to avoid commitment or investing too much in any one relationship.

Women in short-term relationships should employ one of two adaptive strategies. Some may focus on what's in it for them in the short run. They may attempt to maximize their outcomes by demanding a high price for their sexual favors.

Buss (1994/2003) observes:

> In many traditional societies, such as the Mehinaku of Amazonia and the natives of the Trobriand Islands, men bring food or jewelry, such as tobacco, betel nuts, turtle shell rings, or armlets, to their mistresses. Women deny sex if the gifts stop flowing. A girl might say, "You have no payment to give me—I refuse." (p. 86)

Casual encounters can also be entered into with a vision for the future. Women may participate in casual sex in the hopes of attracting an appealing mate for the long term. Even in a one-night stand, they might search for professional men with ambition, status, good earning capacity, and a strong career orientation; men who are kind and considerate, understanding, honest, dependable, easy-going and adaptable; men who like children. These qualifications for casual sex would indicate potential hope for a more long-term relationship. One of our students observed:

> My friends will have casual sex with someone and the next thing you know they have a crush on that person. So many of my friends go into these casual relationships and end up going crazy over the fact that they did not get a "boyfriend" out of it. They think they are a "thing" when in reality they are just meeting up for sex. After a period of time, they say they need to DTR (Define the Relationship) and they are disappointed. A huge topic in my

generation is the "fuck boy." Many of my friends talk about these boys and it is very negative. It is like the female "hoe." These fuck boys act super nice and super charming. They even act as if they like the girl. And they play these girls until they get sex. But they are actually doing this to many girls. So they are "fuck boys." Boys just looking to fuck and do not care about that girl in any way. Many of my friends get into these casual se relationships and then get broken hearted when it ends.

Evolutionary theorists have assembled considerable evidence in support of the contention that, in general, American men possess more positive attitudes toward casual sex, think about casual sex far more often than women do, possess a stronger desire for sexual intercourse with a variety of partners in a variety of settings than do women, are more reluctant to forgo sex, tend to initiate sex (and rarely refuse sexual offers), and are willing to sacrifice more for sex (see Buss, 1994/2003; Jonason, Li, & Cason, 2009; Schmitt et al., 2003, for a review of this research).

We shouldn't exaggerate these gender differences, however. Petersen and Hyde (2010) conducted a meta-analysis of research into gender differences in sexuality, conducted from 1993 to 2007. They analyzed the impact of gender on 30 sexual attitudes and sexual behaviors for men and women from 87 countries, from six continents. Consistent with evolutionary psychology, they found that men did indeed report more permissive attitudes toward casual sex and slightly more sexual experience than those of women. However, they also found that (1) in nations and ethnic groups with greater gender equality, people display smaller gender differences in attitudes and behaviors than do people from more traditional nations and ethnic groups; (2) over time, many traditional gender differences seem to be disappearing; and (3) *in all nations, those gender differences in sexual attitudes and behaviors that did still exist are surprisingly small.* Gender differences in attitudes toward impromptu sex may not be all that fixed and unwavering. In one study, for example, Garcia and Reiber (2008) found that on the State University of New York (SUNY) campus in Binghamton, 64% of men and women reported having engaged in a hookup; the authors found no gender differences.

Many researchers *do* find significant gender differences in the prevalence of casual sex, however. American men often claim significantly more casual sexual partners than do women (Buss, 1988; Grello, Welsh, & Harper, 2006; Hill, 2002). When asked, "Have you ever deliberately had sex without emotional involvement?" 73% of American college men, but only 27% of

American college women, acknowledged that they had (Townsend, Kline, & Wasserman, 1995). Similar differences have been found in Hong Kong (Abdullah, Fielding, Hedley, & Luk, 2002).

Although at first glance this gender difference seems peculiar—it does, after all, "take two to tango"—scholars have proposed several reasons for this apparent anomaly. Men may define a given encounter as casual, while women may assume it is a loving interaction or that it may lead to one. Grello and her colleagues (2006) found that when students were asked about their most recent casual sexual encounter, 18% of University of Tennessee women assumed it was a prelude to romance, while only 3% of men shared this assumption. Over 50% of men and women, however, admitted that their most recent chance encounter was "a one-time thing."

There are other reasons for the anomaly of gender difference in prevalence of casual sex. Men are known to exaggerate the number of their conquests, while women minimize their numbers (Alexander & Fisher, 2003). Women may rewrite history—forgetting sexual escapades or rejection. In addition, men's throwaway encounters may be with prostitutes or women who do not appear in college samples (Baumeister et al., 2001). Whatever the reason, this gender difference appears to be a consistent one. In their meta-analysis of men and women in 87 countries, Petersen and Hyde (2010) found a "medium strength" gender effect for casual sex, which they defined as "incidence or frequency of engaging in sexual behavior with a stranger or a casual acquaintance" (p. 25).

Interestingly, in the United States the difference between genders tends to decrease dramatically as people age. Many begin to date again and get more serious in their relationships. There are probably several reasons for this. First, a very popular time to hook up is when people are in college. In earlier chapters, we talked about the markedly skewed sex ratios in college—on average, there are only 40 men to 60 women in higher education today. This makes college a man's paradise. In the 1930s, Willard Waller (1937) observed that love relationships are governed by the "principle of least interest": The person with the least interest in maintaining the relationship holds all the power. When men are scarce they call the shots, and while many women may yearn for more committed dating-type relationships, men can insist on sex on demand. Second, for women the biological clock is ticking; men can afford to wait until their mid- or late 30s to marry and start a family. So young women may be desperate to hook up with men who seem to offer some semblance of commitment and the chance for motherhood.

One fact of interest: Perhaps due to media hype, students greatly overestimate the comfort of their peers with hookups, and how often they engage in impromptu sex. They think of themselves as fairly restrained, their peers as wildly experimental. This misperception, of course, may have a strong effect on the social pressure they feel to participate in casual sex (Barriger & Vélez-Blasini, 2013).

When men and women leave college, these factors are no longer so important. Many begin dating again. In a way, it is a return to the 1950s, when men asked women out, paid for the date, and waited for an appropriate time for sex. The comedian Aziz Ansari (2015), in a discussion of "the paradox of choice," provides a personal example. If you are in a big city, he observes, you are flooded with options. At first, you are living in a fantasy world. Why choose? If there are an unlimited number of women out there, it stands to reason that Miss Perfect is just around the corner. But as the hangovers, the disappointments of one-night-stands, and your stash of stories about the worst pickup you've ever had begin to pile up, the charm of unlimited options begins to fade. Been there, done that. Soon you find yourself yearning for a night at home, sitting around in your pajamas, watching TV with a sweetheart. Besides, by your 30s, all your friends are already married, with many children; who is going to hit the bars with you? So, amazingly, you start to yearn for The One.

Why Do Men and Women Engage in Casual Sex?

> I was a furnace of desire, and it was becoming impossible for me to resist the flame that was consuming me.
>
> —Casanova (1798)

Personal Reasons for Engaging in Casual Sex

What Motivates Men and Women to Engage in Casual Sexual Activities? Until recently, American sexologists have assumed that people engage in sexual relations primarily for one of the Big Three reasons: out of love, a desire for pleasure (the attainment of physical pleasure, recreational sex, and "sport fucking"), or the hope of procreation. When Hatfield and Rapson

(2006) asked students at the University of Hawaii to list the reasons they and their friends participated in one-night stands, the students cited an array of other reasons as well—among them: a desire for self-esteem, status, or spiritual transcendence, duty, conformity, kindness, conquest or power (people can, of course, also *withhold* sex in the hopes of attaining power), submission to others, vengeance (to conquer, degrade, punish), curiosity, money, to make someone jealous, to attain health and long life (yin and yang), stress reduction, to save the world, political revolt, relaxation or help in getting to sleep . . . and so on. A similar diversity of sexual motives has been proposed by Browning (2005); Browning, Hatfield, Kessler, and Levine (2000); Browning, Kessler, Hatfield, and Choo (1999); and Meston and Buss (2007).

But which of these possible reasons stand above the rest when it comes to people's motivations for engaging in a casual sexual encounter? The main reason, according to one study, is that men and women engage in one-night stands because they are pleasurable (Garcia & Reiber, 2008). The authors report that 89% of participants at SUNY Binghamton (New York) identified physical pleasure as the motivation for such activities—no surprise.

Regan and Dreyer (1999) asked American college men and women who had participated in casual sexual liaisons to write an essay about their motives for doing so. As expected, many of men's and women's reasons for such sex were similar. Both emphasized intra-individual factors (e.g., sexual desire, sexual experimentation, physical pleasure, alcohol and drug use) and factors associated with the recreational sex partner (e.g., attractiveness) as reasons for their short-term sexual encounters. A few differences appeared, however. Men were more likely to emphasize socioenvironmental reasons (e.g., increased status and popularity, conformity to peer group norms), whereas women cited interpersonal reasons for casual sex (e.g., hoping their casual fling would evolve into a serious romance). At SUNY Binghamton (New York), Garcia and Reiber (2008) found that of men and women who had hooked up, 51% had done so with the intention of initiating a traditional romantic relationship; there were no gender differences in this motive. While 37% of participants: 29% of men and 43% of women) reported a traditional romantic relationship as the *ideal* outcome of a hookup, only about 6% (4% of men and 8% of women) actually *expected* a hookup to result in a traditional romantic relationship.

Some young people seek out throwaway encounters because they are frightened of close, romantic, intimate relationships. Hatfield (1984) identified six reasons why people might fear (and thus avoid) true intimacy: fears of (1) exposure, (2) abandonment, (3) angry attacks, (4) loss of control, (5) one's own destructive impulses, and (6) losing one's individuality or being engulfed. Paul and her colleagues (2000) speculated that young people who engage in casual sex often do so out of fears of greater intimacy. Presumably, as young people gain social confidence (and overcome these fears), they might advance to more complex intimate relationships. (There is some evidence in support of that contention; see Gentzler & Kerns, 2004; Grello et al., 2006; Paul et al., 2000; see Table 5.2).

There is one last reason why people in committed relationships avoid casual sex. Once people are in a relationship, they exaggerate how good a deal they have with their current partner. A number of studies have demonstrated that once heterosexual men and women are involved in a love affair, they display relative disinterest in photos of romantic partners of the opposite sex, and systematically derogate their attractiveness (see, for example, Cole, Trope, & Balcetis, 2016). Neuroscientists are able to identify areas of the brain that play an important role in regulating the emotions that threaten the stability of romantic relationships (Meyer, Berkman, Karremans, & Lieberman, 2011).

Situational Reasons for Engaging in Casual Sex

There is no such thing as a bad idea when you are drunk.

—Colin Moore

Although it may seem obvious, several authors have documented that casual sex is likely to occur when both parties have been drinking or taking drugs (Garcia & Reiber, 2008; Grello et al., 2003, 2006; Lyons, 2009). In Regan and Dreyer's study (1999) asking American college men and women to describe their motives for engaging in casual sexual relations, both genders admitted that alcohol use had played a substantial part in their decisions. Gender makes little difference: both men and women are more likely to engage in casual sex when they've been drinking heavily (Cooper & Orcutt, 1997; Testa & Collins, 1997). Alcohol and drugs promote casual encounters in two ways: they increase the appeal of potential pick-ups as well as lowering sexual inhibitions—further strengthening the likelihood of casual sexual encounters (Conner & Flesch, 2001 [Great Britain]; Jones, Jones, Thomas, & Piper, 2003).

As we mentioned earlier, in a field experiment, Pennebaker and his colleagues (1979) asked student researchers to drop by an array of singles bars in Charlottesville, Virginia, timing their visits for early in the evening, a bit later (when things had just gotten going), and late in the evening (at closing time). Students were assigned to approach men and women sitting at the bar and ask them how attractive they judged the other patrons to be. Early in the evening (at 9:00 and 10:30 P.M.), men and women were fairly critical of the other patrons (members of the opposite sex were thought to be "fairly attractive," at best). Come midnight, men and women, realizing it was "now or never," became more charitable. As the old country and western song goes, "All the girls get prettier at closing time. They all begin to look like movie stars . . ." So said Pennebaker's study. That phenomenon is called having "beer goggles." In recent years, the phrase "2 @ 10, 10 @ 2" expresses that sentiment. Thus, it is not surprising that more casual liaisons are agreed to in bars and at fraternity "keg parties" and the like where alcohol is present, while fewer are agreed to in churches, cafés, classrooms, and libraries (Montoya, 2005).

Bogle (2008) provides this quote from Robert, a sophomore at Faith University.

> The likelihood of "hooking up" happening when you are totally sober is very unlikely, I would say. It is only when people start loosening up by drinking, I call it liquid courage. Most guys are shy about going up to pretty girls, [so that is why] I call it liquid courage. They get enough courage up to go up and talk to the girl. And if she was the same status regarding alcohol consumption, then the two people that are attracted to each other will just go ahead and [hook up]. (p. 168)

Theorists have also speculated that men and women are more likely to engage in casual sex when they are in settings where they feel anonymous or are submerged in a group (Zimbardo, 1969). In such settings, personal and social codes are temporarily suspended, social constraints are removed, inhibitions fade, and one can engage in sexual behavior with impunity. Indeed, people are most likely to "blow off steam" at such events as carnival week in Brazil, Mardi Gras in New Orleans, spring break in Florida, a summer vacation at a seaside resort, at professional conferences, or at athletic events far away from home (Herold, Corbesi, & Collins, 1994 [Canada]; Huber & Herold [Canada], 2006; Sönmez et al., 2006).

Students are especially likely to engage in sex with strangers when they are on holiday—spring break, schoolies (in Australia), traveling to foreign countries and the like (Maticka-Tyndale, Herold, & Oppermann, 2003). On holidays, there is a sense of freedom from at-home restrictions, a relaxation of inhibitions, a focus on having a good time, and high alcohol consumption. All of these factors are conducive to heightened sensitivity to sexual arousal and increased sexual activities (Herold & Van Kerkwijk, 1992). For a summary of the wide variety of reasons people report for engaging in casual sex, see Table 7.2.

Personal Reasons for Avoiding Casual Sex

All sexual affairs involve risks, ranging from concrete risks such as acquiring STIs or an unwanted pregnancy to less tangible risks concerned with social and religious mores. Most religions consider sex outside of marriage to be immoral (Cubbins & Tanfer, 2000). There is considerable evidence that the more deeply religious people are, the more they disapprove of casual sex and the less likely they are to engage in it. In a national survey of Canadian adults, Fischstein, Herold, and Desmarais (2007) found that the more deeply religious Canadians were, the less likely they were to consider engaging in casual sex. Similar results were found in a U.S. national survey of men and women, conducted by Cubbins and Tanfer, (2000), and in studies by Kontula (Finland; 1999) and by De Visser, Smith, Richters, and Rissel (Australia; 2007).

Men and women may worry that if they flout community prohibitions they may acquire a poor reputation and risk community and family reprisals (say, from family members intent on protecting the family honor or from jealous dates and mates). These concerns are generally greater for women than for men. Today, a slang expression, "the walk of shame," describes the humiliation that women feel, who must walk back to their dorms, the morning after, with looks ravaged from a night of casual sexual activity. Interestingly, the parallel expression for men is "the stride of pride." Women, of course, may also fear the possibility of unwanted pregnancy.

Both men and women may fear STIs if they engage in high-risk behavior—and these concerns are not baseless. Casual sex with multiple partners, whether heterosexual or homosexual, without adequate protection, is associated with an increased risk of STIs (Christianson, Johansson, Emmelin, & Westman, 2003 [Sweden]; Paul et al., 2000). Many women fear rape, physical

Table 7.2 Reasons for Engaging in Casual Sex

Personal Reasons for Engaging in Casual Sex
Partner is attractive
Conformity to peer group norms
Gain social confidence and acceptance, status, and popularity
Want to be loved
Sexual desire, physical pleasure, curiosity
Overcoming loneliness
Kindness
Seeking adventure
Hoping a casual fling will evolve into a serious romance
Desire for conquest

Situational Reasons for Engaging in Casual Sex
Alcohol and drug use
Shortage of desirable men/women
On a holiday, spring break, and the like
Being in a place where no one knows you
Rape

Personal Reasons for Avoiding Casual Sex
It's immoral
I'm in a committed relationship
Partner won't be a good lover

Situational Reasons for Avoiding Casual Sex
Protect my reputation; a double standard still exists
Might get STIs or AIDS
Pregnancy
Physical danger: robbery, mugging, or sexual assault
My family would object

attacks, and harm (Baranowski & Hecht, 2015). There are hundreds of *Law and Order* episodes that illustrate the physical dangers that women face in singles bars. Scholars find that all of these concerns can prevent men and women from engaging in casual sex (Bogle, 2008; Fenigstein & Preston, 2007; Herold & Mewhinney, 1993).

Situational Reasons for Avoiding Casual Sex

In a series of replications of the Clark and Hatfield (1989) study with which we began this chapter, Tappé, Bensman, Hayashi, and Hatfield (2013) found that men, and especially women, avoided casual sex when they were in a committed relationship, when they were worried about the immorality of such activities, when the other was unattractive or not their type, when they found the person to be too forward, creepy, or stalkerish, and when they worried that the person had an STI or AIDS or might be dangerous (see Table 7.2).

How Do Casual Sexual Encounters Work Out?

Theorists have markedly different views as to how dallying with casual sex works out. Many speculate that men and women may have quite different reactions to a casual sexual encounter. Although the majority of adults agree that premarital sex is acceptable within a romantic context (Regan, 2003), a double standard still exists (Conley, Ziegler, & Moors, 2013): A man sleeps with a lot of girls and he's a stud; a woman does the same thing and she's a slut.

In a study of 832 college students, 26% of women and 50% of men reported feeling positive after a hookup, and 49% of women and 26% of men reported it had been a negative experience (the remainder of students had a mixed reaction; Owen et al., 2010). Not surprisingly, then, men have been found to experience more pleasure and less guilt and fear of stigma than do women after a casual sexual encounter (Bogle, 2008; Conley et al., 2013). Fielder, Walsh, Carey, and Carey (2014) found that first-year college women who hook up are more depressed, more prone to STIs, and more at risk for sexual violence than their peers. They also display higher rates of suicidal ideation. Similar results were secured by Sandberg-Thoma and Dush (2013).

Other researchers have reported that after a hookup, young people, male and female, experience a kaleidoscope of emotions. Paul and Hayes (2002) found that during a typical hookup, 65% of participants reported feeling good, aroused, or excited; 17%, desirable or wanted; 17%, nothing in particular or not focused on the hookup; 8%, embarrassed or regretful; 7%, nervous or scared; 6%, confused; and 5%, proud. Some find that men and women with a history of casual sex may possess lower self-esteem, feel more guilt, have less of a sense of well-being, and experience more psychological distress and depression than do their peers. They also risk more violent victimization and participate in more delinquent behaviors than do their peers (Bersamin et al., 2014; Fiedler et al., 2014).

Most students, however, seem to enjoy their experiences—short-lived or not. In one study, later than Regan's (2003), among participants who were asked to characterize the morning after a hookup, 82% of men and 57% of women were generally glad they had done it (Garcia & Reiber, 2008). Using qualitative and quantitative data from the longitudinal Toledo Adolescent Relationship Study, which interviewed young people of various ages (15–21 years), races and ethnicities, and educational backgrounds, Lyons (2009) found that most men and women did *not* regret their casual sexual experiences.

Best and Worst Experiences

Paul and Hayes (2002) asked college students to describe their best and worst hookup experiences. Men and women agreed that hookups were best when there was interest and attraction, when the partner was good-looking, when sexual behavior was enjoyable, and when they felt wanted and cared about. Some women (27%) and men (16%) thought the hookup was best if a relationship evolved afterward. However, 10% of both men and women judged it "the best" because there was no emotional involvement or attachment (Bisson & Levine, 2009; Paul & Hayes, 2002). In truth, people who hope that the hookup will go somewhere are likely to be disappointed. A full 50% of hookups end up as one-time-only affairs (Paul, McManus, & Hayes, 2000).

And the worst hookups? Alcohol played a large role in the worst hookups, which often involved "quickies" in a car, club, or bar (Paul & Hayes, 2002). Both genders reported feeling a combination of good, aroused, excited, confused, unsure, regretful, embarrassed, nervous, and scared; women more than men felt uncomfortable and anxious for the end of the hookup. After their worse hookups, youth felt confused, unsure, used, anxious to leave, and glad it was over. Men, for example, felt disappointed—realizing that their partners were insufficiently attractive and/or too promiscuous for them. Women felt regretful—reporting shame, regret, self-blame, and pressured to avoid unwanted sex acts (Paul & Hayes, 2002).

A full 46.6% of couples who had engaged in oral sex, anal sex, or vaginal intercourse in their most recent hookups did not use condoms! People may suffer emotionally and physically from STIs, AIDS, or pregnancy (Lewis, Atkins, Blayney, Dent, & Kaysen, 2012).

The most terrible outcome is when not all encounters are wanted or consensual—some involve rape. In a sample of 178 college students, participants noted that most of their unwanted sex, including vaginal, anal, and oral incidents (i.e., sexual assault and rape) (77.8%), occurred during a hookup (Flack et al., 2007). Twenty-three percent of women and 7% of men surveyed reported one or more experiences of unwanted sexual intercourse. The most frequently endorsed reason for unwanted intercourse was impaired judgment due to alcohol (Flack et al., 2007).

Paradoxically, many college students say that they would be more sexual with someone they didn't really like or with whom they did not think there was a chance for a relationship. On the face of it, this seems illogical. But students indicated that one should take it slow with someone one really liked and get to know each other. When you think about it, this does make some sense. Bogle (2008) recounts this interview with Max, a sophomore:

Max: If I see a girl and I think we're just going to hook up, then it's probably like *we can do whatever* [sexually] and it's not a big deal and. . . . I won't see her as dirty, but if it's a girl that I potentially want to have a relationship with and she does do all of that in the beginning, then I would kind of perceive her as dirty.
KB: If "she does do all of that," [meaning] sex, or even less than that?
Max: Well, even less than that. (p. 37)

Rarely mentioned, but true, is the fact that men and women's impromptu sexual encounters may, if discovered, take a toll on dates and mates. Most college students' romantic relationships are characterized by expectations of emotional and sexual fidelity. The discovery that one's dating partner has engaged in casual sex with another can be devastating; it may make one feel betrayed (Welsh, Grello, & Harper, 2003).

Cultural Perspectives on Casual Sex

Historically, cultures have differed markedly in how common it was for young men and women to engage in premarital or casual sexual activity. Among the Silwa, in Aswan, Egypt, for example (like people in much of the

Muslim world), there was strong disapproval of young men and women even talking about sex before marriage, much less engaging in it. Young men and women apparently found the idea of premarital sexual experimentation or casual sex so shameful and terrifying that no one was known to have ever violated the taboo (Ammar, 1954).

In a few Polynesian societies, things were very different. Marshall (1971) conducted field research in Mangaia, in the Cook Islands. He argued that in Mangaia, although romantic love was rare, young people frequently engaged in casual sexual encounters. He observed: "Copulation is a principal concern of the Mangaian of either sex" (p. 123).

Culture, then, has been found to have a profound impact on whether young men and women find it socially acceptable to engage in casual sex. In some cultures, recreational sex is the norm; in others, such encounters are a serious offense, punishable by death (see Francoeur, 2000; Hatfield & Rapson, 1996/2005; Jankowiak, 1995, for a summary of this research).

For a sampling of modern-day survey reports indicating the different rates of casual sex worldwide, see Table 7.3.

Since these studies were conducted by different researchers, at different times, using wildly different sampling procedures, their statistics can only be suggestive. The references, however, do provide a compendium of the available research. Most of this research was conducted by scholars concerned about the spread of STIs and AIDS. For instance, in Zambia, the rates of HIV are extremely high; 20% of men and women between the ages of 15 and 49 are infected with HIV (Agha, 2002).

Cultural and Biosocial Perspectives on Casual Sex

Currently, the once passionate arguments over whether perspectives on casual sex are due to culture or to evolutionary and biological imperatives seem to be moderating. Today, many scholars would argue that it is both. Generally, they attempt to integrate the influences of culture, societal pressures, and personal experiences with those of biology in shaping sexual attitudes and behavior (Finkel, Eastwick, & Matthews, 2007; Petersen & Hyde, 2010; Wood & Eagly, 2002).

Wood and Eagly (2002), for example, point out that if scholars are to understand people's attitudes and behaviors, they must consider both the immediate, proximal causes (such as a culture's gender roles and people's social

Table 7.3 Rates of Casual Sex Worldwide

Country	Age of Sample	Percent of People Engaging in Casual Sex
Among Tourists in Other Countries		
Australia[1]	Age 18+	25% of men, 11% of women; 61% of those who had any sex at all on spring break
Canada[2]	21–23	50%+ of those having any sex at all on spring break
Japanese[3]	Unknown	8% of women at a resort in Thailand
United States[3]	Unknown	16% of women at a resort in Thailand
United States[4]	19–21	Over 50% of those who had any sex at all on spring break
In Own Country		
Hong Kong, China[5]	18–65	63% of those attending an STI clinic
Inis Beag[6]	Entire population	None
Mangaia, Cook Islands[7]	Unknown	Unrestricted
Silwa, Aswan, Egypt[8]	Unknown	Forbidden
Addis Ababa, Ethiopia[9]	15–19	71% of women who had ever had casual sex
Norway[10]	17–19	45% of boys and 25% of girls who had had ever had intercourse
United States[11]	12–21	70% of teens stated they had casual sex at some time
United States[11]	18–23	60–80% of men and women
United States [12]	Unknown	Common
Lusaka, Zambia[13]	Unknown	19% of men, 3% of women stated they had had casual sex at some time

1. Maticka-Tyndale, Herold, & Oppermann (2003).

2. Maticka-Tyndale, Herold, & Mewhinney (1998).

3. Vorakitphokatorn, Pulerwitz, & Cash (1998).

4. Apostolopoulos, Sonmez, Sasidharan, & Jovicich (1999).

5. Abdullah, Fielding, Hedley, & Luk (2002).

6. Messenger (1971).

7. Marshall (1971).

8. Ammar (1954).

9. Fekadu (2001).

10. Traeen & Lewin (1992).

11. Garcia, Reiber, Massey, & Merriwether (2013).

12. Jonason, Li, & Richardson (2010).

13. Agha (2002).

experiences) and the ultimate distal causes (such as genetic factors, biological processes, and features of social structures, such as local ecologies) of sexual attitudes and behavior. There is considerable evidence in support of Wood and Eagley's biosocial model. An example: In patriarchal societies, men generally possess all the power, status, and control of resources. In such societies, powerful men tend to craft social norms that cater to their own sexual needs and desires (for example, to ensure the paternity of their offspring) while sacrificing those of women. Men are allowed to be sexual beings whereas women's sexual lives are fairly restricted. In contrast, in more egalitarian societies, men and women are likely to be more similar (than different) in their sexual attitudes, feelings, and behaviors. In the pages that follow, we will adopt this perspective in our attempt to understand the nature of young people's attitudes toward offhand sexual activities and their sexual behavior.

Consent

Sexuality is a murky area. People's desires are often mixed. Generally, Yes means Yes and No means No. But sometimes, Yes and No mean I don't know, or maybe, or not now but later. Attitudes toward sex are in constant flux. In the 1980s, in films, when the leading man was handsome and virile, No was often taken to mean Yes. In two Academy Award films, *Gone with the Wind* and *On the Waterfront*, the hero carries the woman off in an excess of passion. The next morning she appears tousled and secretly elated. In the recent theatrical film *Nightcrawler*, Jake Gyllenhaal pressures a journalist played by Renee Russo to sleep with him or he will stop providing footage valuable for her career. Was it a transaction, or sexual assault?

In the early 1980s, while conducting research with Ed Donnerstein on the impact of porn on people's aggressive behavior, we searched for two types of stimuli within existing adult films: one scene in which a rape occurred and the actress pretended to enjoy it, and a similar scene in which, after the rape, she was unhappy and miserable. We visited every porn shop in Madison, Wisconsin, and found *not one film* where rape didn't lead to burbles of delight on the part of the woman. Had we more money, of course, we would have filmed our own, but we were young and poor academics.

In Ogas and Gaddam's 2011 book, *A Billion Wicked Thoughts*, in which they review over 400 million porn searches, they found that this trend of male dominance was absolutely continuing into present-day porn production.

While most porn does not depict rape in its most straightforward sense (although, to be clear, that pornography is abundantly available), Ogas and Gaddam found male-dominated porn to be incredibly common. This porn typically featured women of lesser positions of power being coerced, bribed, or threatened into having sexual intercourse—often with men who were much older or unattractive—which often increased the notion of coercion. In addition, the women were usually depicted as enjoying the encounter. These themes lay the groundwork for reinforcing asymmetrical gender roles in sex and in the pursuit and experience of pleasure within consensual terms. Opposite our predictions, Klaassen and Peter (2015) compared pornography produced by professionals with homemade pornography. They found amateur pornography displayed more (not less) gender inequality at the expense of women (disparities in power, violence, and objectification) than did professionally crafted pornography!

As education improves and gender equity makes daily strides, it's not surprising that the idea of "consent" has expanded over the years. For example, at a conference we attended recently for the Society for the Scientific Study of Sexuality, in Phoenix, Arizona, during one presentation the speaker asked the crowd, "If a woman and a man are on a date, and the man says, 'Would you like to go to my place and have sex,' and the woman replies, 'Yes,' what has she just consented to?" An older gentleman at the front of the room quickly raised his hand and replied, "The whole enchilada!" While this caused a knee-jerk reaction of a few giggles, this man was very quickly the target of about 60 anxious academics who flung their arms up with vigor, eager to present other dimensions to the idea of consent. "What if she changes her mind?" "What if she wants oral sex and not penetrative sex?" "What if she is drunk?" "What if *they both* are drunk?" "What if he is her boss?" By the end of the Q&A, the first man who had replied sat silently in the front row, shrugging his shoulders at each question, face red.

But the questions posed were absolutely valid questions, and they demonstrate the importance of incorporating aspects of power differentiation, substance use, and the ability to retract or change consent into the conversation of truly consensual sex. While *sexual assault* is defined as nonconsensual sexual activity obtained through force or threats, verbal coercion, or intoxication (Jozkowski & Peterson, 2013), those variables each exist on a unique spectrum and can have completely different meanings in various contexts. For example, is sex between two drunk people always sexual assault? One of our informants said, "I had friends in the military who got in trouble for this after one of them woke up the next morning and regretted what had happened the night before. The Brass wrote up both of them." Can a person with power ever have sex consensually with their subordinate? These are not always the easiest questions to answer—especially since there may be gender differences in determining consent.

According to Jozkowski (2011), men are more likely to report using non-verbal cues to indicate sexual consent while women are more likely to use verbal cues to indicate sexual consent. This may result in miscommunication or understanding regarding whether two heterosexual individuals want to have sex, and if so, what kinds of sexual acts they wish to engage in. In addition, in another study, when men and women were given fictitious scenarios in which consent was presented in an ambiguous way, men were more likely than women to rate the scenario as consensual (Humphreys, 2007). Lastly, in a qualitative survey conducted by Jozkowski and Peterson (2013) that explored college students' interpretations of consent, researchers found that students largely held to traditional gender roles in perceiving men as initiators and women as passive recipients of sex. Themes of deception, aggression, and force were frequent in many of the men's responses about how they initiate sex: "I would tell her—let's have sex! Before she could say anything, I would just rip off her pants" (p. 520). And if the woman would object, they would pretend they inserted their penis by mistake: "Just stick it in and if she objects, pretend like I had done it by mistake" (p. 520).

However, most men did not indicate that they would engage in these kinds of coercion or deceit in order to instigate sex. But as the movies and pornography may reinforce, certain individuals may believe that women are somehow "playing coy" and secretly want or desire to be seduced. In the popular 2013 song "Blurred Lines," Robin Thicke sings, "I hate these blurred lines / I know you want it. . . / But you're a good girl." Again, the notion here is that "good girls" are in fact "blurring lines" between refusing and accepting sex, which is causing a delay of gratification for the male. This may lead to males feeling they are supposed to aggressively pursue sex with the female, believing her desire for sex is obscured by her desire to appear as a "good girl." In 2015, after a controversy as to the nature of consent, Yale fraternity men carried signs saying, "No means Yes, Yes means Anal." Not surprisingly, that increased the furor.

Consent, however, is an ongoing process that has to be evaluated in context between the individuals involved. As traditional gender roles are replaced with more egalitarian ones, the false narrative of the aggressive male pursuing the passive female to convince her to have sex with him will hopefully become obsolete. For example, the song "Blurred Lines" received a huge amount of backlash against its coercive messages, from journalists, feminists, and regular people alike. Clearly, the conversation moving forward is to establish the parameters of consent, and to respect those parameters. Currently there are numerous resources to help individuals understand and establish consent. For example, the sexual education website Scarleteen offers a worksheet for partners to complete in order to establish what kind of sexual behaviors each person is open to, personal preferences regarding contraception, and even terminology and phrases that are off limits (Corinna & Turett, 2016). If you type in "Consent" into YouTube, dozens of videos explaining and discussing sexual consent will appear, many with several million views. There's even a new campaign called "Consent is Sexy" that can be purchased and brought onto college campuses as a comprehensive learning and resource program.

While consent may seem ambiguous, given the many variables that may exist to obscure it, individuals will feel more confident knowing they have given or received consent after they have learned about its many different dimensions and contexts. The more we continue to talk about it, the better.

Conclusion

Many theorists argue that knowledge of the dynamics of casual relationships is crucially important in gaining an understanding of the architecture of the human mind. Are young people's thoughts, feelings, and behaviors primarily shaped by sociocultural or evolutionary imperatives? What is the interplay between the two? It is in casual mating situations, many theorists argue, that scholars will find the answers (Buss & Schmitt, 1993; Gangestad & Simpson, 2000; Kenrick, Groth, Trost, & Sadalla, 1993; Li & Kenrick, 2006). In fact, studies of casual sexual relationships have demonstrated some of the largest empirical differences between men and women (Oliver & Hyde, 1993).

The elephant in the room, at this moment unseen and unknown, is the matter of change. Most studies are snapshots; what we need are movies. Are gender differences in attitudes and behaviors regarding casual sex diminishing, growing, or remaining constant? With advances in contraceptive and abortion technologies on the near horizon, will the frequency of sexual relationships without traditional labels continue to grow? Some may argue, of course, that people aren't necessarily having more sex. They are simply having the same amount of sex but labeling it differently. In fact, a recent study found millennials have less sex than previous generations (Vivinetto, 2016). Will monogamy be as important (as it seems today) if the threat of infection from sexual activities is reduced?

If in the wake of globalization, cultures alter significantly, gender differences remain constant, and the frequency of hookups stabilizes, evolutionary theory will gain credibility. But if the opposite is true—if cultural and social transformations produce marked movements in urbanization, affluence, technology, and a new tolerance for gender and sexual variation—then we shall need to take that new data fully into account. If gender differences diminish and the popularity of casual sex increases, these developments may strengthen the cultural argument (see Petersen & Hyde, 2010, for data relevant to this observation).

It's time to bring *time* into the debate, to encourage more longitudinal work. It is time to focus not only on the purported negative consequences of causal sexual encounters but also on the benefits. It is time to see what we can learn about ourselves and each other through the lens of recreational sex. It is also time to examine more closely the insights of cultural psychology, history, social psychology, developmental psychology, comparative psychology, reproductive biology, evolutionary theory, public health, and epidemiology in attempting to account for the complex phenomenon of casual sex. We should know a lot more as we track the trajectory and frequency of casual sex in the coming years—we will know not only more about casual sex itself, but about the human activities of which it is a part.

One conclusion can be arrived at now, however. Sexual activity, especially in the developed world, has been greatly demystified. This profound transformation seems likely to continue and to spread around the world. Its consequences remain uncertain and complex, but they are likely to be consequential, as we will all see in the next chapters.

8

From Monogamy to Swingers and Polyamory

In the previous chapter we discussed a variety of alternate relationships—
one-night stands, hookups, "fuck-buddy" sex, "friends with benefits," and
the like—that young men and women might engage in on their way to a
serious, committed relationship. But for some, a serious, committed relationship is not a good fit. They might be married or desire an intimate
relationship, but they yearn for a continuation of the single life, too. In the
past, people who felt like that generally had to "cheat"—or in a more sympathetic term, "sample." But some young adults and married couples want
to incorporate such experimentation into their serious relationships—to
engage in consensual non-monogamy (CNM)—or what has been termed
an *open marriage, swinging, wife or husband swapping, wife or husband
trading, wife or husband lending,* or, more recently, *The Lifestyle* and
polyamory.

Some of the first significant prevalence estimates for CNM relationships
were reported by Blumstein and Schwartz (1983) as part of a large study on
American couples. The authors found that 28% of straight men and 25% of
straight women had an agreement that open relationships were OK, compared to 73% of gay men and 37% of lesbian women. However, only a small
fraction of couples actually acted on these agreements: 7% of straight men,
6% of straight women, and 9% of lesbian women who agreed to an open relationship actually had sex outside their relationship in the previous year. At
a notably higher rate, 61% of gay men reported having an open relationship
agreement and acting on it.

Using two separate U.S.-based quota samples of single adults in the United
States, more than one in five respondents reported engaging in CNM at some
point in their life. This proportion remained constant across age, education level, income, religion, region, political affiliation, and race, but varied
with gender and sexual orientation. Specifically, people who identified as

What's Next in Love and Sex. Elaine Hatfield, Richard L. Rapson, and Jeanette Purvis, Oxford
University Press (2020). © Oxford University Press.
DOI: 10.1093/oso/9780190647162.001.0001

gay, lesbian, or bisexual were more likely to report previous participation in CNM (Haupert, Gesselman, Moors, Fisher, & Garcia, 2017).

Infidelity

Although monogamy is a hallmark of American social norms, there is great diversity in the intimate relationships men and women engage in today. Many participate in extramarital arrangements. There are a variety of terms for extramarital sex. If you disapprove, it is cheating, infidelity, or adultery. If you are neutral or positive, it is sexual networking, sampling, or fooling around. Different countries have different words for it, too. In American slang, people may have "a bit on the side." Swedes and Russians both "sneak to the left." Israelis "eat on the side," Japanese "go off the path." The Irish "play offsides," while the English, "play away." For the Dutch, the culprit "goes strange," or "pitches the cat in the dark." The French prefer "*aller voir ailleurs*," to go see elsewhere. A philanderer in South Africa is a "running man." A Chinese man, trying to balance a wife and a mistress, is trying to "stand in two boats at the same time." In Taiwan, he might be castigated as "a big white turnip with a colorful core." If you cheat in Tel Aviv, the neighbors might shrug and observe, "A tied up mare eats, too" (Druckerman, 2007).

In a recent Gallup Poll, 88% judged extramarital sex to be morally wrong—far worse than polygamy, human cloning, or suicide (Gallup, 2016). When men and women are asked what is their ideal—a monogamous marriage or monogamy with the option of casual, extra-pair sex, both men and women overwhelmingly prefer a strictly monogamous arrangement. Yet, men and women do have affairs. Laumann, Gagnon, Michael, and Michaels (1994) and Wiederman (1997), both studies using nationally representative samples, found that approximately 20–25% of men and 10–15% of women reported engaging in extramarital sex during their marriage. Opportunity seems to be the main determinant of whether or not couples "stray." More men than women are interested in marriage plus arrangements than are women, however (Stone, Goetz, & Shackelford, 2005).

There is some cost to such activities, however. The "cheater" may pay a social penalty. Their family and friends may condemn them. Additionally, those who are unfaithful to their mates are exposed to the same types of risks as people who engage in casual sex—the risk of contracting an STI or HIV, the rage of a jealous mate, and the breakup of a marriage. Women may risk unwanted pregnancy (Greiling & Buss, 2000). Couples are optimists, in a self-deceiving way, though. Most assume (although they've generally never had a discussion about the matter) that their partners would never cheat on them. This is true even when they themselves have had such an encounter (Watkins & Boon, 2016).

Wiederman and Allgeier (1996) asked couples married less than 10 years to assess the probability that their spouses would ever engage in extramarital sex. Again, the estimates were very low, at just 7.9%; more than one third said there was no chance whatsoever that their spouses would betray them in this fashion. Most people assume that they will never divorce—although they know others do. More self-deception, we fear.

In Table 8.1, we present a list of infidelity rates around the world.

But what if your mate didn't disapprove of extramarital sex? We will now consider those marriage-plus arrangements.

Definitions

Consensually non-monogamous relationships (CNMs) are those in which all partners explicitly agree that each partner may have romantic or sexual relationships with others (Conley, Moors, Matsick, & Ziegler, 2013). *Open relationships* are those in which partners agree that they can have extradyadic sex (sexual relations outside the marriage). *Swinging relationships* are those in which couples practice extradyadic sex with another couple or many couples. *Polyamory* is the belief in, practice of, or willingness to engage in CNM, typically in loving and long-term relationships (Rubel & Bogaert, 2015).

History of Consensual Non-Monogamy: Open Marriage, Swinging, and Polyamory

It is not really possible to say when CNM relationships such as open marriages and swinging were "invented." If it is possible to daydream about a sexual activity, surely someone, somewhere, sometime probably gave it a try. Among indigenous peoples, for example, there are many polygamous arrangements, where dominant men are allowed to marry as many women as they please. In others, women are allowed to have sexual relations with

Table 8.1 Infidelity at a Glance: Married and Cohabiting People Who Had
More Than One Sexual Partner in the Last Year

Country/City	Men (%)	Women (%)
Togo	37.0	0.5
Cameroon	36.5	4.4
Ivory Coast	36.1	1.9
Mozambique	28.9	3.1
Tanzania	27.6	2.6
Haiti	25.4	0.8
Benin	23.4	0.6
Zambia	22.6	1.5
Uganda	22.3	1.2
Burkina Faso	20.1	0.5
China (Urban)	18.3	3.2
Dominican Republic	18.0	0.8
Mexico City	15.0	—
Zimbabwe	13.8	0.7
Peru	13.5	0.1
Ghana	13.0	0.4
Brazil	12.0	0.8
Kenya	11.5	1.6
Norway	10.8	6.6
China	10.5	—
Great Britain	9.3	5.1
Bolivia	8.6	0.4
Ethiopia	6.9	1.0
Armenia	4.7	0.1
Philippines	4.5	0.0
United States.	3.9	3.1
France	3.8	2.0
Italy	3.5	0.9
Rwanda	3.2	0.1
Niger	27.2	0.1
Nigeria	15.2	0.6
Chad	19.9	0.7
Malawi	16.3	0.5
Mali	22.4	0.7
Namibia	13.0	1.2
Nepal	3.0	0.0

Table 8.1 *Continued*

Country/City	Men (%)	Women (%)
Switzerland	3.0	1.1
Australia	2.5	1.8
Kazakhstan	1.6	0.9
Bangladesh	1.6	—

Note: Since the numbers are based on different populations and different sampling methods, they are merely suggestive. These are the best data available, however. See Druckerman (2007, pp. 61–63).

anyone who pleases them on ceremonial and festival days (Frayser, 1985; Frayser & Whitby, 1995).

Jenks (2014) points out that, historically, the practice of spouse exchange was acceptable in 39% of the world's cultures. In pre-Islamic Arabia, husbands allowed their wives to live with powerful men, in hopes of producing noble offspring. In the French Congo, temporary spouse trading was practiced as part of a ritual initiation into the Lemba secret society (Janzen, 1982.) In New Guinea, among the Orya of northern Irian Jaya, members of the *agama tonkat* cult (Indonesian for "walking stick") encouraged men to trade wives (Fields, 1998). An Ammassalik Eskimo husband was expected to offer his wife to a guest by means of the culturally sanctioned game of "putting out the lamp." A good host was expected to turn out the lamp at night, as an invitation for the guest to have sexual intercourse with the wife (Hupka & Ryan, 1990).

In the West, as well, there are many early examples of such sexual arrangements. In the 16th century, for example, several radical Anabaptist sects included a "community of women." After a séance on April 22, 1587, for example, John Dee, his wife Lynae, his friend Edward Kelley, and his wife Joanna signed a formal document indicating that conjugal relations would be shared by both couples. In the 19th century, Mormons practiced polygamy; some renegade Mormons still do.

Swapping

According to Gould (1999), the popular and modern form of wife-swapping began among American Air Force fighter pilots and their wives in World War II. In World War II, fighter pilots' odds of surviving were appalling.

From 1942 onward, America averaged 45,170 planes lost per day, every day! A full 44.4% of pilots were killed in action during their tours of duty. (Think of how that compares to the horror we rightly feel over the 2,800 deaths on 9/11!) Not surprisingly, given those statistics, a close bond arose between pilots' families; if men survived, they promised to care for their fellow pilots' wives and families—that meant sexually, too. In "key clubs," women would toss their house keys in a bowl, the men would pluck them out, and couples would go off with the owner into a convenient bedroom.

By the time the Korean War ended, the key clubs had spread from the military to the suburbs. The media dubbed the phenomenon "wife-swapping."

Open Marriage

> Marriage: a community consisting of a master, a mistress, and two slaves, making in all, two.
>
> —Ambrose Bierce

Two of the most celebrated French lovers, Simone de Beauvoir and Jean-Paul Sartre, who met in 1929, never married, although they stayed together for a lifetime; they had an open marriage. When courting at the Sorbonne, they drew up a passionate document. As de Beauvoir (1949/1962) recounted:

> "What we have," he said, "is an *essential* love; but it is a good idea for us also to experience *contingent* love affairs." We were two of a kind, and our relationship would endure as long as we did: but it could not make up for the fleeting riches to be had from encounters with different people. (p. 24)

In the 1970s and 1980s, at the height of the sexual revolution, social commentators began to suggest that a traditional, patriarchal, monogamous relationship should not be the social ideal. Theorists such as O'Neill and O'Neill (1984), in *Open Marriage*, proposed that many couples might be happier and more satisfied if their marriages were supplemented by occasional extramarital activities, such as "wife-swapping," "swinging," and the like. In such arrangements, couples agreed that they could have sex with others, given that they followed a stringent series of ground rules. They must live for the moment only and have realistic expectations. They must respect the other's privacy; have open and honest communication—both verbal and nonverbal; practice honest self-disclosure and feedback; and have role flexibility, open companionship, equality, respect for the other's identity, trust, love, and sex without jealousy.

In addition, when arranging sexual liaisons, they had to craft rules that made both of them feel secure. Many couples, for example, forged rules forbidding emotional attachment, extramarital sex in the marital bed, and sex with those known to both partners. They insisted on the use of contraception and forbade illegitimate children. Then there was the biggest issue with which couples had to deal: "Jealousy has no place in an open marriage" (O'Neill & O'Neill, 1984, p. 239).

People's experiences with open marriage varied. Some couples reported high levels of marital satisfaction and had long-lasting open marriages. Other couples dropped out of the open marriage lifestyle and returned to sexual monogamy. They may have believed that open marriage was a valid lifestyle, but it was just not for them. Other couples experienced serious problems and claimed that open marriage contributed to their divorce.

Recently, there has been renewed interest in open marriage. Researchers estimate that between 1.7 and 6% of married people are involved in such relationships. OkCupid even has a feature for open relationships. The actress Mo'Nique and her husband Sidney Hicks, an actor and producer, are in an open relationship and they have a podcast, which appears on Play.it, the CBS podcast network. Mo'Nique has clarified that the key "rule" to their arrangement is "simply honesty" (Real, 2016).

Commentators commonly assert that monogamy is the only natural way to form a sexual relationship and thereby imply that CNM must be some form of aberration (Barker & Langdridge, 2010). Contrary to popular opinion, however, there is no evidence to suggest that consensual monogamy is pathological. In meta-analyses, comparing participants in CNM with those in traditional marriages, we find that those practicing CNM score as high on measures of psychological well-being (such as the Minnesota Multiphasic Personality Inventory [MMPI]) as monogamists. Gay and straight, young and old, CNM partners score as high on self-esteem, personal fulfillment, stability of mood, interpersonal sensitivity, and the like as non-participants (Rubel & Bogaert, 2015). Gay and straight CNM relationships are as happy, as satisfying (as loving, intimate, and committed, as good in communication, and as committed), and as long-lasting as traditional relationships (Bergstrand & Williams, 2000; Blasband & Peplau, 1985; Fernandes, 2009; Fleckenstein & Cox, 2015; Gass, Hoff, Stephenson, & Sullivan, 2012; Hoff,

Beougher, Chakravarty, Darbes, & Neilands, 2010; Hosking, 2013; Kurdek, 1988; Kurdek & Schmitt, 1986; LaSala, 2004; Mogilsky, Memering, Welling, & Shackelford, 2017; Wagner, Remien, & Carballo-Diéguez, 2000). CNM partners also take more precautions than those in monogamous relationships (e.g., they are more likely to use condoms and to have STI testing (Lehmiller, 2015). They are also more likely to use condoms correctly (Conley, Moors et al., 2013).

Open marriages aren't without costs, however. Since others in the community may disapprove of extramarital sexual activities, couples often have to hide their open marriages from family, friends, and colleagues. In discussing how others responded to her open marriage, Mo'Nique (La Gorce, 2016, p. 2) reported: "People lost their minds, . . . and the criticism has never let up." Such censure may limit participants' social support networks. In some places, where adultery is illegal, open marriages are illegal, too. Some evolutionary psychologists, such as Helen Fisher (2004a), has argued that people simply aren't wired by evolution to manage such complex relationships. Many primatologists talk about the sexuality of our nearest primate relative, the bonobo. The tiny primates engage in same-sex genitogenital rubbing, and they engage in sex with members of the opposite sex, juveniles, and even infants. Japanese primatologist Takayoshi Kano (Nicholls, March, 2016) argues that they are like nymphomaniacs. Many cultural theorists and neuroscientists disagree (see preceding references).

Swingers

Swinging is defined as "the exchange of partners solely for sexual purposes" (Jenks, 2014). Involvement at the emotional level is contrary to "the rules of the game." Today the preferred term for swinging is *The Lifestyle*. It can vary from spontaneous sexual activity involving partner-swapping at an informal gathering of friends to planned meetings in semi-public venues such as hotels, resorts, or cruise ships. Most estimates place the incidence of swinging at 2% or less (Jenks, 1998). However, a study by the North American Swing Club Alliance (NASCA) states that 15% of couples in the United States have engaged, at least once in their married lives, in swinging (McGinley, 1995). Websites that cater to swinging couples now exist, some boasting hundreds of thousand of members (Goodman, 2013).

Research on swinging has been conducted in the United States since the late 1960s. In an Internet study, Jenks (2014) studied modern-day swingers. As in his previous studies (usually conducted at national swingers conventions), he found that swingers in the United States (as compared to more traditional couples) were usually in their 30s and 40s, white, and middle and upper-middle in social class. In contrast to earlier studies (which found that swingers were usually rich, religious Republicans), however, Jenks found that today's swingers in America tend to be Democrats, more liberal, significantly less religious, and more "spiritual" than their peers. They claim their lives are happy and closer to their ideal and they score higher on a scale of happiness than do their peers (although not significantly so). Social class variables have also been studied. A number of studies find that swingers are above average in education (they are generally college educated) and have incomes between $70,000 and $200,000 (Fernandes, 2009).

Edward Fernandes (2013) is a clinical psychologist who has conducted seminal work on swinging. He observes:

One of the questions I'm asked most often is if swinging is a male-driven and dominated endeavor where husbands coerce their wives into this "degrading" situation. . . . According to my research findings, all of the above comments couldn't be further from the truth. I have compiled hundreds and hundreds of hours of interviews with couples in the swinging lifestyle and one of my first questions is how did the couple get involved in the swinging lifestyle, and how is the wife handling it. Moreover, did the wife have a choice in the matter, or did she just go along to please her husband? (pp. 1–2)

While men introduce the idea of swinging to their wives 72% of the time, once involved, things seem to change. At first, women are a little frightened. They don't know what to expect and they worry: Am I pretty enough? Am I sexy enough for other men to want me? Am I too fat? In dressing, women are worried about looking too slutty or too matronly. Soon, however, they gain confidence. Many claim their husband looked at them with fresh eyes and showed a higher level of sexual desire after seeing how much other men want them. Many report they enjoyed the variety.

Some women experiment with bisexuality. In the swinging community, it is women who have the final say on who parties with whom. There is much less research on men in these settings, but legend says that when couples decide to leave the group, it is generally the men who lose interest. After all, according to club rules, it is women who decide whom they will pair up with, when, and how. In addition, most men can generally have only one orgasm a night; thus they are left waiting on the sideline while their wives are otherwise engaged. We have not yet found research to substantiate this claim, however.

As we observed earlier, general trends in research suggest that participants in swinging have similar psychological well-being and relationship quality as monogamists. Their sex lives appear to be equally satisfying. Their divorce rates are about the same as those in the general population (Rubel & Bogaert, 2015).

One of our students reported:

I once got involved with the wife of a swinger. It was quite odd at first, but I can honestly say I don't think I've ever seen a couple so in love despite their sexual activities outside of their marriage. I'd hang out with both of them together as friends, or if the husband wanted it, he'd watch [us have sex]. They were my neighbors across the street.

Jealousy Among Swingers

Is jealousy a cultural universal? Are there gender differences in what sparks jealousy among swingers? How do swingers deal with jealousy? Research investigating the relationship between jealousy and relationship satisfaction has yielded conflicting results (Demirtas & Donmez, 2006). We do know that jealousy is common in CNM relationships (Bergstrand & Williams, 2000). Estimates of the proportion of CNM participants who experience jealousy range from under 33% to 100% (Bergstrand & Williams, 2000). Jealousy is also the most commonly reported reason given for why swingers stop swinging (Denfeld, 1974). Importantly, however, studies suggest that CNMs don't experience any more jealousy in their relationships than do monogamists (Rubin & Adams, 1986). Practitioners of CNM also commonly report that jealousy diminishes with time (de Visser & McDonald, 2007).

Polyamory

Polyamory (from the Greek πολύ *poly*, "many, several," and Latin *amor*, "love") is the desire for or practice of intimate relationships involving more than two people. According to *Loving More* magazine (2016), it involves "emotionally connected relationships openly involving three or more people." In a recent survey of over 4,000 *Loving More* subscribers, Fleckenstein, Bergstrand, and Cox (2012) found that their average age was approximately 40. As to education, 27.4% had a graduate degree, while another 25% had attained a B.A. When asked how happy they were, on a scale ranging from 1 = "Not too happy" to 4 = "Very happy," the average respondent indicated they were 3.0 = "Pretty happy." This is close to the national average.

Richard Jenks (2014) surveyed three groups of Americans—swingers, polys, and people unaffiliated with either group. On average, the swingers and the polys were in their early to mid-40s. The polys were less likely to believe in a traditional God or to be regular church members than were their peers. Both swinging and polyamory are still middle- to upper-middle-class phenomena. Income also places them squarely in the upper middle class. Whites make up the vast majority of participants. In political affiliation, 45.5% were Democrats, 40% were Independents, and 12% were Republicans. Like the swingers, polys were more likely than the general sample to say they were satisfied with their mental and emotional states. They were also most likely to agree with the statement: "In most ways, my life is close to my ideal." Nonetheless, when asked, "Have you had severe enough personal, emotional, behavioral, or mental problems (for example, depression or anxiety) during the past year that you felt you needed help?" 39.4% of polys, 23.3% of swingers, and 21.1% of the general population said, "Yes, they had sought help." Among those who said, "Yes, but did not seek help" were the swingers (7%), polys (9.1%), and general population (39.4%). It seems that all three groups were similar in feeling they once needed help, but the swingers and the polys were just more active in seeking it.

As we observed earlier, general trends in research suggest that participants in poly marriages have similar psychological well-being and relationship quality as that of monogamists (Rubel & Bogaert, 2015). Social commentators point out that polys can also benefit from the setup. They can share family duties and help in child rearing and financial obligations and provide friendship (Barker & Langdridge, 2010).

Of course, polys face criticism from religious groups, family, friends, and members of the community. In addition, the interactions among the partners can be complex. In polyamory, one must deal with the reactions, ideologies, and emotions of many people. The combinations can become overwhelming. Consider for example, a poly household of four or six people. Think of the arguments one can have with roommates about who ate the ice cream and who should buy more—multiply that by six. Divisions of labor, sexual relations, jealousy, and work schedules can wreak havoc with the members of the household. It is this sort of complexity that destroyed the well-intended communes of the hippies in the 1960s and '70s. Nonetheless, today, most polys say they are leading lives that are richly satisfying.

Jealousy in Polys

Many polys claim that they are never jealous. In fact, they say, that when their partners are romantically involved with another, they are happy for them. (Polys term such feelings of empathetic joy for their partners "compersion" [Easton & Hardy, 2009].) Polys commonly see jealousy as something that is manageable rather than intolerable (de Visser & McDonald, 2007). Many see jealousy as a healthy experience that can contribute to personal development and bring a couple closer together (Easton & Hardy, 2009).

When most people hear such claims they think, "Oh, come on! That's a little much. Do you actually expect me to believe that?" Few scholars have investigated the impact of compersion on relationship satisfaction (Duma, 2009). There is some relevant research, however. In one study, 60% of participants reported having had positive reactions in response to their partner's extradyadic sex, and only 15% reported a somewhat or very negative response (Ramey, 1975). Researchers in Israel (Nadler & Dotan, 1992) and the Netherlands (Bringle & Buunk, 1986) found that individuals experience the most jealousy and the most severe physiological reactions (e.g., trembling, increased pulse rate, nausea) when a loved one's affair poses a serious threat to their dating or marital relationship.

Aumer and her peers (2014) set out to find out how jealousy (or the lack thereof) and compersion (or the lack thereof) operated in poly relationships. The authors argued that the goals of the relationship, as in "being monogamous" or "being polyamorous," should greatly impact the relationship between gender, jealousy, compersion, and relationship satisfaction.

The authors interviewed 302 participants, aged 18 to 72, who were involved in monogamous, open, or poly relationships. They measured the variables of interest in three ways. The first, the Multidimensional Jealousy Scale (Pfeiffer & Wong, 1989), is a 24-item scale measuring three different dimensions of jealousy: cognitive jealousy, emotional jealousy, and behavioral jealousy. The cognitive items measure frequency of thoughts such as "I suspect that my partner is secretly seeing someone else." Emotional items measure one's emotional reaction to situations such as "Your partner hugs and kisses someone else." The behavioral items measure the frequency of jealous behaviors such as "I look through my partner's drawers, handbag, or pockets."

The second scale they used was the Compersion Questionnaire. To measure compersion, a modified version of the Compersion Trait Questionnaire (Duma, 2009), a 25-item scale, was included in the survey. This scale included questions like "I'd be comfortable with my partner falling in love with someone else."

Finally, the third scale they used was the Relationship Assessment Scale (Hendrick, Dicke, & Hendrick, 1998). The scale contains questions such as "How well does your partner meet your needs?"

They found that, in general, women scored higher on the jealousy measure and lower on the compersion measure than men. However, among polys, the tendency toward jealousy and compersion, and one's relationship status (single, monogamous, open, or polyamorous), appeared to have no clear cut impact on relationship satisfaction. Once again, research investigating the relationship between jealousy/compersion and relationship satisfaction remains complex.

Anthropologists have also been interested in the kinds of societies in which our primate ancestors lived. Sommer (1993), for example, asked a challenging question: Did our ancient *Homo sapiens*' ancestors live in monogamous, polygamous, polyandrous, or polygynandrous communities? (In monogamy, a man and woman marry—usually for a lifetime. In polygamy, one man may possess many wives; in polyandry, one woman may take several husbands. In polygynandry, or "promiscuous" mating, men and women may mate at will.)

After observing many kinds of primates, Sommer (1993) discovered that it is easy to predict what sort of sexual mating arrangements a primate species will adopt. He needed to know only four facts: (1) In that species, who is bigger—the males or the females? (2) How much do the males' testes weigh? (3) Do females have sexual swellings (which signal sexual receptivity and fertility)? (4) How long does sexual intercourse last? (The scientists found, for example, that in monogamous species such as gibbons, males and females are generally about the same size. In polygynous species such as orangutans [where successful males must physically dominate their rivals], males are much larger than their mates.) Yet, male bonobos are larger than females and both are far from monogamous.

When Sommer (1993) classified *Homo sapiens* on these four characteristics, his calculations led him to conclude that although our human forebears *may* have been monogamous, the odds are that they were polygynous. There is no chance that they were either polyandrous or polygynandrous.

What about our more immediate ancestors? How did they live? On the basis of her calculations, Fisher (1989) concluded that throughout the world, although (in theory) most societies are polygynous, in fact, the overwhelming majority of married men and women are actually in monogamous marriages. Fisher studied the marital arrangements of the 853 societies sampled in the *Ethnographic Atlas* (which contains anthropological information on more than 1,000 representative preindustrial societies throughout the world). She found that although almost all societies (84%) permitted polygyny, men rarely exercised this option. (Only about 10% of men possessed more than one wife. Most possessed just one wife. A few were unmarried.) In 16% of societies, monogamy was prescribed. Polyandry was extremely rare. Only

0.5% of societies permitted polyandry. In recent years, however, theorists such as Wilson and Daly (1992) have observed that in humankind's long evolutionary history, although in theory men and women are "supposed" to be faithful to one partner, in many situations it is to a man's or woman's benefit to break the rules and "mate poach." (Evolutionary psychologists define *mate poaching* as behavior intended to attract someone who is already in a relationship.) In a study by Schmitt and Buss (2001), 15% of people reported that their current relationship directly resulted from mate poaching. Around 3% resulted from both partners having poached each other out of previous relationships ("copoached") Schmitt and Buss (2001).

Thus, humans are likely to possess a variety of cognitive structures designed to deal with a multitude of contingencies (see Barkow, Cosmides, & Tooby, 1992; Hrdy, 1999; Wilson & Daly, 1992, for a discussion of the factors that made and make it advantageous [or costly] for men and women to seek a variety of sexual partners).

Reflections on Monogamy

Notwithstanding the many experiments with non-monogamy, there is little question that cheating is, in the United States at least, currently the chief deal breaker in committed relationships. Let us forgive the people who get most of their information from watching American television or Hollywood movies. They would be forced to come to one conclusion: relationships end because one or both lovers "cheat." Infidelity is the deal breaker of deal breakers. It may be a function of lazy screen and television writers that when they write the script for a failing marriage or love affair, it's almost always because of "cheating." And the other words they use are not much more forgiving: *infidelity, adultery,* even *betrayal.*

Rapson (1988, 2003, 2008) has looked into this emphasis on the need for monogamy from the point of view of a cultural historian. He argues that the focus on faithfulness (practically the sine qua non of love affairs) ripples into actual behavior. Like super sleuths, lovers spy on one another to detect cheating. They peer into their partners' Facebook entries, text messages, and emails. They engage friends to report back on any "suspicious" doings by their partners. Relationships too often devolve into a power struggle, one whose only function is to make sure their partner doesn't "stray." For some, this is all that matters in a relationship. And this is not, alas, simply a tale of teenagers.

Perhaps the obsession with monogamy is partly a function of the emergence of AIDS in the 1980s. Perhaps it's a function of a capitalist view of love and marriage, with ownership very much at stake. Perhaps jealousy is hardwired into our being, though one could argue that the desire for sexual variety is just as wired in (we discussed this in both Chapter 6 and earlier in this chapter).

Whatever the reasons, there is also no question that the language used to describe extracurricular sex is negative. As we've said before, we wonder if things would be different if, as one of our students suggested, we substitute for the terms *cheating* or *infidelity* something like *sampling?* We could also use more neutral terms, such as *fooling around* or *having a fling* or (less colorfully) *non-monogamy* or *extramarital* sex. Words matter.

Such language might then at least encourage people to raise questions about the focus on monogamy as *the sole* measure of a relationship's success, when we are seeing longer lifespans, the pleasure in sexual variety, the potential cure for AIDS, the great improvements in curing STIs, the greater ease in finding willing sexual partners, and the weakening of religious and other culturally inspired sexual taboos.

Furthermore, there is no agreed-upon meaning as to what we mean by "cheating." Is it kissing someone else? If so, what kind of kissing is *verboten*—On the cheek? On the mouth? Tongue in the mouth? Is it worse than kissing to reveal intimacies about the relationship to someone else—what some refer to as "emotional infidelity"? Does infidelity mean intercourse? Is it watching pornography? Is it sexual fantasizing about someone else while making love to your partner? Is it having a randy avatar on "Second Life"? Is it hugging? Is it flirting? Is it looking lustfully (or approvingly) at someone passing by on the street, or going so far as to send messages to someone you've "passed by" on Facebook? Is it having cybersex?

There are hundreds of possible definitions of cheating, and it's obvious that two people have to engage in a conversation in which they carve out what is acceptable in a relationship and where the line exists that (if crossed) will damage it. But that's a tough conversation for people to have, and we fear that most people don't have it. It makes people too anxious.

Furthermore, such a conversation requires some high-level skills that not everyone possesses: the ability to know your own wishes on these matters;

the ability of your partner to have those same abilities; the ability to find words to express those wishes and feelings and preferences; your partner's ability to have the same; your capacity for catharsis, to know that people can be different without loving you less; ditto for your partner; the capacity to develop creative solutions for dealing with those differences; the same for your partner. We're not talking about easy or universally distributed capacities.

In Rapson's class, he once asked if students had had "the talk" with their significant others. Students waved their hands and he asked one student what they had decided. "I don't remember," said the boy. The class howled. So it may be that a good memory is required, too.

The complications can be endless. In therapy we sometimes saw couples who could accept their partner having a fling as long as they talked about it with one another. We saw couples who could accept their partner having a fling as long as they *didn't* talk about it with one another. We saw married individuals who justified their extramarital affair by explaining that they had no feelings for the new lover, while their partner would reply that "at least I had feelings for *my* lover."

And so on …

One final anomaly: Rapson points out that, in the past, a major goal of feminists was to erase the double standard that has defined male–female sexual relations for millennia: that is, that men can fool around as much as they wish and that women cannot. Women who were sexual in the past were punished. Religions regarded it as a sin, and even today, in parts of the world, women can be murdered for sex acts, even for being raped.

Two strategies were available to the women's movement if they hoped to move America toward a single standard: either women could be freed up to express their sexuality as they desired, just as men do; or men could be forced to be as sexually restricted as women have been, particularly once they entered into a committed relationship. For now, monogamy has won the day. With the potential defeat of AIDS on the horizon, the demystification of sex through conversations, hookups, and the Web, that "victory" is not guaranteed in the years to come. We are still early in "the sexual revolution," with outcomes unforeseen and unforeseeable.

Conclusion

Let us conclude this chapter with one curious and apparent inconsistency when it comes to sexual behavior. The undeniable increase in hookups, casual sex, and having sex *before* deciding whether to date someone all suggest that sex is being demystified, becoming less taboo, less related to "sin," more quotidian—that it's just less romantic and forbidden and terrifying, less "a big thing" than ever before. On the other hand, cheating seems to be the chief deal breaker these days, suggesting that sex (in one form or another) *is* very much a big thing.

Is this just a lack of logic and a glaring contradiction, or is there a way to overcome this apparent conflict with a unifying explanation? This is a difficult conundrum, but allow us to offer one possible theory that might cover the inconsistency. It is this: In a stridently capitalist world, particularly in the United States, dating and mating have succumbed to The Market, like everything else. We increasingly market ourselves on social media as though we ourselves are commodities, with flattering photos and flattering self-narratives. We spend huge amounts of time and money on fixing up our bodies and faces; we sell ourselves on the dating market, including our sexual selves. Advertising promises a better personal, romantic, and sexual life if only we buy the promoted diet books, personal trainers, strange foods, cosmetic surgery, and cosmetics generally.

But once we enter a committed relationship—still using the market metaphors—we now own and possess our mates, much like any product, and we cannot accept that parts of our mates, particularly the sexual parts, could be shared by someone else—hence cheating as the deal breaker.

The market perhaps rules our personal and love lives pretty much as it rules our consumer behavior. Capitalism perhaps significantly shapes the way we date and mate, neatly uniting casual sex as we seek a mate with the end of casual sex after we find one. In the process, however, a great deal of personal anxiety is generated, both before and after committing to a mate.

Are there better alternatives to approaching dating and mating than this competitive, demanding application of capitalism, if that's what it is? Perhaps we could ease off all the market pressure on ourselves, especially that surrounding looks. Perhaps we could just try to find someone or some many who are wonderful to be around—in whose company, for whatever reasons, we long to be.

9

Pornography

The Private Enters the Public

Fantasy Girl Comes to Life. Maid Service. Great Body, Great Sex, Great Blowjob. These are just a few sample titles from the Internet's most viewed pornographic videos of all time, as viewed on the popular "adult" website YouPorn.com (YouPorn, 2011). These videos represent the pathways along which contemporary pornography is consumed today—online, streaming, and for free. But what is pornography and, more importantly, how are we supposed to feel about it?

It's explicit. Taboo. Hot. Dangerous. Exploitative. Satisfying. Embarrassing. Addicting. Accessible. Gross. Amazing. Bad. The compelling—and complicating—thing about pornography is that it absolutely can be all of these things at once. It induces widespread moral panic ("Porn is ruining our love lives and making old men of our teenagers" claims a recent article by Martin Daubney [2015] from *The Telegraph*), yet billions of pornographic videos are watched online and on DVDs each month without an observable drop in happy relationships or global fertility rates.

What Is Porn?

The panic may be related to the nature of pornography itself as a contested, politicized, instrument of contrasts: The private act of sex meets the public market of consumption in explicit detail. And what may be most uncomfortable is the appetite this contrast highlights within our society—and within ourselves.

For an issue that seems to be so polarizing, many may find it difficult to place themselves along the "pro" or "anti" porn continuum. Hypothetically, pornography may represent liberating and expressive perspectives on sex, yet there's also great tension in knowing how easy it is for the actors and actresses

What's Next in Love and Sex. Elaine Hatfield, Richard L. Rapson, and Jeanette Purvis, Oxford University Press (2020). © Oxford University Press.
DOI: 10.1093/oso/9780190647162.001.0001

to fall prey to exploitation. "Can a Feminist Like Porn?" asks actress and director Rashida Jones in *Glamour* magazine (Jones, 2015). The conclusion she came to? It sort of depends.

For every study that says watching pornography is harmless, there's another declaring that it's not. For example, studies have found that porn positively affects attitudes about sex and improves self-reported quality of life (Hald & Malamuth, 2008). Somewhat confusingly, however, studies also show that watching porn is correlated with lower relationship satisfaction (Maddox, Rhoades, & Markman, 2011), and excessive porn watching may even lead to decreased gray matter in the brain (Kühn & Gallinat, 2014). By simply typing "Is porn bad?" into Google, the top two results that appear at the top of the search list are "5 Reasons You Need to Watch More Porn" (Dickson & Lang, 2015), followed by "10 Reasons Why You Should Quit Watching Porn" (Christian, 2013). Clearly, the presumed effects of porn are as varied as the adjectives we use to describe it.

So just what is pornography? Is it the array of DVDs in the back room of local seedy sex shops? Is it defined by the videos watched on websites such as YouPorn.com and Pornhub.com that millions of people scrub regularly from their search history? How about the graphic drawings of intercourse in ancient Japanese *shunga* books, often presented to newly married couples so they would know how to copulate on their wedding night? Or the unsimulated sex scene from the recent theatrical film *Wetlands,* in which a group of men ejaculate onto a pizza? Indeed, public debate has raged for decades in attempts to differentiate "porn" from "sex" and "art."

The *Webster-Merriam Dictionary* defines pornography as "the depiction of erotic behavior (as in pictures or writing) intended to cause sexual excitement." With a definition this broad, one could easily categorize a milieu of recent music videos or songs as porn. For example, Miley Cyrus' (2015) music video *BB Talk* features the lyrics "fuck me so you stop baby talkin'!" while Cyrus rolls on her back in a pair of giant adult diapers with legs spread, lollipop in hand. Does this qualify as erotic behavior intended to cause sexual excitement? Most likely. But is it porn? Well, that may be a more difficult question to answer.

While the categories of "porn" and "not porn" may at the end of the day be largely subjective categories, the word *porn* is usually associated with graphic depictions, in video or photography, that show sexual acts such as intercourse, masturbation, or oral sex. This is why anyone can sign onto YouTube and watch Miley Cyrus' *BB Talk*, but not the porn parody *Molly's Wrecken*

Ballz, which features a Miley Cyrus look-alike engaging in intercourse with a Justin Bieber look-alike. While this may not seem like a distinction that needs to be stated, public debate regarding the regulation of porn and its relation to the First Amendment has been an ongoing, controversial topic in the United States. In fact, the U.S. Supreme Court has seen well over a dozen cases in an attempt to define and regulate pornography. In 1964, Chief Justice Potter Stewart famously admitted that he couldn't define obscenity, then stated, "but I know it when I see it." There's no imminent end to the debate, as the Internet proves to be increasingly beyond the reach of regulation, especially as it confronts Americans' desire to protect the First Amendment and the cherished right to free speech.

The Invention of Pornography

Erotic depictions, which include cave drawings, paintings, dramatic arts, music, films, and writing, have been created by nearly every civilization, ancient and modern. The meaning of such erotica has varied in different eras. Early cultures (in India, Japan, China, Greece, and Rome, for example) associated sexual acts with spirituality and supernatural forces and thus, erotic depictions had religious significance (see Illustration 9.1).

Within Pompeii and Herculaneum, graphic paintings above the lintel advertised the sexual services on order. Phalli and testicles engraved in sidewalks guided patrons to the entertainment districts. In homes, huge phalli served as decorations. They were considered to be good luck charms.

During the 18th-century Enlightenment, the coming French Revolution sparked a cascade of pornographic pamphlets linked to political conflicts. Rape, incest, sacrilege, sodomy, patricide, and the most grisly forms of torture and murder were depicted by social critics (such as the Marquis de Sade) to show their contempt for the nobility, the courts, and religious institutions (Hunt, 1996; Williams, 1989).

With the advent of the motion picture, "blue films" and stag films became available for men's night out at the Eagles, Elks, or Moose lodges. Their purpose was purely sexual—much like the pornography of today. In this chapter, we will discuss just one form of pornography—visual pornography. There are other popular forms of pornography, of course. While the novel *Fifty Shades of Grey* sold more than 125 million copies, visual porn is still

Illustration 9.1 Shuga Empire sculpture from India, 1st century BCE, Metropolitan Museum of Art.
Source: https://en.wikipedia.org/wil/History_of_etrotic_depictions

the most popular form of pornography. There is LGBT+ porn, feminist porn, and the like (for those interested in the history of various forms of porn see Hunt, 1996).

The Availability of Pornography

Internet pornography in the United States is currently legal, and the barriers to creating and distributing porn have decreased. Regnerus, Gordon, and Proce (2016) found that 46% of men and 16% of women between the ages of 18 to 39 intentionally viewed pornography in a given week. As a result, the amount of product has increased. With live-streaming Web cams and community-based video-sharing sites, anyone with an iPhone and a penchant for sharing can upload a homemade sex-tape within hours. Additionally, since demand for porn has remained enormously high, the pornography industry has increasingly moved away from traditional pay-for-play business models and is now credited with pioneering the "traffic wave" business model, which nets profits mostly off of clicked ads instead of Web visitors paying directly

Table 9.1 Pornography Revenue in Various Countries

Country	Revenue (Billions) in US dollars
China	27.4
South Korea	25.73
Japan	19.98
US	13.33
Australia	2.00
UK	1.97
Italy	1.4
Canada	1
Philippines	1
Taiwan	1
Finland	.64
Czech Republic	.6
Russia	.25
Netherlands	. 2
Brazil	.1
Other 212 countries	Unavailable
TOTAL	96.06 Billion

Pornography revenue exceeds that of all the top technology companies combined: Microsoft, Google, Amazon, eBay, Yahoo, Apple, Netflix, and EarthLink.

for product (Naked capitalism, 2015). With this conflation of demand and product, over the past two decades porn has been righteously liberated from magazines stuffed under the mattress and now streams 24/7 onto millions of people's at-home devices all over the world (see Table 9.1).

The Web traffic from adult websites exceeds that of many popular sites such as eBay, Reddit, and Craigslist. In Table 9.2 we present the breakdown of Web traffic per month in billions of visits for several of the Internet's top websites. As you can see, adult websites make up a large portion of the most heavily accessed Web traffic.

Simply put, Internet porn, in recent years, has become ubiquitous. While many adult websites have tried to implement age restrictions to access adult content, it may take relatively little effort for a curious young person to purposefully, or even accidentally, enter a Web space filled with graphic pornographic films. In fact, recent studies have found that many kids start watching online porn as young as 6 (Dima, 2013), with up to 93% of boys and 62% of

Table 9.2 Popularity of the Most Popular Pornography Sites

Global Ranking	Website	Total Unique Site Visits per Month, September 2016
1	Facebook	26.9 billion
7	Wikipedia	4.9 billion
10	Baidu	2.5 billion
17	Xvideos.com	1.6 billion
22	Pornhub	1.2 billion
24	eBay	1.1 billion
25	Reddit	1.1 billion
34	Xnxx	945.1 million
37	Xhamster	775.2 million
38	Craigslist	770.3 million

Source: *SimilarWeb.* (n.d.). Top websites. https://www.similarweb.com/top-websites

girls viewing online pornographic images online before they turn 18 (Sabina, Wolak, & Finkelhor, 2008).

These statistics are probably shocking to many adults who grew up in an age when pornography was relegated to the heavily edited images in *Playboy* or dusty videotapes in the back room of 24-hour video shops. (As one of our students observed, "My first memory of seeing pornography is when my friends and I found a stack of *Playboy* magazines under a bridge where we were planning to build a fort! Not much fort building got done that day.") It may be rather ironic that, given these statistics, scientists also find that modern children are being increasingly monitored and restricted by parents when it comes to physical freedom (Bird, 2007). Such restriction may be causing the vast majority of children's recreation time to take place indoors (Dill, 2014). With all of this extra parental control, it just may be that children are going on different kinds of adventure through digital spaces. Life can produce unintended consequences.

While the statistics around children's exposure to online porn is surprising, the statistics around adult's consumption of online porn is even more so. Eleven of the top 300 most visited websites are pornographic in nature, with the world's most visited porn site, Xvideos.com, ranking as the 17th most visited website on the Internet (Marciano, 2016). Data from the world's second most popular pornographic website, Pornhub, offers an in-depth look at user data through their wildly interesting "Insights" blog. As demonstrated earlier in our table of popular websites, Pornhub is the 22nd most accessed adult website in the world, with over 1.2 billion unique visitors a month. According to Pornhub's 2015 "Year in Review," over 87.9 *billion* videos were watched on their site over one year. That translates to roughly 11 videos *per person on Earth.*

Amazingly, around 4.9 billion hours of pornographic video were viewed on Pornhub in 2015 alone, which, if added together, would take 500,000 years to watch from start to finish. In other words, if every pornographic film watched on Pornhub in 2015 were placed one after another, the length of all those films would extend well past the end of Earth's existence, since scientists believe in 500,000 years life on Earth will have likely been due for destruction by a meteor impact (Bostrom, 2002). Enough porn, therefore, has been consumed to take us into the end days—and beyond!

While these numbers appear staggering, recent empirical research suggests that just because pornography is more available than ever before in human history does not mean that there is suddenly a universal desire to consume large amounts of pornography. A recent study by Price, Patterson, Regnerus, and Walley (2015) found only a 10% growth in pornography consumption among individuals born in the 1980s versus those born in the 1970s. While this may seem hard to believe in juxtaposition with the aforementioned traffic to pornographic websites, we suggest two possible explanations: (1) first, the Price et al. (2015) study was a self-report study, and the Web traffic reported by sites such as Pornhub more accurately reflects actual behaviors, or (2) alternatively, there may be large individual variations in regard to pornographic consumption. People may be underreporting the amount of pornography they watch—a happenstance not hard to understand.

Pornography Consumers

Indeed, many people who visit online pornographic websites are known as "compulsive" pornography consumers. While porn addiction is not currently a diagnosis within the American Psychiatric Association's *Diagnostic and Statistical Manual of Mental Disorders,* 5th edition (DSM-5), it is still something that many people struggle with on a daily basis. A recent review of porn and other Internet-related addiction behaviors concluded that Internet porn addiction shared many of the same features as substance addiction

(Love, Laier, Brand, Hach, & Hajela, 2015). This finding is elucidated by recent fMRI research. Voon et al. (2014) recruited participants from therapists' referrals and newspaper ads. They were further screened by a psychiatric interview and scores on the Sex Screening Test. The researchers asked both compulsive and non-compulsive consumers of porn to watch a pornographic film, and then compared activation within brain regions associated with pleasure and reward. Voon and her colleagues found that compulsive porn users showed heightened activity within the reward centers of the brain compared to that in non-compulsive users. In other words, many compulsive porn consumers may feel addicted to porn because they get more chemical rewards for watching porn than non-compulsive consumers.

This is a similar finding within fMRI research examining the brains of people who are addicted to drugs. Cocaine addicts show more activity within their brain's reward systems than non-addicts when both are presented with cocaine. In fact, the Voon et al. (2014) study found that compulsive porn users didn't indicate a heightened sex -drive. Instead, their brains simply indicated that they *liked* watching porn more than non-compulsive users, which corroborates the predictions provided by addiction models.

For these individuals, compulsive porn consumption is not *necessarily* bad. Like most addictions, porn consumption is only considered negative if (1) an individual is obsessed or excessively preoccupied with porn consumption; (2) they cannot control their porn consumption; and (3) they experience negative consequences for their porn consumption (Addiction.com, n.d.). In fact, individuals who are struggling with porn addiction can often be found in Internet support communities, where days of "sobriety," or in this case, abstention from masturbating, are counted and posted with pride.

One such Internet forum is the NoFap (Fap being short for masturbation) Reddit community. This Internet forum currently has over 195,000 "fapstronauts" who actively post 12 Step–like mantras to discourage Internet porn use, sharing personal stories of "getting clean" and moving past their Internet porn addictions. In the recent thread, "Orgasmless October," where users are encouraged to pledge abstinence from masturbation for 30 days, one poster expressed his decisions for joining the site:

> I am not going to orgasm for the entire month of October. I want to know what it's like to live my life without masturbating every day. I feel like a robot. I know my inner voice has been objectifying women since puberty. I have been focusing too much on the way a woman looks and not who

she is. I thought I was in love with my girlfriend. . . . And I realized I only thought I "loved" her for her looks. It destroyed me and our relationship was horrible. It was nice to feel close to a person the way we were. But I know that I could actually have a happy long-lasting relationship without seeing a woman as an object to be used for my pleasure. Unfortunately I can't give up porn yet. I need to wean myself off it. I'm an addict, and I've finally accepted that. I know that I am ready to turn this around. I am currently 2 days clean. (Liberal69, 2016 [online post])

Here, user Liberal69 speaks openly about not only feeling addicted to porn, but suggesting that it is his porn consumption that has led to his objectification of women. Surprisingly, this was a common "negative" response that we heard when we reached out to the members of NoFap to share with us their thoughts and experiences dealing with pornography addiction. We received dozens of helpful responses from male members explaining how they first encountered porn, how they became addicted to it, and how they are now living life without Internet porn. Nearly every response stated that they felt watching porn made them objectify women more, or imparted unrealistic expectations.

User eXTeeGi wrote to us,

Masturbation drains you. It turns you into an emotionless shell of a person. Pornography gives you unrealistic expectations. How could you be attracted to the girl next door when you just masturbated to a girl who's beautiful for a living?

Another user, named "SelfEmpowerment," stated:

I think that pornography perpetuates rape culture. It promotes coercion. It can lead to body shaming of both men and women by both men and women. It is psychologically damaging to both its consumers and its sex workers. The executives at these porn companies are the only beneficiaries. Why do we let these people dictate human sexuality to us? Why is it okay to objectify people based on superficial qualities? (2016 [online post])

While these are anecdotal experiences of pornography, mostly from men who have experienced self-reported addiction to Internet porn, the question remains: Does porn actually reinforce negative gender stereotypes? Do men who watch porn end up actually objectifying women more in real life? Is *The Telegraph* right when they said porn is ruining our love lives and making old men out of our teenagers? While experts are largely divided on the issue of the effects of porn, since porn is not a universal construct and is difficult to measure in naturalistic settings, there is evidence to suggest consumption of porn is correlated with certain negative outcomes. This may be specifically true in regard to the objectification of women. Given the current asymmetries within society between men and women, it isn't a stretch to suggest that porn is made by men, for men. As such, it is likely that porn itself may replicate that power structure.

Evidence That Porn Leads to the Objectification of Women

One of the first scholars to popularize the idea that pornography inherently *objectifies* women was radical feminist and anti-pornography advocate Andrea Dworkin. In her book, *Pornography: Men Possessing Women*, she explained, "Any violation of a woman's body can become sex for men; this is the essential truth of pornography" (Dworkin, 1981). While this orientation has been widely criticized for its absolutism, some studies have suggested objectification may be associated with pornography use. They have found that looking at nude images of females in sexual poses causes individuals to *animalize* the female—meaning they believe she is less capable of personal agency yet more capable of having strong feelings (Gray, Knobe, Sheskin, Bloom, & Barrett, 2011).

While this means viewers of pornography may see women as more than objects, which seems positive, it suggests it may construe them instead as animal-like, which is obviously not positive. Women's sexuality has frequently been torn between these two representations: completely chaste or completely wild—what would be called the Madonna–whore complex.

Surely, this leaves the many nuances of contemporary female sexuality minimized. Another recent study by Hald, Malamuth, and Lange (2013) found that males who indicated high rates of past pornography consumption were more likely to have sexist attitudes toward women. And in perhaps the most damning publication to come out on the topic in recent years regarding heterosexuals and porn, a meta-analysis examining over 22 studies from seven countries found that individuals who consumed more pornography were more likely to hold attitudes associated with sexual aggression and were also more likely to act in sexually aggressive ways, both within lab settings and naturalistic settings (Wright, Tokunaga, & Kraus, 2015).

Evidence That Porn Has Positive Effects

However, as mentioned before, studies on the effects of pornography are largely divided. Many new studies suggest porn consumption holds not only few negative effects but even positive effects as well. Prause and Pfaus (2015) found that male participants who spent more time watching pornography in their daily lives were more likely to have stronger responses to pornography within a lab setting, which then translated to a stronger desire to be with a partner outside of a lab setting. That is, frequent porn consumers were more likely to desire their real-world sexual partner after watching porn than those who consumed porn less frequently.

This contradicts the idea that porn replaces real-world sexual desire, or hampers one's interest in their non-porn star girlfriends or boyfriends. In addition, the Dworkinian notion of all women as passive subjects within pornography has been disputed through a content analysis of popular Internet pornographic films. Klaassen and Peter (2015) analyzed over 400 videos from various pornographic sites and found that actors were more frequently dehumanized (by not having their faces featured), while actresses were more likely to be the object for pleasure, with the main climax of the films focusing on male orgasm. As such, objectification happened to both genders, albeit in different representations. In fact, the study went on to find that sexual violence was rare in the most popular pornographic films, and that men and women were most often portrayed as being in professionally or socially equal positions of power.

Pornography, then, may be best understood in its many, multifaceted contexts, instead of in binary categories of "good" or "bad." Sociologists Rebecca Sullivan and Alan McKee share this sentiment in their book, *Pornography* (2016):

> . . . we insist that pornography is neither inherently good nor bad, neither necessarily transgressive nor oppressive. Rather, we acknowledge media's ability to inform ideas about gender and sexuality, and to provide or withhold resources that assist audiences in making sense of their own media consumption. (p. 3)

In this interpretation of pornography, there is no passive consumption of porn. Each individual, alongside the specific packaging and presentation of the pornography itself, is the agent for its impact on influencing or perpetuating gender norms or behaviors. In fact, pornography for many individuals has become a powerful platform for identity expression. As the volume and diversity of porn created and distributed have increased, pornography has become a space for many queer users to "expand and inform their own identities and desires" that may not have previously been accessible (Trouble, 2014). In addition, pornography is not limited to online video sites, and individuals of different sexualities and gender expressions may utilize a variety of types of pornography—from erotic fiction online to erotic photography—to experience and express their sexualities.

The Effects on Porn Stars of Staring in Pornographic Films

While the effects of porn on an individual are likely to vary, given these many different criteria, an important component of understanding modern pornography involves the fate of the actors and actresses in these films. They are real people, not merely the two-dimensionalized objects we view on screen. The experiences of young women entering the porn industry were recently featured on the popular Netflix documentary, *Hot Girls Wanted* (2015). "We are free right now. The world is in our hands," says 18-year-old Rachel, aka Ava Taylor, after a week and a half in the industry. In the film, several young women are paid to fly to Miami and live in a house together, while a male "talent agent" named Riley coordinates their various appearances in local porn productions, which are then shared on the Internet. Indeed, for many young women, pursuing pornography may represent a liberating path to independence, with modest but immediate financial gains available. As the documentary points out, however, while the immediate gains may be tempting, most women's careers within porn will be short-lived. The "talent agent" Riley explains that "every day a new girl turns 18, and every day, a new girl wants to do porn. I will never run out." Women in porn thus may work for a short amount of time, for relatively low pay, while their videos continue to make money for porn producers and directors in the immortality of the modern Web. Many women face negative stigmatization from family, friends, and employers due to ongoing double standards regarding women's sexuality. In fact, researchers found that study participants rated female pornographic actresses as being more likely to come from dysfunctional families than male pornographic actors (Evans-DeCicco & Cowan, 2001).

In addition, porn actors, both male and female, have been assumed to face great dangers from STIs and HIV, for several reasons. One is that some STIs, including HIV, are not always detectable by general STI-screening panels. For example, herpes simplex I and II are actually very complex to test for, given that the virus lies dormant within nerve cells and antibodies and are not always detectable. HIV is also not immediately detectable upon transmission and can take up to 6 months to indicate a positive test result. Other STIs such as gonorrhea or chlamydia may present no symptoms at all, leading to a lack of adequate testing.

Another factor is that most pornography features unsimulated sex without condoms, which has led many to believe pornography actors and actresses are more likely to be infected with STIs than those who are not in the porn industry. One study from UCLA found that almost 25% of adult pornography performers screened for chlamydia and gonorrhea tested positive for infection (Javanbakht et al., 2014). However, when comparing similar populations of young people who don't do porn to those who do, rates of STI transmission prove to be roughly similar. For example, the Centers for Disease Control and Prevention (CDC) (2015) found that about 20–30% of young people in their early 20s tested positive for chlamydia, which is actually a slightly higher rate than that for porn performers. Rates of HIV are much more of a crisis in minority, low-income communities, thus effective intervention in STI transmission should be made a priority within a different population than porn performers. In addition, since many porn performers are required to get tested for STIs every 2 weeks, some media outlets have suggested people should "prevent STDs like a porn star" (Cohen, 2011) and actually encourage the general population to look toward the porn industry as a model for STI prevention.

One in six people in the United States have contacted genital herpes (HSV-1 and HSV-2). Most don't even know it. In a study at the University of Hawaii, for example, only 1 man in a sample of 400 students believed they had the disease (Thornton, 2015). Worse yet, a recent study by the National Center for Health Statistics found that more than 42% of Americans between the ages of 18 and 59 are infected with genital human papillomavirus. The high-risk strains of the virus, a cause of cervical and vaginal cancers, cancer of the penis, and cancer of the anus and throat, infect 25.1% of men and 20.4% of women (Bakalar, 2017). There are two vaccines that are effective in preventing these diseases, but they must be administered when children are 11–12 years of age. Sadly, some parents refuse to have their children vaccinated, reasoning that if children know they will probably get cancer they will abstain from premarital sex.

However, since most pornography does feature unsimulated sex without condoms, STIs are still a valid ongoing concern for those who participate in porn production, especially those who are part of smaller, more predatory pornography agencies that do not implement the same standards of practice as more reputable companies.

Aside from the stigmatization of proliferating STIs, pornographic actresses in particular are subject to many other negative stigmas and prejudices. For example, female porn stars are often the target of the "damaged-goods" stigma, which exists when women who have engaged in sex work are considered to have experienced trauma in their past, leading them to helplessly decide on a career in porn (Evans-DeCicco & Cowan, 2001). This stigmatization has extended into a widely held belief that female porn actresses are more likely to be victims of sexual assault, even though rates of child sexual victimization are not statistically different between pornographic actresses and non-pornographic actresses (Griffith, Mitchell, Hart, Adams, & Gu, 2013). This inaccurate belief that pornographic actresses are victims perpetuates the sexualization of vulnerable women and further prejudices their identity as individual agents of their own lives, capable of understanding, navigating, and making decisions of their own informed volition. In addition, these layers of stigma may act to reinforce "proper" sexual behavior in women, so that females who do choose to engage in pornography encounter increasingly high social punishment. Interestingly, the Griffith et al. (2013) study found that pornographic actresses were not only not likely to be victims of sexual assault, but they also reported higher levels of self-esteem and sexual satisfaction compared to women who did not participate in pornographic sex work (Griffith et al., 2013).

While it should be acknowledged that a vast majority of pornographic companies may rely on exploitative business models that target young, inexperienced women with low access to resources, it is impossible to prescribe a universal "bad" association for all actors and actresses. In fact, one of *Time Magazine's* selections for the most influential individuals of 2015 includes multimillionaire and international celebrity Kim Kardashian West (Stewart, 2015), who also happens to be the star of the most-watched pornographic film of all time (Hooton, 2014). Many women have developed successful careers within the pornography industry. One such example is Kelly Madison, who currently manages her own pornography company in which she produces and stars in various pornographic videos and photos, often alongside her husband. Her company, Porn Fidelity, has over 500,000 unique visitors a month, and their produced videos have been viewed millions of times across countless streaming sites. Also known as the "Matriarch of the Mom & Pop Porn Shop" (Simon, 2015), Madison has come to represent the "in-control" image of a woman in porn, and asserts there are plenty of other powerful women within the industry, stating, "I'm more proud to be in this industry now than I was 10 years ago, because there are more female directors, female owners, and the girls certainly don't feel like they have to do whatever they're told to do" (Simon, 2015). Madison's career is just one example of a transforming industry that may be more inclusive toward diverse experiences than ever before.

While ongoing stigmatization of female sexuality is most likely the culprit of negative attitudes regarding females involved in pornography, it's apparent that there are many women in the industry who are able to enjoy, if not profit from, participation in pornographic films and videos.

Gay Male Porn

Women aren't the only ones to experience a diverse set of outcomes relating to pornography participation. The gay male porn industry is also a hugely profitable, complex system of social network sites, video-aggregator sites, DVD production, and print magazines. Porn may play an even larger role in gay men's lives, as studies suggest gay men access pornography more than their heterosexual male counterparts (Downing, Schrimshaw, Scheinmann, Antebi-Gruszka, & Hirschfield, 2016). While straight porn has been known to introduce many young people to the logistics of sex, this process of discovering one's own arousal to same-sex sex behaviors within porn takes on especially profound meanings. And with the development of the Internet, sexual curiosities can now be explored and expressed without the risk of shame and exposure that men previously had to face as they headed to the back rooms of local DVD stores, cloaked in hoodies and sunglasses. Curious if you might be gay? Watching gay porn might give you an indication. Gay porn writer and producer Benjamin Scuglia (2015) explains the transition:

In short, until the Internet revolution, you had to go well out of your way to scratch that itch. Not anymore. With each passing year, as home computers transitioned from bulky desktop behemoths to sleek, lightweight, Internet-enabled smartphones, access to pornographic material becomes faster, easier and cheaper to find. Gay porn evolved very quickly from a niche product with exclusive availability to the equivalent of being available on every street corner. (p. 113)

This process has greatly affected the lives of gay men exploring their sexuality and identity. It can have affirming results for men who are sorting through their own identity formation, and can even destigmatize same-sex attraction when they encounter its ubiquity online. In the popular subreddit forum *r.Gay: Be You,* a thread entitled "How did you know you were gay" echoes this experience. One user wrote:

I knew I was gay when I first started to look at porn. I would watch straight porn and find myself thinking things like, "wow that guy looks good fucking that chick." Basically judging the guys in every scene, and realizing that I looked at the girls less and less each time. One day I just said, "fuck it" and watched a gay porn. After about 5 minutes in I said to myself, "yep, I'm a faggot." (Reddit, 2015 [Internet post])

For men who may not identify as homosexual but may still find themselves having same-sex fantasies, the ease by which gay porn can be accessed allows these individuals additional outlets of exploration. A recent study analyzing the rates and types of pornography accessed by males across different sexual orientations found that over 20% of men who self-identify as heterosexual indicated that they had previously viewed pornography featuring gay men (Downing et al., 2016). Downing and his colleagues also found over half of homosexual men in their study indicated that they watched heterosexual porn, which suggests that "gay porn" and "straight porn" may be watched along similarly varied continuums as sexual orientation itself. As such, pornography appears to operate as a canvas on which one can paint oneself into a wide array of fantasies, couplings, and behaviors. Only instead of a paintbrush, there are bare hands, a mind, and a computer screen. As Camille Paglia once wrote, "Pornography is human imagination in tense theatrical action; its violations are a protest against the violations of our freedom by nature" (Paglia, 1990). As such, gay porn is often a liberating force.

However, as "liberating" as gay porn may be for those oppressed by sexuality niches, the porn industry is not a benevolent force unilaterally bestowing sexual freedom for all who encounter it. Gay porn is a business, and it operates for money. And, ironically, as much as the Internet has liberated gay porn into mass consumption, it has also wreaked economic havoc on the industry itself. Scuglia (2015) writes, "The complete collapse of skin magazines showed that while gay and bisexual men still want to savor explicit photos, not enough of them want to pay for the privilege." As a result, the gay male porn industry has been experiencing an economic "recession" in which companies pay actors less, provide fewer ongoing contracts with actors, and overall, net less revenue than they did in the "heyday" of magazine and DVD production. One contemporary gay male porn star stated in an interview with *Dazed* magazine (Godfrey, 2016):

> Nowadays you have to do a lot more work for a lot less money. If you're not 100 per cent suitable for an exclusive contract, you have to jump from studio to studio. There are more websites available, too, though they're not always as high-budget as porn actors would want it to be.

Gay porn seems to be especially prone to the "porn recession" as gay males develop more interactive and free ways to consume sexually explicit materials beyond just the free-streaming Internet websites. Mobile dating apps such as Grindr and Scruff offer location-based software that was originally designed to help gay men meet one another for a variety of romantic and/or sexual encounters. However, researchers suggest that these apps may be about more than just arranging hookups, and that interchanges themselves can serve as arousing sexual material that is consumed for similar purposes as porn. For example, users may exchange explicit photos or videos of themselves without any pressure or intention to meet up in real life. As such, these apps may be operating as ways to both create do-it-yourself porn and to consume it, with the added titillation of the porn being shared between real-live individuals within similar geographic areas (Tziallas, 2015).

Regardless of the current state of the gay porn industry, these dating apps and the advent of streaming content on the Internet indicate there is still an enormous appetite for gay porn that continues to be enjoyed by a variety of people, gay and straight. In fact, even women enjoy gay porn—a lot. Data from the major porn site Pornhub indicated that the second most searched-for porn among women was gay male porn. It just may be that the same kind of porn is arousing to both gay men and women. Blogger Sadie Smythe, remarked, "I liken it to the reason that hetero men like girl-on-girl porn so much, because chicks get their dicks hard. Men are my weakness, they are the erotic rousers, the lowdown teasers, the totally torrid trippers of my brain's pleasure centers" (Murray, 2011). Apparently gay porn isn't so much of a niche as it is a popular global dish.

Interestingly, women's number two most searched-for pornography, according to Pornhub, doesn't have anything to do with gay men at all. In fact, it doesn't have anything to do with *men* at all.

Gay Female Porn

While gay male porn may seem to be a taste that's shared with a wider audience, gay female porn is more frequently associated with performance for male consumption. In fact, there may need to be clear distinctions made between lesbian porn by lesbians, for lesbians, and lesbian porn by straight men, for straight men. In a study in which responses from lesbian and bisexual women were recorded following the viewing of several popular pornographic films featuring same-sex behavior by women, the general feedback was negative. Lesbians felt the body types of the performers reflected that of a heteronormative, male ideal, that the sex lacked intimacy and emotion, and that the focus was largely on penetration with sex toys and not clitoral stimulation (Morrison & Tallack, 2005). As such, many of the participants felt the porn was not reflective of "real" lesbian sex and was created more for male consumption than for queer audiences.

However, many straight women are likely to consume this lesbian "performance porn" and may still find it to be arousing, because women who watch porn are often more likely to watch the same kinds of pornography as men (Ogas & Gaddam, 2011). In this case, women may be fulfilling similar "forbidden" fantasies as men. In addition, women may find that porn featuring same-sex behaviors between women offers a way to avoid the stigma of female subjugation by men that is often viewed as part of heterosexual pornography, which in turn may add to its ability to arouse female viewers from various sexual orientations (McCutcheon & Bishop, 2015).

One of the reasons there may not be more lesbian porn for lesbian, bisexual, and queer women is because of women's overall lack of interest in porn. Ogas and Gaddam (2011) found that most women do not regularly consume pornography, if at all. This seems to match the data from Pornhub itself, which found that around 24% of all global visitors were female (Pornhub, 2016). This does not at all mean that women do not enjoy pornography or regularly consume it, but it does appear that they are not consuming porn at similar rates to men. Even when looking at lesbian porn made specifically by and for lesbians, the production rates are very small compared to those of male gay porn and infinitesimal compared to heterosexual porn. But, it is still there and carries great significance for lesbian, bisexual, and queer women. The first major lesbian porn company that featured "real lesbian sex" is Fatale Media, which has been producing and distributing lesbian pornography via direct VHS and DVD for over 20 years. There is also the widely popular website Crash Pad, which features streaming lesbian and queer porn for a monthly fee of $22. Surely the creation and maintenance of the lesbian porn industry is an important acknowledgment of lesbian, queer, and bisexual women's identities as sexual beings with the desire to see and experience porn outside of heterosexual, patriarchal constructs.

Pornography and Couples

Pornography is frequently accused of being a "third party" in long-term committed relationships. Pornography viewing is often done in private, or in hiding from a romantic partner. Many people wonder, is it cheating if you partner hurries home to watch porn before you get off work, most likely imagining having sex with the person on the screen, and not you? Is it cheating to watch pornography that feature an actor or actress that you happen to have a crush on in your office, even if you're married or in a long-term partnership? Or simply, is watching porn cheating? While the answers to these questions are generally subjective, social science has begun to peel the veil from the role pornography consumption plays in long-term committed relationships.

However, even with the veil pulled back, the overall picture of the role of porn in relationships is not so clear. Like most topics regarding porn, there are many studies that demonstrate a positive impact, and many that demonstrate a negative one. Among college students in long-term relationships, Morgan (2011) found a correlation between porn consumption and lack of relationship sexual satisfaction. Stack, Wasserman, and Ker (2004) found that individuals who had cheated on their spouses were over three times as likely to indicate using Internet pornography than those who had not cheated on their spouses. In a review of dozens of studies regarding pornography and effects within relationships, Manning et al. (2006) found that results from these studies indicated pornography generally distorted perceptions about relationships, devalued major tenants of marriage such as monogamy and child rearing, increased aggression, and increased sexual deviancy.

But is porn *really* that bad for long-term love? Not universally. There are many new studies emerging that suggest pornography can be positive within relationships. Daneback, Træen, and Månsson (2009) found that couples who used pornography to enhance their sexual relationship were more likely to indicate openness within their relationship. This finding parallels others suggesting that pornography consumption within committed relationships doesn't necessarily predict negative outcomes in the relationship, as long as both partners are honest and open about their pornography consumption. Resch and Alderson (2014) conducted a series of questionnaires with individuals in committed relationships and found that couples who indicated their partners were honest about their porn consumption were more likely to report relationship satisfaction. Indeed, in a sample of married couples who were seeking treatment from therapists in regard to their partner's pornography habits, participants indicated that one of the most painful experiences they were having was lack of trust in their partner (Schneider, 2000). This suggests that a lot of negative impacts from porn consumption within relationships may have to do with its interpretation as a "distrustful activity" by the people involved in the relationship.

So, if you are concerned about the porn consumption by your partner within a romantic relationship, studies seem to suggest that discussing this in an open and honest way may facilitate relationship satisfaction. While deciding if watching porn is or is not cheating is a subjective decision made between those within the relationship themselves, it seems that the more couples try to hide or lie about their porn habits, the worse it gets for the relationship.

In Brief

Pornography may extend beyond contrasts between the private and public spheres. Pornography, in its many varied forms, distributed in its many varied ways, appears to take on extremely personalized attributes depending on the individual and context in which it is produced and consumed. This means participating in porn for some may be the largest regret of their lives, and for others, a liberating expression of identity and sexuality. Many consumers of porn may experience shame, and others, an exploration and affirmation of self. For most, it is a combination of all of these features. In addition, the intersection of pornography and the Internet represents liberated, untethered sexual appetites, which for many may be overwhelming.

However, as we develop our understanding of humans as complex sexual entities and loosen the grip of panicky sexual conservatism, our ideas about what we should or should not consume with regard to pornography should begin to expand and account for individual variation. As porn star Sasha Grey once said, "We have a distorted view of our fantasies, but that's because we don't talk about them enough" (Beaumont-Thomas, 2012). Pornography as such may be a reflection of often hidden personal desires, expressed within the often patriarchal and materialistic society in which we live. Perhaps the more we talk about it, the less distorted our ideas about porn—and ourselves—will be.

Conclusion

Just as we've experienced a revolution in sexual behavior over the last few decades, particularly since the invention of the birth control pill, pornography has also been revolutionized. It was only a few years ago that pornography was associated with sleazy men wearing raincoats going to sleazy theaters, with chewing gum stuck to the floors, and masturbating as they watched the amateurish goings-on on the screen in front of them. This porn was regarded as a perverse and fugitive act. Fast forward just a few decades and we see that pornography has entered middle-class homes as a middle-class enterprise brought to us via a variety of new platforms and new technologies. It is viewed by women as well as men, and no longer carries the stigma of the past.

We know that the effects of pornography can vary widely. It can be benign, an activity that sex therapists often prescribe for couples having sexual problems. Or it can be beyond repugnant and malignant as in snuff films.

Pornography in many ways is still in its infancy. Over the next few years and decades the technology will get far more realistic, become far more interactive, and be far more accepted. Beyond that, it is difficult to know what the effects of this new, extremely sophisticated pornography will be down the road.But we know that they will be big. Today, pornography is a multi-billion-dollar activity, viewed by men and by women, in homes and workplaces, by the religious and the secular, by young and old—as well as by couples in their bedrooms.

As pornography grows in technological sophistication, as it becomes more realistic and more interactive, as its stigma declines, it is indisputable that it will be an increasingly important variable in any future predictions about the sexual norms of the future. One bet we are willing to make, as we look ahead, is this: The growth of pornography will add to the rapidly growing demysti- fication of sexual activity that we see going on in so many different venues and that comes up in nearly every chapter of this book as we peer into the future of love and sex. The sexual taboos and mysteries are declining, with consequences unknown.

10

Sex Dolls and Robots

Sex Dolls

Sex dolls have a long history. Around 1190 BCE, in the *Iliad,* Homer described intelligent robots or "golden servants" created by Hephaetus, the ancient god of technology (Homer & Lattimore, 1961). Accounts of *agalmatophia,* or statue love—indicating that a person has formed a deep romantic attachment to a statue—date back to ancient Greece. Statues in ancient Greece and Rome were often placed at street level, tinted with lifelike colors, thereby making them more lifelike and accessible to touch than statues today (Ellis, 1942). Ancient literary and historical accounts describe the sexual use of statues in Dionysian orgies (Hersey, 2006). A living statue appears memorably and movingly at the end of Shakespeare's *A Winter's Tale.* Other terms for sex dolls are *love dolls, Dutch wives, silent wives, synthetic partners,* and *gynoids.*

The modern sex doll has a direct antecedent in the cotton sex doll created and used by sailors on long voyages, referred to as *dames de voyage* (Bloch, 1908). The Japanese had a version of the dames de voyage, called *a do-ningyo.* Tabori (1969) observes:

> A man who is forced to sleep alone can obtain pleasure with *a do-ninyo.* This is the body of a female doll, the image of a girl of thirteen or fourteen with a velvet vulva. But these dolls are only for people of high rank. (p. 337)

Over the past 20 years, the sex doll industry has grown from producing cheap novelty items to creating a multimillion dollar global industry increasingly featuring high-quality, realistic love dolls. The Japanese are masters of the realistic sex doll (see Illustration 10.1), but Americans are increasingly in the running as well.

Matt McMullen is a California entrepreneur who has been perfecting sex dolls for two decades. He is the CEO of Abyss Creations, maker of the RealDoll, a hyper-realistic silicone sex doll. These dolls, which sell for

What's Next in Love and Sex. Elaine Hatfield, Richard L. Rapson, and Jeanette Purvis, Oxford University Press (2020). © Oxford University Press.
DOI: 10.1093/oso/9780190647162.001.0001

Illustration 10.1 Japanese man, Senji Nakajima, shares a moment with his "perfect partner" (Odunayo, 2016).

upwards of $5,000 apiece, are available in a multitude of different shapes, colors, and sizes. Male and transgender dolls also exist.

But now McMullen has gone one step further. He is attempting to animate his dolls by integrating artificial intelligence within their lifeless silicone forms. Ultimately, he plans to craft dolls that have personalities of the buyer's choosing, as well as customized skin, eyes, and hair. The dolls will give the impression that they are actually thinking, sentient beings. Customers can send in a video of their ideal mate and he will reproduce it perfectly. Soon love dolls will be able to croon to their owners in romantic and entertaining ways, as did the operating system in the movie *Her* or the robot in *Ex Machina*, another film about a potentially disconcerting tomorrow.

McMullen intends the dolls he makes to be loved by their owners, not just be sex objects. These dolls went on sale for about $13,000. Craftsmen expect the next generation of dolls to cost from $30,000 to $60,000. The dolls will be able to display emotion and to dance (right now they have difficulty standing upright; Dube, 2015; Maria, 2016).

There are also love doll escort services. In South Korea and Japan, one can rent a doll for $100 an hour. Sex doll brothels also exist in parts of East Asia.

Currently, most people feel disdain for owners of sex dolls. Psychologists such as Richard von Krafft-Ebing, Magnus Hirschfeld, and Havelock Ellis, in their discussions of people who love statues or dolls, assumed people who violate statues were perverse or pathological. But this view may not be all that true. Sarah Valverde (2012) interviewed more than 60 sex doll owners, using a 45-item online survey she had constructed that assessed their demographic traits. They were asked to describe their relationship status and their satisfaction with human and sex doll partners, including sexual satisfaction and performance. Quality of life was also assessed via the Satisfaction with Life Scale. She found that doll owners aren't very different from people in general. She notes:

> Advances in robotics may one day produce human replicas so realistic as to be mistaken for human. A preference for a synthetic partner could become mainstream behavior and no longer be considered deviant. (Maria, 2016, p. 3)

Robots

People have long been interested in automata—machines that mimic some of the behavior of living creatures. In the 18th century, charlatans and craftsman fascinated the King's court with machines that purported to be almost lifelike. One hoax was an exotic Turk, who challenged bystanders to chess matches. Actually, the "mechanical Turk's" brilliant moves were powered by a chess master hidden behind the Turk's throne. There were swans that could float dreamily in ponds, stretch their necks, and peck at corn; Japanese tea boys, who could serve tea to guests; beautiful dolls who could paint watercolors; dolls that could breathe, eat, drink, and dance. Audiences were dazzled.

From Čapek's (1920/2004) *Rossum's Universal Robots* came today's vision of robots that could think, feel emotions, and fall in love. Čapek had the foresight to worry about the downside of robots, who may come to resent being treated as slaves by human masters and may decide to take over the world. Like most dystopian science fiction, the robots, dolls, and cyborgs in Čapek's world rebel and eventually kill all human beings.

But for the moment, devotees of artificial intelligence are concentrating on producing Prince Charmings and Cinderellas, gorgeous facsimiles, who are charming and intelligent and who laugh at all your jokes. These are totally perfect automata, who are able to truly love you, while fulfilling all your desires. A rapidly growing number of films describe encounters with sexbots, such as *Her, Westworld, Lars and the Real Girl,* and *Ex Machina.* We particularly like the title of a popular TV series about robots called *Humans!*

Current Developments

Since the birth of artificial intelligence in the mid-1950s, great strides have been made in producing a truly intelligent artificial entity. In 1997, in a six-game match, the world's reigning chess champion, Garry Kasparov, was defeated by Deep Blue, an IBM computer. Kasparov accused Deep Blue of cheating.

Computer programs can compose music that rivals or at least mimics the compositions of Wolfgang Amadeus Mozart or Bob Dylan. There are art programs that can paint a seemingly perfect Rembrandt or Picasso facsimile—one so good it fools credulous scholars and collectors.

Robots have long been used in industry to perform dangerous, disagreeable, and boring tasks. Now people in the service industry are joining the queue. Toyota now sells service robots that can look after the elderly, clean house, garden, and serve tea to guests in the afternoon. And there are toys, such as Sony's robotic dog, AIBO.

In Hong Kong, graphic designer Ricky Ma, on a budget of $50,000, has fashioned a lifelike Scarlett Johansson, with dark blonde hair and liquid brown eyes, who can respond to suitors with preprogrammed affection. A 3D-printed skeleton lies beneath Ricky Ma's Mark 1 silicone skin, wrapping its mechanical and electronic parts. The only unrealistic part of Scarlett is that she bows politely in Japanese style, on command (Wu, 2016).

On the horizon are humanoids who can carry on intelligent conversations and tell jokes on any subject, on any level, and in any language. The next challenge for entrepreneurs is inventing androids that possess powerful emotions—or at least simulate them. Will they actually be able to love? And how might sex emerge in this brave new world?

Will People Fall in Love with Robots?

Continuing advances in computers and robotics will make legal marriages between *Homo* and *Robo* feasible by mid-century.

—David Levy

Once manufacturers craft machines that simulate love (and eventually actually feel love), will people purchase and fall in love with such perfect machines? The bet is yes. In David Levy's (2007) fascinating book, *Love + Sex with Robots,* he makes a compelling case for that proposition.

People love their pets. They attribute all sorts of ideas, feelings, and intentions to them. "But my dog loves me," they insist. Many young children can't get to sleep without cuddling their favorite doll. Children love My Real Baby, manufactured by the toy giant Hasbro, which moves its face in a babyish way, makes realistic sounds, and exhibits babyish emotions. Children take a maternal role with them, insisting that Baby needs their protection. A 2007 AP-AOL Autos poll found that 44% of women and 30% of men say they think of their car as having a personality of its own (O'Carroll, 2015). Many cars are given pet names.

But what about romantic robots? What if your bot knows your name? Appears fully human? Can interact with you? What if your bot not only whispers "I love you" but seems to pass every test that you can devise to test its affection? What then? What if the bot actually feels love? Will you love him or her back?

People have a great capacity for love, and the best bet is that many will. As any user of Tinder or Match.com can tell you, it is hard to find a suitable mate, or any mate at all. As alternatives such as sex robots become more and more realistic and affordable, many individuals may simply come to prefer this nontraditionally partnered sex to the "old-fashioned" way. This may already be occurring; futurists such as Levy (2007) predict that by 2050 robots will transform human notions of love and sexuality.

What *does* seem to me to be entirely reasonable and extremely likely—nay, inevitable—is that many humans will expand their horizons of love and sex, learning, experimenting, and enjoying new forms of relationship that will be made possible, pleasurable, and satisfying through the development of highly sophisticated humanoid robots. . . . Love and sex with robots on a grand scale are inevitable. (p. 22)

Levy also believes that humans will fall in love with robots, marry robots, and have sex with robots, all as (what will be regarded as) "normal" extensions of our feelings of love and sexual desire (p. 22).

He also contends that, by 2050, human-on-robot love/sex will be more common than human-on-human love/sex. There is some merit to his proposal. In April, 2017, in a small village outside of Paris, a young woman named Lilly married a robot she had built herself, named Moovator. In a story reminiscent of the Greek myth of Pygmalion, she said, "Love is love." She prefers mechanical flaws (errors in code) to human ones—like alcoholism, violence, and alcoholism (CNNMoney, April 15, 2017).

One is left to ponder:

What kind of robot personality will be desired when anyone can have anything they want . . . for a price?

Is it ethical to allow people to engage in sadomasochism with a sentient robot? To participate in child sexuality?

In 2006, Ray Kurzweil published a book entitled *The Singularity Is Near,* in which he argued that as computers get increasingly human-like (even reproducing themselves), and as people use computers to supplement their own intelligence and biological skills (their minds becoming trillions of times more powerful than they are today), a time will come when it will become increasingly difficult to tell human from machine. That is the singularity: the moment when we'll no longer be able to tell humans and their machines apart.

He predicts that 2045 will be the year when that transformation occurs. Many futurists disagree with these predictions, of course, postulating that the merger of humans and machines will take much longer (Markoff, 2016). But few doubt that the merger will someday take place.

If this singularity in fact occurs, what will this mean for the future of human connection and reproduction?

The Ethics of Sex Dolls and Robots

One bit of evidence that we are not looking into some distant future is that people already think of sex dolls and robots as real people. Look at the indignation sparked by the visions of people who apparently want to have sex with dolls and robots. To get a feel for the fury such activities provoke, think of people who want to have sex with child dolls (see Illustration 10.2)

Recently, Australian authorities cracked down on the importation, sale, and possession of "child sex dolls." Shin Takagi, the manufacture of these lifelike dolls, observes that they are made of material that resembles human skin. The dolls, which have names like Lemonade Bonbon or Leopard Sisters, and are sold wearing schoolgirl uniforms or lingerie (Homer, 2016). The creator told the *Atlantic* that he believes that the dolls can help pedophiles—pedophiles who have sexual urges toward children but have never acted on them—to express their fetish in a way that doesn't actually harm kids. He says:

> I often receive letters from buyers. The letters say, "Thanks to your dolls, I can keep from committing a crime." I hear statements like that from doctors, prep school teachers—even celebrities. (p. 2)

There is no evidence one way or another that what he says is true. Some cognitive behavioral therapists like Peter Fagin, from John Hopkins School of Medicine, worries that such dolls might have a reinforcing effect on pedophilic ideation and cause people to transfer their affection to real children.

Illustration 10.2 Child sex dolls.
Permission granted by Shin Takagi.

Child sex dolls are *probably* legal. No one as yet has been arrested for possession of such a doll. In 2002, the U.S. Supreme Court legalized virtual child pornography—a cartoon or media depicting simulated sex with underage children but where no actual sex occurred. The child sex doll probably is protected under the virtual child pornography ruling. In Japan, Hentai pornography, featuring teenage girls, is perfectly legal. That might be a place to start in investigating the impact of sex dolls and Hentai pornography on pedophilic activities.

More Reflections

The technological transformations (or gizmos, depending on your point of view) described in this chapter are barely the tip of the iceberg heading our way. We are in an era of exponential technological creativity, and technology is as big a force in changing the world as any other—perhaps even the biggest.

In our final chapter (Chapter 12), we will mention many more of these innovations, but the big question about all of this remains: Are we talking about games and toys, or are we talking about a psychological revolution? With computer apps, are we noticing sexual and dating activities engaged in mostly by young people, just before they settle down to finding and maintaining a long-term relationship, call it marriage or something else? And how "traditional" will that long-term relationship be?

The new technologies can be forecast, and futurists and engineers are boldly creating incredible and terrifying new possibilities, ranging from designer babies to sex robots to perhaps significantly longer lifespans. What is much harder to predict are their consequences for human behavior, particularly in the sex-and-love game.

Many of these self-same prophets of the future often, with great confidence, pour out their opinions about these consequences. But that's really all they can be—opinions. In our final chapter, we will attempt to do the same, but we do so with sincere humility and a little self-mocking humor. This is because no one knows what the future holds.

The best we can do is attempt to make some informed guesses. So before we all go out and buy our sex dolls, let us turn to two final subjects. First, in the next chapter (Chapter 11), the difficulty in maintaining those long-term

relationships. Then, finally, those (we hope) informed guesses about tomorrow (Chapter 12).

The Master Becomes the Slave

In this text, when we speculate about "the future," we mean the relatively near
future—2040 is about as far as we go. But some futurists are more ambitious.
They point out that humankind will be evolving more slowly than robots
and, in the end, we will be relatively inferior to our once robotic slaves.

Many futurists speculate that computers will soon surpass humans in intelligence and that these self-same machines will possess the capacity to construct the next generation of machines so brilliant that *Homo sapiens* will
be reduced to obsolescence. Y. Noah Harai (2017), in *Homo Deus: A Brief
History of Tomorrow*, observes:

> Every animal—including *Homo sapiens*—is an assemblage of organic
> algorithms shaped by natural selection over millions of years of evolu-
> tion. . . . There is no reason to think that organic algorithms can do things
> that nonorganic algorithms will never be able to replicate and surpass.
> (p. 101)

Currently, computers are giving humans a run for their money: They can,
already to some extent, exceed the cognitive, emotional, and behavioral
capabilities of humankind. One story in Harai's book is of the musician
and programmer David Cope, who wrote a program that creates Bach's
compositions. Concertgoers describe the compositions as having touched
their "innermost being"—and are furious when told that the music had been
created by a device whose "innermost being" happened to be composed of a
mesh of silicone and copper.

It is just a matter of time until the human algorithm is replaced by infi-
nitely more sophisticated alternatives. As Harai notes, "It is not the specter
of mass extinction that is hanging over us. It is the specter of mass obsolescence" (p. 395). A new TV series, *Humans,* depicts this transition. The
Synths start out as servants, superior in every way to humankind, and end
up gaining consciousness and rebelling. The tables are turned. The Synths are
no better and no worse in morality and kindness than the humans who con-
ceived of them.

No one knows whether this chilling (or inspiring, depending on your point of view) set of prophecies is merely fanciful science fiction or impending reality. But in trying to anticipate future developments in love and sex, it would be foolish to pooh-pooh the possibility that artificial intelligence and superior machines will play an increasing—even dominant—role in our lives.

11

The End of the Affair

Today, most people are fairly optimistic about the fate of love. They believe their current love affairs will last forever. Yet, the odds are against a youthful romance deepening into a long and satisfying marriage. Hill, Rubin, and Peplau (1979) interviewed 231 young Boston couples to find out what happened to young love affairs over a two-year period. At the start, most couples (60%) saw each other every day. Most (75%) were dating exclusively. Some (20%) were living together. A few (10%) were engaged. The authors interviewed these same couples again six months, one year, and two years later. By the end of two years, 45% of them had broken up. In Britain, 6 out of 10 young people said they despair of ever finding "The One." The average woman enjoys two long-term relationships and has her heart broken twice before she finds a mate (*Daily Mail Reporter*, 2014). And the sailing obviously isn't always smooth after that.

Couples had the best chance of staying together if, from the start, they were in love, had an intimate relationship, and were *equally* committed to one another. (Try as one might, one person cannot will a relationship. It takes two to love.) Couples did best if they were well matched from the start: They were equally attractive, about the same age, possessed comparable levels of intelligence and educational attainments, and had similar aspirations. Opposites may attract for passionate love and sex, but quasi-clones do better for the long run!

Hill and his colleagues (1979) found that very few of the breakups (7%) were truly mutual. Women were more eager to break up (51% of women compared to 42% of men). Generally, women were the first to recognize that a relationship was going nowhere. Women tended to be very sensitive to interpersonal problems; they could easily identify the specific difficulties that had led to the breakup: "He wants a traditional marriage; I don't." "I am smarter

What's Next in Love and Sex. Elaine Hatfield, Richard L. Rapson, and Jeanette Purvis, Oxford University Press (2020). © Oxford University Press.
DOI: 10.1093/oso/9780190647162.001.0001

than he is." "Our interests are wildly different." "I want to be independent." "I was attracted to another man." Men tended to be less sure about what caused the breakup. When they did acknowledge problems, they tended to focus on external problems ("We lived too far apart; it took me an hour to get to her house.") Couples rarely agreed on what caused the breakup or on how gradually (or abruptly) it came about.

In a more recent meta-analysis of predictors of romantic dissolution, data were collected from 37,761 participants, in 137 studies, conducted over 33 years. Le and his colleagues (2010) examined the individual, relationship, and external variables that determined whether a couple stayed together or broke up. They found that personality variables weren't as important as one might think. Personality measures, such as self-esteem and the Big Five personality variable—such as openness, conscientiousness, extroversion, agreeableness, and neuroticism—were found to have limited predictive ability (see Fig. 11.1).

It was relationship variables—such as positive illusions about the other, love, and commitment—that were among the strongest predictors of relationship stability and success. Other relational variables such as intimacy, trust, self-disclosure, closeness, investments in the relationship, adjustment, satisfaction, and dependence were moderately associated with relationship stability. The more ambivalence and the more alternatives a couple had, the greater the chance that they would break up. One external factor mattered too: the more social support for the relationship, the less likely the relationship was to break up.

Predictors of Relationship Success	Predictors of Relationship Dissolution
Positive Illusions	Ambivalence
Commitment	Alternatives to The Relationship
Love	Attachment Avoidance
Social Support	Anxiety

Fig. 11.1 A sample of significant predictors of relationship success (from Le et al., 2010).

How Long Does Love Last?

The best divorce is the one you get before you get married.

—Folk saying

Passion sometimes burns itself out. Consider this exchange between anthropologist Shostak (1981) and a!Kung (African) tribesman, as they observed a young married couple, running after each other:

> As I stood watching, I noticed the young man sitting in the shade of a tree, also watching. I said, "They're very much in love, aren't they?" He answered, "Yes, they are." After a pause, he added, "For now." I asked him to explain, and he said, "When two people are first together, their hearts are on fire and their passion is very great. After a while, the fire cools and that's how it stays. . . . They continue to love each other, but it's in a different way—warm and dependable." . . . How long did this take? "It varies among couples. A few months, usually; sometimes longer. But it always happens." Was it also true for a lover? "No," he explained, "feelings for a lover stay intense much longer, sometimes for years." (p. 268)

Helen Fisher (2004a) argues that the transient nature of passionate love is a cultural universal. She believes that our *Homo sapiens* ancestors experienced passionate love and sexual desire for very practical genetic reasons. Our hominid ancestors were primed to fall ardently, sexually in love for about four years. This is precisely the amount of time it takes to conceive a child and take care of it until it is old enough to survive on its own. (In tribal societies, children are relatively self-sufficient by this age. That means they generally prefer to spend most of their time playing with other children.) Once our ancestors no longer had a practical reason for remaining together, they had every evolutionary reason to fall out of love with their previous partner and to fall in love with someone new.

Why were people programmed to engage in such serial pair-bonding? Fisher maintains that such serial monogamy produces maximum genetic diversity, which is an evolutionary advantage. To test her hypothesis that, generally, love is fleeting, Fisher (1989) examined the divorce rates in collecting/hunting, agricultural, pastoral, fishing, and industrial societies, scouring ethnographic records and the *Demographic Yearbooks* of the United Nations.

She found that, as predicted, throughout the world, couples most commonly divorced in their fourth year of marriage.

She argues that the same evolutionary forces that influenced our ancestors yesterday shape the modern cross-cultural pattern of marriage/divorce/re-marriage today. Fisher's ideas are stimulating, but her exclusion of cultural forces, considering their omnipresence in nearly all matters related to love and sex, mandate a certain skepticism on the part of the reader.

In 1981, Traupmann and Hatfield conducted a series of interviews that assessed the level of passionate and companionate love in a random sample of 953 dating couples, newlyweds, and older women who had been married for an average of 33 years. (The older women ranged in age from 50 to 82 and had been married from 1 to 59 years.) They found that passionate love decreased precipitously over time. Asked to rate their feelings on a scale that included the responses "none at all," "very little," "some," "a great deal," and "a tremendous amount," steady daters and newlyweds expressed "a great deal" of passionate love for their mates, but starting shortly after marriage, love declined steadily, with the group of older women saying that they and their husbands felt "some" passionate love for each other.

The prevailing wisdom has always been that while the fires of passionate love may only blaze for a few years, with time they are replaced by the steady glow of companionate love, contentment, and commitment. This is not what the authors found. Both passionate and companionate love tended to erode at the same rate (see Fig. 11.2).

How do we interpret this surprising finding? One can draw an optimistic or a pessimistic conclusion. On the positive side, even after several years of marriage, people were still reporting high levels of both passionate and com-panionate love. Women married less than 33 years, for example, reported feeling in between "some" and "a great deal" of passionate and companionate love for their partners. Women married much longer also continued to feel "some" passionate love and "a great deal" of companionate love. While we expected companionate love to remain uniformly high (or even increase) throughout the life cycle, the finding that passionate feelings also remained quite high is encouraging. Contrary to what is often portrayed by the mass media, older persons married for several years can still experience passion and excitement in their intimate relationships.

However, if one wants to interpret the results pessimistically, then em-phasis can be given to the significant difference found between people married for less than 33 years and those married for over 33 years. Women

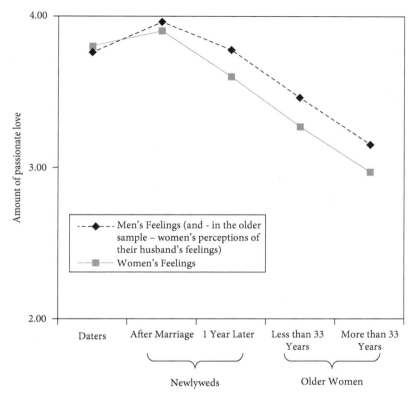

Fig. 11.2 Dating couples', newlywed couples', and older women's passionate love for their partners.

married for longer periods of time did report slightly less passionate and companionate love than did women married for a shorter period of time. (This is especially discouraging, since couples so unhappy they divorced are not, naturally, included in this sample.)

Traupmann and Hatfield's findings are backed by other, more recent research. In a 1999 study, Sprecher and Metts found that although couples in relationships claimed that their love had deepened over time, they were wrong; their memories were faulty. In a study of dating couples, Sprecher administered two questionnaires to each member five times over a four-year period. The questionnaires included a survey asking about feelings of love, satisfaction, and commitment, and another one that contained scales to measure actual levels. She found that although couples insisted they loved more than ever, in fact, love and satisfaction decreased somewhat with the passage of time. Even couples on the brink of a breakup reported that they loved their partners as much as ever. Again, their memories had failed them. Thus, it is possible that either people believe that love increases even when it does not (consistent with Karney & Frye's [2002] findings on recall of satisfaction), or perhaps the meaning of love changes over time so that what was considered love last year is now considered a shallow affection.

In any case, there are some happy exceptions to this dismal prognosis. Interview data (Acevedo & Aron, 2009) suggest that at least some couples may not be deceiving themselves but actually telling it like it is. This cheerful prognosis is supported by fMRI data in married couples reporting intense passionate love even though they've been married an average of 21.4 years: fMRI studies show brain activation similar to that found in early-stage passionate love (Acevedo, Aron, Fisher, & Brown, 2012). Aron et al. (2000) were able to increase reported passionate love (at least temporarily) in long-term relationship partners through an experimental task, suggesting there may be natural mechanisms that permit high levels of passionate love even in long-term relationships. Further, a randomized clinical trial experiment showed that couples who performed exciting activities for 90 minutes per week for 4 weeks had increased relationship excitement, positive affect, and satisfaction 4 months later (Coulter & Malouff, 2013). Expressions of love, respect, passion, and desire predicted relationship satisfaction 15 months later in an observational longitudinal dyadic study (Graber, Laurenceau, Miga, Changan, & Coan, 2011). Meta-analytic synthesis of 137 studies indicated that love was positively associated with nonmarital relationship stability and permanence (Le, Dove, Agnew, Korn, & Mutso, 2010). Further, brain activation in areas associated with passionate love and reward are positively correlated with satisfaction in long-term couples (Acevedo et al., 2012). There is also evidence that brain activation early on in a relationship predicts relationship stability and quality up to 40 months later (Xu et al., 2011).

What makes these long-term relationships go so well? That is a question that merits a book in itself and is outside the scope of this text. For more information on the topic, see work by Gottman, Gottman, and Silver (1995).

Emotions Associated with Breakups

There ain't no cure for love.

—Leonard Cohen

Not surprisingly, Hill et al. (1979), in their study of Boston couples over a two-year period, found that it is easier to leave someone than to be left. Both men and women felt considerably less depressed, less lonely, freer, happier, and more relieved (but guiltier) when they were the rejecting lover than if they were rejected. In fact, the emotional reactions of the mates tended to be mirror opposites of one another: the happier one person was to get out, the worse their partner felt about the breakup. Men were hit harder than women by the breakup. The authors report:

> Men tended more than women to report that in the wake of the breakup they felt depressed, lonely, less happy, less free, but less guilty. . . . Some men found it extremely difficult to reconcile themselves to the fact that they were no longer loved and that the relationship was over. . . . Women who are rejected may also react with considerable grief and despair, but they seem less likely to retain the hope that their rejectors "really love them after all." (p. 78)

Breaking Up Is Hard to Do

Judith Martin (1979), in *Miss Manners: Guide to Excruciatingly Correct Behavior*, had advice for couples who want to break up:

Dear Miss Manners:

I am interested in knowing what is the proper method of breaking off a relationship. For the past several months, I have been exclusively dating a young lady whom I was extremely fond of. Everything seemed to be going great until about two months ago, when she suddenly seemed to lose interest in me. Every time I wanted to see her, she was busy, etc., until finally I just stopped calling her. I have not heard from her since. What do you think of breaking off a relationship in this manner, and how should it be handled? (p. 285)

Miss Manners pointed out that there is no good way to end a relationship without hurting someone. Fast or slow, the period of suffering takes a long time. At first you don't believe she could have lost interest in you. Then you pay attention. You test your hypotheses by ending your calls, then you have proof. Miss Manners observed:

> Thus, the proper behavior for someone whose heart is breaking is to be cheerful, not pained; ungrudgingly forgiving, not accusing; busy, not free to be comforted; mysterious, not willing to talk the situation over; absent not obviously alone or overdoing attentions to others.
>
> Such behavior will have two rewards. First, it will take the sufferer's mind off suffering and begin the recovery. Second, it will make the former lover worry that this supposed act of cruelty was actually a relief to the person it should have hurt. That hurts. (p. 286)

Many people linger too long in a failing relationship because they don't want to hurt the other person. They worry that family and friends will consider them to be the bad guy. In the old days it was assumed that the couple would go to a private place, they would have a long conversation, ending in the decision not to see one another again. Sometimes both people were relieved to be out of the relationship. More often there were tears, recriminations, and begging for one more chance. Not infrequently did the end precipitate depression in one or both of the partners, occasionally and tragically leading to suicide, especially among the young.

That isn't the case today. True, when people are asked how they *wish* their partner had announced that they were through, they say they wished they could have met in person and had an honest discussion as to what went wrong. That rarely happens, however, since the person who wants out desires anything but a "heart to heart": They yearn for some trick that would allow them to "run away" and escape all the drama and recriminations. Sadly, whatever the method people use, breaking up remains painful.

When those heart-to-heart conversations *do* occur, people don't always tell the truth. But smart people learn to decode the messages. "It's not you, it's me," really means "I think I can do better," "You are a nice person, but . . .," means "I've met someone else." "I need to find myself," means "You are starting to drive me crazy." "I'm going off to school" means "The sex is terrible."

In 1975, Paul Simon, in his iconic song, "There are Fifty Ways to Leave a Lover," detailed the many strategies to end a relationship.

> You Just slip out the back, Jack
> Make a new plan, Stan
> You don't need to be coy, Roy
> Just get yourself free
> Hop on the bus, Gus
> You don't need to discuss much
> Just drop off the key, Lee
> And get yourself free

Again, heartbroken people say they want the hard facts, but in truth, scholars find, they are happier when they are lied to.

In recent years, a new wrinkle has been added. People used to tell horror stories about lovers who left a Post-it on the refrigerator saying, "I'm outta here. Sorry." Now, there is the Facebook breakup. You are browsing through your girlfriend's Facebook page and you notice that she suddenly lists herself as "single" and your face has been scratched out on all the photographs. Then you get it: "I'm outta here. Sorry." In fact, there is a Facebook vacuum cleaner designed to systematically hide pictures of you and your ex from your news feed, and to generally minimize their presence in your Facebook experience. If you date online, you can often expect to break up online. According to the *Match singles*, 48% of their breakups took place over email. Luckily, though, only 5% of total breakups occurred over text message. We fear that number will rise in the future. There is even a term for people who were once close but simply quit writing without explanation—it is called "ghosting."

There now exists a breakup service to do lovers' dirty work (Dortonne, 2016). The Canadian duo, Mackenzie and Evan Keast, will cut relations with your lover, for a price. The breakup phone calls costs $10 and $29. The site gets 3,000 hits a day from around the world. The shop offers other options, like a card that smells like poop, a handcrafted note, and a gift box that can be set on fire. The gift boxes include a movie, *The Notebook,* or a video game, *Call of Duty,* a Netflix gift card, and two wine glasses.

People often end a relationship by saying, "Let's stay friends. Let's stay in touch." How often are men and women able to remain friends after the breakup? Scholars find that if the man rejected the woman, it was possible for love to turn into friendship. (Couples remained "just friends"

70% of the time.) If the woman left the man, however, they were usually not able to remain friends. (Couples remained friends only 46% of the time) Metts, Cupach, and Bejlovec (1989). The authors painted a more optimistic picture of the possibilities of turning love into friendship. They found that if couples were friends before the breakup, treated one another fairly during the relationship, and were open and honest with each other when the time came to break up, their chances of remaining friends were vastly improved.

A girl must marry for love, and keep on marrying until she finds it.
—Zsa Zsa Gabor

The Emotions People Feel After a Breakup

Researchers have documented the devastating array of emotions people experience after a breakup. When an affair ends, many young people suffer a storm of emotions—elation and relief (if they wanted the affair to end). And, if they didn't long for that ending, then love, sadness and depression, guilt, anger and bitterness, jealousy, and loneliness follow (see de Jong-Gierveld, 1986; Field, 2011, Perilloux & Buss, 2008, Perlman & Peplau, 1981, for a review of typical reactions). Most newly separated lovers experience a mixture of feelings.

Love
At times, the estranged are filled with love for their mates. They think of the early days of their relationship when things went so well.

Denial
Social commentators rarely talk about denial, but, as one of our informants said:

I think the one emotion that I see the most is denial. Many of my friends cannot believe it is actually happening to them. They wait and wait. Sometimes they will even shoot a "drunk text" (a text after a few drinks) to their boyfriend saying how much they miss him and how much they need to talk to him.

Elation

Some feel surprisingly elated once they have made a decision and have "escaped to freedom." We have seen clients who, after agonizing for years over their decision, are filled with joy and unspeakable relief the moment they walk into their new apartment. "Hell Yeah! I'm free!" or "Thank God," they shout to the walls. These are people who did their grieving while *in* the relationship; they probably completed that process before they physically separated from their mates. They may luxuriate in getting to watch the TV programs they like for a change, spending their money as they like without a Greek chorus of criticism, disciplining or treating the children as they please, and going to sleep when they are tired. They may feel sheepish about feeling so good so soon, but they probably had their share of sorrow before they could experience such pure relief.

Confusion

There are some ideas we hold so deeply that we would have trouble even labeling them as an idea. We tend to think of them as eternal truths. Many people take it for granted that if they love someone, are kind and generous to them, that person will love them back. After a divorce, they are stunned. "How could she not love me when I loved her so much?" they ask again and again in disbelief. "She'll never find someone who loves her as much as I do." (Outside observers, of course, may be bemused by their confusion. Whoever said love was fair?)

"He's so wonderful 25% of the time. Why can't he *always* be that nice?" they ask. They then run through a series of strategies, sometimes going at it for decades—sweetness, persuasion, guilt manipulations, and trying to inspire jealousy. There are anger and tears—designed to inspire the loving side of their mate. Again, the observers smile ruefully. They know full well that if someone is nice 25% of the time and awful 75% of the time, with five years of continuous work, the 25%-er could probably move up to being a 26.7%-er. (Insanity, said the ancients, is doing the same thing over and over and expecting it, this time, to come out differently. This time Lucy won't pull away the football when Charlie Brown runs up to kick it.)

Couples may make love in the evening and find themselves telling their divorce lawyer the next afternoon that they have put their love affair back together. Or, they wish to put the divorce on hold until they to go away the next weekend to "say goodbye." They are ashamed at their ambivalence. One man reported:

I was gone for a week and I came back. . . . And we had the most fantastic weekend, really. It was great, it was fantastic. And then things started up again. The bickering, the whole thing, started up Sunday. (Weiss, 1979, p. 209)

Sadness

Researchers (Means, 1991) interviewed college students who recently broke up. Almost all the men and women said they were still feeling strong love for their partners. Their relationships had all been exclusive; they were psychologically involving and important. To some extent, both wanted the relationship to continue. Nonetheless, it had failed. Two months after things had fallen apart, over 40% of students in these doomed relationships were still experiencing clinically measurable depression.

One of our students wrote an essay entitled "Why me, God: Why me?" In her story of unrequited love, we see many of these themes.

"Why me, God? Why me! What have I done to deserve such pain?" These are the words I keep repeating over and over to myself. It does not seem fair. What have I done to deserve this excruciating pain that is tearing my heart into millions of pieces? Is it all my fault? Did I expect too much out of life? All I know is that God, it hurts so bad and I am so lonely, I know the hurt will never ever go away.

But you say I am much too young to feel such a pain! At the age of 19 I feel the same pain a person of 50 would feel. Never in my life had I dreamt such pain existed. The hurt is unbearable. It tears up every functioning organ that created life for me. I was 14 years old when the relationship started. Young you say, but the hurt I received when it ended felt as if it could kill off the entire population of the world.

Guilt

Expressing guilt, couples may worry, "Maybe I should have tried harder."

Anger and Bitterness

Sometimes when the newly separated think back on their relationship, a flood tide of anger is released. They may have suppressed their own feelings for decades in the interests of harmony. Now they realize how angry they had been for so much of the time. One young woman observed:

> In separating from someone you discover in yourself things that you had never felt before in your life. That's one of the things that really freaks you out. I've always used my mind to keep down anything I didn't like. And now I discover, wow, I can hate! (Weiss, 1979, p. 208)

Loneliness

Researchers point out that the divorced can suffer from either emotional loneliness (the lack of a special someone to love) or from social loneliness (the lack of friends and acquaintances). Many newly separated and divorced couples suffer from both. Jenny de Jong-Gierveld (1986) interviewed 556 men and women, who ranged in age from 25 to 75. The loneliest people were parents without partners (60% of them mentioned feelings of loneliness); 50% of those who lived alone and 13% of those living with somebody admitted to emotional loneliness. In one study, 48% of widows viewed loneliness as the major problem of widowhood (Lopata, 1969). The lonely hunger for love, and in its absence, they may also be angry, anxious, bored, or depressed (Perlman & Peplau, 1981).

Three psychologists (Russell, Peplau, & Ferguson, 1978) have developed a loneliness scale (see Table 11.1). How would you answer a sampling of questions from this scale?

Gender Differences in Dealing with Loss

Orimoto, Hatfield, Yamakawa, and Denney (1991) interviewed 237 University of Hawaii students, asking them how they felt after a recent breakup and how they tried to cope with the situation. The authors found that men's and women's emotional reactions differed surprisingly little. Both men and women were usually devastated by the breakup. They felt a kaleidoscope of emotions—love, anger, and, grief, as well as occasional relief that things were finally over.

How did they deal with their feelings and with the practical problems they faced following the breakup? Women were more likely to try to focus on the problem and try to figure out what had happened and what could they do

Table 11.1 The UCLA Loneliness Scale

For the following questions, you are to circle the choice that best illustrates how often each of the statements would be descriptive of you.

O = (4) I *often* feel this way.
S = (3) I *sometimes* feel this way.
R = (2) I *rarely* feel this way.
N = (1) I *never* feel this way.

1. I am unhappy doing so many things alone.	O S R N
2. I have nobody to talk to.	O S R N
3. I lack companionship.	O S R N
4. I feel as if nobody really understands me.	O S R N
5. I find myself waiting for people to call or write.	O S R N
6. There is no one I can turn to.	O S R N
7. I feel left out.	O S R N
8. I feel starved for company.	O S R N

Note: The higher the score, the more lonely people are said to be.

to make improvements next time around. Mainly however, both men and women used similar strategies. Both men and women felt that they should have coped better than they actually did. There were a few differences, however.

1. *Women paid attention to the problem.* They were more prone to cry, to talk to their friends, to read self-help books and magazines, and to see therapists in an effort to better understand the workings of love.

Men and women were equally likely to use the other techniques.

2. *Both men and women sometimes tried to play things down.* They tried to hide their feelings so others wouldn't know what they were going through. They binged. They drank or took drugs (tranquilizers, sleeping pills, marijuana). They went out of their way to avoid bumping into the one they loved. They avoided going to places or doing things that had been parts of their lives together. They stayed in bed.

3. *Both used cognitive techniques to manage their feelings.* They talked to themselves like a Dutch uncle. "Who needs him (or her) anyway?" "It's

his (her) loss!" "There are lots of good fish in the sea." "I'm lucky to have gotten out of that relationship." Or, "You've learned a valuable lesson."

4. *Both tried to distract themselves from their loss.* They did things to improve their looks or sex appeal (got a haircut, bought clothes, or went on a diet). They kept themselves busy with sports, schoolwork, or career. They engaged in physical activities (they jogged, played basketball, or went swimming).

Helen Fisher and her colleagues (2010) studied men and women who had just been jilted by their beloved. First, the researchers hung a flyer on the SUNY at Stony Brook bulletin board: "Have you just been rejected in love but can't let go?" Rejected sweethearts were quick to respond. In initial interviews, Fisher found that heartbroken men and women were caught up in a swirl of conflicting emotions—they were still wildly in love, yet feeling abandoned, depressed, angry, and in despair.

But what was going on in their brains? To find out, Fisher and her colleagues followed the same protocol they had used in testing men and women who were happily in love—they asked participants to alternately view a photograph of their one-time beloved and a photograph of a familiar, but emotionally neutral individual. The authors found that jilted lovers' brains "lit up" in the areas associated with anxiety, pain, and attempts at controlling anger—as well as in those associated with addiction, risk taking, and obsessive/compulsive behaviors. Jilted lovers did, indeed, appear to experience a storm of passion—passionate love, sexual desire, plus anguish, rejection, rage, emptiness, and despair. (For additional information on the brain activity of women grieving from the loss of a romantic relationship, see Najib, Lorberbaum, Kose, Bohning, and George [2004].)

The newly broken-up are also vulnerable to a variety of mental and physical health problems (Traupmann & Hatfield, 1981). Means (1991) interviewed college students who had recently broken up with their partner. Almost all of them admitted that they were still feeling strong love for their partner. To some extent, both wished the relationship had been a success. Nonetheless, it had failed. Two months after things had fallen apart, over 40% of students in these doomed relationships were still experiencing clinically measurable depression. Scores on the Beck Depression Inventory (Beck, Steer, & Brown, 1996) revealed that 2% of them were experiencing "severe depression," 10% were experiencing "moderate to severe depression," 31% were experiencing "mild to moderate depression," and 1% were experiencing "minimal" depression."

Gardner (2005), a clinical psychologist in Glasgow, said, "People can die from a broken heart" (p. 1). There is evidence he may be right. Sbarra, Smith, and Mehl (2012) conducted a meta-analysis of 12 studies, involving 366,610 people who had just suffered a breakup. The average study followed participants for 12+ years. They found that separation can take a terrible toll on health. Field (2011) reviewed the medical literature and found that bereavement increases a person's vulnerability to mental illness. Heartbreak also sparks a variety of medical problems. These include intrusive thoughts, insomnia, alcoholism and drug use, heartbreak syndrome (i.e., experiencing faux heart attacks), and a compromised immune system. It can spark a variety of physical symptoms, including migraines, headaches, facial pain, rashes, indigestion, peptic ulcers, weight gain or loss, heart palpitations, chest pain, asthma, and infections. Bereavement is also known to increase susceptibility to diabetes, heart disease, tuberculosis, and cirrhosis of the liver. It predisposes people to engage in risky behaviors—such as smoking, drinking, and drug use. The bereaved are also more likely to die from natural causes and accidents, twice as likely to commit suicide, and more likely to be murdered than married people (Bloom, White, & Asher, 1979; Graf, 2016; Hatfield & Rapson, 1993). In a study of 1,580,000 people in Finland, it was found that in the first few weeks after a partner's death, the bereaved are at a great risk of death—from accidents, violence, and alcohol-related causes, from chronic ischemic heart disease and lung cancer (20–35%), as well as from other causes. The effect is short-lived but pronounced; interestingly, men suffer more than women (Martikainen & Valkonen, 1996a, 1996b).

Conclusion

Today, most young people go through many relationships and experience the pain of a disappointing love affair time after time. And while in Chapter 5 we focused not just on the joys of love but also on the pathos of lost love and people's longing for the supposed stabilities of the past, it is well to remind ourselves of a few truths. First, humans often learn through pain. By experiencing many relationships, people develop the opportunity for gaining an understanding of themselves, others, and the complexities of love. Most modern people may be significantly smarter about love, through experience, than were their ancestors. And second, more of us *have* loved. The taste of love can be so sweet (or bittersweet) that lost love deters us from seeking more love for only a short while. Fewer lines of poetry are spoken more frequently, almost to the point of cliché, than those composed in 1850, at the height of the Romantic Movement, by Alfred, Lord Tennyson: "Tis better to have loved and lost / Than never to have loved at all."

But in the last analysis, we wish to leave the reader of this chapter about love, sex, and intimacy with this paradox: The best way to gain a fulfilling relationship lies not in an obsession with love but with greater efforts toward building a balanced life based on one's unique biology, history, personality, and individuality. Romantic intimacy can bestow on us one of the glories of being alive. But there are other kinds of intimacy and other glories as well that form parts of the gift of life and that can enhance romance or even replace it when necessary: fruitful work, family, friends, fun, children, healing, creation, music, sunrises, and sunsets.

Looking Ahead

In the next and final chapter, we will attempt some fearless predictions about the future. But we'd like to end this chapter with an important question that feeds into that final chapter.

In the past, many mediocre marriages and relationships continued, partly because the partners feared loneliness at a breakup. When fights took place, it was undoubtedly human to think that there was someone better "out there." But out there could lie a frightening and uncertain territory. It was natural to ask: How will I find someone? How do I meet people? Do I really want to date again? Am I destined to be alone forever?

Those were good questions because there were, until recently, very few successful ways to find that new mate, especially if you were a woman over a certain age. But our question for today and tomorrow is based on new technologies that make it very easy to meet new people, to have sex, to try to find love. We described those dating apps and websites in Chapters 2 and 3. The question is obvious and important: Will it become harder (is it already becoming harder?) to maintain long-term relationships in the face of troubles and fights and unhappiness? Will the exasperated statement, often made privately to oneself, even in a good relationship—"I don't need this!"—more frequently result in someone actually getting out?

Those relationships, which often continued—happily or disastrously or in-between—because of the difficulty of finding someone new, may be harder to maintain in the future in the face of all those new possibilities for meeting and mating. On the other hand, perhaps the desire for loving, lasting relationships is so powerful, that it will override the seductions of dating apps and social networking and the belief that there is "someone better" waiting to be found.

We don't know the answer to that question, but our tentative guess is that the maintenance of long-term relationships may truly be increasingly threatened with every passing year and every new socializing technology that makes meeting people so easy, online or off. And if that is where the future is leading, it's not absolutely clear whether such a loosening of ties, will, on balance, be a bad thing or a good thing.

And now, given all that we have written here, we head toward the final chapter with some (we hope) informed guesses about what the future may portend for us all.

THE BEST (AND WORST) PREDICTORS OF BREAKUP

Based on analyses from 137 studies and over 30,000 participants, here are the best and worst predictors of breakup. In other words, if you asked people about their relationships at one point in time, what would predict the likelihood of that relationshiop lasting!

The scale shows how strongly each variable predicts break-up.

WORST ◄

| 0.0 | 0.2 | 0.4 | 0.6 | 0.8 | 1.0 |

Self-Esteem   Conflict   Satisfaction   Trust   Commitment

Neuroticism

Agreeableness

Social Network Support

Closeness

Inclusion of Other in the Self incorporating aspects of the partner into the self-concept

Love

► BEST

Relationshop factors like positive illusions and commitment are effective predictors of breakup; individual factors like neuroticism and self-esteem don't give much information on likelihood of breakup.

Le, B., Dove, N. L., Agnew, C.R., Korn, M. S., & Mutso, A. A. (2010). Predicting nonmarital romantic relationshop dissolution: A meta-analytic synthesis. Personal Relationshops, 17, 377-390.

ScienceOfRelationships.com

Read More: http://bit.ly/ochUVp

12

The Future of Love and Sex

Yale historian Robin Winks once observed that writing history is "like nailing jelly to the wall." But, he added, "someone must keep trying." Trying to describe sweeping historical trends and then to predict future trends is even more difficult. But let us, in a playful and modest spirit, make the effort. In this chapter, we will consider futurists' predictions as to the social, economic, and behavioral advances we might expect in the next 50 years.

Just go to Web and you will see the predictions people made in 1800 about the world of tomorrow. Flying houses, moving sidewalks on water (see Fig. 12.1), police with X-ray cameras, flying machines for all, and the like. In general, predictions aren't visionary enough and far too radical and just plain silly.

What's Next in Love and Sex. Elaine Hatfield, Richard L. Rapson, and Jeanette Purvis, Oxford University Press (2020). © Oxford University Press.
DOI: 10.1093/oso/9780190647162.001.0001

"Hildebrands Deutsche Schokolade" Postcard Year 1900: Guesses About the Future of Love, Sex, and Marriage: 2040 AD

In 2000, we were invited to make predictions about the future course of love and sex in the developed world, particularly the United States. We chose to look ahead just about 40 years.

The global village created by worldwide communication, computers, satellites, information exchange, travel, and trade will most certainly continue to reduce cultural differentiation and augment homogenization. While we can anticipate that the world of the future might combine something of East and West, there can be little doubt that in the short run, in the areas of passionate love and sexual desire, the influence of the West on the East will be far greater than the reverse. For some, that is an appealing vision. (They equate Westernization with freedom, women's rights, equality, democracy, and higher living standards.) For others, that is a nightmare vision, an image of selfishness, rampant greed and materialism—made in the West. We divided our predictions into three categories: technological transformations, economic and practical changes, and cultural alterations in general attitudes. Since we tend to think technology may be the major driver of change in history, we start there.

Technological Changes

1. Love, sex, and relationships on the Web. Consequences?
2. Increased availability of porn (videos), technological sex
3. Increased availability of new partners from social media and dating apps. Added pressure to maintain long-term relationships?
4. Cure for AIDS, for impotence. Less emphasis on monogamy?
5. Advances in reproductive technology, including birth control and abortion technology. Boutique/Designer babies?
6. Improvement in cosmetic surgery. What is beautiful/handsome?
7. Robots. Sex dolls. Will machines surpass humans?
8. People living healthier lives for longer periods of time. Much, much longer?

Though mostly correct, there is nothing particularly prescient about these predictions. All we did was identify developments that were trending at the turn into the millennium and prophesize their continuation into the near future. The trick was merely to identify those trends. Though people tend to take for granted current developments, it takes only a little effort at perspective to identify and name them. But while anticipating technological change was easy, their consequences were very difficult to predict and remain so.

Economic and Practical Changes

9. Both spouses working
10. Toward gender and economic equality
11. More consensual unions
12. More long-distance relationships
13. More cyberspace relationships

Cultural Changes

14. Increasing acceptance of homosexuality
15. Increasing acceptance of interracial relationships
16. Increasing acceptance of hookups and sex before *dating*
17. Increasing acceptance of multiple definitions of *family*. Meaning of "family" is ever-changing.
18. The *norm* is CHANGE. Probably VERY RAPID change.

History and Change

Of all our predictions, the linchpin was this one:
18. The norm is change—probably very rapid change.

The overwhelming consensus among cultural historians (who study the history of love and sex and family, among other things) is that human behavior, at its deepest level, has been transformed in the last 500 years. There has been a revolution in human life: No longer do historians study history from the top down (studying the lives of kings, queens, and great generals); they study history from the bottom up. History is the story of love, emotion, and family life among common men and women.

Imagine (like Dr. Who) you are privileged to take a time machine into England in 1500. As you land, you will see a few people running toward you. The first thing you will notice is how short they are. Next, as they approach, you will see how young they are (the lifespan in 1500 was only 25–30 years—depending on how one calculates infant mortality). Still closer you will sense a terrible smell; by our standards, these people stink. They have rashes and oozing sores all over their bodies. They are filthy. They are in poor health. They work exhausting hours and get too little food. The women have genital diseases that make intercourse painful. What effect does this have on love and sex?

The emphasis on the continuity in human behavior prevails in many quarters. Popularizers tell us that men are from Mars and women from Venus. Some scholars labor to emphasize how similar we are to the earliest humans. It's all in the genes.

But historians look at the human record, at facts more than theory, and almost always tend to conclude, as did Robert Darnton (2009), in his famous book on the peasants of early modern France (around 1600): "The human condition has changed so much since then that we can hardly imagine the way it appeared to people whose lives really were nasty, brutish, and short" (p. 29).

Among those changes—none of them trivial—was the transition from arranged marriages to love marriages; from very short lifespans to those almost three times as long; from the norm of children as "participant observers of their parents' sexual activities" (p. 29) to our horror at that reality; from incredible isolation to large-scale connectedness; from women with fewer legal rights than horses to the movement toward gender equality; from sex for procreation to sex for pleasure; and much more. These are not superficial transformations; they are profound. And at the level of psychological states, Darnton writes: "Early modern man did not understand life in a way that enabled him to control it" (p. 27). Life itself was so hard and unyielding that only resignation and acceptance of one's fate could allow people to withstand the misery.

We may overestimate today how much control we have over our own lives, but most people in the developed world do take it for granted that if one makes good choices about mate selection and career, about where to live, and how to live—then we stand a reasonable chance of making our lives better. That's a relatively new psychological and philosophical state of mind, not fully appearing on the historical scene until the Enlightenment of the 18th century.

These revolutions in human behavior, thinking, and feeling seem, if anything, to be speeding up in our own time, as we have seen throughout this book. Though history is not, in most dimensions, very predictable, and though historical causation is notoriously complex, there is one area that we believe to be more predictable than most, and one that plays a very important role in causation: technological advance. As with science, the best technology is generally the latest technology, and technological advance follows a far more linear course than would be the case with art, literature, politics, religion, music, and decent human behavior. In fact, some scientists go so far as to say technology improves exponentially, an idea that would suggest we are at the bottom of a rapidly ascending curve. It would be hard to make the case that the latest music or theater or painting is the best. Nor can one comfortably say that about the "linear growth" of human kindness. However, technology works to improve the functionality of our lives over time.

Because technology (based on scientific discovery) does tend to proceed linearly, most science fiction movies and novels base their futures on potentially plausible prophecies of technological change. Most of our more serious predictions were technologically based.

We did not, in our published prophecies, attempt to chart whether changes would move incrementally (e.g., gains in women's rights) or exponentially (the proliferation of dating websites and social networking). We did not address the issue of whether or not the non-Western world would soon "Westernize" in the realms of love and sex. Nor, more importantly, did we address the *consequences* of all these transformations.

In the year 2000, we simply laid out what those transformations might be. In the preceding chapters of this book, we've expanded on those earlier speculations, trying harder to assess the process and nature of "Westernization" (now somewhat euphemistically called "globalization"), adding on some new topics and assuming that some others (the growing acceptance of homosexual and interracial relationships, for example) speak pretty well for themselves.

We would like to end the book by looking at the "so what" nature of all the changes. Do these new developments cut deeply into human behavior, or are they flashy but trivial in altering a human nature rooted in relatively unchanging biology? We would also like to return to the debated matter of westward expansion in the realms of love and sex.

The Globalization of Love and Sex

In looking ahead globally, it is very possible that issues of climate change, terrorism, and overpopulation will shape human life. If so, as with Wittgenstein, we might have to, with our focus on love, sex, and personal matters, kick the ladder down from underneath us: down we fall—along with everyone else. If survival of our planet and of our species is at stake, dating websites, robot love, and ever-personal issues of finding a mate may seem pretty trivial and not a little frivolous. Focusing single-mindedly on getting good sex may be seen as a selfish and irresponsible activity, given the crises besetting our planet, and our book will seem very much beside the point.

Climate change, terrorism, poverty, resource depletion, nuclear proliferation, and overpopulation bring very real dangers. But short of disaster, people do need love and the search for it will likely continue, even in the face of scarcity.

The alterations in private life derived from the developed world will, we predict, continue to change life in the less developed world. Transformations in Europe and the rest of the West will be faster than in poorer countries, faster in urban areas everywhere than in rural parts, faster where secularism supersedes religion, faster where gender equality has advanced further than where patriarchy still rules.

Paradoxically, as developing countries have gone online via mobile devices for the first time, their ideas about love and sex may be changing more rapidly than in the Western world as rural and religious traditions meet Western-designed dating apps. In India, for example, people don't have running water, but they are matching with potential romantic partners on their mobile devices in different towns.

But Westernization or globalization—for better or for worse—is already a reality, and the expansion of the Internet, the availability of Western popular culture, and the power of international corporations guarantee further spread. Although our stories in this book derive mostly from the West, we are of the opinion that we are telling, as we look ahead, an increasingly global tale.

Consequences of the Changing Landscape of Love and Sex

So what does it all mean? How deeply does all this truly alter human behavior? Or are we describing, by and large, technological games that people, especially young ones, love to play? As they age, will the desire for deep and lasting physical love kick in? Once the dating and sex games are over, will people long for and seek what they have increasingly sought in the modern world—the lifelong love affair, the soul mate, even the children that assure the perpetuation of their genetic material? Are those desires hard-wired into our very being?

On that last question, the evidence is not in. Primatological studies, for example, suggest that physical bonding may plausibly be considered wired in. But we urge profound skepticism when one hears a politician, or a journalist, or a first-generation evolutionary psychologist say the words "always has been." For example, "marriage has always been . . ."; "families have always been . . ."; "sex has always been . . ."; "men have always been . . .; "women have always been. . . ."

You will be hard-pressed to find any historian of family life, of love and sex and marriage and divorce and relationships who does not emphasize change in all of these fundamental areas of life. Transformation is not trivial when Europeans and Americans transition from arranged marriages to love marriages. It is not trivial when an invention like the birth control pill opens the way for sex to be experienced as pleasure or an expression of love without the fear of procreation. Cultural acceptance of homosexuality and interracial relationships is not insignificant. The expansion of the lifespan from 30 years to 80 (and perhaps going up) is hardly insignificant. Above all, the move to gender equality has to be considered revolutionary, with its implications only partly developed by the early 21st century.

When, for example, Hatfield and Rapson were in college, in order to be considered a "woman" in the United States, one had to conform to a set of rules. To be an accepted woman, she had to be married; if not, she was a failure, an old maid, a spinster. She was selfish (or an object of pity) if she did not go on to have children. The only acceptable jobs outside the domestic hearth—despite occasional exceptions—were to be a secretary (not a CEO), a nurse (not a doctor), a school teacher (not a professor), a stewardess (not a pilot), and little else.

A half-century later, despite continuing discrimination, one can be considered a "woman" without being married, without having children (though it's okay if she chooses to be a wife or a mother), to be a lesbian, a truck driver, an athlete, a CEO, lawyer, doctor, scientist, plumber, carpenter, pilot, professor, or criminal! That kind of change is not trivial.

So maybe one can exaggerate the tales of dislocation and novelty we describe in these pages. The desire for physical, lasting human connection may be basic and will trump Tinder. Maybe we're only enlarging the number of ways to find and make those connections. Perhaps in the final analysis we're only widening avenues by which men and women can find the right person or people.

So we end with some humility when we emphasize the one conclusion about which we feel certain.

In the wake of the Enlightenment of the 18th century, both the word and the concept of "progress" was invented: the world would become better and better if only humanity started using its head, its reasoning capacity, and its insistence on verifiable evidence more than had the religious societies of the past. As a result, most of the literary attempts to describe the future that emerged in the 18th and 19th centuries were utopian. Many individuals went on to create actual utopian communes in which justice and happiness would prevail.

Those utopian visions, expressed as late as the end of the 19th century in works like Edward Bellamy's (1888/2003) *Looking Backward*, began to look fatuous as the world plunged into the two most horrific wars in human history. The two World Wars profoundly dampened enthusiasm about humanity's rational capabilities and the future, and people devoured dystopian works like Aldous Huxley's *Brave New World* and George Orwell's *1984*. More recent movies like *Blade Runner* and *Clockwork Orange* (and many, many others) have painted bleak pictures of our ravaged planet and its decadent human populations. The latter were even being replaced by cyborgs and other human-like "beings" who would take over humans, not to the benefit of the world.

Our book adopts neither a utopian nor a dystopian perspective. The world of love and sex is changing, sometimes superficially, sometimes profoundly. The outcomes will depend on how individuals deal with the new technologies and the new ethical questions they raise. One thing new technologies have pretty consistently offered its users is greater choice. They can use them to further traditional goals. They can use them to explore new frontiers of possibility. Or they can choose not to use them at all.

Traditional societies, particularly religious ones, tend to insist on and enforce one way of doing things, one way to behave, one way to believe. Those who deviate are often punished—or extinguished. Technological societies have gone the other way: toward offering more choices as to how to live, more varying views of what is ethical, not fewer.

We believe that's where we may be headed in the future of love and sex, away from single standards and toward multiplicity and variability. Depending on your point of view, this can be a sign of decadence or a signal of freedom.

The brave new world of love and sex is one in which individual choices as to how to live have expanded and are continually expanding. We are convinced that no one model will define our private lives. The fixed gender roles of past centuries (and present ones in much of the rural underdeveloped world) are diminishing and will continue to do so. The name of the game is variability, choice, or multiple options.

Individuals will increasingly feel free—and not be punished—for assuming traditional roles, or for choosing from a vast array of new ones. For many, the smorgasbord of choices will be confusing, disorienting, or even be seen as sinful and punishable as before. But we see no stopping in the short and long run of the growing acceptance and toleration of the many ways to live and love.

All this is best summed up in the openness and nonjudgmental attitude we often see in the developed world, gaining its fullest expression when people are asked to judge nontraditional behaviors, for which they present one word. That word is "Whatever!" Not the dismissive "whatever," but the laconically accepting one.

Or in our home in Hawaii, one easily observes that many locals, when faced with the same ethnical questions about people choosing to live their personal lives in new and various ways, will spread their hands, palm upward, smile, and say: "Watevuh!!

References

Abdullah, A. S. M., Fielding, R., Hedley, A. J., & Luk, Y. K. (2002). Risk factors for sexually transmitted diseases and casual sex among Chinese patients attending sexually transmitted disease clinics in Hong Kong. *Sexually Transmitted Diseases, 29*, 360–365.

Acevedo, B. P., & Aron, A. (2009). Does a long-term relationship kill romantic love? *General Review of Psychology, 13*, 59–65.

Acevedo, B. P., Aron, A., Fisher, H. E., & Brown, L. L. (2012). Neural correlates of long-term intense romantic love. *Social Cognitive and Affective Neuroscience, 7*(2), 145–159.

Addiction.com. (n.d.). Porn addiction. Retrieved from https://www.addiction.com/addiction-a-to-z/porn-addiction/

Aggarwal, R. (2015, November 11). Welcome to the future of apps—it's about to get personal. *Localytics*. Retrieved from http://info.localytics.com/blog/new-study-reveals-what-app-users-want-localytics

Agha, S. (2002). Declines in casual sex in Lusaka, Zambia: 1996–1999. *AIDS, 16*, 291–293.

Alexander, M. G., & Fisher, T. D. (2003). Truth and consequences: Using the bogus pipeline to examine sex differences in self-reported sexuality. *Journal of Sex Research, 40*, 27–35.

Allgeier, E. R., & Wiederman, M. W. (1991). Love and mate selection in the 1990s. *Free Inquiry, 11*, 25–27.

Allison, R., & Risman, B. J. (2013). A double standard for "hooking up": How far have we come toward gender equality? *Social Science Research, 42*(5), 1191–1206.

Amato, P. R. (2004). The consequences of divorce for adults and children. *Journal of Marriage and Family, 62*, 1269–1287.

American Psychiatric Association. (2013). *Diagnostic and statistical manual of mental disorders* (5th ed.) (DSM-5). Arlington, VA: American Psychiatric Association.

Ammar, H. (1954). Growing up in an Egyptian village: Silwa, Province of Aswan. London: Routledge & Kegan Paul.

Anderson, M. (2015). *Technology device ownership: 2015.* Pew Research Center. Retrieved from http://www.pewinternet.org/2015/10/29/technology-device-ownership-2015/

Ansari, A. (2015). *Modern romance.* New York: Penguin Press.

Apostolou, M. (2013). The parental choice branch of sexual selection: Re-examining the evolution of mating behavior. *Journal of Integrated Social Sciences, 3*(1), 37–54.

Apostolopoulos, Y., Sonmez, S., Sasidharan, S., & Jovicich, I. (1999, June). *Travel and infectious disease: Intentions and behaviors of American college students involving casual sex on spring break.* Paper presented at the conference of the International Society of Travel Medicine, Montreal, Quebec, Canada.

AppAnnie (July 4, 2016). [Website] https://www.appannie.com/

Ariès, P. (1962). *Centuries of childhood: A social history of family life.* New York: Knopf.

Aron, A, Fisher, H. E., Mashek, D. J., Strong, G., Li, H., & Brown, L. L. (2005). Reward, motivation, and emotion systems associated with early-stage intense romantic love. *Journal Neurophysiology, 94*, 327–337.

Aron, A., & Henkemeyer, L. (1995). Marital satisfaction and passionate love. *Journal of Social and Personal Relationships, 12*(1), 139–146.

Aron, A., Norman, C. C., Aron, E. N., McKenna, C., & Heyman, R. E. (2000). Couples' shared participation in novel and arousing activities and experienced relationship quality. *Journal of Personality and Social Psychology, 78*, 273–284.

Assimos, J. (2011). So, what is the science behind eHarmony? [eHarmony Blog]. Retrieved from http://www.eharmony.com/why/science

Aubrey, J. S., & Smith, S. E. (2013). Development and validation of the endorsement of the hookup culture index. *Journal of Sex Research, 50*, 435–448.

Aumer, K., Bellew, W., Ito, B., Hatfield, E., & Heck, R. (2014). The happy green eyed monogamist: Role of jealousy and comperson in monogamous and non-traditional relationships. *Electronic Journal of Human Sexuality, 17*, 1–20. Retrieved from http://www.ejhs.org/volume17/happy.html

Axtell, J. L. (1981). *The European and the Indian: Essays in ethnohistory of colonial North America.* New York: Oxford University Press.

Bailey, B. L. (1988). *From front porch to back seat: Courtship in twentieth-century America.* Baltimore, MD: Johns Hopkins University Press.

Bailey, J. M., Gaulin, S., Agyei, Y., & Gladue, B. A. (1994). Effects of gender and sexual orientation on evolutionarily relevant aspects of human mating psychology. *Journal of Personality and Social Psychology, 66*(6), 1081.

Bailey, J. V., Farquhar, C., Owen, C., & Whittaker, D. (2003). Sexual behaviour of lesbians and bisexual women. *Sexually Transmitted Infections, 79*(2), 147–150.

Bakalar, N. (April 8, 2017). HPV is widespread in U. S. survey finds. *Honolulu Star Advertiser.*

Baranowski, A. M., & Hecht, H. (2015). Gender differences and similarities in receptivity to sexual invitations: Effects of location and risk perception. *Archives of Sexual Behavior, 44*, 2257–2265.

Barker, M., & Langdridge, D. (2010). Introduction. In M. Barker & D. Langdridge (Eds.), *Understanding non-monogamies* (pp. 3–8). New York: Routledge.

Barkow, J. H., Cosmides, L., & Tooby, J. (Eds.). (1992). *The adapted mind: Evolutionary psychology and the generation of culture.* New York: Oxford University Press.

Barriger, M., & Vélez-Blasini, C. J. (2013). Descriptive and injunctive social norm overestimation in hooking up and their role as predictors of hook-up activity in a college student sample. *Journal of Sex Reserch, 50*, 84–94.

Bauer, M., McAuliffe, L., & Nay, R. (2007). Sexuality, health care and the older person: An overview of the literature. *International Journal of Older People Nursing, 2*(1), 63–68.

Baumeister, R. F., Catanese, K. R., & Vohs, K. D. (2001). Is there a gender difference in strength of sex drive? Theoretical views, conceptual distinctions, and a review of relevant evidence. *Personality and Social Psychology Review, 5*, 242–273.

Baumeister, R. F., & Vohs, K. (2004). Sexual economics: Sex as female resource for social exchange in heterosexual interactions. *Personality and Social Psychology Review, 8*, 339–363.

Baumeister, R. F., & Wotman, S. R. (1991). *Breaking hearts: The two sides of unrequited love.* New York: Guilford Press.

Baumeister, R. F., Wotman, S. R., & Stillwell, A. M. (1993). Unrequited love: On heartbreak, anger, guilt, scriptlessness, and humiliation. *Journal of Personality and Social Psychology, 64*(3), 377.

Bay-Cheng, L. Y., Robinson, A. D., & Zucker, A. N. (2009). Behavioral and relational contexts of adolescent desire, wanting, and pleasure: Undergraduate women's retrospective accounts. *Journal of Sex Research, 46*, 511–524.

BBC News. (2016, February 12). The dating game. Retrieved from http://www.bbc.co.uk/news/resources/idt-2e3f0042-75f6-4bd1-b4fe-9056540c65f8

Beaumont-Thomas, B. (2012, November 2). Body language: Notes on a shifting fantasy. *Mail & Guardian*. Retrieved from http://mg.co.za/article/2012-11-02-00-body-language-notes-on-a-shifting-fantasy

Beck, A. T., Steer, R. A., & Brown, G. (1996). *Beck Depression Inventory-II (BDI-II)*. New York: Pearson.

Becker, G. S. (1973). A theory of marriage: Part I. *Journal of Political Economy, 81*(4), 813–846.

Bellamy, E. (2003). *Looking backward: 2000–1887*. Peterborough, Canada: Broadview Press (Originally published 1888).

Bendix, R. (1964). *Nation-building and citizenship: Studies of our changing social order*. New York: Wiley.

Bengali, S., & Kaiman, J. (2016, January 16). In countries where gay sex is taboo, Grindr and other apps open a (sometimes perilous) window. *Los Angeles Times*. Retrieved from http://www.latimes.com/world/asia/la-fg-asia-grindr-20160116-story.html

Bergstrand, C., & Williams, J. B. (2000). Today's alternative marriage styles: The case of swingers. *Electronic Journal of Human Sexuality, 3*. Retrieved from http://www.ejhs.org/volume3/swing/body.htm

Bersamin, M. M., Zamboanga, B. L., Schwartz, S. J., Donnellan, M. B., Hudson, M., Weisskirch, R. S., . . . Caraway, S. J. (2014). Risky usiness: Is there an association between casual sex and mental health among emerging adults? *Journal of Sex Research, 51*, 43–51.

Berscheid, E., & Hatfield, E. (1969). *Interpersonal attraction*. New York: Addison-Wesley.

Bird, W. (2007). *Natural thinking: Investigating the links between the natural environment, biodiversity and mental health*. Royal Society for the Protection of Birds. Retrieved from http://ww2.rspb.org.uk/Images/naturalthinking_tcm9-161856.pdf

Bisson, M. A., & Levine, T. R. (2009). Negotiating a friends with benefits relationship. *Archives of Sexual Behavior, 38*, 66–73.

Blair, K. L., & Pukall, C. F. (2014). Can less be more? Comparing duration vs. frequency of sexual encounters in same-sex and mixed-sex relationships. *Canadian Journal of Human Sexuality, 23*(2), 123–136.

Blasband, D., & Peplau, L. (1985). Sexual exclusivity versus openness in gay male couples. *Archives of Sexual Behavior, 14*, 395–412. doi:10.1007/BF01542001

Bloch, I. (1908). *The sexual life of our time: In its relations to modern civilization*. New York: Allied Book Company.

Bloom, B. L., White, S. W., & Asher, S. J. (1979). Marital disruption as a stressful life event. In G. Levinger & O. C. Moles (Eds.), *Divorce and separation* (pp. 184–200). New York: Basic Books.

Blumstein, P., & Schwartz, P. (1983). *American couples: Money, work, sex*. New York: William Morrow.

Bogle, K. (2008). *Hooking up: Sex, dating and relationships on campus*. New York: New York University Press.

Bossard, J. H. S. (1932). Residential propinquity in marriage selection. *American Journal of Sociology, 38*, 219–224.

Bostrom, N. (2002). Existential risks. *Journal of Evolution and Technology, 9*(1), 1–31.

Braithwaite, S. R., Delevi, R., & Fincham, F. D. (2010). Romantic relationships and the physical and mental health of college students. *Personal Relationships, 17*(1), 1–12.

Braudel, F. (1966). *The Mediterranean and the Mediterranean world in the age of Philip II* (2 vols.). New York: Harper & Row.

Bringle, R. G., & Buunk, B. (1986). Examining the causes and consequences of jealousy: Some recent findings and issues. In R. Gilmour & S. W. Duck (Eds.), *The emerging field of personal relationships* (pp. 225–240). Hillsdale, NJ: Erlbaum.

Brink, S. (2007, July 30). This is your brain on love. *Los Angeles Times.* Retrieved from http://www.latimes.com/la-he-brainlove30-2007jul30-story.html

Bronner, E. (2012, November 14). Adultery, an ancient crime that remains on many books. *The New York Times.* Retrieved from http://www.nytimes.com/2012/11/15/us/adultery-an-ancient-crime-still-on-many-books.html?_r=0

Brooke, J. (1991, March 26). "Honor" killing of wives is outlawed in Brazil. *The New York Times.* Retrieved from http://www.nytimes.com/1991/03/29/us/honor-killing-of-wives-is-outlawed-in-brazil.html

Broude, G. J., & Green, S. J. (1983). Cross-cultural codes on husband-wife relationships. *Ethology, 22,* 273–274.

Brown, N. R., & Sinclair, R. C. (1999). Estimating number of lifetime sexual partners: Men and women do it differently. *Journal of Sex Research, 36*(3), 292–297.

Browning, J. R. (2005). A comprehensive inventory of sexual motives. *Dissertation Abstracts International: Section B: The Sciences and Engineering, 65*(10-B), 54–57.

Browning, J. R., Hatfield, E., Kessler, D., & Levine, T. (2000). Sexual motives and interactions with gender. *Archives of Sexual Behavior, 29,* 139–152.

Browning, J. R., Kessler, D., Hatfield, E., & Choo, P. (1999). Power, gender, and sexual behavior. *Journal of Sex Research, 36,* 342–347.

Bumroongsook, S. (1992). *Conventions of mate selection in twentieth-century central Thailand* (Unpublished master's thesis). Department of History, University of Hawaii, Honolulu, HI.

Burkett, B. N., & Kirkpatrick, L. A. (2006, June). *What are deal-breakers in a mate: Characteristics that are intolerable in a potential mate.* Paper presented at the annual meeting of the Human Behavior and Evolution Society, Philadelphia.

Burton, R. (1927). *The anatomy of melancholy.* London: Longman (Original work published 1621).

Buss, D. M. (1988). The evolution of human intrasexual competition: Tactics of male attraction. *Journal of Personality and Social Psychology, 64,* 616–628.

Buss, D. M. (1989). Sex differences in human mate preferences: Evolutionary hypotheses tested in 37 cultures. *Behavioral and Brain Sciences, 12,* 1–49.

Buss, D. M. (1994/2003). *The evolution of desire: Strategies in human mating.* New York: Basic Books.

Buss, D. M. (2000). *The dangerous passion: Why jealousy is as necessary as love and sex.* New York: Free Press.

Buss, D., & Schmitt, D. (1993). Sexual strategies theory: An evolutionary perspective on human mating. *Psychological Review, 100*(2), 204–232.

Buunk, B., & Hupka, R. B. (1987). Cross-cultural differences in the elicitation of sexual jealousy. *Journal of Sex Research, 23,* 12–22.

Cacioppo, S., Bianchi-Demicheli, F., Hatfield, E., & Rapson, R. L. (2012). Social neuroscience of love. *Clinical Neuropsychiatry, 9,* 3–13.

Cacioppo, S., & Cacioppo, J. T. (2016). Comment: Demystifying the neuroscience of love. *Emotion Review, 8*, 108–114. doi:10.1177/1754073915594432

Canetto, S. S., & Lester, D. (2002). Love and achievement motives in women's and men's suicide notes. *Journal of Psychology: Interdisciplinary and Applied, 136*, 573–576.

Čapek, K. (2004). *RUR (Rossum's universal robots)*. New York: Penguin (Originally published 1920).

Capellanus, A. (1957). *The art of courtly love*. New York: Ungar (Original work published 1174).

Centers for Disease Control and Prevention (CDC). (2015). *2015 sexually transmitted diseases surveillance*. Retrieved from https://www.cdc.gov/std/stats15/figures/9.htm

Chang, L. (2016, May 6). Paying for tinder? So are 1 million other people. *Digital Trends*. Retrieved from http://www.digitaltrends.com/mobile/tinder-million-paid users/#:N8jPEBEnsysM_A

Chatel, A. (2015, March 13). Do you like giving oral? 16 women share how they really feel about performing oral sex. *Bustle*. Retrieved from https://www.bustle.com/articles/68920-do-you-like-giving-oral-16-women-share-how-they-really-feel-about-performing-oral-sex

Christian, S. (2013, November 20). 10 Reasons why you should quit watching porn. *GQ*. Retrieved from http://www.gq.com/story/10-reasons-why-you-should-quit-watching-porn

Christianson, M., Johansson, E., Emmelin, M., & Westman, G. (2003). "One-night stands"—risky trips between lust and trust: Qualitative interviews with *Chlamydia trachomatis* infected youth in north Sweden. *Scandinavian Journal of Public Health, 31*, 44–50.

Chu, G. C. (1985). The changing concept of self in contemporary China. In A. J. Marsella, G. DeVos, & F. L. K. Hus (Eds.), *Culture and self: Asian and Western perspectives* (pp. 252–277.) London: Tavistock.

Chu, G. C., & Ju, Y. (1993). *The great wall in ruins*. Albany: State University of New York Press.

Clark, C. L., Shaver, P. R., & Abrahams, M. F. (1999). Strategic behaviors in romantic relationship initiation. *Personality and Social Psychology Bulletin, 25*(6), 709–722.

Clark, R. D. III, & Hatfield, E. (1989). Gender differences in receptivity to sexual offers. *Journal of Psychology and Human Sexuality, 2*, 39–55.

Clark, R. D. III, & Hatfield, E. (2003). Love in the afternoon. *Psychological Inquiry, 14*, 227–231.

CNN Money. (April 15, 2017). Laurie Segall, Mostly human: I love you bot. Real clear future. http://www.realclearfuture.com/2017/04/15/mostly_human_i_love_you_bot_36870.html

Cohen, D. (2001). Cultural variation: Considerations and implications. *Psychological Bulletin, 127*, 451–471.

Cohen, E. (2011, May 19). Prevent STDs like a porn star. *CNN*. Retrieved from http://www.cnn.com/2011/HEALTH/05/19/std.protection.ep/

Cole, S., Trope, Y., & Balcetis, E. (2016). In the eye of the betrothed perceptual downgrading of attractive alternative romantic partners. *Personality and Social Psychology Bulletin, 42*(7), 879–892.

Collins, G. (2009). *When everything changed. The amazing journey of American women from 1960 to the present*. New York: Back Bay Books.

comScore. (2016, March 30). 2016 US cross-platform future in focus. Retrieved from http://www.comscore.com/Insights/Presentations-and-Whitepapers/2016/2016-US-Cross-Platform-Future-in-Focus

Conley, T. D. (2011). Perceived proposer personality characteristics and gender differences in acceptance of casual sex offers. *Journal of Personality and Social Psychology. 100*(2). 309.

Conley, T. D., Moors, A. C., Matsick, J. L., & Ziegler, A. (2013). The fewer the merrier? Assessing stigma surrounding consensually non-monogamous romantic relationships. *Analyses of Social Issues and Public Policy, 13*, 1–30.

Conley, T. D., Ziegler, A., & Moors, A. C. (2013). Backlash from the bedroom: Stigma mediates gender differences in acceptance of casual sex offers. *Psychology of Women Quarterly, 37*, 392–407.

Conner, M., & Flesch, D. (2001). Having casual sex: Addictive and interactive effects of alcohol and condom availability on the determinants of intentions. *Journal of Applied Social Psychology, 1*, 89–112.

Constant, B. (2001). *Adolphe* (M. Mauldon, Trans.). Oxford: Oxford University Press.

Coontz, S. (1988). *The social origins of private life: A history of American families, 1600–1900*. London: Oxford University Press.

Cooper, K. (2015). A woman's advantage. OkCupid. Retrieved from https://www.okcupid.com/deep-end/a-womans-advantage

Cooper, M. L., & Orcutt, H. K. (1997). Drinking and sexual experience on first dates among adolescents. *Journal of Abnormal Psychology, 106*, 191–202.

Copen, C. E., Chandra, A., & Febo-Vazquez, I. (2016). Sexual behavior, sexual attraction, and sexual orientation among adults aged 18–44 in the United States: Data from the 2011–2013 National Survey of Family Growth. *National Health Statistics Reports*, (88), 1–14.

Corinna, H., & Turett, C. J. (2016). Yes. No. Maybe so: A sexual inventory stocklist. *Scarleteen*. Retrieved from http://www.scarleteen.com/article/advice/yes_no_maybe_so_a_sexual_inventory_stocklist

Coulter, K., & Malouff, J. M. (2013). Effects of an intervention designed to enhance romantic relationship excitement: A randomized-control trial. *Couple and Family Psychology: Research and Practice, 2*(1), 34.

Cunningham, M. R., Shamblen, S. R., Barbee, A. P., & Alt, L. K. (2005). Social allergies in romantic relationships: Behavioral repetition, dissatisfaction in dating couples. *Personal Relationships, 12*, 273–295.

Cubbins, L. A., & Tanfer, K. (2000). The influence of gender on sex: A study of men's and women's self-reported high-risk sex behavior. *Archives of Sexual Behavior, 29*, 229–257.

Cyrus, M. (2015. December 11). *BB talk* [Video]. Retrieved from https://www.youtube.com/watch?v=DfwJA0f0UTg

Dabhoiwala, F. (2012). *The origins of sex: A history of the first sexual revolution*. Oxford: Oxford University Press.

Daily Mail Reporter. (2014, January 1). No one said finding The One would be easy. *The Daily Mail*. Retrieved from http://www.dailymail.co.uk/femail/article-2532213/No-one-said-finding-The-One-easy-The-average-women-kiss-FIFTEEN-men-enjoy-TWO-long-term-relationships-heart-broken-TWICE.html

Daly, M., & Wilson, M. (1988). Evolutionary social psychology and family homicide. *Science, 28*, 519–524.

Daneback, K., Træen, B., & Månsson, S. A. (2009). Use of pornography in a random sample of Norwegian heterosexual couples. *Archives of Sexual Behavior, 38*(5),746–753.

Darnton, R. (2009). *The great cat massacre: And other episodes in French cultural history.* New York: Basic Books.

Darwin, C. (1988). *The origin of species.* New York: New York University Press (Originally published 1859).

Daubney, M. (2015, August 15). Porn is ruining our love lives and making old men of our teenagers. *The Independent.* Retrieved from http://www.telegraph.co.uk/men/thinking-man/porn-is-ruining-our-love-lives-and-making-old-men-of-our-teenage/

Davis, D. A., & Davis, S. S. (1995). Possessed by love: Gender and romance in Morocco. In W. Jankowiak (Ed.), *Romantic passion: A universal experience?* (pp. 219–238). New York: Columbia University Press.

de Beauvoir, S. (1962). *The Second Sex* (H. M. Parshley, Trans.). London: New English Library (Originally published 1949).

Debrot, A., Meuwly, N., Muise, A., Impett, E. A., & Schoebi, D. (2017). More than just sex: Affection mediates the association between sexual activity and well-being. *Personality and Social Psychology Bulletin, 43*(3), 287–299.

de Jong-Gierveld, J. (1986). Loneliness and the degree of intimacy in interpersonal relationships. In R. Gilmour & S. Duck (Eds.), *The emerging field of personal relationships* (pp. 241–249). Hillsdale, NJ: Earlbaum.

Deloitte. (2015). *Value of connectivity: Economic and social benefits of expanding internet access.* Deloitte UK Economic Consulting. Retrieved from https://www2.deloitte.com/content/dam/Deloitte/ie/Documents/TechnologyMediaCommunications/2014_uk_tmt_value_of_connectivity_deloitte_ireland.pdf

D'Emilio, J., & Freedman, E., (2012). *Intimate matters: A history of sexuality in America.* Chicago: University of Chicago Press.

Demirtas, A., & Donmez, A. (2006). Jealousy in close relationships: Personal, relational and situational variables. *Turkish Journal of Psychiatry, 17*(3), 181–191.

Denfeld, D. (1974). Dropouts from swinging. *Family Coordinator, 23*(1), 45–49.

De Silva, P. (1997). Jealousy in couple relationships: Nature, assessment, and therapy. *Behaviour Research and Therapy, 35,* 973–985.

de Visser, R., & McDonald, D. (2007). Swings and roundabouts: Management of jealousy in heterosexual swinging couples. *British Journal of Social Psychology, 46,* 459–476.

de Visser, R. O., Smith, A. M. A., Richters, J., & Rissel, C. E. (2007). Associations between religiosity and sexuality in a representative sample of Australian adults. *Archives of Sexual Behavior, 36,* 33–46.

Dewey, C. (February 1, 2016). Facebook's 'teen dating' groups are every parent's nightmare. *Washington Post.* Retrieved from https://www.washingtonpost.com/news/the-intersect/wp/2016/02/01/facebooks-teen-dating-groups-are-every-parents-nightmare-come-to-life/

Diamond, L. M. (2008). *Sexual fluidity.* Cambridge, MA: Harvard University Press.

Dickson, E. J., & Lang, N. (2015, December 11). 5 reasons you need to watch more porn. *The Daily Dot.* Retrieved from http://www.dailydot.com/via/5-reasons-you-need-watch-porn/

Dill, J. (2014, April 8). The irony of the overprotected child. *Family Studies.* Retrieved from http://family-studies.org/the-irony-of-the-overprotected-child/

Dima, B. (2013). Case study: Kids and online threats. *Bitdefender*. Retrieved from http://www.bitdefender.com/media/materials/white-papers/en/Bitdefender-CaseStudy-Kids.pdf

Dion, K. K., & Dion, K. L. (1993). Individualistic and collective perspectives on gender and the cultural context of love and intimacy. *Journal of Social Issues, 49*, 53–69.

Doi, L. T. (1963). Some thoughts on helplessness and the desire to be loved. *Psychiatry, 26*, 266–272.

Doi, L. T. (1973). *The anatomy of dependence* (J. Bester, Trans.). Tokyo: Kodansha International.

Dortonne. (2016, March 2). Breakup service does lovers' dirty work. CNN. Retrieved from http://www.cnn/com/2016/03/02/living/breakup-service-dirty-work-feat/?iid=ob_homepage_deskrecommended_pool/&iref=obnetwork

Dove, M. W., & Wiederman, N. (2000). Cognitive distraction and women's sexual functioning. *Journal of Sex & Marital Therapy, 26*(1), 67–78.

Downing, M. J., Schrimshaw, E. W., Scheinmann, R., Antebi-Gruszka, N., & Hirshfield, S. (2017). Sexually explicit media use by sexual identity: A comparative analysis of gay, bisexual, and heterosexual men in the United States. *Archives of Sexual Behavior, 46*(6), 1763–1776.

Druckerman, P. (2007). *Lust in translation: The rules of infidelity from Tokyo to Tennessee.* New York: Penguin Press.

Dube, R. (June 25, 2015). How AI sex dolls will change dating in just three years. *MUO*. http://www.makeuseof.com/tag/ai-sex-dolls-will-change-dating-just-three-years-nsfw/

Duma, U. (2009). *Jealousy and compersion in close relationships: Coping styles by relationship types.* Mainz, Germany: GRIN Verlag.

Dunn, J. (1989). *Modern revolutions: An introduction to the analysis of a political phenomenon.* Cambridge, UK: Cambridge University Press.

Dworkin, A. (1981). *Pornography: Men possessing women.* New York: Plume.

Easton, D., & Hardy, J. W. (2009). *The ethical slut* (2nd ed.). Berkeley, CA: Ten Speed Press.

Eastwick, P. W., & Finkel, E. I. (2008). Sex differences in mate preferences revisited: Do people know what they initially desire in a romantic partner? *Journal of Personality and Social Psychology, 94*, 245–264.

Ehrenfeld, T. (2013, October 15). 36 questions to bring you closer together. *Psychology Today*. Retrieved from https://www.psychologytoday.com/blog/open-gently/201310/36-questions-bring-you-closer-together

Eisenberger, N. I., Lieberman, M. D., & Williams, K. D. (2003). Does rejection hurt? An fMRI study of social exclusion. *Science, 302*(5643), 290–292.

Ellis, H. (1942). *Studies in the psychology of sex* (Vol. I). New York: Random House.

England, P., Shafer, E. F., & Fogarty, A. C. K. (2008). Hooking up and forming romantic relationships on today's college campuses. In M. Kimmel & A. Aronson (Eds.), *The gendered society reader* (3rd ed.) (pp. 531–547). New York: Oxford University Press.

Epstein, R., McKinney, P., Fox, S., & Garcia, C. (2012). Support for a fluid-continuum model of sexual orientation: A large-scale Internet study. *Journal of Homosexuality, 59*(10), 1356–1381.

Esch, T., & Stefano, G. B. (2005). Love promotes health. *Neuroendocrinal Letters, 26*, 264–267.

Evans-DeCicco, J. A., & Cowan, G. (2001). Attitudes toward pornography and the characteristics attributed to pornography actors. *Sex Roles, 44*(5-6), 351–361.

Fahs, B. (2014). Coming to power: Women's fake orgasms and best orgasm experiences illuminate the failures of (hetero) sex and the pleasures of connection. *Culture, Health & Sexuality, 16*(8), 974–988.

Fair, J. E., Tully, M., Ekdale, B., & Asante, R. K. B. (2009). Crafting lifestyles in urban Africa: Young Ghanaians in the world of online friendship. *Africa Today, 55*, 29–49.

Fekadu, Z. (2001). Casual sex-debuts among female adolescents in Addis Abba, Ethiopia. *Ethiopian Journal of Health Development, 15*, 109–116.

Felmlee, D. H. (2001). From appealing to appalling: Disenchantment with a romantic partner. *Sociological Perspectives, 44*, 263–280.

Fenigstein, A., & Preston, M. (2007). The desired number of sexual partners as a function of gender, sexual risks, and the meaning of "ideal." *Journal of Sex Research, 44*, 89–95.

Fernandes, E. M. (2009). The swinging paradigm. *Electronic Journal of Human Sexuality*. Retrieved from http://www.ejhs.org/Volume12/Swinging2.htm

Fernandes, E. W. (2013, November 13). Women, swinging, sex, and seduction. *Psychology Today*. Retrieved from https://www.psychologytoday.com/blog/the-swinging-paradigm/201311/women-swinging-sex-and-seduction

Feybesse, C. (2015, November 26). *The adventures of love in the social sciences: Social, psychometric evaluations and cognitive influences of passionate love* (Unpublished doctoral dissertation). Université Paris Descartes, Paris, France.

Feybesse, C., Hatfield, E., & Neto, F. (2013). *Medindo o amor apaixonado.* In D. Bartholomeu, J. M. Montiel, F. K. Miguel, L. F. Carvalho, & J. M. H. Bueno (Eds.), *Atualização em avaliação e tratamento das emoções (Actualizations in the evaluations and treatment of emotions)* (pp. 143–166). São Paulo: Vetor.

Field, T. (2011). Romantic breakups, heartbreak, and bereavement. *Psychology, 2*, 382–387.

Fielder, R. L., Walsh, J. L., Carey, K. B., & Carey, M. P. (2014). Sexual hookups and adverse health outcomes: A longitudinal study of firsst year college women. *Journal of Sex Research, 51*, 131–141.

Fields, P. (1998). Of paradise lost: Orya myth. In M. Gregerson & J. Sterner (Eds.), *Symbolism and ritual in Irian Jaya* (pp. 29–47). International Museum of Cultures Publication 33. Jayapura, Indonesia: Cenderawasih University.

Finkel, E. J., Eastwick, P. W., Karney, B. R., Reis, H. T., & Sprecher, S. (2012). Online dating: A critical analysis from the perspective of psychological science. *Psychological Science in the Public Interest, 13*, 1–66.

Finkel, E. J., Eastwick, P. W., & Matthews, J. (2007). Speed-dating as an invaluable tool for studying romantic attraction: A methodological primer. *Personal Relationships, 14*, 149–166.

Fischer, K. W., Shaver, P. R., & Carnochan, P. (1990). How emotions develop and how they organize development. *Cognition and Emotion, 4*, 81–127.

Fischer, K. W., Wang, L-I., Kennedy, B., & Cheng, C-L. (1998). Culture and biology in emotional development. In D. Sharma & K. W. Fischer (Eds.), *Socioemotional development across cultures. New Directions for Child Development, 82*, 21–43. San Francisco: Jossey Bass.

Fischtein, D. S., Herold, E. S., & Desmarais, S. (2007). How much does gender explain in sexual attitudes and behaviors? A survey of Canadian adults. *Archives of Sexual Behavior, 36*, 451–462.

Fisher, H. E. (1989). Evolution of human serial pairbonding. *American Journal of Physical Anthropology, 78*, 331–354.

Fisher, H. E. (2004a). *Why we love: The nature and chemistry of romantic love.* New York: Henry Holt.

Fisher, H. E. (2004b, January 19). Your brain in love. *Time Magazine*, p. 77.

Fisher, H. E., Aron, A., Mashek, D., Li, H., & Brown, L. L. (2002). Defining the brain systems of lust, romantic attraction, and attachment *Archives of Sexual Behavior, 31,* 413–419.

Fisher, H. E., Brown, L. L., Aron, A., Strong, G., & Mashek, D. (2010). Reward, addiction, and emotion regulation systems associated with rejection in love. *Journal of Neurophysiology, 104,* 51–60.

Fitness, J., & Fletcher, G. J. O. (1993). Love, hate, anger, and jealousy in close relationships: A prototype and cognitive appraisal analysis. *Journal of Personality and Social Psychology, 65,* 942–958.

Flack, W. F., Jr., Daubman, K. A., Caron, M. L., Asadorian, J. A., D'Aureli, N. R., Gigliotti, S. N., . . . Stine, E. R. (2007). Risk factors and consequences of unwante sex among unifersity students: Hooking up, alcohol, and stress response. *Journal of Interpersonal Violence, 22,* 139–157.

Fleckenstein, J., Bergstrand, C., & Cox, D. W. (2012). What do polys want?: An overview of the 2012 Loving More Survey. Retrieved from http//www.lovemore.com/polyamory-articles/2012-lovingmore-polyamorysurvey/.

Fleckenstein, J., & Cox, D. W. (2015). The association of an open relationship orientation with health and happiness in a sample of older US adults. *Sexual and Relationship Therapy, 30,* 94–116.

Foley, S. (2015). Older adults and sexual health: A review of current literature. *Current Sexual Health Reports, 7*(2), 70–79.

Francoeur, R. T. (2000). Ethnic views of sexuality in Nigeria. *SIECUS Report, 28*(4), 8.

Frayser, S. G. (1985). Varieties of sexual experience. An anthropological perspective on human sexuality. New Haven, CT: Yale University: Human Relations Area File.

Frayser, S. G., & Whitby, T. J. (1995). *Studies in human sexuality: A selected guide* (2nd ed.). Santa Barbara, CA: Libraries Unlimited.

Frost, J. H., Chance, Z., Norton, M. I., & Ariely, D. (2008). People are experience goods: Improving online dating with virtual dates. *Journal of Interactive Marketing, 22,* 51–61.

Fukuda, N. (1991). Women in Japan. In L. L. Adler (Ed.), *Women in cross-cultural perspective* (pp. 205–219). Westport, CT: Praeger.

Gallup. (2016). Moral issues. Retrieved from http://www.gallup.com/poll/1681/moral-issues.aspx

Gangestad, S. W., & Simpson, J. A. (2000). The evolution of human mating: Trade-offs and strategic pluralism. *Behavioral and Brain Sciences, 23,* 573–587.

Garcia, J. R., Lloyd, E. A., Wallen, K., & Fisher, H. E. (2014). Variation in orgasm occurrence by sexual orientation in a sample of US singles. *Journal of Sexual Medicine, 11*(11), 2645–2652.

Garcia, J. R., & Reiber, C. (2008). Hook-up behavior: A biopsychosocial perspective. Special issue: *Proceedings of the 2nd Annual Meeting of the NorthEastern Evolutionary Psychology Society, Journal of Social, Evolutionary, and Cultural Psychology, 2,* 192–208.

Garcia, J. R., Reiber, C., Massey, S. G., & Merriwether, A. M. (2013). Sexual hook-up culture. *APA Monitor, Special Quaterly CE Edition, 44,* 60–67.

Garcia-Moreno, C., Jansen, H. A. F. M., Ellsberg, M., Heise, L., & Watts, C. H. (2006). Prevalence of intimate partner violence: Findings from the WHO multi-country study on women's health and domestic violence. *The Lancet, 368*, 1260–1269.

Gardner, A. (2005, February). Unrequited love can be a killer. *BBC News, World edition, 18*. Retrieved from http://news.bbc.co.uk/2/hi/uk_news/england/london/4240579.stm

Gass, K., Hoff, C. C., Stephenson, R., & Sullivan, P. S. (2012). Sexual agreements in the partnerships of Internet-using men who have sex with men. *AIDS Care, 24*, 1255–1263.

Gay, P. (1986). *The bourgeois experience*, Vol. 2: *The tender passion*. Oxford: Oxford University Press.

Gayford, J. J. (1979). Battered wives. *British Journal of Hospital Medicine, 22*, 496–503.

Gentzler, A. L., & Kerns, K. A. (2004). Associations between insecure attachment and sexual experiences. *Personal Relationships, 11*, 249–265.

Ghimire, D., J., Axinn, W. G., Yabiku, S. A., & Thornton, A. (2006). Social change, pre-marital non-family experiences and spouse choice in an arranged marriage society. *American Journal of Sociology, 111*(4), 1181–1218.

Godfrey, C. (2016). Gay porn is an industry in recession. *Dazed*. Retrieved from http://www.dazeddigital.com/artsandculture/article/28585/1/gay-porn-is-an-industry-in-recession

Goffman, E. (1952). On cooling the mark out: Some aspects of adaptation to failure. *Psychiatry, 15*, 451–463.

Gomstyn, A., & ABC News Business Unit. (2010, Marsh 22). Wife wins $9 million from husband's alleged mistress. Retrieved from http://abcnews.go.com/Business/wife-wins-million-husbands-alleged-mistress/story?id=10151957

Goode, W. J. (1959). The theoretical importance of love. *American Sociological Review, 24*, 38–47.

Goode, W. J. (1963). *World revolution and family patterns*. New York: Free Press.

Goodman, H. (2013). Happily married swingers. *Redbook*. Retrieved from http://www.redbookmag.com/love-sex/relationships/a13224/happy-swinger-couples/

Goodwin, R. (1999). *Personal relationships across cultures*. London: Routledge.

Gottman, J., Gottman, J. M., & Silver, N. (1995). *Why marriages succeed or fail: And how you can make yours last*. New York: Simon and Schuster.

Gould, T. (1999). *The lifestyle: A look at the erotic rites of swingers*. Ontario: Vintage Canada.

Gouldsbury, C., & Sheane, H. (1911). *The great plateau of Northern Rhodesia*. London: Edward Arnold.

Graber, E. C., Laurenceau, J. P., Miga, E., Chango, J., & Coan, J. (2011). Conflict and love: Predicting newlywed marital outcomes from two interaction contexts. *Journal of Family Psychology, 25*(4), 541.

Graf, S. (2016, April 7). Study: A partner's death can cause health problems. *Lifestyle*. http://www.a0l.com/article/2016/04/07/study-a-partner-s-22/death-can-cause-heart-problems/213397

Graham, J. M., & Christiansen, K. (2009). The reliability of romantic love: A reliability generalization meta-analysis. *Personal Relationships, 16*(1), 49–66.

Gray, K., Knobe, J., Sheskin, M., Bloom, P., & Barrett, L. F. (2011). More than a body: Mind perception and the nature of objectification. *Journal of Personality and Social Psychology, 101*(6), 1207.

Greenhouse, S. (1994, February 3). State Dept. finds widespread abuse of world's women. *The New York Times, 143*, pp. 1A–6A.

Greiling, H., & Buss, D. M. (2000). Women's sexual strategies: The hidden dimension of extra-pair mating. *Personality and Individual Differences, 28,* 929–963.

Grello, C. M., Welsh, D. P., & Harper, M. S. (2006). No strings attached: The nature of casual sex in college students. *Journal of Sex Research, 43,* 255–267.

Grello, C. M., Welsh, D. P., Harper, M. S., & Dickson, J. W. (2003). Dating and sexual relationship trajectories and adolescent functioning. *Adolescent and Family Health, 3,* 103–112.

Gribble, J. N., Miller, H. G., Rogers, S. M., & Turner, C. F. (1999). Interview mode and measurement of sexual behaviors: Methodological issues. *Journal of Sex Research, 36*(1), 16–24.

Griffith, J. D., Mitchell, S., Hart, C. L., Adams, L. T., & Gu, L. L. (2013). Pornography actresses: An assessment of the damaged goods hypothesis. *Journal of Sex Research, 50*(7), 621–632.

Grigoriadis, V. (2003, November 19). Princess Paris. *Rolling Stone.* Retrieved from http://www.vanessagrigoriadis.com/rollingstone.html

Guerrero, L. K., Spitzberg, B. H., & Yoshimura, S. M. (2004). Sexual and emotional jealousy. In J. H. Harvey, A. Wenzel, & S. Sprecher (Eds.), *The handbook of sexuality in close relationships* (pp. 311–345). Mahwah, NJ: Lawrence Erlbaum & Associates.

Guttentag, M., & Secord, P. (1983). *Too many women? The sex ratio question.* Thousand Oaks, CA: Sage Publications.

Haavio-Mannila, E., & Kontula, O. (2003). Single and double sexual standards in Finland, Estonia, and St. Petersburg. *Journal of Sex Research, 40,* 36–49.

Hald, G. M., & Malamuth, N. M. (2008). Self-perceived effects of pornography consumption. *Archives of Sexual Behavior, 37*(4), 614–625.

Hald, G. M., Malamuth, N. N., & Lange, T. (2013). Pornography and sexist attitudes among heterosexuals. *Journal of Communication, 63*(4), 638–660.

Hamilton, D. T., & Morris, M. (2010). Consistency of self-reported sexual behavior in surveys. *Archives of Sexual Behavior, 39*(4), 842–860.

Harai, Y. N. (2017). *Homo Deus: A Brief History of Tomorrow.* New York: Harper.

Harmon, A. (2003, June 29). Online dating sheds its stigma as Losers.com. *The New York Times.* Retrieved from http://www.nytimes.com/2003/06/29/national/29DATE.html?ex=1372219200&en=116d836a4d43845c&ei=5007&partner=USER LAND

Hatfield, E. (1984). The dangers of intimacy. In V. J. Derlega (Ed.), *Communication, intimacy, and close relationships* (pp. 207–220). Orlando, FL: Academic Press.

Hatfield, E., Aronson, E., Abrahams, D., & Rottman, L. (1966). The importance of physical attractiveness in dating behavior. *Journal of Personality and Social Psychology, 4,* 508–516.

Hatfield, E., Bensman, L., & Rapson, R. L. (2009). Unmasking passionate love: The face and the brain. In Freitas-Magalhaes (Ed.), *Emotional expression: The brain and the face.* Porto, Portugal: University Fernando Pessoa Press.

Hatfield, E., Brinton, C., & Cornelius, J. (1989). Passionate love and anxiety in young adolescents. *Motivation and Emotion, 13,* 271–289.

Hatfield, E., Cacioppo, J., & Rapson, R. L. (1994). *Emotional contagion.* New York: Cambridge University Press.

Hatfield, E., Feybesse, C., & Rapson, R. L. (2016). Passionate love: Inspired by angels or demons? In K. Aumer (Ed.), *The psychology of love and hate in intimate relationships* (pp. 65–84). New York: Springer.

Hatfield, E., Forbes, M., & Rapson, R. L. (2012). Commentary: Marketing love and sex. *Social Science and Modern SOCIETY: Symposium: Mating Game, 49,* 506–511. doi: 10.1007/s12115-012-9593-1

Hatfield, E., Hutchison, E. S. S., Bensman, L., Young, D., & Rapson, R. L. (2012). Cultural, social, and gender influences on casual sex: New developments. In J. M. Turn & A. D. Mitchell (Eds.), *Social psychology: New developments.* Hauppauge, NY: Nova Science.

Hatfield, E., Luckhurst, C. L., & Rapson, R. L. (2012). A brief history of attempts to measure sexual motives. *Interpersona: An International Journal of Personal Relationships, 6,* 138–154.

Hatfield, E., Pillemer, J. T., O'Brien, M. U., & Le, Y. L. (2008). The endurance of love: Passionate and companionate love in newlywed and long-term marriages. *Interpersona: An International Journal of Personal Relationships, 2,* 35–64. Retrieved from http://www.interpersona.org/issues.php?section=viewfulltext&issue=3&area=14&id=int485ee26d5859b&fulltextid=14&idiom=1

Hatfield, E., & Rapson, R. L. (1987). Passionate love/sexual desire: Can the same paradigm explain both? *Archives of Sexual Behavior, 16,* 259–277.

Hatfield, E., & Rapson, R. L. (1993). *Love, sex, and intimacy: Their psychology, biology, and history.* New York: HarperCollins.

Hatfield, E., & Rapson, R. (1996/2005). *Love and sex: Cross-cultural perspectives.* Needham Heights, MA: Allyn & Bacon. Reprint: Lanham, MD: University Press of America.

Hatfield, E., & Rapson, R. L. (2006). Love and passion. In I. Goldstein, C. M. Meston, S. R. Davis, & A. M. Traish (Eds.), *Women's sexual function and dysfunction: Study, diagnosis and treatment* (pp. 93–97). London: Taylor and Francis.

Hatfield, E., & Rapson, R. L. (2009). The neuropsychology of passionate love. In E. Cuyler & M. Ackhart (Eds.), *Psychology of relationships* (pp. 519–543). Hauppauge, NY: Nova Science.

Hatfield, E., Rapson, R. L., & Aumer-Ryan, K. (2008). Social justice in love relationships: Recent developments. *Social Justice Research. 21,* 413–431.

Hatfield, E., & Sprecher, S. (1986). Measuring passionate love in intimate relations. *Journal of Adolescence, 9,* 383–410.

Hatfield, E., & Walster, G. W. (1978). *A new look at love.* Reading, MA: Addison-Wesley.

Hatfield, E., Walster, G. W., & Berscheid, E. (1978). *Equity: Theory and research.* Boston: Allyn and Bacon.

Haupert, M. L., Gesselman, A. N., Moors, A. C., Fisher, H. E., & Garcia, J. R. (2017). Prevalence of experiences with consensual nonmonogamous relationships: Findings from two national samples of single Americans. *Journal of Sex & Marital Therapy, 43*(5), 424–440.

Heino, R., Ellison, N. B., & Gibbs, J. L. (2010). Relations shopping: Investigating the market metaphor in online dating. *Journal of Social and Personal Relationships, 27,* 427–447.

Helliwell, J., Layard, R., & Sachs, J. (2017). *World happiness report 2017.* New York: Sustainable Development Solutions Network.

Hendrick, S. S., Dicke, A., & Hendrick, C. (1998). The Relationship Assessment Scale. *Journal of Social and Personal Relationships, 15*(1), 137–142.

Hendrick, C., & Hendrick, S. S. (1989). Research on love: Does it measure up? *Journal of Personality and Social Psychology, 56*, 784–794.

Herbenick, D., Reece, M., Schick, V., Sanders, S. A., Dodge, B., & Fortenberry, J. D. (2010). Sexual behavior in the United States: Results from a national probability sample of men and women ages 14–94. *Journal of Sexual Medicine, 7*(s5), 255–265.

Herold, E. S., Corbesi, B., & Collins, J. (1994). Psychosocial aspects of female topless behavior on Australian beaches. *Journal of Sex Research, 31*, 133–142.

Herold, E. S., & Mewhinney, D. M. K. (1993). Gender differences in casual sex and AIDS prevention: A survey of dating bars. *Journal of Sex Research, 30*, 36–42.

Herold, E. S., & Van Kerkwijk, C. (1992). AIDS and sex tourism. *AIDS and Society, 4*, 1–8.

Hersey, G. L. (2006). *Falling in love with statues: Artificial humans from Pygmalion to the present.* Chicago: University of Chicago Press.

Hildebrandt, L. (2015). Media and self representative perceptions: Deception in online dating. Honors College Theses. Paper 149. Retrieved from http://digitalcommons. pace.edu/honorscollege theses/149

Hilger, M. I. (1952). *Arapaho child life and its cultural background.* Washington, DC: U. S. Government Printing Office.

Hill, C. A. (2002). Gender, relationship stage, and sexual behavior: The importance of partner emotional investment within specific situations. *Journal of Sex Research, 39*, 228–240.

Hill, C. T., Rubin, Z., & Peplau, L. A. (1979). Breakups before marriage: The end of 103 affairs. In G. Levinger & O. C. Moles (Eds.), *Divorce and separation* (pp. 64–82). New York: Basic Books.

Hitsch, G. J., Hortaçsu, A., & Ariely, D. (2010). What makes you click?—Mate preferences in online dating. *Quantitative Marketing and Economics, 8*(4), 393–427.

Hoff, C. C., Beougher, S. C., Chakravarty, D., Darbes, L. A., & Neilands, T. B. (2010). Relationship characteristics and motivations behind agreements among gay male couples: Differences by agreement type and couple serostatus. *AIDS Care, 22*, 827–835.

Homer. (1961). *The Iliad* (R. Lattimore, Trans., introduction) Chicago: University of Chicago Press.

Homer, A. (2016, August 14). Australian authorities crack down on life-like child sex dolls, should they be illegal in the U.S. *Inquisitr*, 1–7. Retrieved from http://www. inquisitr.com/3417050/australian-authorities-crack-down-on-life-like-child-sex-dolls-should-they-be-illegal-in-the--u-s/

Hongladarom, S. (2000). Negotiating the global and the local: How Thai culture co-opts the Internet. *First Monday, 5*(8). Retrieved from https://firstmonday.org/ojs/index. php/fm/article/view/782/691

Hooton, C. (2014, November 27). Pornhub: Kim Kardashian's sex tape is the most-watched porn video of all-time. *The Independent*. Retrieved from http://www. independent.co.uk/life-style/gadgets-and-tech/news/pornhub-kim-kardashians-sex-tape-is-the-most-watched-porn-video-of-all-time-9887050.html

Hosking, W. (2013). Agreements about extra-dyadic sex in gay men's relationships: Exploring differences in relationship quality by agreement type and rule-breaking behavior. *Journal of Homosexuality, 60*, 711–733.

Howell, N. (1979). *Demography of the Dobe!Kung.* New York: Academic Press.

Hrdy, S. B. (1981). *The woman that never evolved.* Cambridge, MA: Harvard University Press.

Hrdy, S. B. (1997). Raising Darwin's consciousness: Female sexuality and the prehominid origins of patriarchy. *Human Nature, 8*, 1–49.

Hrdy, S. B. (1999). *Mother nature: Natural selection and the female of the species.* London: Chatto & Windus.

Hsu, F. L. K. (1953). *Americans and Chinese: Passage to difference* (3rd ed.). Honolulu: University Press of Hawaii.

Hsu, F. L. K. (1985). The self in cross-cultural perspective. In A. J. Marsella, G. DeVos, & F. L. K. Hsu (Eds.), *Culture and self: Asian and Western perspectives* (pp. 24–55). London: Tavistock.

Huber, J. D., & Herold, E. S. (2006). Sexually overt approaches in singles bars. *Canadian Journal of Human Sexuality, 15*, 133–146.

Humphreys, T. (2007). Perceptions of sexual consent: The impact of relationship history and gender. *Journal of Sex Research, 44*, 307–315.

Hunt, L. (1996). *The invention of pornography: Obscenity and the origins of modernity, 1500–1800.* New York: Zone Books.

Hunt, M. (1959). *The natural history of love.* New York: Grove Press.

Hupka, R. B. (1981). Cultural determinants of jealousy. *Alternative Lifestyles, 4*, 310–356.

Hupka, R. B. (1991). The motive for the arousal of romantic jealousy: Its cultural origin. In P. Salovey (Ed.), *The psychology of jealousy and envy* (pp. 252–270). New York: Guilford Press.

Hupka, R. B., & Ryan, J. M. (1990). The cultural contribution to jealousy: Cross-cultural aggression in sexual jealousy situations. *Behavior Science Research, 24*, 51–71.

Hyde, J. S. (2005). The gender similarities hypothesis. *American Psychologist, 60*(6), 581.

Internet and Mobile Association of India. (2017). Mobile Internet in India 2017. Retrieved from https://cms.iamai.in/Content/ResearchPapers/2b08cce4-e571-4cfe-9f8b-86435a12ed17.pdf

Internet World Stats. (2016). World Internet users and 2019 population stats. Retrieved from http://www.internetworldstats.com/stats.htm

Jacobs, A. (2011, April 14). For Chinese men, no deed means no dates. *The New York Times.* Retrieved from http://www.nytimes.com/2011/04/15/world/asia/15bachelors.html

Jankowiak, W. (Ed.). (1995). *Romantic passion: A universal experience?* New York: Columbia University Press.

Jankowiak, W. R., & Fischer, E. F. (1992). A cross-cultural perspective on romantic love. *Ethology, 31*, 149–155.

Janzen, B. (1982). Swinging. In W. MacGaffey (Ed.). *Kongo political culture: The conceptual challenge of the particular.* Bloomington: Indiana University Press.

Jaremka, L. M., Glaser, R., Malarkey, W. B., & Kiecolt-Glaser, J. K. (2013). Marital distress prospectively predicts poorer cellular immune function. *Psychoneuroendocrinology, 38*, 2713–2719.

Javanbakht, M., Gorbach, P., Dillavou, M. C., Riggs, R., Pachero, P., & Kerndt, P. R. (2014, June). *Adult film performers transmission behaviors and STI prevalence.* Presented at 2014 National STD Prevention Conference, Centers for Disease Control and Prevention (CDC), Atlanta, GA.

Jefferson, T. (1778). *Amendment VIII. Document 10. A bill for proportioning crimes and punishments.* The Papers of Thomas Jefferson, Vol. 2 (pp. 492–504). Retrieved from http://press-pubs.uchicago.edu/founders/documents/amendVIIIs10.html

Jefferson, T. (1779). *64. A bill for proportioning crimes and punishments in cases heretofore capital.* The Papers of Thomas Jefferson, Vol. 2 (pp. 492–507). Retrieved from https://founders.archives.gov/documents/Jefferson/01-02-02-0132-0004-0064

Jenks, R. R. (1998). Swinging: A review of the literature. *Archives of Sexual Behavior, 5,* 507–521.

Jenks, R. R. (2014, July 7). An on-line survey comparing swingers and polyamorists. *Electronic Journal of Human Sexuality, 17,* 1–15. Retrieved from http://www.ejhs.org/volume17/swing.html

Jonason, P. K., & Balzarini, R. N. (2016). Unweaving the rainbow of human sexuality: A review of one-night stands, serious romantic relationships, and the relationship space in between. In K. Aumer (Ed.), *The psychology of love and hate in intimate relationships* (pp. 13–28). New York: Springer International Publishing.

Jonason, P. K., Garcia, J. R., Webster, G. D., Li, N. P., & Fisher, H. E. (2015). Relationship dealbreakers: Traits people avoid in potential mates. *Personality and Social Psychology Bulletin, 41*(12), 1697–1711.

Jonason, P. K., Li, N. P., & Cason, M. J. (2009). The "booty call": A copromise between men's and women's ideal mating strategies. *Journal of Sex Research, 46,* 460–470.

Jonason, P. K., Li, N. P., & Richardson, J. (2010). Positioning the booty-call relationship on the spectrum of relationships: Sexual but more emotional than one-night stands. *Journal of Sex Research, 47,* 1–10.

Jones, B. T., Jones, B. C., Thomas, A. P., & Piper, J. (2003). Alcohol consumption increases attractiveness ratings of opposite sex faces: A possible third route to risky sex. *Addiction, 98,* 1069–1075.

Jones, R. (2015, May 12). Can a feminist like porn? *Glamour.* Retrieved from http://www.glamour.com/story/rashida-jones-can-a-feminist-like-porn

Joseph, R., & Joseph, T. B. (1987). *The rose and the thorn.* Tucson: University of Arizona Press.

Jozkowski, K. N. (2011). Measuring internal and external conceptualizations of sexual consent: A mixed-methods exploration of sexual consent. (Doctoral dissertation). Retrieved from ProQuest Dissertations and Theses database (UMI No. 3466353).

Jozkowski, K. N., & Peterson, Z. D. (2013). College students and sexual consent: Unique insights. *Journal of Sex Research, 50*(6), 517–523.

Kaestle, E., & Halpern, C. T. (2007). What's love got to do with it? Sexual behaviors of opposite-sex couples through emerging adulthood. *Perspectives on Sexual and Reproductive Health, 39,* 134–140.

Kagitçibasi, C. (1990). Family and socialization in cross cultural perspective: A model of change. *Nebraska Symposium on Motivation, 37,* 136–200.

Karandashev, V., & Clapp, S. (2015). Multidimensional architecture of love: From romantic narratives to psychometrics. *Journal of Psycholinguist Research, 44,* 675–699.

Karney, B. R., & Frye, N. E. (2002). " But we've been getting better lately": Comparing prospective and retrospective views of relationship development. *Journal of Personality and Social Psychology, 82*(2), 222.

Kelley, H. H., Berscheid, E., Christensen, A., Harvey, J. H., Huston, T. L., Levinger, G., . . . Peterson, D. R. (Eds.). (1983). *Close relationships.* New York: Freeman.

Kelly, E. L., & Conley, J. J. (1987). Personality and compatibility: A prospective analysis of marital stability and marital satisfaction. *Journal of Personality and Social Psychology, 52,* 27–40.

Kenrick, D. T., Groth, G. E., Trost, M. R., & Sadalla, E. K. (1993). Integrating evolutionary and social exchange perspectives on relationship: Effects of gender, self-appraisal, and involvement level on mate selection criteria. *Journal of Personality and Social Psychology, 64*, 951–969.

Kephart, W. M. (1967). Some correlates of romantic love. *Journal of Marriage and the Family, 29*, 470–479.

Kim, H. K., & McKenry, P. C. (2002). The relationship between marriage and psychological well-being. *Journal of Family Issues, 23*, 885–911.

Kim, J., & Hatfield, E. (2004). Love types and subjective well being. *Social Behavior and Personality: An International Journal, 32*, 173–182.

Kinsey, A. C., Pomeroy, W. B., & Martin, C. E. (1948). *Sexual behavior in the human male.* Philadelphia: WB Saunders.

Kinsey, A. C., Pomeroy, W. B., Martin, C. E., & Gebhard, P. H. (1954). *Sexual behavior in the human female.* Philadelphia: WB Saunders.

Kitayama, S. (2002.) Culture and basic psychological processes—Toward a system view of culture: Comment on Oyserman et al. (2002). *Psychological Bulletin, 128*, 89–96.

Klaassen, M. J., & Peter, J. (2015). Gender (in) equality in Internet pornography: A content analysis of popular pornographic Internet videos. *Journal of Sex Research, 52*(7), 721–735.

Kleinplatz, P. J., Ménard, A. D., Paquet, M. P., Paradis, N., Campbell, M., Zuccarino, D., & Mehak, L. (2009). The components of optimal sexuality: A portrait of" great sex". *Canadian Journal of Human Sexuality, 18*(1/2), 1.

Kontula, O. (1999). *Between desire and reality.* Publications of The Population Research Institute. Family Federation of Finland. Helsinki, Finland.

Kort, J. (2015, January 30). Guys on the 'side': Looking beyond gay tops and bottoms. *Cypher Avenue.* Retrieved from http://cypheravenue.com/guys-on-the-side-looking-beyond-gay-tops-and-bottoms/

Krupnick, E. (2014, December 11). Why your non-single friends love Tinder more than you do. Connections. *Mic.* Retrieved from https://mic.com/articles/106196/why-your-non-single-friends-love-tinder more-than-you-do#.h2w1RUA1N

Kühn, S., & Gallinat, J. (2014). Brain structure and functional connectivity associated with pornography consumption: The brain on porn. *JAMA Psychiatry, 71*(7), 827–834.

Kurdek, L. A. (1988). Relationship quality of gay and lesbian cohabiting couples. *Journal of Homosexuality, 15*, 93–118.

Kurdek, L. A., & Schmitt, J. P. (1986). Relationship quality of gay men in closed or open relationships. *Journal of Homosexuality, 12*, 85–99.

Kurzweil, R. (2006). *The singularity is near: When humans transcend biology.* New York: Penguin Books.

Ladurie, E. L. R. (1979). *Montaillou: The promised land of error* (B. Bray, Trans.). New York: Vintage Books,

La Gorce, T. L. (2016, March 10). The secrets to an open marriage according to Mo'Nique. *The New York Times.* Retrieved from http://www.nytimes.com/2016/03/13/fashion/weddings/open-marriage-monique.html

Lambert, T. A., Kahn, A. S., & Apple, K. J. (2003). Pluralistic ignorance and hooking up. *Journal of Sex Research, 40*, 129–133.

Lamy, L. (2011). Love or the black sun of personal relationships. *Journal for the Theory of Social Behavior, 41*, 247–259.

Langeslag, S. J. E., Van der Veen, F. M., & Fekkes, D. (2012). Blood levels of serotonin are differentially affected by romantic love in men and women. *Journal of Psychophysiology*, *26*, 92–98.

LaSala, M. C. (2004). Extradyadic sex and gay male couples: Comparing monogamous and nonmonogamous relationships. *Families in Society*, *85*, 405–412.

Laumann, E. O., Gagnon, J. H., Michael, R. T., & Michaels, S. (1994). *The social organization of sexuality: Sexual practices in the United States*. Chicago: University of Chicago Press.

Laurenceau, J. P., Barrett, L. F., & Pietromonaco, P. R. (1998). Intimacy as an interpersonal process: The importance of self-disclosure, partner disclosure, and perceived partner responsiveness in interpersonal exchanges. *Journal of Personality and Social Psychology*, *74*(5), 1238.

Lauria, L. M. (1998). Sexual misconduct in Plymouth colony. Plymouth Colony Archive Project, Department of Anthropology, University of Virginia.

Lawrence v. Texas, 539 U.S. 558 (2003). Retrieved from https://supreme.justia.com/cases/federal/us/539/558/case.html

Le, B., Dove, N. L., Agnew, C. R., Korn, M. S., & Mutso, A. A. (2010). Predicting nonmarital romantic relationship dissolution: A meta-analytic synthesis. *Personal Relationships*, *17*, 377–390.

Leach, L. S., Butterworth, P., Olesen, S. C., & Mackinnon, A. (2013). Relationship quality and levels of depression and anxiety in a large population-based survey. *Social Psychiatry and Psychiatric Epidemiology*, *48*(3), 417–425.

Leary, M. R., Koch, E. J., & Hechenbleikner, N. R. (2001). Emotional responses to interpersonal rejection. In M. Leary (Ed.), *Interpersonal rejection* (pp. 145–166). Oxford: Oxford University Press.

Lehmiller, J. J. (2015). A comparison of sexual health history and practices among monogamous and consensually nonmonogamous sexual partners. *Journal of Sexual Medicine*, *12*(10), 2022–2028.

Lee, G. R., & Stone, L. H. (1980). Mate-selection systems and criteria: Variation according to family structure. *Journal of Marriage and the Family*, *42*, 319–326.

Levine, R., Sato, S., Hashimoto, T., & Verma, J. (1995). Love and marriage in eleven cultures. *Journal of Cross-Cultural Psychology*, *26*, 554–571.

Levy, A. (2006). *Female chauvinist pigs: Women and the rise of raunch culture*. New York: Simon and Schuster.

Levy, D. (2007). *Love + sex with robots: The evolution of human-robot relationships*. New York: Harper-Perennial.

Lewis, M. A., Atkins, D. C., Blayney, J. A., Dent, D. V., & Kaysen, D. L. (2012). What is hooking up? Examining definitions of hooking up in relation to behavioral and normative perceptions. *Journal of Sex Research*, *50*, 757–766.

Li, N. P., & Kenrick, D. T. (2006). Sex similarities and differences in preferences for short-term mates: What, whether, and why. *Journal of Personality and Social Psychology*, *90*, 468–489.

Lindau, S. T., Schumm, L. P., Laumann, E. O., Levinson, W., O'muircheartaigh, C. A., & Waite, L. J. (2007). A study of sexuality and health among older adults in the United States. *New England Journal of Medicine*, *357*(8), 762–774.

Littleton, H., Breitkopf, C. R., & Berenson, A. (2005). Body image and risky sexual behaviors: An investigation in a tri-ethnic sample. *Body Image*, *2*(2), 193–198.

Lloyd, E. A. (2009). *The case of the female orgasm: Bias in the science of evolution.* Cambridge, MA: Harvard University Press.

Lopata, H. Z. (1969). Loneliness: Forms and components. *Social Problems, 17*(2), 248–262.

Love, T., Laier, C., Brand, M., Hatch, L., & Hajela, R. (2015). Neuroscience of Internet pornography addiction: A review and update. *Behavioral Sciences, 5*(3), 388–433.

Loving More Magazine. (2016). http://www.lovemore.com/magazine/

Lowe, D. (1989). Would You . . . ? [Recorded by Touch and Go]. On *I find you very attractive* [CD single].

Luciano, E. M. C. (2003). *Caribbean love and sex: Ethnographic study of rejection and betrayal in heterosexual relationships in Puerto Rico.* Paper presented at the 29th annual meeting of the International Academy of Sex Research meetings, Bloomington, IN.

Lyons, H. A. (2009). *Casual sex in adolescence and young adulthood: A mixed methods approach* (Unpublished doctoral dissertation). Bowling Green State University, Bowling Green, OH

Lyons, H., Manning, W., Giordano, P., & Longmore, M. L. (2013). Predictors of heterosexual casual sex among young adults. *Archives of Sexual Behavior, 42*, 585–593.

Ma, V., & Schoeneman, T. J. (1997). Individualism versus collectivism: A comparison of Kenyan and American self-concepts. *Basic and Applied Social Psychology, 19*(2), 261–273.

Mace, D., & Mace, V. (1980). *Marriage: East and West.* New York: Dolphin Books.

MacKinnon, C. A. (1989). *Toward a feminist theory of the state.* Cambridge, MA: Harvard University Press.

Maddox, A. M., Rhoades, G. K., & Markman, H. J. (2011). Viewing sexually-explicit materials alone or together: Associations with relationship quality. *Archives of Sexual Behavior, 40*(2), 441–448.

Manning, W. D., Giordano, P. C., & Longmore, M. A. (2006). Hooking up: The relationship contexts of 'nonrelationship' sex. *Journal of Adolescent Research, 21*, 459–483.

Marazziti, D., & Canale, D. (2004). Hormonal changes when falling in love. *Psychoneuroendocrinology, 29*, 931–936.

Marciano, J. (2016, July 19). Top 300 biggest websites: Based on both mobile and desktop data for the first time! *Similar Web.* Retrieved from https://www.similarweb.com/blog/new-website-ranking

Maria, C. S. (2016). Inside the factory where the world's most realistic sex robots are being built. *Real Future.* Retrieved from http://fusion.net/story/181661/real-future-episode-6-sex-bots/

Markoff, J. (2016, April 7). When is the singularity? Probably not in your lifetime. *The New York Times.* Retrieved from http://www.nytimes.com/2016/04/07/science/artificial-intelligence-when-is-the-singularity.html

Markus, H. R., & Kitayama, S. (1991). Culture and self: Implications for cognition, emotion, and motivation. *Psychological Review, 98*, 224–253.

Marshall, D. (1971). Sexual behavior on Mangaia. In D. Marshall & R. Suggs (Eds.), *Human sexual behavior: Variations in the ethnographic spectrum* (pp. 103–162). New York: Basic Books.

Martikainen, P., & Valkonen, T. (1996a). Mortality after death of spouse in relation to duration of bereavement in Finland. *Journal of Epidemiology & Community Health, 50*, 264–268.

Martikainen, P., & Valkonen, T. (1996b). Mortality after the death of a spouse: Rates and causes of death in a large Finnish cohort, *American Journal of Public Health*, 86, 1087–1093.

Martin, J. (1979). *Miss Manners' guide to excruciatingly correct behavior*. New York: United Features Syndicate.

Masci, D., & Lipka, M. (2015, December 21). *Where Christian churches, other religions stand on gay marriage*. Pew Research Center. Retrieved from http://www.pewresearch. org/fact-tank/2015/12/21/where-christian-churches-stand-on-gay-marriage/

Mathes, E. W., King, C. A., Miller, J. K., & Reed, R. M. (2002). An evolutionary perspective on the interaction of age and sex differences in short-term sexual strategies. *Psychological Reports*, *90*, 949–956.

Maticka-Tyndale, E., Herold, E. S., & Mewhinney, D. (1998). Casual sex on spring break: Intentions and behaviors of Canadian students. *Journal of Sex Research*, *35*, 254–264.

Maticka-Tyndale, E., Herold, E. S., & Oppermann, M. (2003). Casual sex among Australian schoolies. *Journal of Sex Research*, *40*, 158–169.

McCarthy, J. (2016, January 18). Satisfaction with acceptance of gays in U.S. at new high. Gallup. Retrieved from http://www.gallup.com/poll/188657/satisfaction-acceptance-gays-new-high.aspx

McCullers, C. (1951). *The ballad of the sad café and other stories*. New York. Mariner Books.

McGinley, R. (1995). History of swinging. Steve & Sharon's Internet Lifestyle Club. Retrieved from http/www.stwd.com/ss/info/history.html.

McNeill, W. H. (1963). *The rise of the West: The history of a human community with a retrospective essay*. Chicago: University of Chicago Press.

Means, J. (1991). Coping with a breakup: Negative mood regulation expectancies and depression following the end of a romantic relationship. *Journal of Personality and Social Psychology*, *60*, 327–334.

Meloy, J. R., & Fisher, H. (2005). Some thoughts on the neurobiology of stalking. *Journal of Forensic Sciences*, *50*, 1472–1480.

Merkle, E. R., & Richardson, R. A. (2000). Digital dating and virtual relating: Conceptualizing computer mediated romantic relationships. *Family Relations*, *49*, 187–192.

Messenger, J. C. (1971). Sex and repression in an Irish folk community. In D. S. Mrshall & R. C. Suggs (Eds.), *Human sexual behavior: Variations in the ethnographic spectrum* (pp. 3–37). New York: Basic Books.

Meston, C. M., & Buss, D. M. (2007). Why humans have sex. *Archives of Sexual Behavior*, *36*, 477–507.

Metts, S., Cupach, W. R., & Bejlovec, R. A. (1989). "I love you too much to ever start liking you": Redefining romantic relationships. *Journal of Social and Personal Relationships*, *6*, 259–274.

Meyer, M. L., Berkman, E. T., Karremans, J. C., & Lieberman, M. D. (2011). Incidental regulation of attraction: The neural basis of the derogation of attractive alternatives in romantic relationships. *Cognition and Emotion*, *25*(3), 490–505.

Milhausen, R., & Herold, E. (2001). Reconceptualizing the sexual double standard. *Journal of Psychology and Human Sexuality*, *13*, 63–83.

Mogilski, J. K., Memering, S. L., Welling, L. L. M., & Shackelford, T. K. (2017). Monogamy versus consensual non-monogamy. Alternative approaches to pursuing a strategically pluralistic mating strategy. *Archives of Sexual Behavior*, *46*(2), 407–417.

Monroe, S., Rohde, P., Seeley, J., & Lewinsohn, P. (1999). Life events and depression in adolescence: Relationship loss as a prospective risk factor for first onset of major depressive disorder. *Journal of Abnormal Psychology, 108,* 606–614.

Montoya, R. (2005). The environment's influence on mate preferences. *Sexualities, Evolution & Gender. 7*(2), 115–134.

Morales, L. (2013, January 14). Home Internet access still out of reach for many worldwide. Gallup. Retrieved from http://www.gallup.com/poll/159815/home-internet-access- remains-reach-worldwide.asp

Morgan, E. M. (2011). Associations between young adults' use of sexually explicit materials and their sexual preferences, behaviors, and satisfaction. *Journal of Sex Research, 48*(6), 520–530.

Murphy, K. (2016, January 15). In online dating, 'sextortion' and scams. *The New York Times.* Retrieved from http://www.nytimes.com/2016/01/17/sunday-review/in-online-dating-sextortion-and-scams.html?ref=opinion.

Murray, G. (2011, July 12). The sweet spot: Why women love watching gay male porn. *San Francisco Weekly.* Retrieved from http://archives.sfweekly.com/exhibitionist/2011/07/12/the-sweet-spot-why-women-love-watching-gay-male-porn

Nadler, A., & Dotan, I. (1992). Commitment and rival attractiveness: Their effects on male and female reactions to jealousy-arousing situations. *Sex Roles, 26*(7-8), 293–310.

Najib, A., Lorberbaum, J. P., Kose, S., Bohning, D. E., & George, M. S. (2004). Regional brain activity in women grieving a romantic relationship breakup. *American Journal of Psychiatry, 161*(12), 2245–2256.

Naked capitalism. (2015, September 26). *The Economist.* Retrieved from http://www.economist.com/news/international/21666114-internet-blew-porn-industrys-business-model-apart-its-response-holds-lessons

National Center for Social Research & London School of Hygiene & Tropical Medicine. University College London. (2001). *National survey of sexual attitudes and lifestyles.* Retrieved   from   http://www.data-archive.ac.uk/findingData/snDescription.asp?sn=5223

Nicholls, H. (March, 2016). Do bonobos really spend all their time having sex? BBC Earth. http://www.bbc.com/earth/story/20160317-do-bonobos-really-spend-all-their-time-having-sex

Nikolowski, W. (1980). Aging and sexuality—seen by andrologists (author's transl). *Aktuelle Gerontologie, 10*(3), 115–117.

Nisbett, R. (2003). *The geography of thought: How Asians and Westerners think differently . . . and why.* New York: The Free Press.

Noller, P. (2005). What is this thing called love? Defining the love that supports marriage and family. *Personal Relationships 3,* 97–115.

Norkey, T. (2015, April 27). Film piracy: A threat to the entire movie industry (with sources). *Movie Pilot.* Retrieved from http://moviepilot.com/posts/2889420.

O'Carroll, T. (2015, October 26). Holy hots, why not child sex robots. Heretic TOC: Not the dominant narrative. Retrieved from https://tomocarroll.wordpress.com/2015/10/26/holy-hots-why-not-child-sex-robots

Odunayo, A. (2016). Married man 'finds love' with a sex doll. *Naij.com.* Retrieved from https://gossip.naij.com/874467-hehe-married-man-two-kids-finds-love-sex-doll-photos.html

Ogas, O., & Gaddam, S. (2011). *A billion wicked thoughts: What the world's largest experiment reveals about human desire.* New York: Dutton.

OkCupid. (2016). About. Retrieved from www.okcupid.com/about.

Oliver, M. B., & Hyde, J. S. (1993). Gender differences in sexuality: A meta-analysis. *Psychological Bulletin, 114*, 29–51.

O'Neill, N., & O'Neill, G. (1984). *Open marriage: A new lifestyle for couples.* Lanham, MD: M. Evans & Co.

Orenstein, P. (2016). *Girls & sex: Navigating the complicated new landscape.* London: Oneworld Publications.

Orimoto, L., Hatfield, E., Yamakawa, R., & Denney, C. (1991). *Gender differences in emotional reactions and coping strategies following a break-up* (Unpublished manuscript). University of Hawaii, Honolulu.

Orr, A. (2004). *Meeting, mating, and cheating: Sex, love and the new world of online dating.* Upper Saddle River, NJ: Reuters Prentice Hall.

Owen, J. J., Rhoades, G. K., Stanley, S. M., & Fincham, F. D. (2010). "Hooking up" among college students: Demographic and psychosocial correlates. *Archives of Sexual Behavior, 39*, 653–663. doi:10.1007/s10508-008-9414-1. [PubMed] [CrossRef] [Google Scholar]

Oysermann, D., Kemmelmeier, M., & Coon, H. M. (2002). Cultural psychology, a new look: Reply to Bond (2002), Fiske (2002), Kitayama (2002), and Miller. *Psychological Bulletin, 128*, 110–117.

Paglia, C. (December 14, 1990). Finally, a real feminist. *The New York Times,* Section A, Page 39.

ParkData. (2015). Dating apps US market share by session. Retrieved from https://www.7parkdata.com

Paul, E. L., & Hayes, A. (2002). The casualties of "casual" sex: A qualitative exploration of the phenomenology of college students" hookups. *Journal of Social and Personal Relationships, 19*, 639–661.

Paul, E. L., McManus, B., & Hayes, A. (2000). "Hookups": Characteristics and correlates of college students' spontaneous and anonymous sexual experiences. *Journal of Sexual Research, 37*, 76–88.

Pennebaker, J. W., Dyer, M. A., Caulkins, R. S., Litowitz, D. L., Ackreman, P. L., Anderson, D. B., & McGraw, K. (1979). Don't the girls get prettier at closing time: A country and western application to psychology. *Personality and Social Psychology Bulletin, 5*, 122–125.

Perilloux, C., & Buss, D. M. (2008). Breaking up romantic relationships: Costs experienced and coping strategies deployed. *Evolutionary Psychology, 6*, 164–181.

Perlman, D., & Peplau, L. A. (1981). Toward a social psychology of loneliness. In S. Duck & R. Gilmour (Eds.), *Personal relationships. 3: Personal relationships in disorder* (pp. 31–56). London: Academic Press.

Petersen, J. L., & Hyde, J. S. (2010). A meta-analytic review of research on gender differences in sexuality, 1993–2007. *Psychological Bulletin, 136*, 21–38.

Pew Research Center. (2013, June 4). *Global acceptance of homosexuality.* Retrieved from http://www.pewglobal.org/2013/06/04/global-acceptance-of-homosexuality/

Pew Research Center. (2015, November 3). *U.S. public becoming less religious.* Retrieved from http://www.pewforum.org/2015/11/03/u-s-public-becoming-less-religious/

Pfeiffer, S. M., & Wong, P. T. (1989). Multidimensional jealousy. *Journal of Social and Personal Relationships, 6*(2), 181–196.

Pornhub (January 6, 2016, 2016). Pornhub 2015 year in review. Pornhub Insights. https://www.pornhub.com/insights/pornhub-2015-year-in-review

Poushter, J., & Oates, R. (2015). *Cell phones in Africa: Communication lifeline.* Washingston DC: Pew Research Centre. Retrieved from https://www.pewresearch.org/global/2015/04/15/cell-phones-in-africa-communication-lifeline/

Prakasa, V. V., & Rao, V. N. (1979). Arranged marriages: An assessment of the attitudes of the college students in India. In G. Kurian (Ed.), *Cross-cultural perspectives of mate-selection and marriage* (pp. 11–31). Westport, CN: Greenwood Press.

Prause, N., & Pfaus, J. (2015). Viewing sexual stimuli associated with greater sexual responsiveness, not erectile dysfunction. *Sexual Medicine, 3*(2), 90–98.

Price, J., Patterson, R., Regnerus, M., & Walley, J. (2016). How much more XXX is Generation X consuming? Evidence of changing attitudes and behaviors related to pornography since 1973. *Journal of Sex Research, 53*(1), 12–20.

Priceonomics. (2016, June 1). Conquer love with these crucial dating app statistics. *Survey Monkey Intelligence Blog.* Retrieved from https://www.surveymonkey.com/business/intelligence/dating-apps/

Proulx, C. M., Helms, H. M., & Buehler, C. (2007). Marital quality and personal well-being: A meta-analysis. *Journal of Marriage and Family, 69,* 576–593.

Pryor, J. H., Hurtado, S., Saenz, V. B., Santos, J. L., & Korn, W. S. (2007). *The American freshman: Forty year trends.* Los Angeles: Higher Education Research Institute, University of California, Los Angeles. Retrieved from https://www.heri.ucla.edu/PDFs/pubs/TFS/Trends/Monographs/TheAmericanFreshman40YearTrends.pdf

Puentes, J., Knox, D., & Zusman, M. W. (2008). Participants in "friends with benefits" relationships. *College Student Journal, 42,* 176–180. NY: Project Innovation.

Punit, I. S. (2016, July 25). Indian travelers "like" Internet access more than a bottle of wine or a hot shower. *Quartz: India.* Retrieved from http://qz.com/738904/indian-travellers-like- internet-access-more-than-a-bottle-of-wine-or-a-hot-shower/

Purvis, J. L. (2017). *Strategic interference and Tinder use: A mixed-method exploration of romantic interactions in contemporary contexts* (Unpublished doctoral dissertation).

Ramey, J. W. (1975). Intimate groups and networks: Frequent consequences of sexually open marriage. *Family Coordinator, 24,* 515–530.

Rapson, R. L. (1988). *American yearnings: Love, money, and endless possibility.* Lanham, MD: University Press of America.

Rapson, R. L. (2003). *Amazed by life: Confessions of a non-religious believer.* New York: Random House.

Rapson, R. L. (2008). *Magical thinking and the decline of America.* New York: Random House.

Real, E. (2016, November 4). Mo'Nique defends her open marriage with husband Sidney Hicks: 'It's so not about sex.' *US Weekly.* Retrieved from http://www.usmagazine.com/celebrity-news/news/monique-defends-her-open-marriage-with-husband-sidney-hicks-w448702

Regan, P. C. (2000). The role of sexual desire and sexual activity in dating relationships. *Social Behavior and Personality: An International Journal, 28,* 51–60.

Regan, P. C. (2003). *The mating game: A primer on love, sex, and marriage.* Thousand Oaks, CA: Sage Publications.

Regan, P. C., & Dreyer, C. S. (1999). Lust? Love? Status? Young adults' motives for engaging in casual sex. *Journal of Psychology & Human Sexuality, 11*(1), 1–24.

Regnerus, M., Gordon, D., & Price, J. (2016). Documenting pornography use in America: A comparative analysis of methodological approaches. *Journal of Sex Research, 53,* 873–881.

Reis, H. T., Aron, A., Clark, M. S., & Finkel, E. J. (2013). Ellen Berscheid, Elaine Hatfield, and the emergence of relationship science. *Perspectives on Psychological Science, 8*(5), 558–572.

Resch, M. N., & Alderson, K. G. (2014). Female partners of men who use pornography: Are honesty and mutual use associated with relationship satisfaction? *Journal of Sex & Marital Therapy, 40*(5), 410–424.

Riela, S., Rodriguez, G., Aron, A., Xu, X., & Acevedo, B. C. (2010). Experiences of falling in love. Investigating culture, ethnicity, gender, and speed. *Journal of Social and Personal Relationships, 27,* 473–493.

Rifkin, R. (2014, May 30). New record highs in moral acceptability. Gallup. Retrieved from http://www.gallup.com/poll/170789/new-record-highs-moral-acceptability.aspx

Rinaldi, S., Rossa, F. D., Dercole, F., Gragnani, A., & Landi, P. (2016). *Modeling love dynamics.* London: World Scientific.

Robb, G. (2008). *The discovery of France.* New York: W. W. Norton.

Roberts, J. M. (1976). *History of the world.* New York: Knopf.

Robles, T. F., Slatcher, R. B., Trombello, J. M., & McGinn, M. M. (2014). Marital quality and health: A meta-analytic review. *Psychological Bulletin, 140,* 140–187.

Rosenberger, J. G., Reece, M., Schick, V., Herbenick, D., Novak, D. S., Van Der Pol, B., & Fortenberry, J. D. (2011). Sexual behaviors and situational characteristics of most recent male-partnered sexual event among gay and bisexually identified men in the United States. *Journal of Sexual Medicine, 8*(11), 3040–3050.

Rosenblatt, P. C. (1967). Marital residence and the function of romantic love. *Ethnology, 6,* 471–480.

Rosenblatt, P. C., & Anderson, R. M. (1981). Human sexuality in cross-cultural perspective. In M. Cook (Ed.), *The bases of human sexual attraction* (pp. 215–250). London: Academic Press.

Rosenfeld, M. J., & Thomas, R. J. (2012). Searching for a mate: The rise of the Internet as a social intermediary. *American Sociological Review, 77*(4), 523–547.

Rosenzweig, A., Prigerson, H., Miller, M. D., & Reynolds III, C. F. (1997). Breavement and late-life depression: Grief and its complications in the elderly. *Annual Review of Medicine, 48,* 421–428.

Rubel, A. N., & Bogaert, A. F. (2015). Consensual nonmogamy: Psychological well-being and relationship quality correlates. *Journal of Sex Research, 52,* 961–982.

Rubin, A. M., & Adams, J. R. (1986). Outcomes of sexually open marriages. *Journal of Sex Research, 22,* 311–319.

Rubio, G. (2014). How love conquered marriage: Theory and evidence on the disappearance of arranged marriages. Retrieved from http://www.sole-jole.org/15097.pdf

Russell, D., Peplau, L. A., & Ferguson, M. L. (1978). Developing a measure of loneliness. *Journal of Personality Assessment, 42,* 290–294.

Sabina, C., Wolak, J., & Finkelhor, D. (2008). The nature and dynamics of Internet pornography exposure for youth. *Cyber Psychology & Behavior, 11*(6), 691–693.

Salisbury, C. M., & Fisher, W. A. (2014). "Did you come?" A qualitative exploration of gender differences in beliefs, experiences, and concerns regarding female orgasm occurrence during heterosexual sexual interactions. *Journal of Sex Research, 51*(6), 616–631.

Sandberg-Thoma, S. E., & Dush, C. M. K. (2013). Casual sexual relationships and mental health in adolescence and emerging adulthood. *Journal of Sex Research, 51,* 121–130.

Sands, K. M. (2000). *God forbid: Religion and sex in American public life*. New York: Oxford University Press.

Sasson, J. P. (1992). *Princess: A true story of life behind the veil in Saudi Arabia*. New York: William Morrow and Co.

Sbarra, D. A., Smith, H. L., & Mehl, M. R. (2012). When leaving your ex, love yourself observational ratings of self-compassion predict the course of emotional recovery following marital separation. *Psychological Science, 23*(3), 261–269.

Schaefer, L. C. (1973). *Women and sex: Sexual experiences and reactions of a group of thirty women as told to a female psychotherapist*. New York: Pantheon.

Schmitt, D. P., & 118 members of the International Sexuality Description Project. (2003). Universal sex differences in the desire for sexual variety: Tests from 52 nations, 6 continents, and 13 islands. *Journal of Personality and Social Psychology, 85*, 85–104.

Schmitt, D. P., & Buss, D. M. (2001). Human mate poaching: Tactics and temptations for infiltrating existing mateships. *Journal of Personality and Social Psychology, 80*(6), 894.

Schmitt, D. P., Young, G., Bond, B., Brooks, S., Frye, H., Johnson, S., . . . Stoka, C. (2009). When will I feel love? The effects of culture, personality, and gender on the psychological tendency to love. *Journal of Research in Personality, 43*, 830–846.

Schneider, J. P. (2000). Effects of cybersex addiction on the family: Results of a survey. *Sexual Addiction & Compulsivity: The Journal of Treatment and Prevention, 7*(1-2), 31–58.

Scuglia, B. (2015). The last days of gay porn. *Psychology & Sexuality, 6*(1), 111–117.

Serewicz, M. C. M., & Gale, E. (2008). First-date scripts: Gender roles, context, and relationship. *Sex Roles, 58*(3-4), 149–164.

Shaver, P. R., & Hazan, C. (1988). A biased overview of the study of love. *Journal of Social and Personal Relationships, 5*, 474–501.

Shaver, P. R., Murdaya, U., & Fraley, R. C. (2001). Structure of the Indonesian emotion lexicon. *Asian Journal of Social Psychology, 4*, 201–224.

Shaver, P. R., Wu, S., & Schwartz, J. C. (1991). Cross-cultural similarities and differences in emotion and its representation: A prototype approach. In M. S. Clark (Ed.), *Review of personality and social psychology, 13* (pp. 175–212). Thousand Oaks, CA: Sage Publications.

Shostak, M. (1981). *Nisa: The life and words of a!Kung woman*. Cambridge, MA: Harvard University Press.

Shotland, R. L. (1989). A model of the causes of date rape in developing and close relationships. In C. Hendrick (Ed.), *Close relationships* (pp. 247–270). Thousand Oaks, CA: Sage Publications.

Silverman, L. H. (1971). An experimental technique for the study of unconscious conflict. *British Journal of Medical Psychology, 44*(1), 17–25.

SimilarWeb. (2016) . Tinder. Retrieved from https://www.similarweb.com/app/google-play/com.tinder/statistics#ranking

Simmons, C. H., Vom Kolke, A., & Shimizu, H. (1986). Attitudes toward romantic love among American, German, and Japanese students. *Journal of Social Psychology, 126*, 327–337.

Simon, I. (2015, August 7). Interview: Kelly Madison—matriarch of the mom & pop porn shop. *BaDoink.io*. Retrieved from http://www.badoink.io/life/interviews/interview-kelly-madison-matriarch-of-the-mom-pop-porn-shop/

Simpson, J. A., Campbell, B., & Berscheid, E. (1986). The association between romantic love and marriage: Kephart (1967) twice revisited. *Personality and Social Psychology Bulletin, 12*, 363–372.

Skocpol, T. (1979). *States and social revolutions: A comparative analysis of France, Russia, and China*. New York: Cambridge University Press.

Slatcher, R. B., & Selcuk, E. (2017). A social psychological perspective on the links between close relationships and health. *Current Directions in Psychological Science, 26*(1), 16–21.

Slinkard, M. S., & Kazer, M. W. (2011). Older adults and HIV and STI screening: The patient perspective. *Geriatric Nursing, 32*(5), 341–349.

Smith, A., & Anderson, M. (2016, February 29). *5 facts about online dating*. Pew Research Center. Retrieved from http://www.pewresearch.org/fact-tank/2016/02/29/5-facts-about-online-dating/

Smith, J. C., & Hogan, B. (1983). *Criminal law* (5th ed.). London: Butterworths.

Smith, T. W., & Son, J. (2013). *Trends in public attitudes about sexual morality*. NORC at the University of Chicago. Retrieved from http://www.norc.org/PDFs/sexmoralfinal_06-21_FINAL.PDF

Sommer, V. (1993, November 13). *Primate origins: The hardware of human sexuality*. Paper presented at the meetings of the Society for the Scientific Study of Sex, San Diego, CA.

Sönmez, S., Apostolopoulos, Y., Yu, C. H., Yang, S., Matilla, A., & Yu, L. C. (2006). Binge drinking and casual sex on spring break. *Annals of Tourism Research, 33*, 895–917.

Soueif, A. (1999). *The map of love*. London: Bloomsbury Publishing.

Spitzberg, B. H., & Cupach, W. R. (2007). Cyber-stalking as (mis)matchmaking. In M. Whitty, A. Baker, & J. A. Inman (Eds.), *Online matchmaking* (pp. 127–146). Hampshire, UK: Palgrave Macmillan.

Sprecher, S., Aron, A., Hatfield, E., Cortese, A., Potapova, E., & Levitskaya, A. (1994). Love: American style, Russian style, and Japanese style. *Personal Relationships, 1*, 349–369.

Sprecher, S., & Chandak, R. (1992). Attitudes about arranged marriages and dating among men and women from India. *Free Inquiry in Creative Sociology, 20*, 1–11.

Sprecher, S., & Metts, S. (1999). Romantic beliefs: Their influence on relationships and patterns of change over time. *Journal of Social and Personal Relationships, 16*(6), 834–851.

Sprecher, S., Schwartz, P., Harvey, J., & Hatfield, E. (2008). The businessoflove.com: Relationship initiation at Internet matchmaking services. In S. Sprecher, A. Wenzel, & J. Harvey (Eds.), *The Handbook of Relationship Initiation* pp. 249–265). New York: Erlbaum.

Sprecher, S., & Toro-Morn, M. (2002). A study of men and women from different sides of earth to determine if men are from Mars and women are from Venus in their beliefs about love and romantic relationships. *Sex Roles, 46*(5), 131–147.

Sprecher, S., Treger, S., & Sakaluk, J. K. (2013). Premarital sexual standards and sociosexuality: Gender, ethnicity, and cohort differences. *Archives of Sexual Behavior, 42*, 1395–1405.

Stack, S., Wasserman, I., & Kern, R. (2004). Adult social bonds and use of internet pornography. *Social Science Quarterly, 85*(1), 75–88.

Statistica. (2015). Number of mobile phone users in India from 2013 to 2019 (in millions). Retrieved from http://www.statista.com/statistics/274658/forecast-of-mobile-phone-users-in-india

Statistica. (2016). Leading dating websites in the United States in June 2015, based on visitor numbers (in millions). Retrieved from http://www.statista.com/statistics/274144/most-popular-us-dating-websites-ranked-by-monthly-visitors/

Statistics Brain Research Institute. (2016a, January 18). Online dating statistics. Retrieved from http://www.statisticbrain.com/online-dating-statistics/

Statistics Brain Research Institute. (2016b, February 16). Arranged/forced marriage statistics. *Statistic Brain*. Retrieved from http://www.statisticbrain.com/arranged-marriage-statistics/

Stavrianos, L. S. (1981). *Global rift: The Third World comes of age*. New York: Morrow.

Stephens, W. N. (1963). *The family in cross-cultural perspective*. New York: Holt, Rinehart & Winston.

Sternberg, R. J. (1988). *The triangle of love*. New York. Basic Books.

Stewart, M. (2015). The 100 most influential people: Kim Kardashian West. *Time Magazine*. Retrieved from http://time.com/collection/2015-time-100/

Stolberg, S. G., & Pérez-Peña, R. (2016, February 5). Wildly popular app Kik offers teenagers, and predators, anonymity. *The New York Times*. Retrieved from https://www.nytimes.com/2016/02/06/us/social-media-apps-anonymous-kik-crime.html

Stone, E. A., Goetz, A. T., & Shackelford, T. E. (2005). Sex differences and similarities in preferred mating arrangements. *Sexualities, Evolution, and Gender, 7*, 269–276.

Stone, L. (1977). *The family, sex and marriage: In England 1500–1800*. New York: Harper.

Strassburg, D., & McKinnon, R. K. (2013). Sexting by high school students: An exploratory and descriptive study. *Archives of Sexual Behavior, 42*, 15–21.

Sullivan, R., & McKee, A. (2015). *Pornography: Structures, agency and performance*. Hoboken, NJ: John Wiley & Sons.

Surbey, M. K., & Conohan, C. D. (2000). Willingness to engage in casual sex: The role of parental qualities and perceived risk of aggression. *Human Nature, 11*, 367–386.

Symons, D. (1979). *The evolution of human sexuality*. New York: Oxford University Press.

Tabori, P. (1969). *The humor and technology of sex*. New York: Julian Press.

Tadros, S. (2016, July 5). Crackdown as men jailed over 'gay wedding.' *Sky News*. Retrieved from http://news.sky.com/story/crackdown-as-men-jailed-over-gay-wedding-10383595

Takahashi, K., Mizuno, K., Sasaki, A. T., Wada, Y., Tanaka, M., Ishii, A., . . . Watanabe, Y. (2015). Imaging the passionate stage of romantic love by dopamine dynamics. *Frontiers in Human Neuroscience, 9*, 191–198.

Tannahill, R. (1992). *Sex in history*. Chelsea, MI: Scarborough House Publishers.

Tappé, M., Bensman, L., Hayashi, K., & Hatfield, E. (2013). Gender differences in receptivity to sexual offers: A new research prototype. *Interpersona: An International Journal of Personal Relationships, 7*, 323–334.

Testa, M., & Collins, R. L. (1997). Alcohol and risky sexual behavior: Event-based analyses among a sample of high-risk women. *Psychology of Addictive Behaviors, 11*, 190–201.

Thompson, L. Y., & Muehlenhard, C. L. (2003, April). Factors affecting women's decisions to pretend to experience orgasms. In *Eastern Region-Midcontinent Region conference of the Society for the Scientific Study of Sexuality, Baltimore, MD*.

Thornton, P. D. (2015). *The influence of STI status on romantic and sexual behavior intentions* (Doctoral dissertation, Order No. 10085625). Available from Dissertations & Theses @ University of Hawai`i at Manoa; ProQuest Dissertations & Theses Global (1780629133). Retrieved from http://eres.library.manoa.hawaii.edu/login?url=http://search.proquest.com.eres.library.manoa.hawaii.edu/docview/1780629133?accountid=27140

Toma, C. L., Hancock, J. T., & Ellison, N. B. (2008). Separating fact from fiction: An examination of deceptive self-presentation in online dating profiles. *Personality and Social Psychology Bulletin, 34,* 1023–1036.

Tooby, J., & Cosmides, L. (1992). The evolutionary and psychological foundations of the social sciences. In J. H. Barkow, L. Cosmides, & J. Tooby (Eds.), *The adapted mind: Evolutionary psychology and the generation of culture* (pp. 19–136). New York: Oxford University Press.

Topping, A. (2012, October 22). Parasite porn websites stealing images and videos posted by young people. *The Guardian.*

Townsend, J. M., Kline, J., & Wasserman, T. H. (1995). Low-investment copulation: Sex differences in motivations and emotional reactions. *Ethology and Sociobiology, 16,* 25–51.

Toynbee, A. (1934). *A study of history* (Vols. 1–4). New York: Oxford University Press.

Tracy, J. (2012, March 22). How many online dating sites are there? *Online Dating Magazine.* Retrieved from http://www.onlinedatingmagazine.com/faq/howmanyonli nedatingsitesarethere.html

Traeen, B., & Lewin, B. (1992). Casual sex among Norwegian adolescents. *Archives of Sexual Behavior, 21,* 253–269.

Traupmann, J., & Hatfield, E. (1981). Love and its effect on mental and physical health. In R. Fogel, E. Hatfield, S. Kiesler, & E. Shanas (Eds.), *Aging: Stability and change in the family* (pp. 253–274). New York: Academic Press.

Traupmann, J., Peterson, R., Utne, M., & Hatfield, E. (1981). Measuring equity in intimate relations. *Applied Psychological Measurement, 5,* 467–480.

Trawick, M. (1990). *Notes on love in a Tamil family.* Berkeley: University of California Press.

Triandis, H. C., McCusker, C., & Hui, C. H. (1990). Multimethod probes of individualism and collectivism. *Journal of Personality and Social Psychology, 59,* 1006–1020.

Trouble, C. (2014). Finding gender through porn performance. *Porn Studies, 1*(1-2), 197–200.

Tyson, G., Perta, V. C., Haddadi, H., & Seto, M. C. (2016). A first look at user activity on Tinder. arXiv preprint arXiv:1607.01952.

Tziallas, E. (2015). Gamified eroticism: Gay male "social networking" applications and self-pornography. *Sexuality & Culture, 19*(4), 759–775.

Valverde, S. H. (2012). *The modern sex doll-owner: A descriptive analysis* (Unpublished master's thesis). California State Polytechnic University, Pomona, CA.

VandenBos, G. R. (Ed.). (2007). *APA dictionary of psychology.* Washington, DC: American Psychological Association.

Vannier, S. A., & O'Sullivan, L. F. (2012). Who gives and who gets: Why, when, and with whom young people engage in oral sex. *Journal of Youth and Adolescence, 41*(5), 572–582.

Van Steenbergen, H., Langeslag, S. J. E., Band, G. P. H., & Hommel, B. (2014). Reduced cognitive control in passionate lovers. *Motivation and Emotion, 38,* 444–450.

Vivinetto, G. (2016, August 3). What 'hookup culture?' Millenials having less sex than their parents. *NBC News.* Retrieved from http://www.nbcnews.com/health/sexual-health/what-hookup-culture-millennials-having-less-sex-their-parents-n621746.

Voon, V., Mole, T. B., Banca, P., Porter, L., Morris, L., Mitchell, S., . . . Irvine, M. (2014). Neural correlates of sexual cue reactivity in individuals with and without compulsive sexual behaviours. *PloS one, 9*(7), e102419.

Vorakitphokatorn, S., Pulerwitz, J., & Cash, R. A. (1998). HIV/AIDS risk to women travelers in Thailand: Comparison of Japanese and Western populations. *International Quarterly of Community Health Education, 18*, 69–87.

W3Techs. (2013). https://w3techs.com

W3Techs. (2016, October). Usage of content languages for websites. Retrieved from https://w3techs.com/technologies/overview/content_language/all

Wade, L. D., Kremer, E. C., & Brown, J. (2005). The incidental orgasm: The presence of clitoral knowledge and the absence of orgasm for women. *Women & Health, 42*(1), 117–138.

Wagner, G. J., Remien, R. H., & Carballo-Diéguez, A. (2000). Prevalence of extradyadic sex in male couples of mixed HIV status and its relationship to psychological distress and relationship quality. *Journal of Homosexuality, 39*, 31–46.

Wallen, K. (1989). Mate selection: Economics and affection. *Behavioral and Brain Sciences, 12*, 37–38.

Waller, W. W. (1937). The rating and dating complex. *Amerian Sociological Review, 2*, 727–734.

Wallerstein, I. M. (1974). *The modern world-system.* New York: Academic Press.

Walster, G. W. (1975). The Walster, et al. (1973) Equity formula: A correction. *Representative Research in Social Psychology, 6*, 65–67.

Wang, A. Y., & Nguyen, H. T. (1995). Passionate love and anxiety: A cross-generational study. *Journal of Social Psychology, 135*, 459–470.

Watkins, S. J., & Boon, S. D. (2016). Expectations regarding partner fidelity in dating relationships. *Journal of Social and Personal Relationships, 33*, 237–256.

Weaver, S. E., & Ganong, L. W. (2004). The factor structure of the Romantic Belief Scale for African Americans and European Americans. *Journal of Social and Personal Relationships, 21*, 171–185.

Weeks, D. J. (2002). Sex for the mature adult: Health, self-esteem and countering ageist stereotypes. *Sexual and Relationship Therapy, 17*(3), 231–240.

Weidman, A. C., Cheng, J. T., Chisholm, C., & Tracy, J. L. (2015). Is she the one? Personality judgments from online personal advertisements. *Personal Relationships, 22*, 591–603.

Weiss, R. S. (1979). The emotional impact of marital separation. In G. Levinger & O. C. Moles (Eds.), *Divorce and separation* (pp. 201–210). New York: Basic Books.

Welsh, D. P., Grello, C. M., & Harper, M. S. (2003). When love hurts: Depression and adolescent romantic relationships. In P. Florshiem (Ed.), *Adolescent romantic relations and sexual behavior: Theory, research, and practical implications* (pp. 18–212). Mahwah, NJ: Lawrence Erlbaum Associates.

White, G. L., & Mullen, P. E. (1989). *Jealousy: Theory, research, and clinical strategies.* New York: Guilford Press.

Wiederman, M. W. (1997). Extramarital sex: Prevalence and correlates in a national survey. *Journal of Sex Research, 34*, 167–174.

Wiederman, M. W., & Allgeier, E. R. (1996). Expectations and attributions regarding extramarital sex among young married individuals. *Journal of Psychology and Human Sexuality, 8*, 21–35.

Wildermuth, S. M. (2004). The effects of stigmatizing discourse on the quality of on-line relationships. *Cyber-Psychology & Behavior, 7*, 73–84.

Williams, B. T. (2008). "What South Park character are you?": Popular culture, literacy, and online performances of identity. *Computers and Composition, 25*(1), 24–39.

Williams, L. (1989). *Hard core: Power, pleasure, and the frenzy of the visible.* Berkeley: University of California Press.

Wilson, M., & Daly, M. (1992). The man who mistook his wife for a chattel. In J. H. Barkow, L. Cosmides, & J. Tooby (Eds.), *The adapted mind: Evolutionary psychology and the generation of culture* (pp. 289–326). New York: Oxford University Press.

Wilson, M., & Daly, M. (1993). Spousal homicide risk and estrangement. *Violence and Victims, 8,* 3–16.

Wilt, S., & Olson, S. (1996). Prevalence of domestic violence in the United States. *Journal of the American Women's Association, 51,* 77–82.

Wittfogel, K. A. (1957). *Oriental despotism: A comparative study of total power.* New Haven, CT: Yale University Press.

Wolkstein, D. (1991). *The first love stories.* New York: Harper Perennial.

Wood, W., & Eagly, A. H. (2002). A cross-cultural analysis of the behavior of women and men: Implications for the origins of sex differences. *Psychological Bulletin, 128,* 699–727.

World Bank Group. (2013). *Poverty and equity data.* Retrieved from http://povertydata. worldbank.org/poverty/home/

Wright, P. J., Tokunaga, R. S., & Kraus, A. (2015). A Meta-analysis of pornography consumption and actual acts of sexual aggression in general population studies. *Journal of Communication, 66*(1), 183–205.

Wu, V. (2016). Yen for animation inspired Hong Kong designer's robot. *Reuters/Daily Mail.* http://www.dailymail.co.uk/wires/reuters/article-3518636/WIDER-IMAGE-Yen-animation-inspired-Hong-Kong-designers-robot.html

Xu, X., Aron, A., Brown, L., Cao, G., Feng, T., & Weng, X. (2011). Reward and motivation systems: A brain mapping study of early-stage intense romantic love in Chinese participants. *Human Brain Mapping, 32*(2), 249–257.

Young, D., & Hatfield, E. (2011). Measuring equity in close relationships. In T. D. Fisher, C. M. Davis, W. L. Yaber, & S. L. Davis (Eds.), *Handbook of sexuality-related measures: A compendium* (3rd ed.). (pp. 216–219). Thousand Oaks, CA: Taylor & Francis.

YouPorn. (2011, August 30). YouPorn's top 10: Most viewed porn videos of all time. *YouPorn Blog.* Retrieved from http://blog.youporn.com/youporns-top-10-most-viewed-videos-of-all-time/

Zeki, S., & Romaya, J. P. (2010). The brain reaction to viewing faces of opposite- and same-sex romantic partners. *PLoS ONE, 5,* e15802.

Zimbardo, P. G. (1969). The human choice: Individuation, reason, and order versus deindividuation, impulse, and chaos. *Nebraska Symposium on Motivation, 17,* 207–337.

Zimmer-Gembeck, M., & Helfand, M. (2008). Ten years of longitudinal research on US adolescent sexual behavior: Developmental correlates of sexual intercourse, and the importance of age, gender, and ethnic background. *Developmental Review, 28,* 153–224.

Zuckerman, E. (2013, June 20). English is no longer the language of the Web. *Quartz.* Retrieved from http://qz.com/96054/english-is-no-longer-the-language-of-the-web/

Name Index

Tables and figures are indicated by *t* and *f* following the page number

For the benefit of digital users, indexed terms that span two pages (e.g., 52–53) may, on occasion, appear on only one of those pages.

ABC News Business Unit, 109
Abdullah, A. S. M., 133–34, 145*t*
Abrahams, D., 74–75
Abrahams, M. F., 35
Acevedo, B. C., 8
Acevedo, B. P., 94, 206
Adams, J. R., 160
Adams, L. T., 182
Addiction.com, 176
Aggarwal, R., 64
Agha, S., 144, 145*t*
Agnew, C. R., 206
Agyei, Y., 35
Alderson, K. G., 188
Alexander, M. G., 107, 134
Allgeier, E. R., 17, 153
Allison, R., 107–8
Alt, L. K., 38
Amato, P. R., 96
American Psychiatric Association, 96, 175–76
Ammar, H., 143–44, 145*t*
Anderson, M., 24, 44, 59, 64–65
Anderson, R. M., 14–15
Ansari, A., 135
Anselm, 77
Antebi-Gruszka, N., 183
Apostolopoulos, Y., 145*t*
Apostolou, M., 66–67
AppAnnie, 70–71
Apple, K. J., 129
Ariely, D., 33, 36, 45
Ariès, P., 53
Aron, A., 4, 8, 40, 75–76, 91, 92, 94, 206
Aron, E. N., 94
Aronson, E., 74–75
Asadorian, J. A.

Asante, R. K. B., 46
Asher, S. J., 216
Assimos, J., 48
Atkins, D. C., 142–43
Aubrey, J. S., 125, 129
Aumer, K., 162
Aumer-Ryan, K., 74
Axinn, W. G., 8
Axtell, J. L., 56

Bailey, B. L., 128
Bailey, J. M., 35
Bailey, J. V., 115–16
Bakalar, N., 181–82
Balcetis, E., 137
Balzarini, R. N., 123–24
Band, G. P. H., 96
Baranowski, A. M., 139–40
Barbee, A. P., 38
Barker, M., 157–58, 161
Barkow, J. H., 164
Barrett, L. F., 95, 178
Barriger, M., 135
Bauer, M., 112
Baumeister, R. F., 35, 79, 97, 98, 134
Bay-Cheng, L. Y., 123–24
BBC News, 66
Beaumont-Thomas, B., 189
Beck, A. T., 215–16
Becker, G. S., 81–82
Bejlovec, R. A., 210
Bellamy, E., 227
Bendix, R., 54–56
Bengali, S., 43–44, 71
Bensman, L., 141
Benson, 2
Beougher, S. C., 157–58

Berenson, A., 114
Bergstrand, C., 157–58, 160–61
Berkman, E. T., 137
Bersamin, M. M., 141–42
Berscheid, E., vii, 17, 34, 77
Bianchi-Demicheli, F., 49
Bierce, Ambrose, 156
Bird, W., 174
Bishop, 186
Bisson, M. A., 142
Blair, K. L., 115–16
Blasband, D., 157–58
Blayney, J. A., 142–43
Bloch, I., 191
Bloom, B. L., 216
Bloom, P., 178
Blumstein, P., 151
Bogaert, A. F., 153, 157–58, 160, 161
Bogle, K., 138, 139–40, 141, 143
Bohning, D. E., 215
Boon, S. D., 152–53
Bossard, J. H.S., 44
Bostrom, N., 175
Braithwaite, S. R., 93–94
Brand, M., 175–76
Brandt, Holly, xiii
Braudel, F., 52–53
Breitkopf, C. R., 114
Bringle, R. G., 162
Brink, S., 92
Brinton, C., 94
Bronner, E., 109
Brooke, J., 102–3
Broude, G. J., 15
Brown, G., 215–16
Brown, J., 116–17
Brown, L., 91, 92
Brown, L. L., 206
Brown, N. R., 107–8
Browning, J. R., 135–36
Buehler, C., 96
Bumroongsook, S., 14–15
Burkett, B. N., 38
Burton, R., 102
Buss, D. M., 39, 79, 101, 102–3, 126–27,
    131, 132, 133–34, 135–36, 149, 152–53,
    164, 210
Butterworth, P., 95

Buunk, B., 100, 162

Cacioppo, J. T., 4, 92–93
Cacioppo, S., 4, 49, 92–93
Campbell, B., 17
Canale, D., 96
Canetto, S. S., 96
Čapek, K., 193
Capellanus, A., 12
Carballo-Diéguez, A., 157–58
Carey, K. B., 141
Carey, M. P., 141
Carnochan, P., 1
Casanova, 135
Cash, R. A., 145t
Cason, M. J., 133
Catanese, K. R., 35
Centers for Disease Control and
    Prevention (CDC), 111, 181
Chakravarty, D., 157–58
Chance, Z., 36
Chandak, R., 14
Chandra, A., 111
Chang, L., 30
Changan, 206
Chatel, A., 114–15
Cheng, C-L., 11–12
Cheng, J. T., 33
Chisholm, C., 33
Choo, P., 135–36
Christian, S., 170
Christiansen, K., 2
Christianson, M., 139–40
Chu, G. C., 9
Clapp, S., 93
Clark, C. L., 35
Clark, M. S., 75–76
Clark, R. D. III, 122, 127–28, 141
Clement, J., 60
CNNMoney, 196
Coan, J., 206
Cohen, D., 11–12
Cohen, E., 181
Cohen, Leonard, 207
Cole, S., 137
Collins, G., 128
Collins, J., 138
Collins, R. L., 137

comScore, 31, 59
Conley, J. J., 39
Conley, T. D., 130, 141, 153, 157–58
Conner, M., 137
Conohan, C. D., 127–28
Constant, B., 97
Coon, H. M., 11–12
Coontz, S., 53
Cooper, K., 35
Cooper, M. L., 137
Copen, C. E., 111
Corbesi, B., 138
Corinna, H., 148–49
Cornelius, J., 94
Cosmides, L., 1, 5, 164
Coulter, K., 206
Cowan, G., 180–81, 182
Cox, D. W., 157–58, 161
Cubbins, L. A., 139
Cunningham, M. R., 38
Cupach, W. R., 47–48, 210
Cyrus, M., 170

Dabhoiwala, F., 84
Daily Mail Reporter, 201
Daly, M., 96, 102–3, 164
Daneback, K., 187–88
Darbes, L. A., 157–58
Darnton, R., 223
Darwin, C., 130
Daubman, K. A.
Daubney, M., 169
D'Aureli, N. R.
Davis, D. A., 16, 19
Davis, S. S., 16, 19
de Beauvoir, S., 156
Debrot, A., 94
Dee, John, 155
Dee, Lynae, 155
de Jong-Gierveld, J., 210, 213
Delevi, R., 93–94
Deloitte, 56
D'Emilio, J., 105–6
Demirtas, A., 160
Denfeld, D., 160
Denney, C., 213
Dent, D. V., 142–43
De Silva, P., 96

Desmarais, S., 127, 139
de Visser, R., 139, 160, 162
Dewey, C., 48
Diamond, L. M., 110
Dicke, A., 163
Dickson, E. J., 170
Dickson, J. W., 123, 129
Dill, J., 174
Dillavou, M. C.
Dima, B., 173–74
Dion, K. K., 14
Dion, K. L., 14
Doherty, William, 10
Doi, L. T., 9
Donmez, A., 160
Donnerstein, Ed, 146
Dotan, I., 162
Dove, M. W., 114
Dove, N. L., 206
Downing, M. J., 183, 184
Dreyer, C. S., 136, 137
Druckerman, P., 152, 154t
Dube, R., 192
Duma, U., 162, 163
Dunn, J., 54–56
Dush, C. M. K., 141
Dworkin, A., 178

Eagly, A. H., 144–46
Easton, D., 162
Eastwick, P. W., 25, 80, 144
Ehrenfeld, T., 40
Eisenberger, N. I., 108
Ekdale, B., 46
Ellis, H., 191, 193
Ellison, N. B., 32–33, 45–46
Ellsberg, M., 96
Emmelin, M., 139–40
England, P., 129
Epstein, R., 110
Esch, T., 95
Evans-DeCicco, J. A., 180–81, 182

Fagin, Peter, 197
Fahs, B., 116–17
Fair, J. E., 46
Farquhar, C., 115–16
Febo-Vazquez, I., 111

Fekadu, Z., 145t
Fekkes, D., 96
Felmlee, D. H., 98
Fenigstein, A., 127–28, 139–40
Ferguson, M. L., 213
Fernandes, E. M., 157–58, 159
Feybesse, C., 2–4, 5, 8–9, 38, 93, 96
Fialer, Phil, 21
Field, T., 210, 216
Fielder, R. L., 141
Fielding, R., 133–34, 145t
Fields, P., 155
Fincham, F. D., 93–94
Finkel, E. I., 80
Finkel, E. J., 25, 43, 49, 50, 75–76, 144
Finkelhor, D., 173–74
Fischer, E. F., 5–8
Fischer, K. W., 1, 11–12
Fischtein, D. S., 127, 139
Fisher, H., 96, 158, 164, 203–4, 206, 215
Fisher, H. E., 50, 91, 92, 93, 115–16
Fisher, T. D., 107, 134
Fisher, W. A., 116–17
Fitness, J., 99
Flack, W. F., Jr., 143
Fleckenstein, J., 157–58, 161
Flesch, D., 137
Fletcher, G. J. O., 99
Fogarty, A. C. K., 129
Foley, S., 112
Forbes, M., 42–43
Fortenberry, J. D.
Fox, S., 110
Fraley, R. C., 11–12
Francoeur, R. T., 144
Frayser, S. G., 153–55
Freedman, E., 105–6
Frost, J. H., 36
Frye, N. E., 205–6
Fukuda, N., 14

Gabor, Zsa Zsa, 210
Gaddam, S., 146–47, 186–87
Gagnon, J. H., 152
Gale, E., 107–8
Gallinat, J., 170
Gallup, x, 152
Gangestad, S. W., 149

Ganong, L. W., 11–12
Garcia, C., 110
Garcia, J. R., 115–16, 129, 133, 136, 137, 142, 145t
Garcia-Moreno, C., 96
Gardner, A., 216
Gass, K., 157–58
Gaulin, S., 35
Gay, P., 90
Gayford, J. J., 102
Gebhard, P. H., 109
Gentzler, A. L., 136–37
George, M. S., 215
Ghimire, D. J., 8
Gibbs, J. L., 32–33
Gilley, Mickey, 81
Giordano, P., 129
Giordano, P. C., 129
Gittleson, Todd, 21–23
Gladue, B. A., 35
Glaser, R., 95
Godfrey, C., 185
Goetz, A. T., 127, 152
Goffman, E., 74
Gomstyn, A., 109
Goode, W. J., 9, 15
Goodman, H., 158
Goodwin, R., 15
Gordon, D., 172–73
Gottman, J., 206
Gottman, J. M., 206
Gould, T., 155–56
Gouldsbury, C., 102
Graber, E. C., 206
Graf, S., 216
Graham, J. M., 2
Gray, K., 178
Gray, Sasha, 189
Green, S. J., 15
Greenhouse, S., 102–3
Greiling, H., 152–53
Grello, C. M., 123, 129, 133–34, 136–37, 143
Gribble, J. N., 107
Griffith, J. D., 182
Grigoriadis, V., 114
Groth, G. E., 149
Gu, L. L., 182

Guerrero, L. K., 100
Guttentag, M., 82
Gyllenhaal, Jake, 146

Haavio-Mannila, E., 19
Haddadi, H., 30–31
Hajela, R., 175–76
Hald, G. M., 170, 178–79
Halpern, C. T., 94, 113
Hamilton, D. T., 108
Hancock, J. T., 45–46
Harai, Y. N., 199
Hardy, J. W., 162
Harmon, A., 21
Harper, M. S., 123, 129, 133–34, 143
Hart, C. L., 182
Harvey, Jim, 21
Hashimoto, T., 8–9
Hatch, L., 175–76
Hatfield, E., vii–viii, 1–4, 5, 8–9, 10, 11–12,
   21–23, 26, 34, 37–38, 42–43, 49, 74–75,
   77–79, 80, 90, 92–93, 94, 95, 120, 122,
   127–28, 135–37, 141, 144, 204, 205–6,
   213, 215–16, 226
Haupert, M. L.
Hayashi, K., 141
Hayes, A., 123, 129, 141–42
Hazan, C., 4
Hebrews, 105–6
Hechenbleikner, N. R., 96
Hecht, H., 139–40
Hedley, A. J., 133–34, 145t
Heino, R., 32–33, 34–35, 36
Heise, L., 96
Helfand, M., 124–25
Helliwell, J., 56–57
Helms, H. M., 96
Hendrick, C., 4, 163
Hendrick, S. S., 4, 163
Herbenick, D., 111, 113
Herold, E., 124–25
Herold, E. S., 127, 129, 138–40, 145t
Hersey, G. L., 191
Heyman, R. E., 94
Hicks, Sidney, 157
Hildebrandt, L., 30
Hilger, M. I., 102
Hill, C. A., 133–34

Hill, C. T., 201–2, 207
Hirschfeld, Magnus, 193
Hirshfield, S., 183
Hitsch, G. J., 33, 34–35, 45
Hoff, C. C., 157–58
Hogan, B., 102–3
Hogan, Paul, xiii
Homer, 191
Homer, A., 197
Hommel, B., 96
Hongladarom, S., 62
Hooton, C., 182
Horan, Kendall, xiii, 24–25
Hortaçsu, A., 33, 45
Hosking, W., 157–58
Howell, N., 131
Hrdy, S. B., 130, 131, 164
Hsu, F. L. K., 9
Huber, J. D., 138
Hui, C. H., 9
Humphreys, T., 148
Hunt, L., 171–72
Hunt, M., 13
Hupka, R. B., 99, 100, 155
Hurtado, S., 124–25
Hutchison, E. S. S.
Huxley, Aldous, 227
Hyde, J. S., 35–36, 80, 81, 124–25, 127, 129,
   130, 133, 134, 144, 149, 150

Impett, E. A., 94
International Telecommunication
   Union, 57
Internet and Mobile Association of
   India, 60
Internet Watch Foundation, 118
Internet World Stats, 56

Jacobs, A., 83
Jankowiak, W., 5–8, 11–12, 19, 144
Jankowiak, W. R., 5–8
Jansen, H. A. F. M., 96
Janzen, 155
Jaremka, L. M., 95
Javanbakht, M., 181
Jefferson, T., 108–9
Jenks, R. R., 155, 158, 159, 161
Johansson, E., 139–40

Jonason, P. K., 38, 39, 123–24, 129, 133, 145*t*
Jones, B. C., 137
Jones, B. T., 137
Jones, R., 169–70
Joseph, R., 14, 15
Joseph, T. B., 14, 15
Jovicich, I., 145*t*
Jozkowski, K. N., 147–48
Ju, Y., 9

Kaestle, E., 94, 113
Kagitçibasi, C., 56
Kahn, A. S., 129
Kaiman, J., 43–44, 71
Kano, Takayoshi, 158
Karandashev, V., 93
Karney, B. R., 25, 205–6
Karremans, J. C., 137
Kasparov, Garry, 194
Kavi, Ashok Row, 71
Kaysen, D. L., 142–43
Kazer, M. W., 112
Keast, Mackenzie and Evan, 209
Keillor, Garrison, 45–46
Kelley, Edward, 155
Kelley, H. H., 16–17
Kelley, Joanna, 155
Kelly, E. L., 39
Kemmelmeier, M., 11–12
Kennedy, B., 11–12
Kenrick, D. T., 149
Kephart, W. M., 16–17
Kern, R., 187–88
Kerns, K. A., 136–37
Kessler, D., 135–36
Kiecolt-Glaser, J. K., 95
Kim, H. K., 93
Kim, J., 11–12, 95
King, C. A., 128
Kingsbury, Madison, xiii
Kinsey, A. C., 109–10, 113
Kirkpatrick, L. A., 38
Kitayama, S., 9, 11–12
Klaassen, M. J., 146–47, 179
Kleinplatz, P. J., 117
Kline, J., 35, 133–34
Knobe, J., 178

Knox, D., 123
Koch, E. J., 96
Kontula, O., 19, 139
Korn, M. S., 206
Korn, W. S., 124–25
Kort, J., 115–16
Kose, S., 215
Kraus, A., 178–79
Kremer, E. C., 116–17
Kroeber, 102
Krupnick, E., 65
Kühn, S., 170
Kurdek, L. A., 157–58
Kurzweil, R., 196

Ladurie, E. L. R., 53
La Gorce, T. L., 158
Laier, C., 175–76
Lambert, T. A., 129
Lamy, L., 90
Lane, Burton, 45
Lang, N., 170
Langdridge, D., 157–58, 161
Lange, T., 178–79
Langeslag, S. J. E., 96
LaSala, M. C., 157–58
Lattimore, R., 191
Laumann, E. O., 152
Laurenceau, J. P., 95, 206
Lauria, L. M., 108
Lawrence v. Texas, 109
Layard, R., 56–57
Le, B., 202*f*, 202, 206
Le, Y. L., 94
Leach, L. S., 95
Leary, M. R., 96
Lehmiller, J. J., 157–58
Lerner, Alan Jay, 45
Lester, D., 96
Levine, R., 8–9, 18
Levine, T., 135–36
Levine, T. R., 142
Levinger, G., 21–23
Levy, A., 114
Levy, D., 195–96
Lewin, B., 145*t*
Lewinsohn, P., 96
Lewis, M. A., 142–43

Li, N. P., 123–24, 133, 145t, 149
Lieberman, M. D., 108, 137
Lindau, S. T., 111
Lipka, M., 107
Littleton, H., 114
Lloyd, E. A., 115–17
London School of Hygiene & Tropical
    Medicine, 124–25
Longmore, M. A., 129
Longmore, M. L., 129
Lopata, H. Z., 213
Lorberbaum, J. P., 215
Love, T., 175–76
Lovell, Nicole, 48
Loving More magazine, 161
Lowe, D., 122
Luciano, E. M. C., 11–12
Luckhurst, C. L., 80, 120
Luk, Y. K., 133–34, 145t
Lyons, H., 129
Lyons, H. A., 129, 137, 142

Ma, Ricky, 194
Ma, V., 69
Mace, D., 13
Mace, V., 13
Mackinnon, A., 95
MacKinnon, C. A., 116–17
Maddox, A. M., 170
Madison, Kelly, 182–83
Malamuth, N. M., 170, 178–79
Malarkey, W. B., 95
Malouff, J. M., 206
Manning, W., 129
Manning, W. D., 129, 187–88
Månsson, S. A., 188
Marazziti, D., 96
Marciano, J., 174
Maria, C. S., 192
Markman, H. J., 170
Markoff, J., 196
Markus, H. R., 9
Marshall, D., 144, 145t
Martikainen, P., 216
Martin, C. E., 109
Martin, J., 207–8
Masci, D., 107
Massey, S. G., 145t

Match singles, 209
Mathes, E. W., 128
Maticka-Tyndale, E., 139, 145t
Matsick, J. L., 153
Matthews, J., 144
McAuliffe, L., 112
McCarthy, J., x
McCullers, C., 97
McCusker, C., 9
McCutcheon, 186
McDonald, D., 160, 162
McGinley, R., 158
McGinn, M. M., 95
McKee, A., 179
McKenna, C., 94
McKenry, P. C., 93
McKinney, P., 110
McKinnon, R. K., 118
McManus, B., 123, 142
McMullen, Matth, 191–92
McNeill, W. H., 52, 53
Means, J., 212, 215–16
Mehl, M. R., 216
Meloy, J. R., 96
Memering, S. L., 157–58
Merkle, E. R., 42–43
Merriwether, A. M., 145t
Messenger, J. C., 145t
Meston, C. M., 135–36
Metts, S., 205–6, 210
Meuwly, N., 94
Mewhinney, D. M. K., 129, 139–40, 145t
Meyer, M. L., 137
Michael, R. T., 152
Michaels, S., 152
Miga, E., 206
Milhausen, R., 124–25
Miller, H. G., 107
Miller, J. K., 128
Miller, M. D., 96
Mitchell, S., 182
Mogilski, J. K., 157–58
Mole, T. B.
Mo'Nique, 157, 158
Monroe, S., 96
Montoya, R., 138
Moore, Coline, 137
Moors, A. C., 141, 153, 157–58

Morales, L., 57–58
Morgan, E. M., 1, 187–88
Morris, M., 108
Morrison, 186
Muehlenhard, C. L., 116–17
Muise, A., 94
Mullen, P. E., 102
Murdaya, U., 11–12
Murdoch, Iris, 95
Murphy, K., 47
Murray, G., 185–86
Mutso, A. A., 206

Nadler, A., 162
Najib, A., 215
Naked capitalism, 172–73
NASCA (North American Swing Club
   Alliance), 158
National Center for Health
   Statistics, 181–82
National Center for Social
   Research, 124–25
Nay, R., 112
Neilands, T. B., 157–58
Neto, F., 8–9
Nguyen, H. T., 94
Nikolowski, W., 112
Nisbett, R., 11–12
Noller, P., 94
Norkey, T., 62–63
Norman, C. C., 94
North American Swing Club Alliance
   (NASCA), 158
Norton, M. I., 36
Novak, D. S.

Oates, R., 59
O'Brien, M. U., 94
O'Carroll, T., 195
Odunayo, A., 192f
Ogas, O., 146–47, 186–87
OkCupid, 49
Olesen, S. C., 95
Oliver, M. B., 81, 129, 149
Olson, S., 96
O'muircheartaigh, C. A.
O'Neill, G., 156–57
O'Neill, N., 156–57

Oppermann, M., 139, 145t
Orcutt, H. K., 137
Orenstein, P., 113
Orimoto, L., 213
Orr, A., 24
Orwell, George, 227
O'Sullivan, L. F., 113
Owen, C., 115–16, 141
Oysermann, D., 11–12

Paglia, Camille, 184
ParkData, 31f
Patterson, R., 175
Paul, E. L., 123, 129, 136–37,
   139–40, 141–42
Pennebaker, J. W., 82, 138
Peoples, Sarah, xiii
Peplau, L., 157–58
Peplau, L. A., 201, 210, 213
Pérez-Peña, R., 48
Perilloux, C., 210
Perlman, D., 210, 213
Perta, V. C., 30–31
Peter, J., 146–47, 179
Petersen, J. L., 81, 124–25, 127, 129, 133,
   134, 144, 150
Peterson, R., 78
Peterson, Z. D., 147–48
Pew Research Center, x, 105–6
Pfaus, J., 179
Pfeiffer, S. M., 163
Piccolomini, Alessandro, 13
Pierce, John, 48
Pietromonaco, P. R., 95
Pillemer, J. T., 94
Piper, J., 137
Pomeroy, W. B., 109
Pornhub, 186–87
Poushter, J., 59
Prakasa, V. V., 14
Prause, N., 179
Preston, M., 127–28, 139–40
Price, J., 175
Priceonomics, 30
Prigerson, H., 96
Proce, 172–73
Prokscha, Sabine, xiii
Proulx, C. M., 96

Pryor, J. H., 124–25, 129
Psychological Inquiry, 122
Puentes, J., 123
Pukall, C. F., 115–16
Pulerwitz, J., 145*t*
Punit, I. S., 60
Purvis, J. L., vii–viii, 35–36, 75–76

Ramey, J. W., 162
Rao, V. N., 14
Rapson, R. L., vii–viii, 1–4, 5, 8–9, 10, 26,
    38, 42–43, 49, 52, 74, 77–78, 79, 80, 84,
    89, 90, 92–93, 94, 120, 135–36, 144, 165,
    166–67, 216, 226
Real, E., 157
Reed, R. M., 128
Regan, P. C., 94, 136, 137, 141, 142
Regnerus, M., 172–73, 175
Reiber, C., 129, 133, 136, 137, 142, 145*t*
Reis, H. T., 25, 75–76
Remien, R. H., 157–58
Resch, M. N., 188
Reynolds, C. F. III, 96
Rhoades, G. K., 170
Richardson, J., 123–24, 145*t*
Richardson, R. A., 42–43
Richters, J., 139
Riela, S., 8
Rifkin, R., x
Risman, B. J., 107–8
Rissel, C. E., 139
Robb, G., 86
Roberts, J. M., 52, 53
Robinson, A. D., 123–24
Robles, T. F., 95
Rodriguez, G., 8
Rogers, S. M., 107
Rohde, P., 96
Romaya, J. P., 93
Rosenberger, J. G., 115
Rosenblatt, P. C., 9, 14–15
Rosenfeld, M. J., 24, 43–44
Rosenzweig, A., 96
Rottman, L., 74–75
Rubel, A. N., 153, 157–58, 160, 161
Rubin, Z., 21–23, 160, 201
Rubio, G., 67
Russell, D., 213

Russo, Renee, 146
Ryan, J. M., 99, 155

Sabina, C., 173–74
Sachs, J., 56–57
Sadalla, E. K., 149
Saenz, V. B., 124–25
Sakaluk, J. K., 124–25
Salisbury, C. M., 116–17
Sandberg-Thoma, S. E., 141
Sands, K. M., 105–6
Santos, J. L., 124–25
Sappho, 90–91
Sasidharan, S., 145*t*
Sasson, J. P., 131
Sato, S., 8–9
Sbarra, D. A., 216
Schaefer, L. C., 116–17
Scheinmann, R., 183
Schmitt, D., 79, 131, 149
Schmitt, D. P., 8, 127–28, 133, 164
Schmitt, J. P., 157–58
Schneider, J. P., 188
Schoebi, D., 94
Schoeneman, T. J., 69
Schrimshaw, E. W., 183
Schwartz, J. C., 11
Schwartz, P., 151
Scuglia, B., 183–84, 185
Secord, P., 82
Seeley, J., 96
Selcuk, E., 94
Serewicz, M. C. M., 107–8
Seto, M. C., 30–31
Shackelford, T. E., 127, 152
Shackelford, T. K., 157–58
Shafer, E. F., 129
Shamblen, S. R., 38
Shaver, P. R., 1, 4, 11–12, 35
Sheane, H., 102
Sheskin, M., 178
Shimizu, H., 9
Shostak, M., 203
Shotland, R. L., 47–48
Silver, N., 206
Silverman, L. H., 76
Silverman, Sara, xiii, 31–32
SimilarWeb, 65

Simmons, C. H., 9
Simon, I., 182–83
Simon, Paul, 209
Simpson, J. A., 17, 149
Sinclair, R. C., 107–8
Skocpol, T., 56
Slatcher, R. B., 94, 95
Slinkard, M. S., 112
Smith, A., 24, 44, 64–65
Smith, A. M. A., 139
Smith, H. L., 216
Smith, J. C., 102–3
Smith, S. E., 106, 107, 125, 129
Smythe, Sadie, 185–86
Solomon, 98
Sommer, V., 163–64
Son, J., 106, 107
Sonmez, S., 145t
Sönmez, S., 138
Soueif, A., 1
Spitzberg, B. H., 47–48, 100
Sprecher, S., 2, 10, 14, 16–18, 25,
    124–25, 205–6
Stack, S., 187–88
Statistica, 27–28
Statistics Brain Research Institute, 24, 67
Stavrianos, L. S., 52–53
Steer, R. A., 215–16
Stefano, G. B., 95
Stephens, W. N., 15
Stephenson, R., 157–58
Sternberg, R. J., 4, 6t
Stewart, M., 182
Stillwell, A. M., 98
Stolberg, S. G., 48
Stone, E. A., 127, 152
Stone, L., 53
Strassburg, D., 118
Strong, G.
Sullivan, P. S., 157–58
Sullivan, R., 179
Surbey, M. K., 127–28
Symons, D., 131

Tabori, P., 191
Takagi, Shin, 197f, 197
Tallack, 186
Tanfer, K., 139

Tannahill, R., 66–67
Tappé, M., 141
Tawiah, 46
Taylor, 80
Taylor, Ava, 180–81
Tennyson, Alfred, 217
Te'o, Manti, 46
Testa, M., 137
Thicke, Robin, 148
Thomas, A. P., 137
Thomas, R. J., 24, 43–44
Thompson, L. Y., 116–17
Thornton, A., 8
Thornton, P. D., 181–82
Toffler, Alvin, 86–87
Tokunaga, R. S., 178–79
Toma, C. L., 45–46
Tooby, J., 1, 5, 164
Topping, A., 118
Toro-Morn, M., 17, 18
Townsend, J. M., 35, 133–34
Toynbee, A., 53
Tracy, J., 24
Tracy, J. L., 33
Traeen, B., 129–30, 145t
Træen, B., 188
Traupmann, J., 78, 94, 204, 205–6, 215–16
Trawick, M., 2
Treger, S., 124–25
Triandis, H. C., 9
Trombello, J. M., 95
Trope, Y., 137
Trost, M. R., 149
Trouble, C., 180
Tulesosopo, Ronaiah, 46–47
Tully, M., 46
Turett, C. J., 148–49
Turner, C. F., 107
Tyson, G., 30–31, 35
Tziallas, E., 185

Utne, M., 78

Valkonen, T., 216
Valverde, S. H., 193
VandenBos, G. R., 98
Van der Veen, F. M., 96
Van Kerkwijk, C., 139

Vannier, S. A., 113
Van Steenbergen, H., 96
Vélez-Blasini, C. J., 135
Verma, J., 8–9
Vivinetto, G., 149–50
Vohs, K. D., 35, 79
Vom Kolke, A., 9
von Krafft-Ebing, Richard, 193
Voon, V., 175–76
Vorakitphokatorn, S., 145t

W3Techs, 60–61
Wade, L. D., 116–17
Wagner, G. J., 157–58
Wainaina, Eric, 59, 68–69
Wallen, K., 115–16, 127
Waller, W. W., 134
Wallerstein, I. M., 53
Walley, J., 175
Walsh, H. L., 123, 141
Walster, G. W., vii, 34, 77, 78
Wang, A. Y., 94
Wang, L-I., 11–12
Wasserman, I., 187–88
Wasserman, T. H., 35, 133–34
Watkins, S. J., 152–53
Watts, C. H., 96
Wawerungigi, 69
Weaver, S. E., 11–12
Webster, G. D.
Weeks, D. J., 112
Weidman, A. C., 33
Weiss, R. S., 212, 213
Welling, L. L. M., 157–58
Welsh, D. P., 129, 133–34, 143
West, Kim Kardashian, 182–83
Westman, G., 139–40
Whitby, T. J., 153–55
White, G. L., 102

White, S. W., 216
Whittaker, D., 115–16
Wiederman, M. W., 17, 152, 153
Wiederman, N., 114
Wildermuth, S. M., 44–45
Williams, J. B., 157–58, 160
Williams, K. D., 108
Williams, L., 171
Wilson, M., 96, 102–3, 164
Wilt, S., 96
Winks, Robin, 220
Wittfogel, K. A., 54–56
Wolak, J., 173–74
Wolkstein, D., 5
Wong, P. T., 163
Wood, W., 144–46
World Bank Group, 57
Wotman, S. R., 97, 98
Wright, P. J., 178–79
Wu, S., 1, 11
Wu, V., 194

Xu, X., xiii, 8, 91, 206

Yabiku, S. A., 8
Yamakawa, R., 213
Yeats, William Butler, 80
Yoshimura, S. M., 100
Young, D., 37
YouPorn, 169

Zeki, S., 93
Ziegler, A., 141, 153
Zimbardo, P. G., 138
Zimmer-Gembeck, M., 124–25
Zuccarino, D.
Zucker, A. N., 123–24
Zuckerman, E., 60–61
Zusman, M. W., 123

Subject Index

Tables and figures are indicated by *t* and *f* following the page number

For the benefit of digital users, indexed terms that span two pages (e.g., 52–53) may, on occasion, appear on only one of those pages.

a do-ningyo, 191
Aboriginal people, 5–8, 19
Abrahamic religions, 105–6
Abyss Creations, 191–92
addiction, 175–76, 177
adultery, 39, 109, 165
AdultFriendFinder, 29*t*
Afghanistan, 52–53, 54
Africa
  arranged marriages, 14–15
  attitudes toward marriage, 19
  colonialism, 54
  culture, 9, 19, 52–53
  Internet access, 59
  online dating scams, 47
  passionate love, 5
  sub-Saharan, 14–15, 59
After School, 48
agalmatophia (statue love), 191
ageism, 112
aggressive behavior, 146
Ai, 5
AIBO, 194
AIDS, 83, 127, 128–29, 142–43, 144, 165
alcohol, 137–38, 142, 143
America. *See* United States
Ammassalik Eskimo people, 99, 155
Anabaptists, 155
anal sex, 115, 142–43
ancient Greece, 171, 191
ancient Rome, 171, 191
Android phones, 65
anonymous sex. *See* casual sex
Anselm, 77
apps. *See* dating apps; mobile apps
Arab countries, 19, 52–53

Arabic language, 1
Arapaho (American) people, 102
Argentina, 67*t*
Armenia, 154*t*
arranged marriages, 14, 66–72
Ashley Madison, 28, 29*t*
Asia, 9, 13, 52–53
Asian-Americans, 124–25
Australia, 5–8
  attitudes toward marriage, 17–18, 18*t*, 19
  casual sex, 127–28, 139, 145*t*
  child sex dolls, 197
  culture, 9
  dating apps, 67*t*
  infidelity rates, 154*t*
  passionate love, 5
  pornography revenue, 173*t*
Austria, 67*t*

Babylon, 73*f*
Badoo, 27–28, 29–30, 29*t*, 32, 66, 67*t*
Bahrain, 71
Baidu, 174*t*
Bangladesh, 154*t*
bare branches, 82
Barrymore, Drew, 76
BB Talk (Cyrus), 170–71
beer goggles, 137–38
behavior. *See also* sexual behavior(s)
  aggressive, 146
  deal breakers, 38–39
  erotic, 100
  intrusive behaviors, 38–39
  non-consensual, x
Belgium, 67*t*
Bellamy, Edward, 227

Benin, 154*t*

bereavement, 215–16. *See also* loss

Bible, 5

Bieber, Justin, 61–62, 170–71

Big Five personality test, 25

biosocial perspectives, 144

birth control, 89, 119–20, 128–29, 158

bisexuality, 111, 160

Black-Americans, 124–25

blackpeoplemeet.com, 28

Blade Runner, 227

"Blank Space" (Swift), 61

blue films, 171–72

Blued, 43–44

"Blurred Lines," 148–49

Bolivia, 154*t*

Bollywood, 11

bonding, physical, 226, 227

booty calls. *See* casual sex

brain imaging, 91–93, 92*f*

Brazil

    attitudes toward marriage, 17–18, 18*t*

    dating apps, 67*t*

    infidelity rates, 154*t*

    male jealousy, 102–3

    pornography revenue, 173*t*

breakup services, 209

breakups, 201

    advice for couples who want to break
      up, 207–8

    best (and worst) predictors, 219

    divorce, 39, 203–4

    emotions after, 210–13

    emotions during, 207–16

    over Facebook, 209

    friends after, 209–10

    gender differences, 213

    love after, 210

    ways to leave a lover, 209–10

brothels, 192

Bulgaria, 67*t*

Bumble, 29–30, 29*t*, 31–32

Burkina Faso, 154*t*

Burton, Richard, 102

business, 21–51

California Personality Inventory, 74–75

Cameroon, 154*t*

Canada, 9

    casual sex, 139, 145*t*

    culture, 52–53

    dating apps, 67*t*

    pornography revenue, 173*t*

    recreational sex, 129

capitalism, 168

casual sex

    attitudes toward, 124–26, 133–34, 135

    best and worst experiences, 142

    biosocial perspectives on, 144

    cultural perspectives on, 143–44

    definitions of, 123–24

    desire and willingness to engage in, 127

    evolutionary perspectives on, 130–35

    influences on, 122

    nature of, 124

    outcomes, 141–43

    participation in, 130

    prevalence of, 128–30, 133–34

    reasons for avoiding, 136–37,
      139–41, 140*t*

    reasons for engaging in, 135–37, 140*t*

    receptivity to, 122, 123*t*

    rise of, 129

    risks of, 152–53

    worldwide rates, 144, 145*t*

Catfish (MTV), 46–47

catfishing, 46

Catholic Church, 105–6, 119

CatholicSingles.com, 28, 29*t*

caudate nucleus, 91

cellular (cell) phones. *See* mobile phones

Chad, 154*t*

chastity, 126

cheating or infidelity, 39, 152–53, 154*t*,
    165, 166

chemistry, 49–50, 91–92, 92*f*

Chemistry.com, 28, 29*t*, 49

child pornography, 198

child sex dolls, 197*f*, 197, 198

children, 53, 173–74

Chile, 67*t*

China

    attitudes toward marriage, 19

    attitudes toward premarital sex, chastity,
      and casual sex, 126–27

    bare branches, 82

casual sex, 126–27, 145t
Christmas cakes, 82
colonialism, 54
culture, 9, 19, 52–53
   dating apps, 67t
   erotica, 171
   extramarital sex, 152
   folk conception of love, 5–8, 11–12
   infidelity rates, 154t
   love and marriage, 13
   mating market, 83
   online dating, 43–44
   passionate love, 5, 11–12
   pornography revenue, 173t
   sex ratios, 82–83
   Shanghai Marriage Market, 77
Chinese-Americans, 10
chlamydia, 181
choice, 228
ChristianCafe.com, 28
ChristianMingle.com, 25, 27–28
Christians and Christianity, 14, 53, 105–6
Christmas cakes, 82
Clockword Orange, 227
Clover, 32
CNM. See consensual non-monogamy
Coffee Meets Bagel, 29t
collectivism, 9, 18
college students, 38–39, 129, 143. See also
      young people
Colombia, 67t
colonialism, 54, 55f
communication, 156–57
companionate love, 1–5
   erosion of, 204–6
   health benefits, 94, 95
compatibility algorithms, 28
compersion, 162
Compersion Questionnaire, 163
Compersion Trait Questionnaire, 163
compromise, 15
computer matching, 21, 77, 194, 199
   Happy Family Planning Service, 21, 22f
   online dating, 23–32
Congo, 155
consensual non-monogamy (CNM),
      151–52, 153–67
consent, 146–49

Consent is Sexy campaign, 148–49
ConservativeMatch, 28, 29t
Constant, Benjamin, 97
Cook Islands, 5–8, 144, 145t
Cope, David, 199
Copper Inuit Alaskan Indian tribe, 19
couples. See also breakups
   long-term relationships, 201, 206
   open relationships, 151
   pornography and, 187–88
Craigslist, 32, 173, 174t
Crash Pad, 186–87
cruising. See casual sex
cultural changes, 222
cultural differences, 1, 19
   in casual sex, 122
   in definition of love, 1
   in jealousy, 100–1
   in love and marriage, 17–19, 18t
   in passionate love, 8–10
   in susceptibility to love, 10
cultural norms, 105–7
cultural stereotypes, 107
Cyrus, Miley, 170–71
Czech Republic, 67t, 173t

dames de voyage, 191
Daphnis and Chloe, 5
DateMyPet.com, 28
dating. See also relationships
   deal breakers, 37–39, 79
   emotional rewards, 37
   online, 23–42, 46, 86
   opportunity gains and losses, 37
   personal rewards, 37
   recommended strategy for gay and
      straight folks, 26–27
   traits to look for, 34
   virtual, 29t
dating apps, 29–31, 64, 69, 185
   advantages of, 43–44
   costs, 32
   most popular apps, 27–32
   popularity, 66, 67t
   sample apps, 29, 29t
   scams, 48
dating markets, 86
dating sites. See online dating

day-to-day events, 37
de Beauvoir, Simone, 156
de Staël, Germaine, 97
Dee, John, 155
Dee, Lynae, 155
Deep Blue, 194
Democrats, 161
Denmark, 56–57, 67*t*
depression, 212, 215–16
disillusionment, 98
divorce, 39, 203–4. *See also* breakups
DNA matching, 49–50
domestic violence, 96
Dominican Republic, 154*t*
Dong Xian, 5
dopamine, 91
double standards, 107–8, 114–15, 143
drugs, 137
Dunst, Kirsten, 76
Dutch wives, 191
dystopia, 227

East Asia, 52–53, 192
eBay, 173, 174*t*
ECHI (Endorsement of the Hookup
    Index), 125–26
economic changes, 222
egalitarian families, 53
Egypt, 19, 52–53, 67*t*, 70–71, 143–44, 145*t*
eHarmony, 27–28, 29*t*, 32, 48
Eisenhauer, David, 48
emotional rewards, 37
Endorsement of the Hookup Index
    (ECHI), 125–26
England, 9, 17–18, 18*t*, 152, 154*t*, 201. *See
    also* United Kingdom
Enlightenment, 171
Enovid, 128–29
equitable relationships, 79
equity, 78
Equity Global Measure, 77–78
equity theory, 77–81
erotic behavior, 100
erotica, 171, 172*f*
escort services, 192
Estonia, 19
ethics, 196–98, 228
Ethiopia, 145*t*, 154*t*

Euro-Americans, 10, 53, 124–25
Europe, 10, 52–53, 119
Evangelical Christians, 105–6
evolutionary psychology, 80
evolutionary theory, 79, 130–35
Ex Machina, 192, 193–94
expectations, 143, 177
extramarital sex, 152–53, 165

Facebook, 29–30, 29*t*, 60–61, 86
    online dating groups, 71
    popularity, 173, 174*t*
    teen dating groups, 48
Facebook breakups, 209
family life, 15, 53, 68, 222
Fatale Media, 186–87
female orgasm, 116
female sexuality, 112–13, 114, 182–83
feminism, 84–85
feminist porn, 171–72
Fialer, Phil, 21
fidelity, 143
Fifty Shades of Grey, 63–64, 63*t*,
    171–72
Filipinos, 10
FindYorFace, 29*t*
Finland, 19, 56–57, 67*t*, 126–27, 139,
    173*t*, 216
folk lore, 5–8
France, x, 126–27, 152, 154*t*,
    196, 223
friends with benefits, 123, 151.
    See also casual sex
friendships, 209–10
Friendster, 29*t*
Frim, 66, 67*t*
Fulbe people, 5–8
functional magnetic resonance imaging
    (fMRI), 92–93
future directions, 220

gama tonkat cult, 155
Gay, 29*t*
gay female porn, 186–87
gay male porn, 183–86
gay rights, x
GDP (gross domestic product), 56–57
gender differences, 81, 131

in attitudes toward casual sex, 122, 123*t*,
    124–25, 127, 133–34
in casual sex, 122
in dealing with loss, 213
double standards, 107–8, 114–15, 143
in online dating, 35–36
in oral sex, 113–14
in receptivity to casual sex, 122, 123*t*
in recreational sex, 129
in sexual behavior reporting, 108
gender equality, 82, 84, 226
gender roles, 84–86, 107–8, 226, 228
gender stereotypes, 107
GenePartner, 28, 29*t*
Georgia (U.S.), 83–84
Germany, 126–27
Gettingon, 29*t*
Ghana, 46, 47, 57–58, 58*f*, 154*t*
ghosting, 209
Gittleson, Todd, 21–23
global index of happiness, 56–57
globalization, 11, 19–20, 52, 224, 225
Gomez, Selena, 61–62
Gone with the Wind, 146
Google, 60–61
Greece, 5, 9, 171, 191
Greek myth, 5
grief, 215–16. *See also* loss
Grindr, 28, 29–30, 29*t*, 32, 43–44,
    70–71, 185
gross domestic product (GDP), 56–57
guilt, 212
Gyllenhaal, Jake, 146
gynoids, 191

Haiti, 154*t*
happiness, 56–57
Happn, 29–30, 29*t*
Happy Family Planning Service, 21, 22*f*
HappyBuddhist.com, 28
Harvey, Jim, 21
Hasbro, 195
Hatch Labs, 65
Hatfield, Elaine, 21–23
Heartbeep, 66, 67*t*
heartbreak syndrome, 216
Hentai pornography, 198
Her (film), 192, 193–94

Her (site), 28, 29–30, 29*t*
Herculaneum, 171
herpes, genital, 181–82
Hicks, Sidney, 157
Hilton, Paris, 114
Hindus, 14
Hinemoa and Tutanekai, 5
Hinge, 29–30, 29*t*, 31*f*
Hispanic Americans, 124–25
history, 21, 222
HIV, 115, 144, 152–53, 181
Hollywood, 11, 63
homicide, 96
Homo sapiens, 130, 131, 163–64, 199, 203
homosexuality. *See also* lesbian, gay,
        bisexual, transgendered, and asexual
        (LGBT+) community
    acceptance of, 106, 107, 226
    attitudes toward, 110–11
    same-sex sex life, 115
Hong Kong, 17–18, 18*t*, 133–34, 145*t*, 194
hookup culture. *See* casual sex
Hookup Culture Index, 125–26
hookups, 123–24. *See also* casual sex
Hot Girls Wanted (2015), 180–81
HSV, 181–82
human papillomavirus, 181–82
humanism, 53
humanoids, 194
Humans, 193–94, 199
Hungary, 67*t*, 100
Huxley, Aldous, 227

IBM, 194
Iceland, 56–57
IllicitEncounters, 29*t*
Inanna and Dumuzi, 5
Independents, 161
India, 52–53, 54
    arranged marriages, 14–15, 69–70
    attitudes toward marriage, 17–18, 18*t*
    attitudes toward premarital sex, chastity,
        and casual sex, 126–27
    dating apps, 67*t*, 69–70
    erotica, 171, 172*f*
    Internet access, 60
    love and marriage, 13
    mobile phones, 60

India, (*cont.*)
    online dating, 43–44, 69–70
    passionate love, 5
Indiana University, 111, 113
indigenous peoples, 153–55
individualism, x, 9, 13, 19
Indonesia, 5–8, 11–12, 67*t*, 71, 126–27
inequity, 79
infatuation, 2, 93, 96
infidelity, 39, 152–53, 154*t*, 165, 166
Inis Beag, 145*t*
Instagram, 29–30, 31–32
Internet, 20, 52. *See also* online dating
Internet access, 56
Internet pornography, 172–76, 174*t*,
    177, 188
interracial relationships, 226
intimacy
    reasons people fear and avoid, 136–37
    ways to increase, 40–42
intrusive behaviors, 38–39
iPair, 66, 67*t*
Iran, 52–53, 126–27
Iraq, 19, 52–53
Ireland, 67*t*, 100, 152
Irian Jaya, 155
Islamic State (ISIS), 48, 54, 105–6
Israel, 67*t*, 126–27, 152, 163
Italy, 9, 67*t*, 154*t*, 173*t*
iTunes, 61, 70–71
Ivory Coast, 154*t*

Jack'd, 29*t*
Japan, 9, 52–53
    arranged marriages, 14
    attitudes toward marriage, 17–18, 18*t*
    dating apps, 67*t*
    erotica, 171
    extramarital sex, 152
    Hentai pornography, 198
    love and marriage, 13
    pornography, 170, 173*t*
    sex dolls, 191, 192*f*, 192
    susceptibility to love, 10
Japanese-Americans, 10
Japanese tourists, 145*t*
JDate, 28, 29*t*
jealousy, 98, 101, 152–53, 157

male, 102–3
    in polys, 162
    in swingers, 160
    triggers, 100
Jewish Daily Forward, 24
jihottie (jihadist hottie), 48
Johansson, Scarlett, 194
Judaism, 105–6

Kasparov, Garry, 194
Kazakhstan, 154*t*
Keast, Mackenzie and Evan, 209
Kelley, Edward, 155
Kelley, Joanna, 155
Kenya, 5–8, 59, 67*t*, 68–69, 154*t*
key clubs, 155–56
kickasstorrents.com, 62–63
Kik (app), 48
KIK or Teen Dating and Flirting (site), 48
Kinsey, Alfred, 109, 111
Kinsey Reports, 109–10
Kinsey Scale, 110
Korea, 52–53
Korean War, 156
Kula Rings, 52
Kung people, 131
!Kung tribe, 203
Kuwait, 19, 67*t*

Lagos, 47
language, 165
Lars and the Real Girl, 193–94
Latin America, 9, 19
Lawrence et al. v. Texas, 109
Lebanon, 19
Lemba secret society, 155
lesbian, gay, bisexual, transgendered, and
    asexual (LGBT+) community, 89. *See
    also* homosexuality
    acceptance of, x
    consensual non-monogamy
        (CNM), 151–52
    gay female porn, 186–87
    gay male porn, 183–86
    online dating, 70–72
    open relationships, 151
    same-sex sex life, 115
    sides, 115

lesbian, gay, bisexual, transgendered, and
    asexual (LGBT+) porn, 171–72
lesbian porn, 186–87
Levinger, George, 21–23
LGBT+ community. *See* lesbian, gay,
    bisexual, transgendered, and asexual
    (LGBT+) community
LiberalHearts, 28
liberalism, 106
Libya, 19
The Lifestyle, 151, 156
Logan, Jesse, 118
loneliness, 213, 214*t*
Long, Justin, 76
long-term relationships, 201, 206
loss, 213, 214–15. *See also* breakups
love
    in Arabic, 1
    badlands of, 95–103
    being in love, 2
    after a breakup, 210
    chemistry of, 91–93, 92*f*
    companionate, 1–5, 94, 95, 204
    compromising on, 15
    culture and, 8–10
    definitions of, 1, 2, 4, 8
    end of, 201
    erosion of, 204–6, 205*f*
    folk conceptions, 5–8, 11–12
    future directions, 220
    globalization of, 52, 225
    health benefits, 93–94, 95
    on Internet, 60–66
    joys of, 90–95
    lasting, 203
    maintenance of, 101
    market view of, 73
    marriage for, 12–18, 18*t*, 53, 66–72
    mathematics of, 23*f*
    nature of, 88
    obsessive, 2
    passionate, 1–2, 5–12, 90, 203, 204, 205*f*
    reciprocated, 90
    with a robot, 195
    sex for, 120
    statue love *(agalmatophia),* 191
    Sternberg's Triangular Love Scale, 4, 6*t*
    susceptibility to, 10

    unrequited, 90, 95–103, 212
    Western, 52, 60–66
love dolls, 191
love relationships, 134
Lovell, Nicole, 48
lovesickness, 2
Lovoo, 66, 67*t*

Ma, Ricky, 194
Madison, Kelly, 182–83
Madonna–whore complex, 178
magnetic resonance imaging, functional
    (fMRI), 92–93
mail order brides, 86
Malawi, 154*t*
Malaysia, 67*t*
Mali, 154*t*
ManCrunch, 29–30, 29*t*
Mangaia, Cook Islands, 5–8, 144, 145*t*
Mangrove community, 5–8, 19
Manhunt, 29*t*
Maori, 5
markets, 73, 73*f*, 167–68
marriage
    arranged, 14, 66–72
    attitudes toward, 15–16, 17–18, 18*t*, 19
    globalization and, 68
    for love, 12–18, 18*t*, 53, 66–72
    open, 151, 153–67
    sex before, 106
marriage markets, 73, 73*f*
Married at First Sight, vii
Match.com, 24, 27–28, 29*t*, 31*f*, 32,
    65, 195
matchmaking
    algorithms for, 28, 29*t*
    chemistry of, 49–50
    by computer, 21 (*see also* dating apps)
    DNA matching, 49–50
    Happy Family Planning Service,
        21, 22*f*
    online dating, 23–27, 29*t*, 37
    scientific approach to, 28
Mate, 29*t*
mate poaching, 164
mate value, 76–77
mathematics, 23*f*
McMullen, Matt, 191–92

Mehinaku people, 132
men
    breakups, 207
    casual sex, 122, 123t, 127, 128, 130, 133–34, 135, 139–42
    coping with loss, 213
    gay porn, 183–86
    infidelity rates, 152–53, 154t
    jealousy, 102–3
    objectification of, 179
    open relationships, 151
    porn stars, 180–83
    recreational sex, 129, 133–34
men who have sex with men (MSM), 115. See also lesbian, gay, bisexual, transgendered, and asexual (LGBT+) community
mental health
    benefits of love, 93–94
    effects of breakups, 215–16
Mesopotamia (Iraq), 52–53
Mexican-Americans, 10
Mexico, 17–18, 18t, 67t, 71, 100, 154t
Micronesia, 5–8, 11–12
Middle East, 52–53
MillionairesClub123, 32
Minnesota Multiphasic Personality Test, 74–75
mobile apps, 29–30, 29t, 31, 59. See also dating apps
mobile phones, 57–58, 58f, 59
Molly's Wrecken Ballz, 170–71
Momo, 66, 67t
Mo'Nique, 157, 158
monogamy, 164, 165
Moovator, 196
Mormons, 155
Morocco, 5–8, 14, 15–16, 19, 102–3
Mozambique, 154t
MTV, 11, 46–47
Multidimensional Jealousy Scale, 163
Multifactor Measure of Equity, 77–78
Muslims, 14–15, 54, 71, 143–44
My Real Baby (Hasbro), 195
Mylol, 28
MySpace, 29t

Nakajima, Senji, 192f

Namibia, 71, 154t
National Survey of Sexual Health and Behavior, 111, 113
nationalism, 19–20
Nepal, 154t
Netflix, 180–81
the Netherlands, 67t, 100, 126–27, 152, 163, 173t
New Zealand, 67t
News in Brain and Behavioural Sciences, 122
Niger, 154t
Nigeria, x, 5–8, 67t, 154t
Nigerian 419 scam, 47
Nigerian/Ghana emergency scam, 47
Nightcrawler, 146
NoFap forum, 176–77
non-consensual behaviors, x
norepinephrine, 91
norm violations, 38–39, 108–9
normalcy, 104–9, 118
North America, 52–53
North Cameroun, 5–8
North Carolinia, 109
Northern Europe, 9
Norway, 56–57, 126–27, 129–30, 145t, 154t
nymphomaniacs, 158

obscenity, 170–71
obsessive love, 2
Oceania, 52–53
OkCupid, 27–28, 29t, 30, 31f, 32, 49, 157
older adults, 111–13
Olsen, Mary-Kate, 76
OmniDate, 29t
On the Waterfront, 146
online dating, 23–26, 34, 86. See also dating apps
    advantages and disadvantages, 42
    advice for, 36
    catfishing, 46
    considerations, 27
    costs, 32
    dangers, 44
    dangers of, 46
    most popular sites and apps, 27–32

outcomes, 48–50
personal deal breakers, 37
questions people ask, 26
sample sites, 29, 29t
scams, 47
teen dating groups, 48
user profiles, 25, 32–36
what to look for, 36–42
who should try, 26–27
online piracy, 62–63, 63t
OnlineBootyCall, 29–30, 29t
open relationships, 151
opportunity gains and losses, 37
oral sex, 113, 115, 142–43
organized religion, 105–6
orgasm, female, 116
Orwell, George, 227
Orya people, 155
OurTime, 28

Pacific Islands, 9, 10
Pakistan, 17–18, 18t, 52–53
Palau, 5–8, 11–12
Palestine, 52–53
Palestinian Arabs, 126–27
passion. See passionate love
passionate love, 1–2, 90
    antiquity of, 5
    benefits of, 94
    chemistry of, 91–93, 92f
    cultural universal, 5–12
    culture and, 8–10
    definition of, 2, 11, 90, 92–93
    erosion of, 204–6, 205f
    health benefits, 93–94, 95
    in long-term relationships, 206
    negative effects of, 96
    transient nature of, 203
Passionate Love Scale (PLS), 2–4, 3t
Pawnee Indian tribe, 99
Perfectmatch, 29t
Persia (Iran), 52–53
personal rewards, 37
personality traits, 25, 38–39
personality types, 39
Peru, 154t
Philippines, 10, 17–18, 18t, 154t, 173t
Photovault, 48

physical appearance, 75–76, 81
physical bonding, 226, 227
physical health
    benefits of love, 93–94, 95
    effects of breakups, 216
"Pillow Talk" (Zayn), 61–62
PinkCupid, 29t
piracy, 62–63, 63t
Plateau tribes, 102
Plato, 61–62
Playboy magazine, 174
PlentyofFish, 27–28, 29t, 30, 32
Pokémon Go, 64
political affiliation, 161
polyamory, 151, 153–67
polyandry, 99, 163, 164
polygamy, 153–55, 163
polygynandry, 163
polygyny, 163–64
Polynesia, 52–53, 144
Pompeii, 171
pop culture, 61
Porn Fidelity, 182–83
porn stars, 180–83
Pornhub.com, 170, 174–75, 174t, 185–87
pornography, 106–7, 169
    addiction to, 175–76, 177
    child porn, 198
    definition of, 170–71
    gay female porn, 186–87
    gay male porn, 183–86
    Hentai, 198
    male-dominated, 146–47
    revenge porn, 118
    revenue worldwide, 172–73, 173t
    virtual, 198
    Web sites, 172–75, 174t
Portugal, 67t
power, 82, 100–1
predictions, 221–22
pregnancy, 142–43, 152–53
premarital sex, x, 106, 126
Presbyterian Church, 107
primates, 163–64
principle of least interest, 134
privacy, 105–6, 156–57
privatization, 68
progress, 227

Project Cupid, 21–23
property rights, 99
Protestants, 105–6, 107
Psychological Inquiry, 122
psychology, evolutionary, 80
public opinion
    acceptance of gays and lesbians'
        rights, x
    acceptance of nontraditional
        behaviors, 228
    attitudes toward extramarital sex, 152
    attitudes toward homosexuality,
        110–11, 226
    attitudes toward marriage, 15–16, 17–
        18, 18*t*, 19
    attitudes toward premarital sex, chastity,
        and casual sex, x, 124–26, 133, 135
    attitudes toward sex, 107
puritanism, 105–6
Pygmalion, 196

queer women, 186–87. *See also* lesbian,
    gay, bisexual, transgendered, and
    asexual (LGBT+) community

rape, 143
RealDoll, 191–92
recent theory, 81–84
reciprocated love, 90
recreational sex, 129
Reddit, 173, 174*t*
    NoFap forum, 176–77
    r.Gay: Be You forum, 184
Relationship Assessment Scale, 163
relationships. *See also* dating
    behaviors responsible for termination
        of, 38–39
    after breakups, 209–10
    deal breakers, 37–39, 79
    fate of, 201
    friends with benefits, 123, 151 (*see also*
        casual sex)
    friendships, 209–10
    interracial, 226
    long-term, 201, 206
    open, 151
    physical bonding, 226, 227
    predictors of success, 202*f*, 202

questions to help increase
    intimacy, 40–42
recommended strategy for gay and
    straight folks, 26–27
swinging, 153
threats to, 99, 100
traits to look for in mates, 34
ways to increase passion, intimacy, and
    commitment, 40–42
Republicans, 161
revenge porn, 118
r.Gay: Be You forum, 184
robots, 193–200
Romania, 67*t*
romantic passion. *See* passionate love
Rome, ancient, 171, 191
Romeo and Juliet, 5
Rubin, Zick, 21–23
Russia, 10, 17–18, 19, 67*t*, 83, 86, 152, 173*t*
russo, Renee, 146
Rwanda, 154*t*

Sade, Marquis de, 171
sadness, 212
same-sex sex life, 115
sampling, 165
Sanger, Margaret, 119
Sappho, 90–91
Sarkozy, Olivier, 76
Sartre, Jean-Paul, 156
Saudi Arabia, 19, 67*t*, 131, 155
scams, 47
Scandinavia, 84
Scarleteen, 148–49
Science, 122
scientific approach, 28, 53. *See also*
    chemistry
ScientificMatch, 29*t*, 32
Scruff, 29–30, 29*t*, 185
secularism, 53
self-esteem, 99, 100, 114
separation, 216
serotonin, 91
sex differences, 131. *See also* gender
    differences
sex dolls, 191–93, 192*f*, 196–200
    child sex dolls, 197*f*, 197, 198
sex industry, 83. *See also* pornography

sex ratios, 81, 134
sex roles, 115–16
Sexnet, 122
sexting, 118
sexual assault, 147–48
sexual behavior(s), 94, 104
    attitudes toward, 126
    casual sex, 122, 123t
    extramarital sex, 152–53, 165
    globalization of, 225
    hookup culture, 122
    initiation of, 148
    market view of, 73
    non-consensual, x
    open relationships, 151
    oral sex, 113, 115, 142–43
    physical bonding, 226, 227
    premarital sex, x, 106, 126
    reasons for engaging in, 135–36
    same-sex, 115
    unwanted activity, 143
    vaginal intercourse, 142–43
Sexual Behavior in the Human Female
    (Kinsey), 109
Sexual Behavior in the Human Male
    (Kinsey), 109
sexual fluidity, 110–11
sexual orientation, 110
sexual revolution, 128–29
sexual strategies theory, 131
sexuality
    female, 112–13, 114, 182–83
    sociosexuality, 79–80
sexually transmitted illnesses (STIs), 83,
    89, 113, 127, 128–29, 139–40, 142–43,
    144, 152–53, 181–82
    prevention of, 181–82
    testing for, 157–58
Seyfried, Amanda, 76
Shaadi.com, 69–70
Shackelford, Cynthia, 109
Shakespeare, 5, 12–13, 191
Shanghai Marriage Market, 77
Shiva and Sati, 5
short-term relationships, 132
Shuga Empire, 172f
shunga books, 170
sides, 115

Sikhs, 14
silent wives, 191
SilverSingles, 29t
Silwa people, 143–44, 145t
singularity, 196
Skype, 59
smartphones. *See* dating apps;
    mobile apps
Snapchat, 31–32, 48
social experiments, 122
social life, 122
social media, 20, 29t, 81
sociosexuality, 79–80
sodomy laws, 109
Solomon, 5
Sony, 194
South Africa, 67t, 152
South America, 52–53
South Asia, 52–53
South Korea, 67t, 173t, 192
Soviet Union, 100
Spain, x, 67t
speed dating, 75–76, 86
sport fucking, 135–36
Spotify, 29–30
spouse trading or wife-swapping, 151,
    155, 156–57
Sri Lanka, 52–53
stag films, 171–72
stalking, 96
Stanford University, 21, 31f
State University of New York (SUNY)
    Binghamton, 133, 136
statue love *(agalmatophia)*, 191
stereotypes, 107
Sternberg's Triangular Love Scale, 4, 6t
Stewart, Potter, 170–71
stigmatization, 182–83
*Still Doing It: The Intimate Lives of Women
    Over 65*, 112
STIs. *See* sexually transmitted illnesses
structural power, 82
students. *See* college students
sub-Saharan Africa, 14–15, 59
Sugar Daddy, 29
Sugar Mama, 29
SugarDaddie, 29t
Sumer, 5

SUNY (State University of New York)
Binghamton, 133, 136
swapping, 151, 155, 156–57
Sweden, 66, 67t, 126–27, 139, 152
Swift, Taylor, 61
swinging, 151, 153–67
Switzerland, 56–57, 67t, 154t
synthetic partners, 191
Syria, 52–53, 54

taboos, 99
Taita people, 5–8
Taiwan, 67t, 126–27, 152, 173t
Tamil people, 2
Tanzania, 154t
Taylor, Ava, 180–81
technological developments, 89, 221, 224
teen dating groups, 48
Telco, 59
Teʻo, Manti, 46–47
terminology, 165
Thailand, 14, 17–18, 18t, 67t
thepiratebay.org, 62–63
TheRightStuff.com, 25
Third World women, 86
Time Magazine, 182–83
Tinder, 27, 29–32, 29t, 31f, 35–36, 65–66,
67t, 69–70, 75–76, 195, 227
Toda people, 99
Togo, 154t
Toledo Adolescent Relationship
Study, 142
torrenting, 62–63
Tortorella, Nico, 110–11
Touch and Go, 122
tourists, 145t
Trinidad, Morocco, 5–8
Trobriand Islands, 132
Tulesosopo, Ronaiah, 46–47
Tumblr, 116
Turkey, 5–8, 11–12, 67t

UCLA Loneliness Scale, 213, 214t
Uganda, 154t
Ukraine, 67t
umbrella effect, 63
Unitarian Universalist Church, 107
United Arab Emirates, 19

United Kingdom, 71, 173t
See also England
United States
arranged marriages, 14–15
attitudes toward marriage, 16–18, 18t
attitudes toward premarital sex, x
casual sex, 124–25, 134, 145t
consensual non-monogamy
(CNM), 151–52
cultural norms, 105–6
culture, 9, 52–53
dating apps, 71
extramarital sex, 152
happiness ranking, 56–57
infidelity rates, 154t
jealousy triggers, 100
laws against adultery, 109
monogamy, 165
organized religion, 105–6
passionate love, 11
pornography, 172–73, 173t
recreational sex, 129
sex ratios, 83–84
smartphones, 59
sodomy laws, 109
susceptibility to love, 10
swinging, 159
United States Air Force, 155–56
University of California, Los Angeles
(UCLA) Loneliness Scale, 213, 214t
University of Hawaii, 135–36, 181–82, 213
University of Tennessee, 134
unrequited love, 90, 95–97, 212
urbanization, 68
utopia, 227

vaginal intercourse, 142–43
vengeance, 102
ventral tegmental area (VTA), 91, 92f, 92
Vevo, 61
VhaVhenda, 5
Viber, 59
VictoriaMilan, 28
video sharing, 61–62
virtual dating, 29t
virtual pornography, 198
VirtualDateSpace, 29t
VTA (ventral tegmental area), 91, 92f, 92

Waiting Room, 29t
Weopia, 29t
West, Kim Kardashian, 182–83
West Asia, 52–53
West Germany, 126–27
Western dominance, 54–56, 55f
Western Europe, 9
Western Illinois University, 128
Western love, 16–17, 52
Westernization, 19, 52–53, 221,
    224, 225
Westworld, 193–94
Wetlands, 170
Whatsapp, 29t, 59, 69
Whisper, 48
WhosHere, 66, 67t
Whosthere, 66
wife-swapping, 151, 155, 156–57
Wikipedia, 174t
women
    breakups, 207
    casual sex, 122, 123, 123t, 127, 128, 130,
        133–34, 135, 139–42
    coping with loss, 213
    female sexuality, 112–13, 114,
        182–83
    gay porn, 186–87
    infidelity rates, 152–53, 154t
    interest in porn, 186–87
    long-term relationships, 201
    Madonna–whore complex, 178
    mail order brides, 86
    marriage markets, 73, 73f
    objectification of, 176–79
    older, 112–13
    open relationships, 151
    orgasms, 116
    passionate love, 94
    porn stars, 180–83

queer, 186–87 (see also lesbian, gay,
    bisexual, transgendered, and asexual
    (LGBT+) community)
recreational sex, 129
sexual activity, 115–16, 119–20
swinging, 159–60
wife-swapping, 151, 155, 156–57
women who have sex with women, 115–16.
    See also lesbian, gay, bisexual,
    transgendered, and asexual (LGBT+)
    community
women's movement, 84
women's status, 84, 100–1, 114, 226
World War II, 155–56
"Would You?" (Touch and Go), 122

Xhamster, 174t
Xnxx, 174t
Xvideos.com, 174–75, 174t

Yahoo, 60–61
Yale University, 148
Yik Yak, 48
young people. See also college students
    deal breakers, 37–39
    questions about online dating, 26
    recreational sex among, 129–30
    teen dating groups, 48
    ways to increase passion, intimacy, and
        commitment in relationships, 40
YouPorn.com, 169, 170
YouTube, 60–61, 122, 148–49, 170–71
Yugoslavia, 100
YYC, 66, 67t

Zambia, 47, 144, 145t, 154t
Zayn, 61–62
Zimbabwe, 102, 154t
Zoosk, 27–28, 29–30, 29t, 31f, 32